The Irish Wake

And
The Irish Wedding

Corner Stones of Irish Life
Foundations of the Irish Personality
A Guide for Preparation and Understanding
©Conrad Jay Bladey, 2020.

The Irish Wake and the Iirish Wedding Corner Stones of Irish Life
Foundations of the Irish Personality
A Guide for Preparation and Understanding
©Conrad Jay Bladey
Hutman Productions, 2020
ISBN: 9781732083059
Cover
Above- Last Appearance of Teddy O'Rafferty, Robert Criukshank,1789-1856
Below- Candidates for Marriage or The Cleric's Interruption by Howard Hemlick 1881

Irish Wake
Schall, 1841

Introduction

This book expands and combines two of our first publications. I have included more commentary and description. It is hoped that these improvements will help the reader to experience these customs as they developed over time. The commentaries have come from many points of view. Please consider them not as political and cultural statements but as stories recording observables by specific individuals in specific times. Focus on the observables, that is artifacts of celebration within the commentaries. They are the treasures, our legacy having been carried carefully over the centuries.

Contents

Strawboy Suit
E. Estyn Evans, <u>Irish Folk Ways</u>

Part 1: The Irish Wedding

PÒsadh
&
Bainis

The
Guide to the
The Traditional
Irish
Wedding

©Conrad Jay Bladey
Hutman Productions 2020
ISBN: 9781732083059

Introduction

Welcome to my Treasury of the Traditions of Irish Weddings

Before we get started, I would like to offer a few thoughts concerning Irish Weddings and Weddings in general. The customs documented below come from a wide variety of Irish regional traditions. Some of these traditions are practiced today while others have been neglected. I have tried to avoid listing traditions that are recent or commercial. Where there is any doubt, I have indicated it in the text. I would like to encourage you to consider the old ways and to give them new life. Customs and traditions are simply component parts which you can dust off and join together to make your own masterpiece. Don't be overly concerned about finding all the pieces of the puzzle. Some pieces are probably lost. Make the event your own and have fun!

Beware, weddings are not just parties. If fun was the only purpose, they would have never survived the centuries. Weddings are complex artifacts that have been developed from smaller artifacts which were created and cared for over the centuries. The wedding fulfilled important basic cultural needs dating from the dawn of time. Before culture, in the darkness where the dark folkloric landscape was close at hand there were no stories or traditions. Individuals were on their own. Common problems had no solutions. How would we get people together to protect new members, enculturate them and keep the culture alive? How could the different roles of husband and wife be combined for their most efficient application? Who would be responsible for the new family unit and the children it may produce? Without marriage of some form there would have been no obligations to address these issues. People bonded together to help each other and produce children also needed to bond with other members of the culture who might provide a second line of defense for the children. In the dark folkloric landscape, one could not disclose these essential relationships. Learning was difficult--trial and error. Marriage provided ways to disclose the hidden structures so that they might be addressed by the culture. In the 21st century marriage is still difficult. It is an imperfect human construct. However, the aspects of the dark folkloric landscape it began to disclose still surround us. So, before you get to fun and entertainment remember the groundwork and artifacts of tradition laid down so long ago by our ancestors. Be sure that your event preserves his legacy as best you can. Do the social networking, exchange skills and things like recipes and stories. Plug into the cultural grid so necessary to prosper through time avoiding the unseen obstacles in the dark world. Once that is accomplished then, you can have fun.

Each and every wedding should be unique and in some way personal. I hope that you will use this work as a resource from which to build a new and personal wedding from the old parts. Allow your own creativity to work with the traditions that have come down through the centuries. Try your best to use as many of the old parts as possible.

In planning the wedding, you should also consult your family traditions as they currently exist. Perhaps you are fortunate enough to have ancient traditions preserved within your own heritage, which you do not find in this document. You should of course treasure these. For those planning to get married in Ireland I would direct you to the regulations I have included here. Be sure to contact the governments involved as soon as possible. Planning ahead is essential. A wedding in Ireland can be a wonderful thing but it will not take care of itself.

Another point worth considering is the range of historical traditions which have come down to us from the heritage of Ireland. Many today for example think of Ireland in terms of Ancient Celtic traditions. While a Celtic-styled wedding is a wonderful thing, (see the survey of Brehon law below) Ireland through the ages has produced many different styles and traditions. Dublin for example reached the height of its cultural importance in the 1700s. Wonderful gowns, fantastic crystal and harp music have come down to us from this period. Additionally, the Victorian age in Ireland was also a period of high culture which has given us its own patterns and fashions including Ulster linen, lace and of course Guinness Stout. So....in planning your event please consider the entire palette of possibilities. In this publication I have included, generally, old and documented traditions. Some of these traditions need your help if they are to survive. I hope that you will be able to bring some of them back to life and that they will help to enrich your event and help to form new traditions. Remember that the planning phase is also an enjoyable and most memorable aspect of any wedding. Enjoy your quest for the perfect Irish wedding.

Good luck and let us know how your event went!

Some Gaelic Terms

The Act of the Irish Government giving the rights of marriage is known as- *An tAcht um Pósadh.*
The term for Marriage is *pósadh* which comes from the Latin *Sponsare* which was first used in the 11-12th century.
The term used by the Gaelic legal system is *lanamnas.*Its use dates to c.800. As weddings became more public the term *bainis* was used.

-Arbuthnot, Sharon, "The Language of Marriage", In: Marriage and the Irish, Salvador Ryan, Ed., 2019, p. 1.

As you can see-the tradition has gone on for a while!

A First toast for you:

May you never lie, steal, cheat or drink. But if you must lie, lie in each other's arms. If you must steal, steal kisses. If you must cheat, cheat death. And if you must drink, drink with us your friends----

-Traditional

Flann O'Brien takes a Humorous look at the process....

The Irish sure do enjoy their weddings. They also enjoy writing about them! There is humor in the spectacles created by love! Everyone planning an Irish wedding should see the classic, yet politically incorrect, movie The Quiet Man and each should read what Flann O'Brien has written on the subject. I present an excerpt below:

From The Poor Mouth Chapter 6

After pondering the matter (marriage) for another year, I approached the Old-Fellow once more.

-Honest fellow! Said I, I'm two years waiting now without a wife and I don't think I'll ever do any good without one. I'm afraid the neighbors are mocking me. Do you think is there any help for the fix I'm in or will I be all alone until the day of my death and everlasting burial?

Boy! Said the Old-Fellow. 'Twould be necessary for you to know some girl.
If that's the way, I replied, where do you think the best girls are to be got?
In the Rosses without a doubt!

The Sea-cat entered my mind and I became a little worried. However, there is little use denying the truth and I trusted the Old-fellow.

If 'tis that way, said I in a bold voice. I'll go to the Rosses tomorrow to get a woman.
The Old-Fellow was dissatisfied with this kind of thing and endeavored for a while to coax me from the marriage-fever that had come upon me but, of course, I had no desire to break the resolution which was fixed for a year in my mind. He yielded finally and informed my mother of the news. "-Wisha! Said she," "the poor creature!

If he manages to get a woman out of the Rosses, said the Old-Grey Fellow, how do we know but that she'll have a dowry?

Wouldn't the likes of that be a great help to us at present in this house when the spuds are nearly finished and the last drop reached in the end of the bottle with us?

"I wouldn't say that you haven't the truth of it!" Said my mother.

They decided at last to yield completely to me. The Old Fellow said that he was acquainted with a man in Gweedore who had a nice curly-headed daughter who was as yet unmarried although the young men from the two sandbanks were all about her, frenzied with eagerness to marry. Her father was named Jams O'Donnell and Mabel was the maiden's name. I said that I would be satisfied to accept her.

The following day the Old-Fellow put a five noggin bottle in his pocket and both of us set out in the direction of Gweedore. In the middle of the afternoon we reached that townland after a good walk while the daylight was still in the heavens. Suddenly the Old-fellow halted and sat down by the roadside.

"Are we yet near the habitation and enduring home of the gentleman, Jams O'Donnell?" Asked I softly and quietly, querying the Old-Fellow.

-"We are!" Said he. "There is his house over yonder."
"Fair enough," said I. "Come on till we settle the deal and get our evening spuds. There's a sharp hunger on my hunger".
"Little son!" Said the Old-fellow sorrowfully, "I'm afraid that you don't understand the world. 'Tis said in the good books that describe the affairs of the Gaelic paupers that its in the middle of the night that two men come visiting if they have a five-noggin bottle and are looking for a woman. Therefore we must sit here until the middle of the night comes". "But 'twill be wet tonight. The skies above are full."

"Never mind! There's no use for us trying to escape from fate, oh, bosom friend!"
We did not succeed in escaping that night either from fate or the rain. We were drenched into the skin and to the bones. When we reached Jams O'Donnell's floor finally, we were completely saturated, water running from us freely, wetting both Jams and his house as well as everything and living creature present. We quenched the fire and it had to be rekindled nine times.

Mabel was in bed (or had gone to her bed) but there is no necessity for me to describe the stupid conversation carried on by the Old-Fellow and Jams when they were discussing the question of the match. All the talk is available in the books which I have mentioned previously. When we left Jams at the bright dawn of day, the girl was betrothed to me and the Old Fellow was drunk. We reached Corkadoragha at the midhour of the day and were well satisfied with the night's business....."

---From:<u>The Poor Mouth.</u>Flann O'Brien,Trans Patrck Power,Viking,New York,1973.pp.79-84

A good and healthy way to look at the tradition. You can't just take it out of the book or use it literally. You must tailor your own event from the pieces.

Quotes from the Quiet Man, John Ford

Hugh Forbes:
Then, a toast: May their days be long and full of happiness; may their children be many and full of health; and may they live in peace... and freedom.

Thornton:
There'll be no locks or bolts between us, Mary Kate... except those in your own mercenary little heart!

Mary Kate Danaher:
What manner of man is it that I have married?
Hugh Forbes:
A better one, I think, than you know, Mary Kate

Mary Kate Danaher:
Well, we just started a-courtin', and next month, we, we start the walkin' out, and the month after that there'll be the thrashin' parties, and the month after that...

The Celtic Marriage

Going Celtic

That which we know about Celtic marriage comes to us from the ancient legends and the surviving statutes and customs of Brehon law. Both were written down during Christian times but they are filled with pagan Celtic aspects which are fascinating and beautiful. If you wish to plan a Celtic-style wedding please take a few moments to read the descriptions of people provided by the ancient Irish tales. These will give you clues as to dress and color and style. I would strongly recommend reading those tales as found in the translations collected by Cross and Slover in their work <u>Ancient Irish Tales.</u> In these tales you will also find references to feasts and celebrations which will help you to set the scene. There are many small things you can do which will add a Celtic character to your wedding. The Celtic period lasted longer in Ireland than anywhere else so you have a choice of settings ranging from the Prehistoric to early modern times; however, as time went on Celtic lifeways became more European. It is important to know that an ancient Celtic Wedding need not be anything like the traditional Mediaeval banquet as re-created in all of those castles. It can be something special in its own right.

Time of year? -Cormac Mac Cullenan (9th century A.D.) wrote that November was the month favoured for weddings. This month was popular because of the nature of pastoral cultures. It was the time when resources were at their highest level and work minimal.

Foods of the Early Celtic period are not the same as those of the Middle Ages, but they are just as much fun! In any case there were no potatoes! Oatmeal, however, was available. The shellfish of the British Isles were described by the Romans, especially the oysters. Almost anything that lived was cooked and eaten: deer, wild pig, elk, wild ox, bear, beaver, sheep, goats, cattle, pigs, boar.... Cabbages and other native vegetables were also an important part of the diet. The classical writers who encountered the Celts were amazed at their capacity for strong drink. The most prized drink was imported wine from Italy prepared with cumin. The most popular beverage was wheaten beer made with honey or without. It was called *corma.* A common cup was used. We have one record of an impressive feast, that of King Louernius of Gaul:

> *...he made a square enclosure one and half miles each way, within which he filled vats with expensive liquor and prepared so great a quantity of food that for many days all who wished could enter and enjoy the feast prepared, being served without a break by the attendants.*-(Ross, 1972)

For another good description of preparations for feasting and celebration see the ancient Irish tale *Bricriu's Feast.*

Good sources for recipes of the Celtic Period are:

Food & Drink in Britain : From the Stone Age to the 19th Century ., C. Anne Wilson

Art, Culture and Cuisine : Ancient and Medieval Gastronomy.,Phyllis Pray Bober

Food in Antiquity, Mike Dobson John Wilkins (Editor) David Harvey (Editor) F. D. Harvey (Editor).

Brehon Law was the system of interpreted law used by the ancient Celtic peoples to organize their lives. Scholars have noted that the Brehon law very carefully planned for all aspects of the marriage equation. Perhaps the tenets of Brehon law will help you to structure your marriage and relationships. Be advised that Brehon law is no longer the law of the land anywhere on the Isle of Ireland. We have another section below which addresses contemporary legal requirements both in the Republic and in the Province.

Here are some highlights of the ancient Brehon law and ancient Irish Tradition:

Wooing
1.This has is not found in ancient early Irish law tracts.

The Wooing of Emer

Stories of Wooing can be found in The Wooing of Emer (The Book of Dun Cow)
First a council is held to determine how the hero Cuchulainn should be married off.
The benefits of marriage to the tribe were discussed. Then he is introduced to nine girls who are eligible. CuChulainn rejects them and then goes off to find his own and then finds Emer. After conversing with Emer in test conversation he goes off to mature and prove himself and then returns to marry Emer. Then the bride price is paid and the union is created as was traditional.

The Wooing of Deirdre

Neesha (Noise) sees her and talks of her as a "summer heifer." Deirdre discusses the prophesies and other arrangements but then threatens Neesha and the bond is made.

The Marriage Contract:

Who could not Marry:
1.A barren Man -This could be grounds for annulment of marriage.
2.An Unarmed Man.
3. A man in Holy orders who had an obligation to celibacy (enforced from the fifth century)
4. A churchman or bishop. (the only reason given is to make the list equal 7 parts)
5. A rockman- a man without land or who was not a freeman.
6. A very fat man- one too obese to perform the sexual act.

7. A *claenán*- a "perverted little wretch" which meant someone who told a woman's bed secrets.

A man of standing must have a *cétmuinter* or chief wife (that is the first one he marries) The *aire forggaill* or highest noble grade had "a chief spouse according to the law." The same is true for the *aire túise* or next in rank and the *aire désa* the lowest of the noble ranks. Even the highest ranking commoner or *bóaire* would have to have a chef spouse of equal rank.

Keating notes that young boys and girls of age to be married were kept apart at the Fair of Tailten until their marriage contracts were drawn up. A part of the area where the fair was held in County Meath was referred to as "hillock of the Bride Price" and was the place where dowries were paid. There is also a place there called Marriage Hollow where marriages were performed.

As referred to in the ancient stories, in particular the Wooing of Emer, girls were to be married off starting with the oldest with youngest being married last. This custom also appears in the "Origin of the Boru Tribute."

In the ninth century Cormac Mac Cullenan noted that the favorite time for weddings was November. This time of year corresponds to the time of maximum wealth for pastoral peoples.

The Honor price of a spouse was half that of the husband. This is only for *cétmuinters*. In addition to *cétmuinters* there were concubines or *dormuine* (entitled to one quarter of a spouse's honor price.)

There were ten sexual partnerships or *lánamnus* recognised by law:

1. Union of equal rank (ideal)
2. Woman supported by the property of the man (partners are of different classes).
3. Man was supported by a woman's property (man must do the work that is not a kept man)
4. A woman received in place of a wife (concubine) had specific rights. There are several titles: *dormuine,ben charrthach* (loved-woman).
5. A man keeps temporary company with another woman, neither supports the other.
6. Abducted woman-specific legal rights. Her offspring have rights.
7. Wandering soldier and his woman: these were not tied to the land yet they were recognised and had rights.
8. Union of Deception- such as a union made by man while woman was asleep. The man had obligations to woman and child.
9. Forced union-the guilty party was punished in relation to the honour of the girl and family. Any children born were recognised.
10. Union of levity- involving idiots or lunatics.

23

Due in a marriage of a *cétmuinter* was:

1. *Coibche*- The principal dowry. It is the same as the word to buy in 9ᵗʰ century Irish. This was paid to the father of the girl. The father then divided it with the *áige fine* or head of kindred. This was paid each year until the girl reached the age of twenty-one but only if the marriage lasted that long. In the second year the woman received one third of the amount. Her father and his superior divided the rest. Each year the wife kept a larger part. This became her own personal property and was derived from the property of the male. This provided the wife with enough resources to be independent after 21 years.
2. *Tinól*- A wedding present dowry given by friends. Composed of cattle, which were the chief form of wealth. This was divided between bride and her father with the father receiving one third.
3. *Tinchor*- Household goods given to the woman
4. *Tinnscra*- Bride Price or dowry. Given to the father of the bride if she was from outside of the *tuath*. This could be objects of gold, silver, copper or brass. This was meant to be transportable, unlike cows or household goods.

The Duties of Husband and Wife under contract:

The woman must give the man *toil ocus genus ocus bangnim. toil*= sexual desire, *genus*= chastity or reserving sexual experiences for the husband. *Bangnim*= woman-deed or sexual relations.

The man is only required to provide *fergnim* or the virile act.

The wife must respect the primacy of the man along with his leadership, as those are the due powers of manhood. She can take an oath against him. The contract does not negate the other rights of the woman.

The contract must be made with the knowledge of both parties. In regard to the contract of fostering of children the wife had an equal and direct voice and the contract must be settled jointly.

When united in an equal partnership or *comthigerna* (co-lord) both must jointly provide resources for great festivals and work together in buying and breeding cattle. Every aspect of life and property must be arranged for jointly. The Brehon laws governed all aspects of life and operated to ensure that the wife is not exploited.

Divorce

No Fault
1. Illness makes marriage impossible. A disease causes separation
2. One of the parties must make a pilgrimage.
3. A physical disfigurement or injury which can not be cured as determined by a Brehon, physician or nobleman.
4. Having to leave to find a friend or avenge aggression or similar cause.
5. Loss of sanity

6. The parties are barren.
7. Death

Separation with Compensation – The *coibche* can be taken when:

1. Husband circulates a false story.
2. Husband circulates a satire about the wife.
3. Woman is blemished by a blow.
4. Woman is repudiated for another.
5. Woman deprived of sexual intercourse or if husband prefers servant boys when this is not necessary for him.
6. Woman is given a charm by man so she will sleep with him.
7. Woman who is not fed.
8. If any of the causes which would bar a man from marriage was discovered after the fact.

If a woman leaves her husband for an unlawful reason she is then classified as a person without protection under Brehon law.

If the woman leaves for sufficient reason then she is entitled to her property. The couple determines this. There is no special court. If the woman leaves for an unacceptable reason then she must return all coibche gifts and her relatives must also return such gifts.

We end our discussion of Brehon law here but to learn of other provisions especially in regard to children and other matters see: <u>Sex and Marriage in Ancient Ireland.</u>, by Patrick C. Power, Dufour, 1997.

A Survey of Celtic Marriage Ceremonies.

In Chapter V. some remarks have been offered on the intercourse of the sexes, when speaking of the *mercheta mulierum*. The Celts, it has been there said, are charged with a neglect of their women, and a disregard to the proper regulation of the married state, that could but ill accord with the condition of a people in any degree civilized. Ten or twelve Britons, it is said, espoused a virgin each, and taking up their abode together, they lived in promiscuous cohabitation, but the children of each woman was considered as belonging to the man who had originally married the mother. The custom which continued until lately in some parts, and yet subsists among a few of the rudest, who sleep all together on straw or rushes, according to the general ancient practice, there is reason to believe, led to the aspersion cast on the British and Irish tribes. How natural it must have been for a casual observer to suppose from seeing men and women reposing in the same place, that the marriage rites were not in force. To judge of the ancient inhabitants by the rudest of the present Highlanders and Irish, who often sleep in the same apartment, and are some times exposed to each other in a state of semi-nudity, we should not come to a conclusion unfavorable to their morality, for this mode of life is not productive of that conjugal infidelity which St. Jerome and others insinuate as prevalent among the old Scots. Solinus, indeed, says the

women in Thule were common, the king having a free choice; and Dio
says the Caledonians had wives in common: yet these assertions may
well be disputed. Strabo describes the Irish as extremely gross in this
matter; O'Conner says polygamy was permitted; and Derrick tells us
they exchanged wives once or twice a year; while Campion says they
only married for a year and day, sending their wives home again for any
slight offence; but notwithstanding the attempt of Sir William Temple to
show the advantages of such loose connexion, it is reasonable to believe
that it did not exist, at least to the extent represented. Nations that
are even in a savage state are sometimes found more sensitive on that
point of honor than nations more advanced in civilisation; and all, perhaps,
that can be admitted is, that certain formalities may have been
practised by the Britons, from which the bundling of the Welsh, and
the hand-fisting in some parts of Scotland, are derived. The conversation
which took place between the Empress Julia and the wife of a
Caledonian chief, as related by Xiphilin, certainly evinces a grossness and
indelicacy in the amours of the British ladies, if true; but it appears to
be a reply where wit and reproof were more aimed at than truth. The
case of the Empress Cartismandua shows the nice feeling of the Britons
as to the propriety of female conduct. The respect of the Germans for
their females, and the severity with which they visited a deviation from
virtue, have been described; and the farther testimony of Tacitus may
be adduced, who says that but very few of the greatest dignity chose to
have more than one wife, and when they did, it was merely for the honor
of alliance. It may here be stated that the Gaël have no word to
express cuckold, and that prostitutes were, by Scots' law, like that of
the ancient Germans, thrown into deep wells; and a woman was not permitted
to complain of an assault if she allowed more than one night to
elapse before the accusation.

The Gauls, according to Caesar, had no sexual intercourse before
twenty. The Germans were equally long before they partook of connubial
happiness; they married in the prime of life, and the parties were
matched in stature as well as disposition, and this was not only with a
view to their own happiness, but to insure a fine family.

The ceremonies of courtship and marriage among the Celts were not
tedious, but the latter was never consummated without consulting the
Druidess and her purin, which was five stones thrown up and caught on
the back of the hand, called, says Vallancey, by the Irish, *Seic seona*,
now corrupted into jackstones." The ancient Irish presented their lovers
with bracelets of womens' hair. Duchomar, a Caledonian hero,
recommends his suit to Morna, by saying he had slain a stately deer
for her. The Gauls brought a portion equal to that of the women, and
the united product was reserved for the survivor.t. Among the Germans
the husband gave the wife a dowery— oxen, and a horse accoutred, a
shield, with a sword and javelin; and the parents attended to approve of
these presents, by whose acceptance the damsel was espoused. The
oxen in the same yoke, we are told, indicated that the wife was hence

forth to be a partner with the husband in his hazards and fatigues. The arms which she received, with certain others which she also, it appears, brought to her husband, she preserved for her sons, whose wives might again receive them. The father of a bride among the old Highlanders gave his arms to his son-in-law. Spelman remarks that the Irish dowers were bestowed exactly in the manner of the old Germans.

The Highlanders give dowers according to their means, cattle, provisions, farmstocking, &c.; and where the parents are unable to provide sufficiently, it is customary in Scotland for a newly-married couple to "thig," or collect grain, &c. from their neighbors, by which means they procure as much as will serve for the first year, and often more. The portion of a bride is called a *tocher*. The wedding feasts are scenes of great mirth and hospitality. It is often the case that they are "siller

* Brande's Pop. Ant. xlviii. * Bello Gall. vi. 17. # Tacitus.
60

bridals;" otherwise, those in which the parties are paid for the entertainment, which is sometimes resorted to as a means of raising a few pounds to begin the world with; but the feasts are generally free, and consist of an abundance of every thing. In the Highlands the company occasionally get breakfast, dinner, and supper, and there is sometimes so numerous an attendance that many sheep are killed for their entertainment.

A Mull wedding feast is thus described:—a long table is placed in a barn or outhouse, on which is set, at convenient distances, meat, with eggs, oatbread, and potatoes, and near every third person a. whole cheese and a lump of butter; the whisky, or other liquor, is provided by the bridegroom, but the rest of the entertainment is furnished by the parents of the bride. In Tiri, another of the Western Isles, a respectable marriage feast was provided with a profusion of mutton, turkeys, geese, ducks, fowls, custards, puddings, vegetables, butter, cheese, oatbread, milk, and whisky, all provided by the parents of the bride, except she has only a mother, in which case the bridegroom is thought bound to bear the expense."

In the Isle of Man, the relations always bring something to a mar riage feast. On one platter you may sometimes see a dozen capons, on another six or eight fat geese—sheep and hogs are roasted whole, and oxen cut up in quarters.f

Dr. Henry says that within twenty or thirty years, when a party in Orkney agreed to marry, they went to the temple of the moon, which was semi-circular, and there the woman fell on her knees and invoked Woden, a singular relict of superstition. The ring was a badge of the married state among the Celts, and was worn both in Gaul and Briton on the middle finger. That used among the Northern nations seems to have been nearly as large as to admit the whole hand.

A marriage company, among the Galatians, all drank out of the same
cup. When the German bride entered in the morning she was clothed
in a white robe, and was crowned with herbs and flowers, particularly
vervain, which was sacred to Venus. A Lusitanian woman was taken
into the house with a sort of violence, her husband dragging her from
the arms of her brother, and she was preceded to her new residence by
a person who implored the favor of Hymen to the happy couple.
A very ancient custom of carrying off a wife by force, remains in
some parts of Ireland to this day. In 1767, a girl was carried off in the
county of Kilkenny, but was rescued and married to another party.
The disappointed lover raised his friends, and, provided with arms, they
besieged the house, in order to recover the prize, and although they
were beaten off it was not before lives were lost.

A Scotish bride was expected to show a reluctance, and require a
certain degree of violence, which was neither thought unbecoming in
the man, nor a hardship to the woman; many instances being fond of

* Mrs. Murray's Guide. On this subject "the Bridal of Caolchairn," by Mr. Hay,
will be read with interest. t Waldron's Hist. p. 169.

happy unions, accompanied with apparent force and cruelty. The practice
was sometimes, however, carried too far, and the real violence
which was used constituted the *raptus,* or forcible abduction of women,
of which so many instances occur in the legal history of the country.
The unfortunate Lovat was accused of this crime, in having married,
without the lady's consent, and actually cut her dress from her person
with a dirk An old north country song, entitled "Lord Saltoun and
Achanachie," alludes to a similar act of deforcement,

"When she was married she would na' ly down,
But they took out a knife and cut off her gown."

One of the sons of the celebrated Rob Roy was hanged for carrying
off the heiress of Balfron, more, however, apparently against her friends'
consent than her own, for she lived some time contentedly with him in
the Highlands.

In the pastoral districts of Ireland the parents and mutual friends
meet on a hill side, usually midway between their respective dwellings,
and there drink "the agreement bottle" of whisky. This settled, the
father, or next of kin to the bride, sends round to his neighbors and
friends, and every one gives his cow or heifer, by which means the portion
is soon raised. Caution is, however, taken of the bridegroom on
the day of delivery for restitution of the cattle, should the bride die
childless, in which case, within a stipulated time, each receives back
his own; care being thus taken that no man get rich by frequent marriage.
On the day of "home bringing," the bridegroom and his friends

ride out to the place of treaty, where they meet the bride, and the custom of old was to cast short darts at the bride's company, but at such a distance as seldom to occasion any wounds; "yet it is not out of the memory of man that the Lord Hoath on such an occasion lost an eye. This custom is now obsolete." "

The following observances at a wedding in Wales, if not entirely disused, are fast dying away. Some weeks previous, a person well known in the parish, went round inviting all, without limitation or distinction, to attend. The company assembled the evening previous to the ceremony at the bride's father's, the bridegroom arriving accompanied by music. The bride and her retinue were then shut up in a room, and the house doors being locked, the company made loud demands for admittance until the bride's maid opened a window and assisted the bridegroom to enter, after which the doors were opened and the party admitted. After a few hours dancing and a refreshment of oatcake and spiced ale, the bride's maid and company retired: the bridegroom returning early next day with all his friends, preceded by a harper playing "come haste to the wedding." They were joined by the bride at her father's, who, along with her brother or other male relation, took their station behind

* That is about 1682. Sir H. Pier's Description of Westmeath, ap. Vallancey's Coll. i. p. 122.

the bridegroom, with their retinue of friends, and all proceeded to church. On leaving the church the harper played "joy to the bride groom," and the bride and her maid having changed partners, they all went to a part of the churchyard, if such there was, unappropriated for interment, and there danced to the tunes of "the beginning of the world," and "my wife shall have her way." They then adjourned home where various sorts of bread, ale, and cheese, were prepared, and a collection for the bride was made, a benevolence which was not always in money; sometimes the friends and neighbors went the night before, carrying presents of grain, meal, cheese, &c. It is a practice among the better sort in these days for the bride to remain with her parents for some weeks, and when she goes to her husband, the furniture which she has provided, and which is called *starald*, is removed with much ceremony, every article being moved in succession, according to fixed rules. The next day the young couple are attended by the younger part of their friends, and this is called a *turmant.*" When parties separated in this country, by Hwyel's laws, the property was equally divided. There are several other observances that are to be referred to the original Britons, such as the cake broken over the head of the Scot's bride, on her first entering her future residence. It is a curious practice of newly married women to commence spinning and preparing linen for their shroud. The bard who attended a marriage was entitled to the bridegroom's plaid and bonnet.

Many superstitious movements and notions were occasioned by a woman's confinement, that are not worth observance. In some parts of the Highlands, we learn from Mrs. Murray, when near her time, a large knife and a spade were laid under the bedstead, and beneath the pillow was placed the bible, while salt was plentifully strewed about the doors to avert the fairies. These unearthly creatures derive the Gaëlic name, *sithich,* from *sith,* a sudden attempt to grasp, which accords with their known propensity to carry off children. They lived under little green mounts, called *sith dhuin,* which are still approached by the Highlanders with veneration, certainly from the supposed residence of these beings, and not from their being "hills of peace," as Dr. Smith thinks. The Gallic women delighted in a numerous family.t The mode of rearing children has been described. They were inured to hardship and brought up in military virtue, and rude, but imposing, simplicity of manners. No rights of primogeniture, or undue partiality, engendered feelings of discord and contention—they were alike excluded from mix ing in society, or even appearing before their parents in public, until they were able to bear arms. The children of the Germans were held in the same estimation by their mother's brother as by their father, which, says Tacitus, was an inviolable tie.

* A. B. Table Book, ii. 793.
f The Thracian women laid their new born children on the earth and wept over them. Les diff. Moeurs, &c. 1670.
The Druids, elevating their minds to the most sublime conceptions,

-The Scotish Gaël, Or, Celtic Manners: As Preserved Among the Highlanders ... James Logan,1833.

Marriage Lore

From: Traces of the elder faiths in Ireland : a folklore sketch : a handbook of Irish pre-Christian traditions, Wood-Martin, W. G. (William Gregory), 1901, v2, p.26.

CHAPTER II.
MARRIAGE LORE.

AN old Icelandic author states that, into a certain island in one of the Irish lakes, no female of any animal, including the human species, was allowed to enter. This rule seems to have been enforced, not only in Ireland, but in various parts of Europe. Curson, in his Monasteries of the Levant, states that " no female animal of any sort is admitted to any part of the peninsula of Mount Athos ; and since the days of Constantino the soil of the holy mountain has never been contaminated by the tread of a woman's foot." Moore has immortalised this idea in the legend of Glendalough, where St. Kevin hurls Kathleen into the waters for daring to intrude on his presence and on his mediations; yet

" Soon the saint, yet, ah ! too late, Felt her love, and mourned her fate."

It has been wittily remarked of this most strictly moral man.

' ' If hard lying could gain it, he surely gained heaven ; For on rock lay his limb , and rock pillow'd his head, Whenever this good holy saint kept his head ; And keep it he must, even to his last day, For I 'm sure he could never have thrown it away."

St. Senan also inexorably hunted away the fair sex,

" But legends hint that had the maid Till morning light delay'd, And given the saint one rosy smile, She ne'er had left his lonely isle."

St. Columbkille seems likewise to have been credited with a horror of women. He detested even cows on their account, and would not allow one to come within sight of the walls of his monastery, because, as he explained: "Where there is a cow there must be a woman, and where there is a woman there must be mischief." Writers, almost without exception, depict the early Irish saints as of most exemplary character. Whether the long past ages in which they lived " lent enchantment to the view," and hid from modern gaze little episodes in the lives of other saints not quite as correct as the two foregoing examples, it is now impossible to say. Let us suffice that, in point of morality, they contrast most favourably with the picture drawn of Scottish monks by Sir Walter Scott :

" The living dead, whose sober brow Oft shrouds such thoughts as thou hast now, Whose hearts within are seldom cured Of passions by their vows abjured ; When under sad and solemn show Vain hopes are nursed, wild wishes glow."

The exclusion of women from sacred localities is a practice far older than Christianity. They were prohibited by the Romans from entering the temples of Hercules, the reason for which is given by Plutarch and Macrobius. Irish examples could be multiplied to any extent. The monks of Iniscathy Abbey from its foundation to its demolition are said never to have permitted a woman to enter the island. A lady having requested speech with a monk, he replied " What have women to do with monks? We will neither admit you or any other woman into the island." The lady replied " If you believe Christ will receive my soul, why do you turn away my body?" "That," he answered, " I verily believe, but we never permit any woman to enter this place, so God preserve you. Return to the world lest you be a scandal to us, for however chaste you may be you are a woman."

" Cui Praesul, Quid faeminis Commune est cum monachis ? Nee te, nee ullam aliam - Admittimns in insulam.
Tune ilia ad Episcopum ; Si meum credis spiritum Posse Christum suscipere, Quid me repellis corpore?
Credo inquit, hoc optime, Sed nullae unquam faeminae Hue ingressam concedimus ; Esto : salvet te Dominus.
Redi iterum ad saeculum, Ne sis nobis in scandal um : Et si es casta pectore Sexum habes in corpore."

There are, however, some still surviving fragmentary relics of ancient customs pointing to a state of things having formerly existed in Ireland resembling those still prevalent in some parts of the East, as well as in Africa. A night spent in one of the old churches at Termonbary, near Lough Ree, or passed in a cleft in the rock at the source of the river Lee, by a married woman who had not been blessed with issue, proved as effective in removing barrenness as did ever the prolific shadow of Rabelais' Abbey Steeple ; and is it not strange that, although the- early Christian missionaries are reputed to have held women in holy abhorrence, a visit to one of their " beds " was usually a favourite religious exercise of devout women, who imagined that by lying in it and turning thrice round, at the same time repeating certain prayers, a favourable answer would be granted to their maternal requests. Amongst some African tribes a man is at liberty to return his wife to her family and demand repayment of her purchase money if she bear no children. However, before doing so, he must send her to the " bed " of a fetichman ; but if, after that, she still remains barren, the woman's family are bound to take her back and repay her price to the disappointed Benedict. Almost any number of Irish " Saints' " or " Priests' Beds " might be enumerated ; a few shall suffice. A writer, describing the Island of Devenish in the year 1815, says that " a few paces to the north of St. Molaise's house is his ' bed," which is a stonetrough (coffin) sunk level with the surface of the ground, six feet in length and fifteen inches wide, in which people lie down and repeat some prayers, in hope of relief from any pains with which they may be affected. About 100 paces north of St. Mary's Abbey is St. Nicholas's Well, to which many resort for relief, repeat some prayers, and leave a rag suspended on a bush near it." In the parish of Killady, county Cork, is St. Ita's Well, where "rounds " are still paid. An oblong hole in the ground not far distant is called "St. Ita's Bed," where, " if child-bearing women roll themselves, they will not suffer the pains of childbirth. Needless to add, no decent woman would do this in public, but I am told several come here privately on by-days for that purpose, or take home a handful of the earth from the " Bed " for the purpose of rubbing it around their bodies in the name of the Holy Trinity." About the year 1873 the Rev. James Page thus describes a scene at the station called " St. Patrick's Bed," on Croagh Patrick '' All the devotees do not go there none but those that are barren and the abominable practices committed there ought to make human nature, in its most degraded state, blush. This station course is forty yards in circumference. Bound this they go seven times, then enter the bed, turn round seven times, take up some small pebbles, and bring them home, in order to prevent barrenness, and to banish rats and mice. The greater part of those who go through this station stop upon the hill all night that they may sleep in the bed." On Inishmore, now called Church Island, in Lough Gill, county Sligo, are the ruins of a church founded by St. Loman in the sixth century. In a rock, near the door of the church, there used to be a depression or cavity in a slab of rock called " Our Lady's Bed." This was a favourite resort of devout women, who imagined that by lying in it, turning thrice round, and at the same time repeating certain prayers, a favourable answer would be granted to their maternal requests. This belief has long ceased, the island is no longer used as a burial place, and the " Bed" has disappeared, or cannot now be identified. In one of the wild desolate islands off the Western coast there is, according to Lady Wilde, a stone receptable called " The Bed of the Holy Ghost." Many people go from the mainland for the purpose of passing a night in this " bed," believing that " it heals all diseases," and that " it brings good luck to all, and to women the blessing of children." The small stones on the top of the Ballymascanlan Cromleac, near Dundalk, locally known as the " Pulleek Stone," are thrown by the credulous, who believe that if one rests there the thrower will be married before the expiration of the year. This is an excellent example of a world-wide superstition, for J. F. Campbell records having found in Japan small piles of stones at the foot of every image and memorial stone, and on every altar by the wayside. Another traveller, describing the ceremony which gives birth to these heaps of stones, states that women who desire children make pilgrimages to a sacred stone on the holy hill of Nikko and throw pebbles at it. If they succeed in hitting it their wish is granted. He maliciously adds that they seem very clever at the game. He also describes a seated statue of Buddha, at Tokio, whose knees women fling stones with the same object, and further relates that the grotesque statues guarding the entrance of another temple were covered with pellets of chewed paper shot through the bars of the railing which surrounded the idols. A successful shot implied the attainment of the spitter's wish. In Upper Brittany pins are thrown into the holy well of St. Goustan by those who wish to be married within the year; the pins stick point downward into the bottom of the well if the prayer is to be granted. Girls still resort to a little shrine on the beach at Perros Guirec, in Lower Brittany. The postulant, her prayer concluded, sticks a pin into the wooden statue of the saint, which is riddled with pin-holes, and her wish for a husband is infallibly granted within a year. Similar rites are observed in Poitou and Alsace, and the like practices exist almost all over France, or have died out, in many places, only recently. In an island near Achill there is a holy well at which no female is allowed to draw water. It must be handed to her by a male, be he even an infant, whose hand she should place within her own in laying hold of the vessel when drawing the water which may be afterwards used for the ordinary purpose of everyday life. Numerous anecdotes are recounted of the misfortunes which have happened to women who persisted in drawing water from this well. An old man who lived for many years on this island solemnly declared that he had, on several occasions, cleaned out the well after women had taken water from it, and that on each occasion it was full of blood and corruption. From the time he commenced to clean out the well until the task was accomplished, no water flowed into it; but as soon as the cleansing was finished, clear spring water immediately burst forth. According to an ancient legend, quoted by Professor O'Curry, the River Shannon originated from the profanation of a sacred pagan well by a woman. Women wrere not permitted to wash their feet in holy wells, though men were allowed to do so, for the Irish held a great many superstitions relative to water in which feet had been dipped.

In Nennius' Historia Britonum, the Mill of Kilkeary in Ossory is described as the thirty-second wonder of Ireland. This ancient mill would neither grind on the Sabbath, nor would it grind stolen grain, and women dare not enter it. The site of this semi-sacred edifice is now occupied by a modern building, and for its present characteristics the miller can answer. In many localities it was forbidden to bury men and women in the same cemetery. The prohibition still occasionally survives as at Inishniurray ; and it is an almost universal belief that if a woman be buried in the men's ground, the corpse will be removed during the night, by unseen hands, to the women's cemetery, and vice versa. The custom of separate burial is derived from very ancient times, for the old pagans had, in some instances, separate burying places for the two sexes. A little to the north of Buttevant, on a height overlooking the road, stands an ancient conical sepulchral tumulus, styled in Irish " the mound of the boys." A tumulus of corresponding dimensions, called " the mound of the girls," is in the immediate vicinity. This idea of supposed pollution by contact with women appears to be much the same in all ages, and all the world over. In the present day the movements of the fleet of trading canoes belonging to some of the natives of New Guinea are governed by minute and elaborate regulations on this subject. No woman is allowed on board any canoe for two months previous to its sailing, and during the entire period of absence the leading men in each canoe must abstain from all intercourse with the fair sex. So much similarity and so many correspondences exist in the every-day routine prevailing among races generally considered distinct, that the ethnological differences they exhibit are of little weight when what they possess in common is taken into consideration. To unravel the tangled skein of primitive life as it formerly existed in Ireland, we must look to the tribes of Central Africa, of America, the hillmen of India, and the Pacific Islanders. With many of these we find marriage laws unknown, the family system undeveloped, and the only acknowledged blood relationship that through females. " These facts of to-day are, in a sense, the most ancient history. In the science of law and society, 'old' means not old in chronology, but in structure; that is most archaic which is nearest to the beginning of human progress considered as a development, and that is most ' modern ' which is farthest removed from that beginning." In the whole range of legal symbolism there is no trait more remarkable than that of capture in marriage ceremonies, nor is there any the meaning of which has been less studied. The Rev. Edward Chichester, A.M., writing in 1815, on ancient customs in the parish of Culdaff, county Donegal, says that there were many which appeared extraordinary, though not confined to any one district of Ireland, the most singular he mentions being elopement previous to matrimony, and that notwithstanding the absence of all difficulties which might stand in the way of the union of the lovers. " The symbol of capture occurs whenever, after a contract of marriage, it is necessary for the constitution of the relation of husband and wife that the bridegroom or his friends should go through the form of feigning to steal the bride, or carry her off from her friends by superior force. The marriage is agreed upon by bargain, and the theft or abduction follows as a concerted matter of form to make valid the marriage. The test then of the presence of the symbol in any case is, that the capture is concerted, and preceded by a contract of marriage. If there is no preceding contract, the case is one of actual abduction." Those who approach the study of this interesting subject with unbiassed minds will readily perceive that there must have existed an early period of lawlessness, in which it was with women as with other kinds of property, " that he should take who had the power, and he should keep who can " ; that wives were first obtained by force, then by theft, and later by trade and bargain. The question of ancient marriage customs in Ireland has not been grappled with by antiquaries, and it is probable that, when the solution has been attained, it will exhibit matrimonial alliance in the Emerald Isle in a very different light from that in which it has been hitherto depicted by an extravagantly eulogistic school of writers. Sir Henry Piers, in a Description of Westineath written about the year 1682 and published in *Collec. de Rebus-Hi.*, vol. i., p. 122, says regarding Irish marriages, that " especially in those counties where cattle abound, the parents and friends on each side meet on the side of a hill, or, if the weather be cold, in some place of shelter about midway between both dwellings. If agreement ensue, they drink the ' agreement bottle,' as they call it, which is a bottle of good usquebaugh (whiskey), and this goes merrily round. For payment of the portion, which is generally a determinate number of cows, little care is taken. The father or next of kin to the bride sends to his neighbours and friends *sub mutuae vidssitudinis obtentu*, and everyone gives his cow or heifer, and thus the portion is quickly paid. Nevertheless, caution is taken from the bridegroom on the day of delivery for restitution of the cattle in case the bride dies childless within a certain day, limited by agreement; and in this case every man's own beast is restored. Thus care is taken that no man shall grow rich by frequent marriages." In the present day the routine is somewhat as follows :

Some desirable partner for their son is discovered by his parents desirable either in respect of the amount of her fortune, in cash or kind, or the land she possesses. The families are generally strangers to each other; so, to put the matter in train, it becomes necessary to engage the services of an intermediary to place the proposal before the young woman's parents. The professional "match-maker " is usually elderly, shrewd, calculating, and versed in all the arts of country diplomacy. The commission given, he calls as if by accident, and without making any definite proposal, sketches an outline of the desired arrangement. Negotiations and the all-important question of the fortune follow, and here occurs the match-maker's opportunity, as his services are, usually rewarded in proportion to the terms he obtains, so ample play is given to his powers of "blarney" and wealth of argument. If the girl is possessed of a fortune, the novelty of the transaction comes in, as the dowry passes, not into the estate of the young couple, but into the pocket of the bridegroom's parents, who, in consideration, agree to assign the farm to their son, charged with certain payments.

A traveller in Ireland, about the year 1830, describes a rustic marriage festival which he came on by chance one evening in the wilds of Kerry. The account is thus summarised by Lady Wilde: "A large hawthorn tree that stood in the middle of a field, near a stream, was hung all over with bits of coloured stuff, while lighted rush candles were placed here and there amongst the branches, to symbolise, no doubt, the new life of brightness preparing for the bridal pair. Then came a procession of boys marching slowly with flutes and pipes made of hollow reeds, and one struck a tin can with a stick at intervals, with a strong rhythmical cadence. This represented the plectrum. Others rattled slates and bones between their fingers, and beat time, after the manner of the *Crotolistrai* a rude attempt at music, which appears amongst all nations of the earth, even the most savage. A boy followed, bearing a lighted torch of bog-wood. Evidently he was Hymen, and the flame of love was his cognisance. After him came the betrothed pair hand-in-hand, a large square canopy of black stuff being held over their heads the emblem, of course, of the mystery of love, shrouded and veiled from the prying light of day. Behind the pair followed two attendants, bearing high over the heads of the young couple a sieve filled with meal, a sign of the plenty that would be in their house, and an omen of good luck and the blessing of children. A wild chorus of dancers and singers closed the procession; the chorus of the epithalamium and grotesque figures, probably the traditional fauns and satyrs, nymphs and bacchanals, mingled together with mad laughter and shouts and waving of green branches.

The procession then moved on to a bonfire, evidently the ancient altar, and having gone round it three times, the black shroud was lifted from the bridal pair, and they kissed each other before all the people, who shouted and waved their branches in approval. "Then the preparations for the marriage supper began; on which, however, the traveller left them, having laid some money on the altar as an offering of good-will for the marriage future. At the wedding supper there was always plenty of eating and drinking and dancing, and the feast was prolonged till near morning, when the wedding song was sung by the whole party of friends standing, while the bride and bridegroom remained seated at the head of the table. The chorus of one of these ancient songs may be thus literally translated from the Irish:
" 'It is not day, nor yet day, It is not day, nor yet morning; It is not day, nor yet day, For the moon is shining brightly.'
" Another marriage song was sung in Irish frequently, each verse ending with the lines:
" ' There is sweet enchanting music, and the golden harps are ringing and twelve comely maidens deck the bride-bed for the bride.'
" A beautiful new dress was presented to the bride by her husband at the marriage feast, at which also the father paid down her dowry before the assembled guests ; and all the place round the house was lit by torches when night came on, and the song and the dance continued till daylight, with much speech-making and drinking of poteen. All fighting was steadily avoided at a wedding, for a quarrel would be considered a most unlucky omen. A wet day was also held to be very unlucky, as the bride would assuredly weep for sorrow throughout the year. But the bright warm sunshine was hailed joyfully, according to the old saying :
'" Happy is the the bride that the sun shines on; But blessed is the corpse that the rain rains on.'
"On the day of bringing home, the bridegroom and his friends ride out and meet the bride and her friends at the place of meeting. " Having come near to each other, the custom was of old to cast short darts at the company that attended the bride, but at such distance that seldom any hurt ensued ; yet it is not out of the memory of man that the Lord of Howth, on such an occasion, lost an eye."

Even at the commencement of this century, countrymen, when going to a marriage, generally rode on horseback, each having behind him a woman seated on a pillion; the bride was mounted behind the best man ; the bridegroom, however, rode alone. That old world relic of barbarism, the pursuit and capture of the bride, then still existed. The latter pretended to run away, pursued by the bridegroom ; and even yet the bridal party usually set out for a long drive, the bride and bridegroom, bridesmaid and best man, being on the first car, the guests following in an order which usually depends upon the respective merits and speed of their horses. This drive was sometimes called " dragging home the bride." Sometimes the term was applied to the drive from the parent's house to that of her husband. f Weddings were made the occasion of great festivities, usually followed by a dance kept up till the greater number of the guests were stretched upon the floor through the combined effects of fatigue and other causes. In remote parts of the country, " straw boys " still appear at the house disguised in tall conical- shaped straw masks (fig. 8), decorated with stripes of red and green cloth ; they also wear white shirts and red petticoats set off with many coloured ribbons. The leader dances with the bride, the next in rank with the bridesmaid, and the remainder of the band find partners as best they can. They are usually well entertained and treated to drink. They formerly demanded money, nd indulged in boisterous play; but in most localities this is a thing of the past. Lord Kames, in Sketches of the History of Man, states that the following marriage ceremony was in his day (1807), or had till shortly before, been customary among the Welsh : " On the morning of the wedding day, the bridegroom, accompanied with his friends on horseback, demands the bride. Her friends, who are likewise on horseback, give a positive refusal, upon which a mock scuffle ensues. The bride, mounted behind her nearest kinsman, is carried off, and is pursued by the bridegroom and his friends with loud shouts. It is not uncommon, on such an occasion, to see two or three hundred sturdy Cambro Britons riding at full speed, crossing and jostling, to the no sinall amusement of the spectators. When they have fatigued themselves and their horses, the bridegroom is suffered to overtake his bride. He leads her away in triumph, and the scene is concluded with feasting and festivity." In Roman history, the story of the rape of the Sabines should be accepted as a mythical tradition of the ancient way of procuring wives by force, and, as might naturally be expected, the story, differing slightly in form, is to be found in the folk-lore of many tribes and in many places. In the Irish Nennius there is a

Fio. 8.
Wedding Dance Mask. Slightly less than quarter real size.

\rape of wives by the Picts from the Gael, and the Irish are also represented as giving three hundred women to the Picts, conditional on the succession to the crown amongst the Picts being through females only : " ' There were oaths imposed on them, By the stars, by the earth, That from the nobility of the mother Should always be the right of the sovereignty. The story of the oaths is, no doubt, a fable to explain the *descensus per umbilicum* of the Picts. But in ' Duan Gircanash,' a poem on the origin of the Gaedhel, reciting the same event, the Pints' are represented as stealing the three hundred wives:
"'Cruithne, son of Cnig, took their women from them It is directly stated Except Tea, wife of Hermion, Son of Miledh.'

   And in consequence of the capture, the Gael, being left wifeless, had to form alliances with the original tribes of Ireland:

" ' There were no charming noble wives For their young men; Their women having been stolen, they made alliance With the TuathaDea.'"

Mr. C. Staniland Wake, in Marriage and Kinship, remarks : " In the Book of Aicill, under the head of ' Abduction without leave,' it is said that the child of a woman who had been abducted without leave from her family, unless begotten more than a month after the abduction, belonged not to the abductor, but the mother's family. If the mother had been forcibly abducted it belonged to them absolutely, and they might refuse to sell it to the abductors ; but if the mother had consented to the abduction he could force her family to sell. Where there had been an abduction without leave, the woman's family were allowed a month to bring the man to terms about her, or to reclaim her. If there was no contract, and the woman remained with her abductor longer than that period, her family lost their right to the offspring. Here we have different phases of marriage by capture, forcible abduction, abduction without the consent of the woman herself, and abduction without leave of her family, which, no doubt, was wanting also when the consent of the woman had not been obtained. From the reference to the consent which was necessary to take the children from the woman's family and give them to their father it may be thought that abduction with the leave first had of the woman's family was recognised. The arrangement referred to was made, however, after the abduction, a month being fixed by custom as the term within which it ought to be come to, or the woman brought back by her family." In this case there does not appear to be any such symbolical capture, or abduction by arrangement, as Dr. MacLellan's theory requires. There was actual capture, which was afterwards compounded for, but as the contract came after the abduction, the facts do not come within the theory according to which " the marriage is agreed upon by bargain, and the theft or abduction follows as a concerted matter of form, to make valid the marriage. It comes rather within the statement that ' if there is no preceding contract, the case is one of actual abduction.' " In the 21st chapter of Deuteronomy, verses 10-14, we have the full description of marriage by capture as practised amongst the Israelites. Every detail, even to the paring of the nails of the captive before marriage, is identical with one of the Arab methods of terminating the widow's period of seclusion and allowing her to marry again. The general conclusion which may be drawn from these and other allied facts, taken as a whole, may be interpreted as evidence of a gradual progress from a state of Totemism and female kinship, always tending upwards from that condition, exhibiting the development of human society as an evolution, moving, at different epochs, with varying rapidity. Mr. John F. MacLennan, M.A., in Primitive Marriage, points out that " as civilization advanced, the system of kinship through females only, was succeeded by a system which acknowledged kinship through males also, and which in most cases passed into a system which acknowledged kinship through males only." The Editors of the Senchus Mor appear to be of opinion that Patria Potestas did not enter into old Irish law, for they say (vol. ii., p. 4, preface) that " the provisions of the Irish family law do not appear to have any connection with the ancient Eoman law. The Irish law demands for the mother a position equal with the father, and there is no trace of the exercise of that arbitrary power which was wielded by a Roman father over the members of his family." In the laws of Ireland there was thus, according to this evidence, no trace of Patria Potestas. Many English writers allege that in former times the population living in remote parts of Ireland paid very little attention to the tie of matrimony in fact, Keating admits the accusation, for he remarks : " With regard to what is charged upon the Irish by other writers, that they very religiously observe their - matrimonial contracts for the space of a year, and think they may then lawfully dissolve them, it is sufficient to reply that this opinion prevailed only among the rude and unpolished part of the people, who despised the discipline of the Church, and denied the authority of their ecclesiastical superiors." A " Teltown Marriage " is an expression often used in Meath to describe an irregular marriage in the present day, and a somewhat similar custom to that now to be described existed in Scotland, Wales, and part of England till very lately. If a couple who had been married for a twelvemonth disagreed, they returned to Teltown, to the centre of a fort styled Eathdoo, placed themselves back to back, one facing the north, the other the south, and walked out of the fort a divided couple free to marry again. (What numbers would now take advantage of this simple ceremony were it but legally efficacious !) Another ancient idea was that people should not marry in the autumn in "binding" time, for they were sure to be unbound afterwards, and the bride and bridegroom should go out of the church door together, as in many localities it is believed that the first to go out will be the first to die. There are also ill-disposed women, or witches, who by weaving spells during the wedding service prevent any children being born of the marriage. Their general manner of proceeding is to tie a knot on a string for every word uttered during the ceremony. Other traces of Pagan wedding customs still linger. " Giving away the bride " is a relic of the time when the bride was really sold ; the promise of the bride in the marriage service to obey her husband was, at one time, no mere form ; the bride's veil is a reminder that in days of old she was really shrouded from head to foot ; rice poured over the newly married couple is doubtless a substitute for the staple food of the country, and a token of a hope that they may always have a sufficiency ; old shoes were thrown after brides long before the introduction of Christianity, so that throughout the entire ritual of wedding observances, there is probably nothing that has not been hallowed by centuries of Paganism. At the commencement of this century it was customary, in the parish of Culdaff, county Donegal, for an infant at its birth to be forced to swallow spirits, and it was immediately afterwards suspended by the upper jaw upon the midwife's fore-finger. This ceremony was performed for the purpose of preventing a disease which the people styled " headfall." Another custom, not -merely local, but found in other parts of the kingdom, was noticed" by the Rev. Edward Cupples in the county Antrim. When his parishioners brought children to be baptized, a piece of bread and cheese was concealed in the infant's clothes. If several children were brought to the font at -the same time, the males were first presented to the clergyman.

Strangest of all strange customs is that of the Couvade, the custom which obliges the husband to take to his bed when a child is born, sets the doctor to dose him, the woman to nurse, and his friends to visit him. No certain information has as yet, it is believed, been obtained relative to the present continuance of this custom in Ireland, but the prominent position held by the mother in Irish birth-rites is very remarkable. Solinus recounts how, before the Christian era, the Irish mother puts the " food on the sword of her husband, and lightly introduces the first particle (auspicium) of nourishment into the little child's mouth with the point of the sword, and with gentle vows, expresses a wish that he may never meet death otherwise than in wars and amid wars." The Eev. F. A. Potter, in his description of the parish of Eathconrath, in the county Westmeatn, in the year 1819, mentions the fact of all the married women calling themselves by their maiden names, and this is still common in Ulster. To the present day, in many places, women, although married, retain their maiden names, and in times not very remote often followed their mother's rather than their father's kindred. The study of this habit may, in time to come, unravel the tangled skein of this folk custom ; but apparently the Couvade was prevalent in Ulster at a very remote period, for in one of the early centuries of the Christian Era, when the Northern Province was invaded by Maev, Queen of Connacht or the Western Province, she found all the adults confined to bed, so that no one, save the champion Cuchullin (Coolin) and his father, were able to defend the country against the invaders. This inactivity and inertia of the Northerns was interpreted by the light of a custom which seemed to render it intelligible. This singular inaction is accounted for in a tale entitled CeasnaiiUtean Uladh, or the " Childbirth debility of the Ulstermen." In the Book of Leinster it is recounted that Macha, wife of Crunniuc, was compelled to run in a chariot race with the horses of Conor, notwithstanding her earnest entreaty for a postponement of the contest on the plea that she was soon to become a mother. Her prayers were unavailing. After she had passed the goal she gave birth to twins, upon which she cursed the Ulstermen, and inflicted them yearly, at a certain season, with labour pains for five days and four nights (or four days and five nights). This was styled the Noinden Ulad. This incident is recited to account for the debility of the Ulstermen, when the Province was invaded by the celebrated Connacian Queen. It may be well to explain that the term Couvade or " hatching" comes from Beam, where the custom is so named. Even in the present day in Ireland, women before childbirth often wear the coat of the father of the expected arrival, with the idea that this will make the father share some of the pains of labour, and thus mitigate those of the mother. Women also often place the trousers of the father of the child round their neck, the effect of which is also to lighten their pains. In the same way, in India, amongst the Kukis, the doctor, not the patient, swallows the medicine. The custom of the Couvade is still practised in Southern India, in Yunnan, in China, in Borneo, Kamschatka, Greenland, and by many tribes of North and South America. *~A traveller in Guiana in the year 1763 thus describes the custom of the Couvade there prevailing : " When the wife lies in for the first time, the husband is obliged to keep his hammock, which is drawrn up to the ridge of the house, and he is suffered to have no nourishment but a little cassava wheat and some water. When they let him down, they cut him in several parts of his body with some sharp instrument, made either of the fin of a fish or the tooth of some animal. Sometimes also they give him a, sound whipping. Till this ceremony is performed upon the birth of the first child, the husband is the slave of his father-inlaw, and as soon as it is over he is obliged to enter into the service of some old Indian, and quit his wife for some months. During this time he is not allowed to eat venison, pork, nor game of any kind: neither is he allowed to cleave wood, under a. notion that it may hurt the infant. This servitude is terminated by a great festival, at which the husband is again put into possession of his liberty and his wife." Descent can be easily proved from the mother, whilst it is, as a general rule, impossible to know the paternity of an infant. Whenever relationship is traced through females only, the custom may be safely regarded as a remnant of savagery ; for it should be borne in mind that in primitive times a child was considered to belong to the tribe generally, afterwards it came to be looked on as the property of the mother, then of the father, whilst it is only in modern times that it is looked on as related to both. When a state of society was reached in which the father took the place previously held by the mother, the father instead of the mother came to be regarded as the parent. In the altered state of the case the father would, on the birth of the child, be bound by this idea to be careful of what he did or what he ate, for fear the child might be injured, and in this way the curious ceremony of the Couvade may have originated. In classical literature there are clear illustrations of it; so also among the Tibareni, a tribe on the south coast of the

Black Sea, among the Cantabri in the North of Spain and in Corsica. Mr. C. Staniland Wake, writing on the Couvade, directs attention to the fact that Dr. E. Tylor was of opinion that the custom " implicitly denies that physical separation of ' individuals ' which a civilized man would probably set down as a first principle common by nature to all mankind. ... It shows us a number of distinct and distant tribes deliberately holding the opinion that the connection between father and child is not only, as we think, a mere relation of parentage, affection, duty, but that their very bodies are joined by a physical bond, so that what is done to the one acts directly upon the other." Professor Max Muller offers the curious suggestion that the Couvade custom arises from some " secret spring in human nature " which led the husband at first to be " tyrannised over by his female relations, and afterwards frightened into superstition. He then began to make a martyr of himself till he made himself really ill, or took to his bed in self-defence." Sir John Lubbock sees in that custom a connection with the change which he supposes to have taken place from female to male kinship. He says: " As soon as the change was made, the father would take the place held previously by the mother, and he, instead of she, would be regarded as the parent. Hence, on the birth of a child, the father would naturally be very careful what he did, and what he ate, for fear the child be injured." The suggestion made in this passage is carried further by M. Giraud-Teulon, who regards the Couvade as an imitation of nature, intended to give a colour to the fiction that the father had brought forth the child, and was for it a second mother, such a pretence being the only way in which a bond between the father and his child could be established. The French writer shows that " adoption by the imitation of nature " was practised among the Eomans down to the first century of the empire. This was with a people who recognised relationship through both father and mother, and it was not a true instance of the Couvade. " So far, moreover, from this custom having any relation to a change from female to male kinship, it is most strongly pronounced among peoples having preferably a system of kinship through females. This is the case with the Arawaks and Caribs of British Guiana, and probably with the Abipones of Paraguay. M. Giraud-Teulon dwells on the domestic superiority of women among the Basquees with whom a husband n'entre dans la maison que pour reproduire et travailler pour la bien de sa femme." " This ' reproduction ' furnishes the explanation of the custom in question. With some of the Brazilian tribes, when a man becomes a father he goes to bed instead of his wife, and all the women of the village come to console him for ' *la peine et douleur qu'il a eu de faire cet enfant.*' This agrees with the idea entertained by so many peoples that the child is derived from the father only, the mother being merely its nourisher. When such an idea is held, it is not surprising if, as among the Abipones, the belief is formed that ' the father's carelessness influences the new-born offspring, from a natural bond and sympathy of both,' or if the father abstains, either before or after the child's birth, from eating any food or performing any actions which are thought capable of doing it harm. Still more so, if the child is regarded, as is sometimes the case, as the reincarnation of the father, a notion which is supported by the fact, pointed out by Mr. Gerald Massey, that in the Couvade the parent identifies himself with the infant child, into which he has been typically transformed. The explanation given by Prof. Douglas of the Couvade as practised by the aborigines in the Chinese province of Kwei-chow agrees with that view. He states that the father goes to bed with the infant for a month, ' the idea being that the life of the father and child is one, and that any harm happening to the father will affect injuriously the well-being of the infant'." Thus we see that the Couvade was practised by tribes represented then as backward in civilization, and in modern times by savages in many widely separated countries. This curious custom has been found at all times in many parts of the world, and in countries so distant from one another as to preclude the idea of imitation ; hence it seems that, however absurd the custom may appear, yet there must be a sentiment in human nature, at some stage of its development, of which it is the outcome. The daily life routine of a present day savage is regulated by many strange customs, which, however foolish they may appear to us, are regarded by the practiser as of vital importance to his own welfare ; and these customs are in reality but the sterile or growth-arrested germs which, under more favourable conditions, have in civilized communities evolved into highly complicated legal and religious codes. Finally the practice of the Couvade may be accounted for, partly on the idea of the child belonging exclusively to the father, and partly on the want of distinction in the savage mind between objective and subjective relations, whilst it has been also suggested that the malignant demons plotting against mother and child were considered to be tricked in this substitution of the man for the woman ; but C. Tomlinson, F.E.S., suggests that such a practice " could not have originated in the motives above referred to, but rather in the necessities of humanity in the early history of the race, when the man shared with the woman the exhausting function of suckling the child. From long disuse, the lacteal organ has become rudimentary in men generally, but occasionally exceptions are to be met with." He then enumerates many instances, both with regard to tribes and to individuals, and states that on submitting to a physiologist the question whether at some remote period of the history of the human race man did not share with woman the task of suckling the infant, he was referred to Darwin's Descent of Man (chap, vi., 2nd ed.), in which this subject is treated at length, and to which the reader is also referred. A most interesting Paper on "Lactation," by John Knott, M.D., M.R. C.P.I., &c., has lately appeared in the Medical Press, vol. cxix., pp. 578-580, 608-610. Classic antiquity presents instances of nations tracing their descent through the female line only. For examples, Herodotus (Clio, clxxiii) states that the Lycians "have one distinction from which they never deviate, which is peculiar to themselve ; they take their names from their mothers, and not from their fathers. If anyone is asked concerning his family, he proceeds immediately to give an account of his descent, mentioning the female branches only." Over the different companies into which the Cretans were divided, a woman presided who had the care and management of the whole family: this female government arose from their pretended descent from Thetis. According to Plutarch, Bellerophon slew a wild boar which had destroyed the cattle and crops of the Xanthians, but who nevertheless gave him no reward for the exploit. He thereupon prayed Neptune to blight their crops, which the god did, until moved by the supplications of the female population, Bellerophon prayed a second time to Neptune to remove the curse. To commemorate this a law was enacted amongst the Xanthians, that they should take their names from their mothers and not from their fathers. The story is, however, evidently invented to account for the peculiarity of having descent reckoned through females only. The old-world idea of pollution through contact with women is neatly ridiculed in the reply of Theano, wife of Pythagoras, to a person who inquired of her what time was required for a woman to become pure : " She is pure immediately if the man be her husband ; but if he be not her husband, no time will make her so." A very common superstition is that a marriage lacks validity unless solemnized with a gold ring. In a small country town, in the south of Ireland, a local jeweller used to keep a few wedding rings for hire, and when couples, who were too poor to purchase one of the necessary precious metal, were about to be married, they procured, for a small sum, the temporary loan of a ring, it being returned to the jeweller immediately after completion of the marriage ceremony. In very poor localities it is customary for the same gold ring to do duty for many marriages, for which purpose it is placed in the custody of some fairly comfortably circumstanced individual. It is regarded as most unlucky if the wedding ring slips off the finger of the newly married wife either through accident or carelessness ; another superstition is that when a wedding ring has worn so thin as to break in two, the woman or the husband will die, that the wedding ring and married life wear away *pari passu*,

"Perhaps, we have here an answer to the often-asked question of modern days, ' Why do ladies encumber themselves with such heavy wedding rings ? ' Another common notion is, that if a wife should be unfortunate enough to break her wedding ring, she will shortly lose her husband." The wedding ring is, it is stated, worn on the fourth finger, in accordance with a very ancient but erroneous belief that an artery ran direct from this finger to the heart. " This," Wheatly says," is now contradicted by experience, but several eminent authors, as well Gentiles as Christians, as well physicians as divines, were formerly of this opinion, and therefore they thought this finger the properest to bear the pledge of love, that, from thence, it might be conveyed, as it were, to the heart." According to the old proverb: " As your wedding-ring wears, your cares will wear away."

Wedding Strawboys, Co. Sligo C., 1900-1910, William Green

Here is an attempt by a 19th century scholar to interpret the tradition. You can see how each generation has colored interpretation in their own way. You can feel free to do the same.

Lady Wilde, <u>From Ancient Legends, Mystic Charms and Superstitions of Ireland</u>., Ticknor and Co., Boston, 1887.

In old times in Ireland it was thought right and proper to seem to use force in carrying off the bride to her husband. She was placed on a swift horse before the bridegroom, while all her kindred started in pursuit with shouts and cries. Twelve maidens attended the bride, and each was placed on horseback behind the young men who rode after the bridal pair. On arriving at her future home, the bride was met on the threshold by her bridegroom 's mother, who broke an oaten cake over her head, a good augury of plenty in the future. In the mountains where horses cannot travel, the bridal party walk in procession; the young men carrying torches of dried bogwood to light the bride over the ravines, for in winter the mountain streams are rapid and dangerous to cross.

The Celtic ceremonial of marriage resembles the ancient Greek ritual in many points. A traveler in Ireland some fifty years ago, before politics had quite killed romance and ancient tradition in the hearts of the people, thus describes a rustic marriage festival which he came on by chance one evening in the wilds of Kerry:-

A large hawthorn tree that stood in the middle of a field near a stream was hung all over with bits of coloured stuff, while lighted rush candles were placed here and there amongst the branches to symbolize, no doubt, the new life of brightness preparing for the bridal pair. Then came a procession of boys marching slowly with flutes and pipes made of hollow reeds, and one struck a tin can with a stick at intervals, with a strong rhythmical cadence. This represented the plectrum. Others rattled slates and bones between their fingers, and beat time, after the manner of the Crotolistori--a rude attempt at music, which appears amongst all nations of the earth, even the most savage. A boy followed, bearing a lighted torch of bogwood.

Evidently he was Hymen, and the flame of love was his cognizance. After him came the betrothed pair hand-in-hand, a large square canopy of black stuff being held over their heads; the emblem, of course, of the mystery of love, shrouded and veiled from the prying light of day.

Behind the pair followed two attendants bearing high over the heads of the young couple a sieve filled with meal; a sign of the plenty that would be in their house, and an omen of good luck and the blessing of children.

A wild chorus of dancers and singers closed the procession; the chorus of the epithalamium, and grotesque figures, probably the traditional fauns and satyrs, nymphs and bacchanals, mingled together with mad laughter and shouts and waving of green branches.

The procession then moved on to a bonfire, evidently the ancient altar; and having gone round it three times, the black shroud was lifted from the bridal pair, and they kissed each other before all the people, who shouted and waved their branches in approval.

Then the preparations for the marriage supper began, on which, however, the traveler left them, having laid some money on the altar as an offering of good-will for the marriage future. At the wedding supper there was always plenty of eating and drinking, and dancing, and the feast was prolonged till near morning, when the wedding song was sung by the whole party of friends standing, while the bride and bridegroom remained seated at the head of the table. The chorus of one of these ancient may be thus literally translated from the Irish--

> *"It is not day nor yet day,*
> *It is not day, nor yet morning:*
> *It is not day, nor yet day,*
> *For the moon is shining brightly."*

Another marriage song was sung in Irish frequently, each verse ending with the lines--

"There is sweet enchanting music, and the golden harps are ringing; And twelve comely maidens deck the bride-bed for the bride."

A beautiful new dress was presented to the bride by her husband at the marriage feast; at which also the father paid down her dowry before the assembled guests; and all the place round the house was lit by torches when night came on, and the song and the dance continued till daylight, with much speech-making and drinking of poteen. All fighting was steadily avoided at a wedding; for a quarrel would be considered a most unlucky omen. A wet day was also held to be very unlucky, as the bride would assuredly weep for sorrow throughout the year. But the bright warm sunshine was hailed joyfully, according to the old saying--

> *"Happy is the bride that the sun shines on;*
> *But blessed is the corpse that the rain rains on."*

-Editor's note- does it not seem that the customs of the cake and the grain described above are more Scottish traditions than Irish. This account however is older than most I have read.

Before and Without Arrangement!

I'd wed you without herds, without money, or rich array.
And I'd wed you on a dewy morning at day-dawn gray.- Sir Samuel Ferguson

Now here is an example of a custom of the ancient days which folks might not be comfortable with today. It does however reflect the variety of tradition and makes for good conversation.

From:*Curious Customs of Sex and Marriage.,* George Ryley Scott, Torchstream Books, London. P.44.

An interesting reference to bundling as practiced in Ireland occurs in a book entitled <u>The Stranger in Ireland</u>, written by John Carr, who says:

" One evening, at an inn where we halted we heard a considerable bustle in the kitchen, and upon inquiry, I was let into a secret worth knowing. The landlord had been scolding one of his maids, a very pretty plump little girl, for not having done her work; and the reason which she alleged for her idleness was, that her master having locked the street door at night, had prevented her lover enjoying the rights and delights of bundling, an amatory indulgence which, considering that it is sanctioned by custom, may be regarded as somewhat singular, although it is not exclusively of Welsh growth. The process is very simple: the gay Lothario, when all is silent, steals into the chamber of his mistress, who receives him in bed, but with the modest precaution of wearing her under petticoat, which is always fastened at the bottom, not infrequently, I am told by a sliding knot. It may astonish a London gallant to be told that this extraordinary experiment often ends in a downright wedlock- the knot which cannot slide. A gentleman of respectability also assured me that he was obliged to indulge his female servants in these nocturnal interviews, and that, too, at all hours of the night, otherwise his whole family would be thrown into disorder by their neglect; the carpet would not be dusted nor would the kettle boil."

Richard Twiss, in his book: **A Tour in Ireland** in 1775, also says that bundling was prevalent among the common people in some parts of Ireland; and as evidence of a similar custom existing in Holland quotes a passage from the travels of Van Egmont and Heyman.

Running Away....

In Ireland at one time it was considered fitting, according to Sampson, that the groom should *"run away with the bride."* Jeaffreson (1872) in his interesting work Brides and Bridals, mentions a curious practice observed some two centuries ago in West Meath, in which a number of the bridegroom's friends approached the bride's party, when it was usual to make a sportive show of hostility to the cavaliers who advanced on horseback for the purpose of surrendering her to her hands. *"Being come near each other"* said Piers, *"the custom was of old to cast short darts at the company that attended the bride, but at such distance that seldom any hurt ensued. Today it is not out of the memory of man that the Lord of Hoath on such an occasion lost an eye."*

From the accounts of contemporary writers it is apparent that in connection with these Irish weddings, however good might be the match, it was thought little of if the bridegroom did not first seize and carry off the bride. The couple spent some days, marked by jollification, among friends of the bridegroom, and then returned to the home of the bride's parents. Herethey were visited by relations and friends laden with gifts, for the most part consisting of bottles of whisky, as contributions to a second jollification; on the conclusion of which the couple proceeded to their new home, to commence their married life together.

Running For the Bottle

The Irish wedding was always an occasion of great hilarity, jollity and mirth. Among other scenes attending it, running for the bottle was much practiced. It was usual for the wedding parties to ride to the residence of the clergyman to have the ceremony performed.
In their absence, the father or the next friend prepared, at the bride's residence, a bottle of the best spirits that could be obtained, around the neck of which a white ribbon was tied. Returning from the clergyman's, when within one or two miles of the home of the bride, some three or four young men prepared to run for the bottle. Taking an even start, their horses were put at full speed, dashing over mud, rocks, stumps, and disregarding all impediments. The race, in fact, was run with as much eagerness and desire to win, as is ever manifested on the turf by our sporting characters. The father or next friend of the bride, expecting the racers, stood with the bottle in his hand, ready to deliver to the successful competitor. On receiving it, he forthwith returned to meet the bride and groom.
When met, the bottle was first presented to the bride, who must taste it at least, next to the groom, and then handed round to the company, every one of whom was required to swig it.

-Kircheval, Samuel, The History of The Valley of Virginia,1850.

Ancient Capture....

That the practice (of marriage by capture) was of great antiquity in Ireland is indicated by an old poem of that country, Duan Gircanash, which makes reference to three hundred women being carried off into enforced marriage by the Picts from the Gaels. One of the verses narrates: Cruithne, son of Cuig, took their women from them. It is directly stated-- Except Tea, wife of Hermion, Son of Miledh.

Finding themselves thus deprived of their women, the Gaels finally made an alliance with the aboriginal tribes of Ireland, as we are told in the following quatrain:

There were no charming noble wives
For their young men;
Their women having been stolen, they made alliance
With the Tuatha Dea.

-From: **Strange Customs of Courtship and Marriage** by William J. Fielding, The New Home Library, New York. P. 239.

Don't walk behind me, I might not lead you
Don't walk in front of me, I might not follow you,
Just walk beside me and be my friend.

-Traditional Irish Saying

Temporary

John O'Donovan (1806-1861) wrote of the Teltown Marriages:

A number of young men went into the hollow to the north side of the wall, and an equal number of marriageable young women to the south side of the wall which was so high as to prevent them from seeing the men; one of the women put her hand thro' the hole in the gate and a man took hold of it from the other side, being guided in his choice only by the appearance of the hand. The two were thus joined hands by blind chance were obliged to live together for a year and a day, at the expiration of which time they appeared at the Rath of Telton and if they were not satisfied with each other they obtained a deed of separation, and were entitled to go to Laganeeny again to try their good fortune for the ensuing year.

Preparing   the   Way

Marriage in Ireland through the centuries was much more than merely a union between two individuals. Throughout centuries of Irish history and prehistory marriage represented the creation of a new unit of production, a new extension of civilization into the wilderness or the maintenance of an existing unit. Marriage changed the community. The union had to be right and it had to be supported with the wealth of the community at large. Civilization at the very edge of the world depended upon it. Marriages were often extension of political arrangements on one level while on another the new families which were created became units of production upon which many others in the community depended. It is no wonder that the Irish spent so much of their social time together concerned with consulting with all of the dimensions of the cosmos in order to make sure that the union would be the right one. This process could have been a withdrawn and mysterious ordeal, but such is not in keeping with the nature of the Irish culture. As you will see below preparing the way for marriage was turned into the life of every party, gathering and seasonal celebration. Preparation became a reason for life itself and a source of excitement and entertainment. I hope that the customs documented below will help you to add joy and excitement to the process which leads to the marriage ceremony. Get everyone involved and have fun!

Divination!

Irish women have many customs, which predict the one to marry. One method is to boil an egg hard, remove the yolk, fill the cavity with salt, and eat the whole of it. Then go to bed without speaking or drinking anything. If the Lover appears in a dream, offering water to quench the maiden's thirst, he is to be accounted faithless. The *"faggot charm"* is to go on Hallowe'en or Midsummer Eve at midnight to the wood stack, and draw out a stick. If it is straight and even, your husband will be gentle and kindly; if knotted, he will be churlish; and if bent and twisted, a crabbed old man.

The nutshell charm is a very old one. Take two nuts (generally chestnuts) and name them silently-one for yourself and one for your lover. Place them on the bars of the fire and watch. If they burn quietly and steadily, you will gain a faithful love; if your companion nut jumps away from you, you will be disappointed; and if your own nut should move, your love will pass.

W h o   Will   It   Be.......?

Divination is perhaps one of the most popular forms of entertainment in the Irish Tradition. Divination occurs in connection with all major celebrations especially around Samhain (Oct.31). The frequent use of divination relates to the belief that the other world past and future were only barely cut off from the present and could be entered by means of divination. Try a few of these to find out if you can predict the identity of the marriage couple! I include these rituals not only for the purposes of divination but to convey a sense of the meaning of the wedding in Irish culture. In a small village planning for marriage was a continual part of everyday life. At all gatherings and everywhere one turned the women of the village would be at work thinking about your eventual wedding. This tradition has distinct links to the culture of the ancient Celts. From these divinations you can also come to understand how the people thought of their world. As you read them try to imagine the gatherings involved and the excitement of the revelations.

-J.B.Arthur, <u>Ulster Folklife</u>, 1957, p43, wrote:

"In addition to the crosses, imitation ladders and spinning wheels are also woven from the rushes, (of St. Brigid's Day Feb. 1), two or three rushes each being used for the purpose. That night the young men and young women sleep with these under their pillow, the men having the spinning wheels and the women the ladders. One's future partner would subsequently first be seen climbing a ladder or spinning at a wheel."

These were often exchanged as love tokens- the man made the ladder; the girl made the spinning wheel. They exchanged these and then if they dreamed of each other will be sure to marry- Danaher, Kevin, The Year in Ireland., Mercier, Minneapolis,1972.

"Marriage in May was considered most unlucky. On the other hand, May-Eve was one of the nights when marriage divination might be successful. The girl who looked at the reflection of the "young May Moon" in her mirror or in a well might see her future husband looking over her shoulder. -Danaher, Kevin, The Year in Ireland., Mercier, Minneapolis, 1972, p.125.

Lady Wilde wrote in **Ancient Cures, Charms and Usages**, *1890 (p.106-7)*

"On May morning, before sunrise go out to the garden, and the first snail you see take up, and put it on a plate sprinkled lightly with flour, place a cabbage-leaf over, and so leave it till after sunrise, when you will find the initial letters of your lover's name traced on the flour.(this can be done between two plates as well) "Should the snail be quite within his house when you take him up, your lover will be rich; but should the snail be almost out of his shell, then your future husband will be poor, and probably will have no house or home to take you to when you wed him. Therefore take good heed of the warning given to you by the snail, or avoid trying your future fate if you are afraid of the result."

On page 101 she says:

"Among others it is thought right and proper to have the threshold swept clean on May-Eve. Ashes are then lightly sprinkled over it, and in the morning the print of a foot is looked for. If it turn inward a marriage is certain, but if outward then a death will happen in the family before the year is out."

Sir William Wilde wrote in **Irish Popular Superstitions**, *(* p. 49) of the Midsummer fire:

"As the fire sunk low, the girls tripped across it to procure good husbands;.
"In many places and especially in south Leinster, young men and women joined hands in couples and jumped together.....the onlookers took it for granted that there was some intention of marriage between the pair and the wiseacres claimed to be able to foretell the outcome from the way in which the flames flickered as the couple jumped."

-Danaher, Kevin, The Year in Ireland., Mercier, Minneapolis1972, p.144.

On St. John's Eve or between St. John's Eve and Old St. John's day or little St. John's Day (June 29- July 4) *"Yarrow (Achillea millefolium) was gathered....for medicinal use . It was also used in marriage divination by girls who recited while plucking it these words:*

Good morrow, good yarrow, good morrow to thee
Send me this night my true love to see
The clothes that he'll wear, the colour of his hair
And if he'll wed me.
The plant was put under the pillow and the girl dreamed of her future husband

-Danaher, Kevin, The Year in Ireland., Mercier, Minneapolis, 1972. p..148.

   Of the last sheaf of the End of the Harvest: *" The last sheaf was held by many to affect the destiny of its cutter....Some held that whoever cut or bound it would die unmarried. In county Carlow the girls were asked each to have a stroke at it with a reaping hook, and she who felled it at one blow would be married within the year.*

"-Danaher, Kevin, <u>The Year in Ireland</u>*., Mercier, Minneapolis,1972. p. 191.

Around Samhain (Oct. 31) :

"the custom of roasting beans and nuts. The girl who placed the bean watched where this would leap, some ambitious youth perhaps making a wide front on the landscape....Many a maiden and many a youth secretly spread shift or shirt before a fire and watched from safe coign of vantage to see who would turn these articles late at night. The reel of thread was cast into a lime kiln to find out who would wind it up again......As a girl, one November Eve, she ate up a salt herring in three bites in the hope that her future husband might appear to her in a dream offering her a drink of water. When she confessed this high crime, the parish priest said: "Were you not afraid that the devil would choke you?.....a ring concealed in one of the cakes (Bairin Breac-a fruit cake) *foretold (early) marriage"*

- Danaher, Kevin, <u>The Year in Ireland</u>., Mercier, Minneapolis,1972.202.

M.J. Murphy in **At Slieve Gullion's Foot**, P. 45 writes:

"A marriage ring was often mixed in the champ. Here boys and girls gathered round a pot on the floor, and armed with big spoons, tried to be first to get the ring in their mouths. The winner would be married ere next Hallow Eve..." Sometimes a little circle of withy was used instead of a wedding ring.

Danaher, Kevin, The Year in Ireland., Mercier, Minneapolis1972, p. 219.

The: **Journal of the Kildare Archaeological Society**, 1908, p.448 describes two other games-

"Two hazel-nuts ,walnuts or chestnuts, or even two grains of wheat, were selected and named after some boy and girl who were supposed to be courting. They were then placed side by side on a bar of the grate, or in the turf-ashes, and according as to whether they burned quietly, or jumped apart from one another, so would be the future before them"...Four plates having been set down on a table, water was poured into one, a ring placed on another, some clay in the third, and in the fourth was placed either some straw, salt, or meal. A person would then be blindfolded and led up to the table, and into whichever plate he or she placed their hand, so would their future turn out. The water signified migration, the ring marriage, the clay death, and the fourth plate prosperity. On re-arranging the order of the plates others would be blindfolded and led up in like manner."

"In county Kerry two beans were named for couples, first heated and then dropped into a vessel of water, with the words:
"Piosam, Pósam, Lánamha phóire, I méisin uisce, I lár na teine, Is tá mo lánamha pósta.
"Piosam, Poisam, A pair of beans in a dish of water in the middle of the fire And my pair are married"

"If both beans sank at once, then the named pair are sure to marry and live in harmony. If one sinks and one floats, they will not marry, if both float they will marry and quarrel."-

-Danaher, Kevin, The Year in Ireland., Mercier, Minneapolis1972. p.220.

Miss. A. Watson notes in **Folklore**, 1893, p.361-2:

"When we were children Hallow Eve was always an occasion for practicing mysterious rites, the end and aim of each being to foretell the future. The first thing always was to get an old iron spoon, filled with lead in scraps; this was held over a hot fire till it melted. Then a key which must be the hall-door key, was held over a tub of cold water and the hot lead was poured through the wards of the key. The lead cooled in falling through the water, and when it had all settled in the bottom of the tub, the old nurse proceeded to read its surface.........the lead would take the form of the trade or profession of the future husband. "

In Ancient Legends of Ireland Lady Wilde on p. 111. describes another game:
"Another spell is the building of the house. Twelve couples are taken., each being made of two holly twigs tied together with a hempen thread; these are all named and struck round in a circle in the clay. A live coal is then placed in the centre, and whichever couple catches fire first will assuredly be married. Then the future husband is invoked in the name of the Evil One to appear and quench the flame.On one occasion a dead man in his shroud answered the call, and silently drew away the girl from the rest of the party. The fright turned her brain, and she never recovered her reason afterwards."
Bryan Merryman of County Clare describes a divination in his long Irish poem: *Cúirt an Mheadhon Oídhche* (lines 287-306)

> *No trick of which you'd read or hear*
> *At dark of moon, or where it's clear,*
> *At shrove or Samhain or through the year,*
> *That I've not tried to find my dear!*
> *Under my pillow I've kept all night*
> *A stocking stuffed with apples tight,*
> *For hours a pious fast kept up*
> *Without a thought of bite or sup.*
> *My shift I'd draw against the stream*
> *In hope of my sweetheart to dream.*
> *The stack I'd sweep without avail*
> *Left in the embers hair and nail.*
> *The flail against the gable laid.*
> *Under my bolster put the spade.*
> *My distaff in the oats would lie.*
> *I'd drop spun yarn in the lime-kiln's eye*
> *Flax seed upon the road I'd fling.*
> *A cabbage head to bed I'd bring.*
> *There is no trick of these I mention*
> *That I've not tried for the Devil's intention. "*

....All the things mentioned were to induce a dream of the future partner....bairin breac, the first spoonful of colcannon ...the last left on the plate....were sometimes put into the left stocking of the girl and then the stocking was tied with her own right garter or with nine ivy leaves. While this was being done he following words were said:

> *"Nine ivy leaves I place under my head*
> *to dream of the living and not of the dead,*
> *to dream of the man I am going to wed,*
> *and to see him tonight at the foot of my bed"*

Fasting and inducing thirst was found to be another way to cause dreams. The partner to be would be seen offering a drink. Salt herring eaten at bedtime, salted porridge or flour, salt and soot would also work. If you dried out your shift on the riverbank, the figure of the lover will be seen on the opposite bank, or his face reflected on the water. Others said that it must be hung up to dry, and the watching girl would see her future husband turning it during the night. Sometimes a young man would dip and dry his shirt in this way to see his future wife.

If you sweep around the base of the corn stack with a broom three times you will see your future partner or his name will be spoken aloud. Sometimes you just have to walk around the stack three times.

Drop hair and nail clippings into the last embers of a fire and you will have a dream of your husband or wife to be.

A flail or spade will bring a vision of the man. A cuigeal or distaff of the spinning wheel should be placed in the corn-drying kiln to reveal the same.

Drop a ball of woolen thread into the pit of a limekiln and wind it back slowly. If the string caught the girl asks who is holding it and the voice of the future husband should answer.

You can also drop a ball of yarn out the window and according to General Vallency in

Collectanaea de Rebus Hibernicus, *xii, 460* the Pater Noster should be said backwards while winding in the thread.

If a girl went to the crossroads at night and sprinkled flax seed on the road or put a *súgán* across it her intended husband would step across it at midnight.

If an apple is peeled in one long strip and then it is let fall on the ground it will form the initials of a future husband. If a girl eats an apple in front of a mirror the future husband will be seen looking over the girl's shoulder.

If you wash your face but do not dry it before bed the lover will appear in a dream proffering a towel.

Put the letters of the alphabet on pieces of paper. Float these face downwards on a basin of water. In the morning they should be found to have sunk to the bottom and those which have turned over to show the letters will show the initials or spell the name of the future spouse.

"A daring girl might take a mouthful of water, and holding it in the mouth without swallowing, creep close to the door or window of a neighbour's house and listen until the name of a young unmarried man was mentioned in the conversation by somebody within. When by virtue of the charm this youth would become her husband. A grain of wheat held between the teeth was believed by some to be equally potent."

"Three stalks of corn pulled from the stack at the dead of night could also tell their tale. The first two were discarded, but the state of the third ear would surely reveal, by its form and size, how rich and how handsome would be the desired husband or wife."

—Danaher op.cit. p.224.

A head of cabbage, pulled up by the root gave much information on the crucial marriage question: A.J. Pollock, in **Ulster Folklife**, 1960, 62 gives a version from County Down of this very widespread custom:

"The girls were blindfolded and sent out in pairs, hand in hand, up the garden or field and told to pull the first cabbage they found. Its size and shape-whether it was big or small, straight or crooked - would indicate the shape and nature of their future spouse. If there was only a little they would be poor. The taste of the "custoc", i.e. the heart would tell them his temper and disposition, according to whether it was sweet or bitter. Finally the "runts" or stems were hung above the door, each was given a number and the name of a boy friend, for example Barney might be the name given to the third runt. If Barney was the third person to enter the house on the night, this was considered to be a good omen."
Other versions go further and say that if the young man indicated in the charm can by some means be induced to eat part of the same cabbage head, he will inevitably lead the girl to the altar."

A.J. Pollock in the source cited above also gives this charm from the County Down p.63:

"If none of these charms worked you could always try to "winnow three wechts of nothing", the wecht being the skin of a winnowing tray. You had to go alone to a barn, open both doors and take them off their hinges. This was important, for the Being that would appear might otherwise shut the doors and do you harm. You then took the wecht and went through the motions of winnowing corn in a strong wind. This was repeated three times, and on the third occasion an apparition would pass through the barn, in at the "windy" door and out through the other. The face would be that of your future husband, and the clothes he wore and the tools he carried would tell you both his occupation and station in life."

The **Journal of the Kildare Archaeological Society**, *1908,449* mentions a similar charm:

"A boy would go to a barn and sow oats along its floor, in the name of the devil, from one end to the other. Having done that, he would go to the door, open it, and expect to see the fetch of his future wife standing outside. Instances have been known where, in place of the fetch, a coffin has appeared, and this foretells to the beholder that he will not be alive on that night twelve-month."

Another charm from County Down comes from R.H. Buchanan in: *Ulster Folklife*, *1963, 68.:*

"In many parts of Co. Down salt was used in another way. Here the girl would sprinkle salt on the four corners of the bed and repeat the following verse:

> *"Salt, salt, I salt thee*
> *In the name of God in unity.*
> *If I'm for a man or a man for me*
> *In my first sleep may I see him*
> *The colour of his hair, the clothes he'll wear*
> *The day he weds with me"*

Rose Shaw, in **Carleton's Country**, 57, writing of the Clogher Valley in county Tyrone mentions again the ladders and spinning wheels of rushes:

"Also they had made wee ladders with rushes cut in the Three Counties Hollow, and they would hang the ladders above their beds that night- a sure way for a girl to see "himself" walk up the ladder in her dreams."

Cáit Ni Bhrádaigh in **Beáloideas**, 1936,268-9 notes:

> *"Put three knots on the left garter, and at every knot say:*
> *"This knot, this knot ,this knot to see*
> *The thing I never saw yet.*
> *To see my love in his array*
> *And what he walks in every day,*
> *And what his occupation,*
> *This night may I in my dream see*
> *And if my love be clad in green,*
> *His love for me it is well seen,*
> *And if my love be clad in grey,*
> *His love for me is far away.*
> *And if my love is clad in blue,*
> *His love for me is very true."*

> *"Go to bed, place the knotted garter under your pillow, and you will see your future husband in a dream."*
> *"Cut nine stalks of yarrow with a black-handled knife. When all are gone to bead say:*
> *"Good morrow, good morrow, my pretty yarrow!*
> *I pray before this time to-morrow*
> *You will tell who my true love shall be*
> *The clothes that he wears, and the name that he bears,*
> *And the day that he'll come to wed me"*

On New Years Eve put out holly and ivy leaves, or a sprig of mistletoe under a pillow to bring a dream of the future husband you can recite:

"Oh, ivy green and holly red,
Tell me, tell me whom I shall wed!
-Danaher, Kevin, The Year in Ireland., Mercier, Minneapolis, 1972 .p222.

Maybe you will have success if you do some special things at special places:

Kilmaolcheader church,Dingle, Co. Kerry- Ogham standing stone with hole near the top. Those putting fingers through the hole become engaged.

Loch Derg, Co.Donegal- go there nine times and you will find a husband

The Metal Man, Co. Waterford, Tramore Bay- Girls who hop around the man three times will be married in a year.

Then there is always the traditional pancake predictor…..

Shrove Tuesday Pancake Tossing (Hall, 1841-3)

On Shrove Tuesday the oldest girl tosses the first pancake. If this is done correctly, she will be a good match in the current year.

So as you see, thinking about it well in advance is important. There is a dynamic quality of anticipation built into the old traditions. The wonder of it all is an important aspect.

What Irish magpies foretold:
One for sorrow; two for mirth;
three for a wedding;
four for a birth.-Irish Proverb

Courtship and Arrangement

The most traditional of Irish weddings follows a match made for economic and political purposes by the father of the groom. The contrast of this custom with the divinations of the women is interesting one. The father chooses from one of his sons for a son to be married. His choice is important, as the son to be married will inherit the farm. In early times the land could be and was subdivided endlessly so that all received a portion. This practice was forbidden, as small land holdings became uneconomical and land scarce. Later it was the obligation of the farmer to "settle" only one son "on the land."

A young man looking for a young lady would work through his friends and from friends to relatives with the setting for such discussions being the markets or public houses.

Eventually all families become involved. Once a lady is recommended the man will send a "speaker" to her to determine her fortune and suitability. If the speaker and the woman's family are convinced that it would be a good match the speaker will be given a go ahead to "draw it down" He returns to the young man's house and arranges a meeting between the two fathers and the young man. At the meeting the first drink is called by the young man; the second by the young lady's father.

The young lady's father asks the speaker of the dowry price. The girls father inquires as to the nature of the home, the farm, the livestock and the situation of the farm.

How many cows, sheep, horses? What sort of garden? What sort of water supply? Is it far from the road? Or on it? What kind of house and what sort of roof- slate or thatch? Near a chapel - a school?

If a nice place and eight cows, near the road, the fortune of 350 pounds may be asked. The young lady's father offers 250 then the father throws off 50 . then the speaker divides the 50 between them so now it's 275 then the young man insists on 300- but maybe he will think of it....if she is a good housekeeper. They drink until intoxicated.

After the fortune is arranged they then set a place and time for the young people to see one another. The young lady takes her friends, brother, mother and father.

The young man takes his friends and the speaker. If they like each other they will set a date to come see the land. If things aren't right they simply say they do not suit, not revealing details.

The day before the girl's people come to see the land, preparations for a feast are made. Geese are killed, the house whitewashed, whiskey and porter bought. The cows are fed and sometimes cows are borrowed to make things look good.

A goose generally served as a meal for the feast of introduction. The goose was plucked while family members discussed married life with the girl. Sometimes this meal was known as : "Aitin' the Gander." the Bindings or the agreement of marriage was sketched out.. This agreement would detail the rights of the relatives.

The girl's family comes and the land is walked. The young man sends his best friend to show the girl's father round making sure the bad points are not shown. If the girl's father likes the land he will join in the feast until night.

The next day they go to the attorney to get the writings between the parties concluded. The father agrees to sign over the land. After that the wedding can go forward.

"In ancient Ireland it is said to have been the custom for the man to give the woman he wanted to marry a bracelet woven of human hair. Her acceptance of it was symbolic of accepting the man, linking herself to him for life. The use of some strands of hair in love-lockets, usually curled into a circle, has been a custom down to modern times. In the bracelet, as in the ring, we have the circle--the link symbolizing union unbroken without end"

From: **Strange Customs of Courtship and Marriage** by William J. Fielding, The New Home Library, New York, p.26.

"The purchase of the bride was customary among the ancient Celts. In Ireland the bride-price (called coibche) consisted of various objects, such as articles of gold, silver or bronze, clothes or horse bridles, cattle or swine, land or houses. Installment payment was not unusual, the husband making a yearly remittance after marriage until his obligation was fulfilled"

-From: **Strange Customs of Courtship and Marriage** by William J. Fielding, The New Home Library, New York. P.263.

"Among the Irish peasants the professional match-maker or "cosherer" is still to be found, and some very quaint customs survive. If a girl's fiancé dies, it is the custom for her to solemnly "give back her promise" before witnesses, holding the dead man's hand. There is also much fairy folklore in Ireland and it is said that if a bridegroom unbuttons one button of the right knee, the little people cannot harm him. In parts of Mayo and Leitrim there is a strange survival of a wedding dance with a straw mask or sometimes a straw petticoat. A band of nine "strawboys," as they are called, visits the bride's home on the wedding eve, and one dances with the bride and the rest with the other girls present. They are followed by nine more also masked, and it is considered unlucky if any of them are recognized."

-From: **A Short History of Marriage** By: Ethel, L.Urlin,1913, Omnigraphics, Detroit, 1990 p.195.

You will read more about the "strawboys" in the chapter on the wedding itself.

The Irish have been guided throughout the centuries by their ancient Irish tales.

Once when Naoisi was outside alone Deidre slipped out to him as if she were going past him and he did not recognize her.
"That's a nice heifer that's going by me," he said.
"Heifers ought to be by," she said, "wherever there are no bulls,"
"You have the bull of the province," he said, meaning the King of Ulster.
"I'd choose between you, " she said ,"and take a little young bull like you."
"No," he said. "Not after Cathbad's prophecy!"
"Are you saying that because you don't want me?"
"I am surely," said he.
She made a rush at him and grabbed his two ears.
"Then two ears of shame and mockery on you," she said, "unless you take me with you."
"Go on , woman! " he said.
"You'll have it," she said.

Annon 9th cent. Trans Frank O'Connor.

In Co. Limerick, around harvest time, bachelors must wear a shamrock and the houses of girls to be married must be painted blue.

In Co. Donegal a man who wanted to marry a particular girl would go to the girl's residence with friends and toss his cap into the house. Tossing the cap back out was a negative response.

In Co. Westmeath- Jumping the Bezum or twig/broom meant that the two people would be marrying.

While many do not care for formalities, they are traditional and add excitement to the preparations.

Courtship in Ireland is said to be that period during which a girl decides whether or not she can do any better.-Traditional Saying

An old blessing for a young man: That you might have nicer legs than your own under your table before the new spuds are up.

The Deadline:
Shrove Tuesday

The matchmakers worked hard to arrange things between Epiphany, also known as Little Christmas, until Shrovetide. Shrove Tuesday was the absolute deadline. The entire community would look forward to this season for announcements of celebration and feasting to come. These announcements would also be important indicators of the future prosperity of the community and the perpetuation of the culture on the frontiers of civilization.

As young Rory and Moreen were talking
How Shrove Tuesday was drawing near;
For the tenth time he asked her to marry;
But says she, "Time enough till next year,"
Then ochone I'm going to Skellig
O Moreen what will I do?
Tis the woeful road to travel
And how lonesome I'll be without you

.-Traditional in: P.W. Joyce,English as we Speak it in Ireland, Wolfhound,1988.

Shrovetide is the most important time for country marriages. The time was almost exclusively the only time marriages were performed. Lent was such a strictly kept season that it had to be avoided at all cost. Shrove Tuesday was the very end of the season. Marriage during Lent was banned by the Council of Trent in the 16th century. The council however, in its ruling, referred to ancient customs which had already prohibited Lenten marriages. In Ireland the prohibition is many centuries old.

W.Shaw Mason wrote in: Parochial Survey of Ireland., Dublin, 1814-19.

"For a fortnight before Shrove Tuesday, the great day for weddings it is the practice for persons in disguise to run through the street of Ballymahon, from seven to nine or ten'oclock in the evenings announcing intended marriages or giving pretty broad hints for matchmaking, in these words, "Holla, the bride- the bride, A.B. to C.D." &c,; these jokes sometimes prove true ones."

"You're off to the Rock, I suppose?" "Don't miss the Boat." "Who will you be taking on the excursion?"

Are you on the Skellig List?
You see....on the Skellig islands Easter was observed one week later than on the mainland. If you missed the Shrove Tuesday deadline there was still one last chance-
You could go and get married on the Skelligs.

Skellig Lists- These were made by a bard of those who should be married that year before Shrove Tuesday. Those on the list were to have made a pilgrimage to St. Finnian's monastery on Great Skellig Rock. Sometimes the lists were made into songs by local authors. These were printed, sold and distributed throughout the community. The printing was done anonymously. Sometimes the list was made into a poster which advertised the departure of a sea cruise to the Skelligs complete with the names of the unmarried passengers!

In Cork City on Shrove Tuesday eve two boys take a rope and chase a girl and try to capture her with the rope. This was called Skellicking. If the girl is captured the boys pretend to take her to the Skelligs. Sometimes men would capture the unmarried and dunk them in water, calling that "going to the Skelligs".

Procrastinators beware! On the other hand...the Skelligs are not that terrible a place! They would be a beautiful setting for weddings. The islands are topped by wonderful ruins of the ancient monasteries of the Celtic church; however, you should realize that part of the procedure requires that you walk barefoot to the rocks which are located off the Kerry coast. When you go be sure to bring back blocks of *bog-deal,* or oak which has been preserved in the bog. This was a prized variety of firewood reserved for special fires of celebration. This, then, is your penalty for not getting married on time!

And, also, be careful! In addition to being forced to the Skelligs you may find yourself covered with ash or find a bag of ash attached to you or thrown at you on Ash Wednesday. In north Galway and southeastern Mayo you could get salt thrown on you. It was said to be a preservative to keep you fresh until the next wedding season! Sometimes bachelors in County Donegal would wake up to find a scarecrow effigy of a wife set up across from their houses. One time in Waterford a crowd took a large log into town, gathered up the unmarried and tied them to it. Be careful not to be sent to a person's house for a pancake sieve because in Monaghan sending one from house to house on such a search was a practical joke played on the unmarried. Sometimes unacceptable marriages were also attacked at this time. Marriages of convenience or for financial gain brought hecklers blowing on trumpets and making noise to your door.

Marriage was so important for the community at large that those who should be married, but were not, received a considerable amount of public ridicule. Older men who had not yet married were called *boys*. Once one married, one could be called a *man*. Only women who married could attain the rank of *Matron*. Sometimes parents were to blame and kept their sons *boys* for years before finally deciding to hand over the farm to them and permit marriage. This practice has accounted for severe psychological disorders amongst the rural unmarried men of Ireland. An excellent source for this is the book by Nancy Scheper-Hughes, <u>Saints Scholars and Schizophrenics. Mental Illness in Rural Ireland.</u>,University of California Press.Berkley,1979.

On Chalk Sunday, which is the first Sunday after Shrove Tuesday, bachelors were marked with a streak of chalk on their Sunday coats. Chalking was done by children to taunt the bachelors. Those who were older and still unmarried were popular targets and they found that their clothing was marked with many chalk lines. Sometimes it was worse than chalk as as *rattle,* the colouring dye used for marking sheep, was used. This was hard to remove from clothing. The customs of chalking probably did little to improve the mental state of the elderly *old boys;* however, the custom lasted well into the 1930s and perhaps beyond. Sometimes children just chalked each other on the day as a form of amusement.

Clearly one avoided marriage at one's own risk. Such was the importance of marriage in old Ireland. Now you will know why on *domhnach na Smúit* or Puss Sunday, the First Sunday in Lent the unmarried come out of church wearing a *Smút* or scowl (Pus also means scowl!). For them it would truly be as it is called in Kilkenny: *Domhnach na nDeóirin* or Sunday of the little tears. –*Source: Danaher,op.cit. p. 43-51.*

Proceedings of the American Philosophical Society, May 3, 1889,
Shrove Tuesday, the Lenten Season and Easter, James Mooney, p 386.

..The customs pertaining to the Lenten season, with the attendant festivals of Shrove Tuesday…
..The Roman feast of Minerva took place about the middle of March, and was celebrated by public amusements, and was also a favorite time for getting married.
This statement still holds good throughout all Catholic countries, where
marriages are prohibited by the Church during the succeeding six weeks of
Lent. On this subject the same author says: "It is also remarkable that
in the Irish-speaking districts more marriages take place at this season
than at any other period of the year. The feasts and the marriages are at
present ascribed to the near approach of the season of Lent; but perhaps,
like the other popular festivities of the year, they had their origin
in something more remote, though now forgotten." t Back of all mythology the
custom probably has its explanation in the fact, as stated by the poet, that
" In the spring the young man's fancy lightly turns to thoughts of love."
It is popularly expected that all the marriageable young folks shall have

been mated before Lent, and on this, the last day of grace, the young men
in Cork, Waterford and other towns of the south, were formerly accustomed
to go through the streets in bands, carrying ropes, with which they
caught any unlucky girl who had "mist her chance," and pulld her a
few rods along the road, after which she was releast. This was called taking her to Skellig to
get married, the allusion being to the Skellig rocks on the coast of Kerry, formerly a noted
place of pilgrimage, toward the end of the Lenten season, for young women who desired
good husbands.
This " taking to Skellig" has supplanted an older and rougher pastime,

* Smiddy, Druids, 112.
t Idem, 112-3.

practiced in the south about fifty years ago and known as "drawing the
log." Any unmarried young folks of either sex who were so unfortunate
as to be caught on the streets on this day were compelled to drag a heavy
timber at the end of a rope, followed by crowds of men and boys armd
with shillelaghs and shouting, "Come draw the log, come draw the log,"
while keeping step to the music of a piper in attendance. In Hall's "Ireland,"* this custom is
assigned to the following day, Ash-Wednesday, which is obviously a mistake.
In Clare, it is said that all the disappointed young women--and, for
that matter, the disappointed young men as well-are in a bad humor on
Shrove Tuesday night, and their soreness continues to increase all week,
so that by Sunday they can be distinguisht by the "puss " on their countenances. Hence, the
first Sunday in Lent is there known as "Puss Sunday," and mischievous boys delight in
marking the backs of the unfortunate ones with flour or chalk so as point them out to the
whole congregation. This practice exists also in Kerry, where there is a popular legend that
on the night of Shrove Tuesday, all the disappointed lovers of both sexes shoulder their
burden of wasted hopes and blighted affections under the form of a bundle of gads or rods
and repair to the banks of a mystic river, known, on this account, as *Sruts an na
ngadaraid'e (siluhawnna ngodheree)*, or the "stream of the gads," where they get rid of their
troubles by throwing the whole load of affliction into the water. Going
to Srut'dn na ngadaraid'e is the Kerry equivalent for going up Salt river.
In the evening, the young folks-and the old ones as wel-gather round
the turf fire to learn, by " tossing the pancake," what is to be the result
of their future marriage ventures. A crock of batter having been prepared, a part is pourd out
on the pan to form the first cake, which is consignd to the care of the oldest unmarried
daughter. At the proper time, she turns the cake with a dextrous toss up the chimney, and if
it comes down smoothly on the other side in the pan, she can hav her choice of a husband
whenever she likes. If, on the other hand, it falls into the ashes or comes down with a corner
doubled over, she cannot marry for at least a year. This is also regarded as an omen of il
fortune with an accepted lover, and so strong is this feeling that engagements have even
been broken
off for no other reason. The lucky tosser of the first cake at once shares
it with the other girls. On eating it there is generally found in one slice
the mother's wedding ring and in another a piece of furz, both having
been put into the batter before baking. Whoever gets the ring wil be
most happy in her future choice, while the other will remain unmarried.
A similar custom exists in England and Scotland.

* Hall, Ireland, i, 315.
t Ibid.
Mooney.] 388 [Iay 3,

If a newly married woman hasn't moved to her new home before Lent she should stay put till Easter. -Irish Proverb

Time for a Proposal:

Just when you think everything is arranged you still need a proposal!

Let us start with a little Irish Gaelic to make things authentic. Gaelic can add a lot to the atmosphere and sincerity of both the proposal and the wedding itself. With a little practice you can look up and master the pronunciation. Gaelic is really written in code. The alphabet was fitted to an oral language when people started to write things down. Once you learn the rules of eclipses and aspiration you can pronounce almost anything. Just be sure that you lean the difference between the broad and slender vowels. A good book to use as a guide to pronunciation is:

Progress In Irish., Ni Ghrada,Mairead Brown and Nolan,Dublin.

This dictionary will be of assistance:
O'Siochfhradha,N.O., Learners Irish-English/ English Irish Dictionary., Comhlach Oideachais na Neireann tta.

Remember! Little children can speak perfect Irish and do so all over the Isle of Ireland. You can too! A good way to master the pronunciation is to make up a guide on a piece of paper or cardboard and use it as a bookmark. If you check the pronunciation each time you encounter a word in Gaelic you will learn in no time.

A rún! (uh ROON) lit.,   O! love!

A ghrá! (uh GHRAW) lit.,	O! love!
A chumann! (uh KHU-muhn) lit.,	O! affection!
A mhuirnín! (uh WOOR-neen) lit.,	O! sweetheart!
A chroí! (uh KHREE) lit.,	O! heart!
A chuisle! (uh KHWISH-luh) lit.,	O! pulse!
A stór! (uh STOHR) lit.,	O! treasure!
A thaisce! (uh HASH-kyuh) lit.,	O! treasure!
A chiste! (uh HISH-chuh) lit.,	O! treasure chest!
A rún mo chroí!	O! love of my heart!
A chuisle mo chroí!	O! pulse of my heart!
A chiste is a stór!	O! treasure chest and treasure!
A mhuirnín dílis!	O! true sweetheart!

Now on to the golden phrases:

Irish Gaelic, English, and Scots Sayings

An bpósfaidh tú mé? Will you marry me?
Pósfaimis! Let's get married!
Engaged to be maried--Tá mé geallta do--(name)
Lámh is focal a thabhairt dá chéile-- to be betrothed to each other
"I do"-- Gabhaim agus glaicim é (or í) mar c(h)éile
 fáinne pósta -- wedding ring
When you are married and have a large family: Tá mé pósta agus céasta. (I'm married and crucified!)

And then some other helpful words:

A chara=Friend
Anam Cara=soul mate
Bainis= Wedding/Reception
Bean Cleamhnais = Female matchmaker
Breá= Excellent
Croi=Heart
Cuireadh=invitation
Thabharfainn fuil mo chroi duit=I'd give you my heart's blood
Fear Cleamhnais- matchmaker, Man
Flaithiúil/flaithiúlacht Generous/generosity
Gealltanas pósta- engangement
Grá/titim I ngrá le= to fall in love with
Grá mo chroi= my heart's love
Leannán=lover
Le meas- in affection
Mo grá thú-I love you (literally my love to you)
Pósadh- Marriage

Fáinne pósta = wedding ring
Is fearr pósta é- he is a married man
Is mise a fear céile- I am her husband

And then of course a proverb in Irish Gaelic:
"Más mian leat cáineadh pós, Más mian leat moladh faigh bás."
If you want to be blamed get married, if you want to be praised - drop dead!
-Old Irish Proverb

Here are a few traditional lines of proposal in English:

Would you like to be buried with my relatives?
Would you like to hang your washing out next to mine?
Come to live in my heart and pay no rent.

Those who are linked to the tradition of Ulster and the Province of Northern Ireland will have to look into the Ulster Scots language.
Here is a book which should be helpful:

Robinson, Philip (1997): Ulster-Scots: A grammar of the traditional written and spoken language; Belfast (Northern Ireland): Ulster-Scots Heritage Council (218 York Street, Belfast, Northern Ireland, BT15 1GY; 01232 - 746939); 230 pp

While not exactly Ulster Scots, here are some Scots phrases which may be relevant:

Be guid tae ma dochter e.
Be good to my daughter, won't you.

Ye dinna gang for that kin o lassie, na?
You don't go for that sort of girl, no?

Git yokit tae.
Get started with / married to.

Her tung wad clip cloots.
She has a sharp tongue.

Lang mey yer lum reek.
Live long and healthy.

Monie wirds, muckle drouth.
Much talking makes one thirsty.

She's better nor she's bonnie.
She's better than she's pretty.

She's her mither's t'ae ee.
She's the apple of her (mother's) eye.

   Trail the weeng.
Have an illicit love affair.

Some Proverbs:

A bonnie bride is suin buskit an a short horse is suin wispit.
A pretty bride needs little decoration; a small horse little grooming.

Monie ane for land, taks a fuil bi the haund.
Many marry for money.

Better ma freends thinks me fremmit as fashious.
Better my friends think me stranger due to seldom visits than troublesome due to too many.

Greeting for Newly-weds.

Happie fit.

When parting.

        Heist ye back.
        Return soon.

The Wedding

At last after a lifetime of wondering and then following the ritual of arrangement it is time to put together the wedding itself. There is a wide range of choices to be made. Let us explore them.....

The House

"A house with three contiguous apartments is selected for a wedding: the reason of this is to preserve a distinction between the classes of company expected. The best apartment is reserved for the bride and bridegroom, the priest, the piper, and the more opulent and respectable guests as the landlord, his family and the neighbouring gentry, who are always invited and usually attend on such occasions. The second apartment is appropriated for the neighbours in general: and the third, or an outhouse, is devoted to the reception of buckaughs, shulers, and other beggars. When the marriage is celebrated two collections are raised amongst the guests, the first for the priest, the other for the piper. The assembly does not take place until late in the evening, when the marriage ceremony is performed, and the festivities seldom conclude before day-break the next morning."- T. Crofton Croker, Researches in the South of Ireland, Irish Academic Press, 1981. p. 235

One of the most important roles played by the Irish Pub is that of serving as social hall. In small rural villages houses were not usually large enough to accommodate many guests but generally each village had a pub or inn nearby. The important thing was to fit everyone, even the poor and homeless, into the party somehow!

Special Places in Ireland for weddings:
The four "*gallawns*" (standing stones), Island of Cape Clear, Comillane townland. One of these is called *Cloch na Geallúna* or trysting stone. This stone has a hole in it through. The couple joins hands through the hole.

The Clothing

This will be determined by the style you select for the wedding in general. As we noted in our introduction there are many periods of costume for which Ireland is famous. There are some general recommendations based upon custom but it is important to explore the history of Irish costume. Start with collections of famous artworks. There are books of Irish interiors featuring popular designs from all periods. Explore the re-creations of ancient Irish costume and then once you have explored select the right kind of style of costume for you.

Here are some traditional suggestions.
Bride: Wear your best dress. Just decorate it up or, have the village or local seamstress make a dress for you. Color=Blue , Fabric=silk if you can find it.
Anne of Brittany set the trend for all white wedding gowns in 1499. White is a recent color preference. Generally in Ireland gowns were simply the best dress owned, with jewelry, embroidery and lace, tags, ribbons, knots, tassels or other ornaments known as "Shingerleens".
But there is always the exception:Mourne O'Glanny married Aran Roe in a cloak of red (11th century).

A Groom of the 16th century would wear a bright yellow silk shirt, pleated with an embroidered linen jacket. Trousers were worn tight. Cloaks were also popular.
Linen and lace were always popular materials because they were traditionally made in Ireland. The Irish have always been fond of artistic metalwork especially brooches.

To help in your search through the costume treasures of Ireland I would suggest that you take a look at these books which contain many illustrations of all periods of Irish costume design.

Dress in Ireland: A History ., Mairead Dunlevy, Irish Books & Media, 2000.
Ireland Art into History., ed. Brian P.Kennedy and Raymond Gillespie,Roberts Rinehart,1994.
The Irish, ed. Leslie Conron Carola, Hugh Lauter Levin, 1993.

The Ring

In addition to the ring you should also have a coin to exchange.
While this might not be an old tradition it has become popular: Exchange coins following exchange of wedding bands. If the coins clink this will be lucky for the production of children.

T h a t   Ring!

While the most important symbol of marriage and most popular wedding ring is the Claddagh Ring, many more ancient Celtic designs created centuries before
also convey the values expressed in the marriage ceremony.   Such designs are infinite patterns of interlace and abstract patterns. Rings in these ancient patterns also make very fine wedding rings. The Claddagh design seems regrettably to be everywhere and is very popular being found on everything from toilet paper to door mats. Perhaps it is too popular.   If the Claddagh design is important for you by all means use it. If however you wish to find a unique design there are many craftsmen inspired by the ancient Celtic traditions who can produce hand crafted designs of great meaning and in authentic traditional style. Seek them out at Celtic festivals and via the Irish Trade Bord in New York. They have an 800 toll free number.

All About Claddagh Rings

 It is said that the Claddagh ring is a symbol of love, friendship and loyalty.

The Ring began life as the traditional marriage ring of "Fishing Kings of Claddagh". (the fishermen of the Claddagh - a small village on Galway Bay) who are remembered for refusing to go out to fish to feed those who were starving during the potato famine. It is said to then have had the meaning "in love and friendship let us reign." In the 17th and 18th centuries the ring grew in popularity outside of the local region of the Claddagh and Galway Bay. The heart was worn towards the wrist if the person was married, otherwise it was worn pointing towards the fingertips.

The first known maker of the ring was Richard Joyce around 1690. Joyce was had once been captive in Tunis where he acquired his noted skills as a goldsmith.

Claddagh Rings come in many varieties and materials. The FAQ of soc.culture.irish newsgroup has recorded some of the many stories of the ring. I have provided them for you below. After you read them please read my version which follows. It has come to me through many years as an instructor being asked the stories of the ring.

Tales of the Claddagh:

(a)
Way back in the "sandy mists" of time, so the story went, it seemed, there was a king. This king was madly in love with a peasant woman, but as she was of a lower class the love had to go unrequited. In dread despair the king killed himself and had his hands lopped off and placed around his heart as a symbol of his undying love for the woman.

(b)
It symbolizes love (heart), friendship/faith (hands) and loyalty (crown). Two hands Joined together in love and Crowned by the Glory of Christ.

(c)
There was a Dublin version of this Ring that appeared some 100 years back with two hands and two hearts but no crown. Some call this Version the Fenian Claddagh.

(d)
The Crown to The Father, The Left hand to the Son, and the Right Hand the the Holy Ghost. This Explanation is directly Correlative to the Shamrock, one of the Earliest Symbols of the Holy Trinity among the Irish.

(e)
Some will say Beathauile is the Crown, Anu is the Left hand, and the Dagda Mór is the Right hand and the Heart is the Hearts of all mankind and that which gives the everlasting music to the Gael.

(f)
As legend has it, the town developed the ring (originally a sigil to be painted on ships and sails) to be worn by sailors of Claddagh. When these sailors would run into other fishermen in their waters, they would check for the sigil, and if they did not find it, they would kill them.

(g)

The original Claddagh ring is generally attributed to one Richard Joyce, a native of Galway, who while being transported as a slave to the plantations of the West Indies was captured by Mediterranean pirates and sold to a Moorish goldsmith who trained him in his craft. In 1689 he was released and returned to Galway and set up his shop in the Claddagh. (The Claddagh is said to be the oldest fishing village in Ireland). By tradition the ring is taken to signify the wish that Love and Friendship should reign supreme. The hands signify friendship, the crown loyalty, and the heart love.

The ring has become popular outside Connemera since the middle of the 19th century- its spread being helped by the vast exodus from the West during the great Famine in 1847-49. These rings were kept as heirlooms with great pride and passed from mother to daughter. Today, the ring is worn extensively across Ireland, either on the right hand with the heart turned outwards showing that the wearer is "fancy free" or with the heart turned inwards to denote that he or she is "spoken for".
The pride of place is on the left hand, with the heart turned in, indicating that the wearer is happily married.

Conrad Bladeys Folk Tale of the Meaning of the Claddagh Design:

As one who has worked as an instructor lo these many years teaching the Irish about their own culture- a virtual lost cultural luggage department finding folklore and customs lost on the way to these shores....

I have long wondered about the relationship of the Claddagh design to the Irish Americans I have met. In every class, in every semester someone, usually someone of Irish descent, inquires: "Mr.Bladey I have this beautiful ring. ....I would like to know....and in some cases....I took this course to find out the story of the Claddagh Ring."
Being a professional I calmly and politely tell following tale.....

The American Folk Tale of the Claddagh Ring

One day long ago.....a man and a woman both on vacation in Ireland chanced to meet in beautiful Galway City on the shores of the breathtaking Galway Bay. The man was handsome; the girl...... beautiful.
They had many things in common and were soon out on the town sampling the wonderful oysters and stout for which the city is famous. Late into the evening they drank and ate at the sessions and then later still they danced

until the wee hours at the ceili at the church hall. They had such a good time
that they found themselves the next morning in the same bed....shocked and being
fervent Catholics and mindful of the rules of the Pope of Rome the pair realized
that they would have to go straight off and get married once they reached America.
Their love was strong and true and they set out the next morning to purchase a
pair of rings for the wedding. And being in Galway there is of course, no other
alternative save the Galway ring, itself the scourge of the world of the Irish and of
others.

They found just such a ring in a quaint and very cute jeweler's shop near the old
town of Claddagh, a part of Galway not far from the Spanish Arch.
They picked out a wonderful and very expensive pair of identical rings and they sat down
with the ancient, rose-cheeked jeweler to have them sized.

As the jeweler sized the rings the jeweler told the pair a wonderful cute (and totally
false and contrived) story of the rings, and, asked if they would like the story on a presentation
fake vellum scroll which goes with a special more costly presentation package for the rings,
complete with seaweed-flocked ring boxes. They agreed and paid the $1,000 extra for the
presentation package. Much impressed, they thanked the jeweler and left to pack, for both
had canceled their hotel rooms and had made arrangements to fly back home immediately.

Upon returning to America the couple immediately summoned all of their
friends and quickly brought over to the bride's home her cousin the priest
and the wedding was arranged. It went very well considering the haste
and the priest read out the story of the rings in his rich southern USA brogue
as part of the ceremony. He read from the mock parchment scroll the silly
story of the rings.

The crowd was impressed with the tale. They asked for it to be told again
and again at the reception and as many photos were taken of the rings as of
the two who were married! At last everyone went home and the pair set off
on their new life.

Ten years later in memory of the occasion the two thought to celebrate their
anniversary with a party to which all of the original guests were invited.
Everyone turned up and halfway through the party a few of the guests called
once again for the charming story of the ring!

The room went silent, as the couple became the focus of attention. But the silence lasted and
lasted, and the pair went red-faced and could hardly say
a word. At last tearfully the bride spoke. "I am afraid I don't know the story
of the rings." With that an audible gasp came from all in attendance and then
in an instant all the many guests rushed from the room nearly causing a panic.

The couple had not seen or heard from any of their friends from that they
until.....they took my course and heard the story of the ring. Once they

had regained it they notified their friends and once again they all returned
to a celebration this time for the couple's 50th anniversary. By that time all of their friends
and some of them with grandchildren all had Claddagh rings, but they had all, lost the story....
and so the cry went out in utmost earnest this time....

TELL US THE TALE OF THE RING!!!!

And so the elderly bride in an elderly voice told the silly story of the ring and they all went
home within the Irish tradition to...... forget it once again!

So that is the American Folk Version of the Story of the Claddagh ring
which in fact is the story of a story, which is almost always forgotten!

Whatever your particular taste you will find an Irish traditional ring of great meaning and
value. It is worth seeking one out.

Borrowed Rings

Some poorer couples might borrow a wedding ring in order that the ceremony
properly performed. One Tyrone man, whose mother was housekeeper to a priest recalled:

*"My mother was the housekeeper in the Beragh parish, there was a new
Priest ordained then, and my mother was just widowed at the time, and
she went to him as a housekeeper. And the weddings at that time was at
8 O'clock in the morning, And manys a one came to the church without a
wedding ring, And Fr. McGrath used to say to my mother, 'We're having
a wedding this morning, give us your ring in case.' And I remember my
mother saying, she says, 'That ring of mine has married dozens and
dozens of people."*

Rings might also be hired, and it has been claimed that in parts of Ireland 'it is
believed unless the wedding ring be golden, the marriage lacks validity. If the
people are too poor to purchase the circlets made of precious metal, hoops of
gold were hired It was claimed that a Munster shopkeeper considerably augmented
his income by renting rings to couples to use during the wedding ceremony
 Some brides were married by having the loop of a door key, either to the new home or to
the church, slipped on to the finger. This was usually a matter of expediency for those who
could not afford a more expensive ring, but it could carry greater implications of
stigmatism, as sometimes it was understood that a couple who had been living together
were pressurized into marriage…

-Ballard, Linda May, <u>Forgetting Frolic Marriage Traditions in Ireland,</u> p. 73.

Music for the Irish Wedding

As with many things in traditional cultures, Music should be something which is created as much by the guests and family as by the professional musician. While hiring musicians is a long-[1]respected custom, you should also encourage your guests and your family to bring along their instruments and songs. Dancers also should be encouraged. Having a piper or professional musician at a wedding is a popular custom, however, it is important to select the right variety of piper or musician for the Irish wedding. There are two types of pipes: Scottish Highland Pipes and Irish Uilleann Pipes (often known as the Elbow pipes as they are played via a bellows under the elbow.) The latter is the most appropriate type of piper for the Irish Wedding. The Uilleann Pipes are much sweeter than the Highland Pipes and do not have the "war" connotation that the Scottish Highland Pipes have. A word here about dress for the musicians: pipers in traditional villages would not dress in kilts. These individuals would be well dressed in peasant garb and sometimes not well dressed at all. They were largely itinerant moving from place to place over the roads. If you absolutely must have someone in a kilt be aware that the traditional Irish kilt is not a tartan but a plain "saffron" color. Another popular instrument for weddings is the harp. Here again one must take care to try to find a "Celtic" harp which is much smaller than most other harps and has the appropriate tone. Fiddlers, Concertina Players, Flute Players, Drummers and Tin Whistle players should also be welcome. The Tin Whistle when well-played can add a very special and very Irish quality to any wedding. It is important of course, that you make the musicians very welcome at the wedding reception. This will extend the music dramatically in some cases!

As for tunes, well....there are many which are suitable. These days the "Irish Wedding Song" is popular. I have included it below, however, there are many fine tunes and songs and even whole Masses from which to choose. Be aware that almost every Irish tune can be played slowly as an air. It is entirely appropriate to take your favorite dance tune and slow it down, add ornaments and play it dramatically. Above all be sure to ask all those taking part in the wedding ceremony from the Priest to the ring bearers and parents which songs they would like to hear. Any music played by a traditional Irish group of musicians will, naturally, sound great!

Here is my list (derived from an Internet poll of Irish Musicians):

Tune Song List

---

[1]

I Heard the Voice of Jesus Say, (tune: Star of County Down)
Be Thou My Vision,
Danny Boy and various lyrics to the tune of Danny Boy
The Celtic Alleluia (not very traditionally Celtic-Oregon Catholic Press)
Celtic Mass, (Oregon Catholic Press)
Anything written by Fr. Liam Lawton, especially a CD called Sacred Story.
The Spinning Wheel Song
The Rose of Tralee
The Darlin' Girl From Clare
The Snowy-Breasted Pearl
I Know My Love (by his way of walkin')
The Sally Gardens
Raglan Road
Old Maid in the Garret
Easy and Slow
Let Him Go, Let him Tarry
My Singing Bird
The Limerick Rake
My Bonny Boy is Young But He's Growing
Maids When You're Young (never wed an old man)
The Old Woman From Wexford.
My Lovely Rose of Clare
The Wild Rover
Mary From Dungloe
The German Clockwinder
Bunch of Thyme Go Lassie Go
If I Was A Blackbird
On the Banks of the Roses
Spancil Hill
She Moved Through The Fair
The Lark in the Clear Air
The Mountains of Mourne
McBreens Heifer
Red Haired Mary
The Zoological Gardens
I Courted Biddy Magee
The Queen of Connemara (in a cot in Connemara there's a wife and wee one praying)
I had Thou Be my vision.
She moved through the fair
Give me your hand (Tamhair dom do lamb),
Carrickfergus, ...any slow Irish airs.
Aifreann Baile Nua (The Newtown Mass O'Brien)
Donal Agus Morag
Dark Inniseoghan

Three Irish Masses:
Mass - Sean O' Riada

St. Patrick's Mass- Philip Green
Celtic Mass- Christopher Walker

Pop Songs
Of course in the contemporary world one is bound to run into the old chestnuts of the
popular genres. I list these so that the musicians might be prepared for every eventuality.

"Sure, She's Irish"
Did Your Mother Come from Ireland?
My Little Claddagh Ring
You're the One (air)
The Humour Is On me Now
Happy Are We All Together
Believe Me if All those Endearing Young Charms
An Irish Lullaby
Silver Threads Among the Gold

Some Notation
A word about tempo. In traditional music adaptation is the watchword! A fast tune can be a
march or if you like the melody enough it can be a wonderful slow air. If dancers are ready
you can change it into a dance or a waltz. It is up to you. No one way is correct! My
general rule of thumb is that if no one is dancing make it a wonderful rich and ornamented
slow air full of thought and contemplation. Then when someone gets up to dance or, if you
are in need of a procession, adapt accordingly. By all means use your own ornamentation
and have fun with the music.

The Bride's Favorite Jig
Traditional

Haste to the Wedding
Traditional

Tabhair Dom Do Lámh = Give Me Your Hand
Traditional/Rory Dall Ó Catháin

Sheebeg and Sheemore=The Small Fairy Hill and the Large Fairy Hill   O'Carolan

O'Carolan's Concerto   O'Carolan

March of the Kings of Laois   Rory O'Moore

Carrickfergus

Music Sources

If you are going to be using recorded music I would recommend the following:

The Best of the Chieftains., The Chieftains., Columbia, Legacy,
ck 48693- good for the reception-lively

Carolan's Receipt., Derek Bell., Shanachie 79013- good quiet parlor music

Flight of the Green Linnet., Various. Rkodisc RCD 20075.- Good variety of celtic music.

Fire in the Kitchen., Various BMG, 09026 631332- Good music for a celebration.

Lark in the Morning., Various., Tradition TCD1001- Traditional at the root.

Anuna., Anuna, Celtic Heartbeat Atlantic, 827332- Sacred and Secular sounding Sacred.

The Vow, Various., Druid Stone., North Star Music., NS0113.,-A good collection of Irish Romantic and Wedding music.

Important Traditional Songs

Clancy's Wooden Wedding

Five years ago last Sunday night when Clancy took a wife
'twas Little Bridget Haley who would stick to him for life
and he gave a wooden wedding the event to celebrate
and he sent out invitations to his friends both small and great

Now everyone was supposed to bring a present made of wood
some of the things they brought were bad and some were very good
but everyone who came they did the very best they could
when Clancy had a weddin' made of wood

There was all kinds of wood brought to the house that night
hard wood, soft wood and kindling wood delight

there was wood and wooden shavings enough to fill a bed
'twas brought to Clancy's house when he was five years wed

Now the first one to get there was Tim O'Hoolihan,
he brought for a present a Japanese fan
then came Maloney just as neat as a pin
he brought a cradle for to rock the baby in

O'Brien brought a sawhorse handsomely engraved
O'Toole brought a cord of wood for which he didn't pay
Murphy brought the clothespins and Ryan brought a broom
and it looked as though a lumberyard exploded in the room

Wood that came from China, wood that came from Spain
wood from Jerusalem across the ragin' main
wood that came from Russia sent by the Csar
wood that came from Ireland enough to build a car
wood that came from England, wood that came from Wales
wood that came from Scotland, wood that came from jails

They passed around the whiskey and they passed around the ale
and if the glasses wasn't big enough they used a wooden pail
Everyone was feelin' good no one was feelin' dry
all around the glory and the glory it was high
someone asked Clancy, "Would he sing a song?"
Clancy said he would, but his voice was gone
Up jumped Maloney and he gave a recitation
all about the kind of wood that grew in every nation
"Begorra such a racket I can't keep it mum!"

O'Brien called Maloney an educated bum
well up jumped Maloney and he gave him such a whack
it raised up a hump in the middle of his back
that was the signal and they all began to fight
and the women hollared, "Murder!" and they said it wasn't right

Murphy threw the poker and it hit O'Hoolihan
O'Brien threw the kettle and he threw the frying pan
Patrick lost his false teeth and through the window dove
Maloney sat down on a red hot stove

Well there was all kinds of wood went flyin' through the air
Brady hit O'Grady with the round of a chair
Murphy took Sullivan and threw him on the bed
stabbed him with a clothespin and left him there for dead
Police got twenty five and thirty got away.
They took then up before the judge the very next day
he judge looked them over as before them they stood
he gave them sixty days in jail...now they're all sawing wood

-Traditional

Crosby's Irish Wedding Song

THE IRISH WEDDING.

SURE won't you hear what roaring cheer Was
spread at Paddy's wedding O, And how so gay they
spent the day, From churching to the
bed-ding O? First, book in hand, came
Father Quipes, With the bride's dad-da, the

Bai - lie O, While the chaunter with the

merry pipes Struck up a lilt so gai-ly O.

Tiddery teddery, &c.

Now there was Mat, and sturdy Pat,
And merry Morgan Murphy O,
And Murdock Mags, and Tirlogh Skaggs,
M'Loughlin, and Dick Darfey O;

171

And then the girls, rigg'd out in white,
Led on by Ted O'Reilly O,
While the chaunter, &c.

When Pat was ask'd if his love would last,
The chapel echo'd with laughter O,
By my soul, says Pat, you may say that,
To the end of the world and after O;
Then tenderly her hand he gripes,
And kisses her genteelly O,
While the chaunter, &c.

Then a roaring set at dinner were met,
So frolicsome and so frisky O,
Potatoes galore, a skirrag or more,
With a flowing madder of whisky O;
Then round to be sure didn't go the wipes,
At the bride's expense so gaily O,
While the chaunter, &c.

And then at night, O what delight
To see them capering and prancing O!

An opera or ball were nothing at all,

    Compar'd to the stile of their dancing O;

And then to see old Father Quipes

    Beating time with his shillelah O,

        While the chaunter, &c.

And now the knot so sucky are got,

    They'll go to sleep without rocking O,

While the bridesmaids fair so gravely prepare

    For throwing of the stocking O:

Dacadorus we'll have, says Father Quipes,

    Then the bride was kiss'd round genteelly O

While to wish them good fun, the merry pipes

    Struck up a lilt so gaily O.

-Crosby's Irish Musical Repository: A Choice Selection of Esteemed Irish Songs, Adapted for the Voice, Violin and German Flute, 1810.

Sheelah's Wedding,

Crosby lyrics

Well, the time being settled, to church they were carried,
With some more lads and lasses, to see the pair married,
'Who vow'd that too long from the parson they tarried ;
For who would such sweet things be scorning?
Then at church, arrah, yes, you 'may fancy them there ;
Sure the priest tied them fast, you may very well swear;
And when it was done
Och, what laughing and fun
Took place about something, and throwing the stocking;
While the blythe boys and girls
Talk'd of ringing the bells,
On St Patrick's day in the morning;
Now at home safe and snug, and the wedding-day over,
Sure the bride and the bridegroom were both left in clover,
Which Paddy so pleas'd, that hereafter a rover,
Och, he swore he should ever be scorning.
For Paddy, d'ye see, was so fond of his wife,
That he vow'd they'd be cozy and loving for life;
While so frisky they'd sing, 'Summer, winter, and spring
Arrah, would they, because in nine months, or about it, .
Why, a sweet little Pat

May squall out, and all that
On St Patrick's day in the morning.

-Traditional

41

=====

SHEELAH'S WEDDING.

Air—St Patrick's Day in the Morning.

Och, I sing of a wedding, and that at Dun-

lea-ry, And a wed-ding's no time to be

moping and drea-ry; So a wed-ding took

place be-tween Pat and his dea-ry, Who

long had at Cu-pid been frowning. But at

42

length, d'ye see, they resolv'd to be tied. Paddy

Shan-non the bridegroom, and Shee-lah the

bride: For, d'ye mind, af-ter that, Whispers

Sheelah to Pat, "Arrah, dear, how I blush: but I

" may have a ba-by; And then, love," says

she, " Oeh, how hap-py we'll be, On St

" Patrick's day in the morning !'"

- Crosby's Irish Musical Repository: A Choice Selection of Esteemed Irish Songs, Adapted for the Voice, Violin and German Flute, 1810.

The Irish Wedding Song

This is a modern traditional song of great popularity which is often requested.
This version comes from a friend's wedding where in the old way it was sung from
memory.

Here they stand hand in hand they've exchanged wedding rings

This day is their day of dreams and of plans, and all that them love
just have to say.

May God bless these two who married today

In goodness and bad times in sickness and health.

May they know that riches you don't need for wealth and help them
face problems they'll meet on from this day.

Oh God bless this twosome we married today

May they find peace of mind comes to each one who is kind.

May the poor times ahead become glories in time

May all of their kids be happy all-ways

Oh God bless this household that started today

As they will grow may they know all the love that was shown

And as life it gets on shorter may their own feelings grow

Wherever they travel wherever they range

May God bless these partners we married today

*You can substitute first names of bride and groom in the last line of song
as in god bless...and ....

There is also an "Irish Wedding Song" by Ian Betteridge to which
this traditional version is related.

Whatever your preference-- let there be plenty of lively music. Bring everyone into the
performance.

The Wedding of Ballyporeen.

Descend, ye chaste nine, to a true Irish Bard,
You're old maids, to be sure, but he sends you acord.
To beg you'll assist a poor musical elf,
With a song ready-made, he'll compose it himself;
About maids, boys, a priest, and a wedding,
With a crowd you could scarce thrust your head In;
A supper, good cheer, and a bedding,
Which happened at Ballyporeen.

Twas a fine Summer's morn, about twelve in the day.
All the birds fell to sing, all the asses to bray,
When Patrick, the bridegroom, and Oonagh, the bride
In their beat bibs and tuckers, set oil, side by side.
O, the pipers play'd first in the rear, sir.
The maid blushed, the bridesmen did swear, sir;
O, Lord: how the spalleens did stare, sir.
At this wedding of bally poreen.

They were soon tacked together, and home did return.
To make merry the day at the sign of the churn;
When they sat down together, a frolicsome troop,
O, the bunks of old Shannon ne'er saw such a group.
There were turf-cutters, threshers, and tailors.
With harpers. and pipers, and nuilors,
And pedlers. and smugglers, and sailors,
Assembled at Ballyporeen.

There was Bryan MacDermot and Shaughnessy's brat.
With Terence and Triscol, and platter-faced Pat;
There was Norah Macormic and B-yan O'Lynn,
And the fat, red-haired cook-maid, who lives at the inn.
There was Shelah, and Larry, the genius,
With Pat's uncle, old Derby Dennis;
Black Thady and crooked Macgennis,
Assembled at Ballyporeen.

Now the bridegroom sat down to make an oration,
And he charmed all their souls with his kind botheration;
They were welcomed, he said, and he swore, and he cursed.
They might eat 'till they swelled, and might drink till they burst.
The first christening I have, if I thrive, sirs,
I hope you all hither will drive, sirs;
You'll be welcome all, dead or alive, sirs,
To the christening at Ballyporeen.

Then the bride she got up to make a low bow,
But she twittered, and felt so-she could not tell how-
She blushed And she stammered-the few words she let fall.
She whispered so low that she bothered them all.
But her mother cried: "What, are you dead, child?
O, for shame of you. hold up your head, child;
Though sixty, I wish I was wed, child,
O, I'd rattle all Ballyporeen."

Now they sat down to meat-Father Murphy said grace,
Smoking hot were the dishes, and eager each face;
The knives and forks rattled, spoons and platters did play,
And they elbowed and jostled, and wollopped away.
Rumps, chines, and fat sirloius did groan, sirs.
Whole mountains of beef were cut down, sirs;
They demolished all to the bare bone, sirs.
At this wedding at Ballyporeen.

There was bacon and greens, but the turkey was spoiled.
Potatoes dressed both ways, both roasted and boiled;
Hog's puddings, red herrings-the priest got the snipe,
Culcannon pies, dumplings, cod, cow-heel and tripe.
Then they ate 'till they could cat no more. sirs.
And the whiskey came pouring galore, sirs;
O, how Terry Macmants did roar, sirs,
O, he bothered all Ballyporeen.

Now the whiskey went round, and the songsters did roar,
Tim sung "Paddy O'Kelly," Nell sung "Molly Asthore;"
Till a motion was made that their songs they'd forsake,
And each lad take his sweetheart, their trotters to shake.
Then the piper And couples advancing,
Pumps, brogues, and bare feet fell a prancing;
Such piping, such figuring and dancing,
Was ne'er known at Ballyporccn.

Now to Patrick, the bridegroom, and Oonagh, the bride.
Let the harp of old Ireland be sounded with pride;
And to all the brave guests, young or old, gray or green,
Drunk or sober, that jigged it at Ballyporcen.
And when cupid shall lend you his wherry,
To trip o'er the conjugal ferry,
I wish you may be half so merry
As we were at Ballyporeen.

The Wedding of Ballyporeen

Book: P.M. Haverty - One Hundred Irish Airs, vol. 1 (New York, 1858, No. 4, p. 2)

Food For Irish Weddings

A man interested in a girl because of her cookery was called a Belly Bachelor –Ulster Saying

As I have noted earlier there is a considerable variation in the style of Traditional Irish Weddings. They can range from the Celtic Inspired to the ornate Georgian and Victorian. There are also degrees of class and economic status to choose from as well. So too with food for the wedding. It can come from the Celtic Campfire or from the Grand Hotel. While catering is traditional one must not overlook the importance of the institutions of the Village Ceili and the traditional Irish Teatime.

It is traditional for local celebrations to hire the room in the local pub. The Ceili tradition calls for foods prepared by the community and brought in for the celebration. These can range from main courses such as spiced beef, beef and Guinness, mutton, and lamb stew to picnic foods such as savory meat pies, sausage rolls and sandwiches. Desserts would include the wedding cake but would also include the full range of traditional favorites such as Guinness Cake, Whiskey Cake, and the Queen of Puddings. Find out what people can make and ask them to bring it. The Ceili also calls for a variety of entertainments. Music of course is traditional but also traditional are games and storytelling.

The Irish tea time is also an institution, which often finds itself as part of a wedding celebration. It is important to select the correct tea. Traditionally Irish tea is a blend of High Mountain Grown Ceylon and Assam leaves. One should always use bulk tea and never use tea bags. When looking for bulk tea it is not necessary to find the fancy varieties with all sorts of additives. Simply ask for Irish Breakfast Tea or Irish Blend. This tea is generally served with good cream which is put into the cup. About 1/3 of the cup is cream. For a wedding one would also try to find fancy sugars. If a large tea urn is not available then it is fun to assemble a variety of teapots. These can be donated by your guests and can add a lot of color to the event. The tea must be strained so you will need at least one tea strainer per pot. It also must be steeped for 5 minutes before pouring out. Always bring the pot with the tea in it to the hot water.

In addition to the tea itself one should also provide a wide assortment of tea time treats. Scones, cakes and breads with sides of real butter and assorted jellies, jams and marmalades should be laid out. One can have one's tea spread at any time during the day. It is good to always have a pot on whenever people are standing around waiting. The tea can also be laid out during the meal for those who finish early or stay late.

May God give you luck and put a good man in your way, and if he is not good, may the wedding whiskey be drunk at his wake.

-Traditional Irish saying.

I have included the traditional wedding cake recipe as well as several traditional tea time treats and main courses. The essence of the traditional tea time is a wide variety of selections.

Irish Spiced Beef

Ingredients:20 cloves, 2 tsp ground allspice or cinnamon, 6 Shallots, 2 tsp Prague Powder(can be obtained from the Sausage Maker-26 Military Rd, Buffalo,N.Y. 14207), 1 Pound Kosher Salt (coarse), 1 tsp black pepper, three tsp. ground mace, 7-8 lb. beef. 2-3 bay leaves, ground nutmeg, Two Pints Guinness Stout. Instructions:1. Grind all dry ingredients and mix. 2. Add finely chopped shallots. 3. Rinse beef and place in plastic or glass container (avoid iron). 4.Take one seventh of the spice/salt mixture and rub it all over the meat. Place meat back into container, cover and set out on the back porch or in a cool spot- if too warm outside place in fridge.5. Each day for seven days rub the meat with one-seventh of the mixture, turn over and re-cover. Leave the liquid that forms with the meat. 6. At the end of seven days place meat and liquid into a big pot. Add water to top up and cover the meat and boil until the meat is tender.(a fork should just barely be able to lift up strands of meat-don't over do it!) Change water adding clean water and boil for another 30 minutes. 7.Then add veg-large carrots, onions, and potatoes. Cook until almost done-about 20 minutes. Add two pints Guinness Stout and boil for another 10-20 minutes.
You can eat this hot or leave to cool overnight. Place meat into colander with weight on it and plate or dish under it.

Beef With Guinness

Beef With Stout The Only way to Cook Beef-sometimes add oysters!
Ingredients: 1/4 lb. Butter,1 pound beef chuck cut into 1x2 inch pieces.1 large sweet onion-sliced thin, a bouquet garni (thyme, sage, parsley, bay leaf,)1/4 teaspoon salt.1/4 teaspoon black pepper,1 cup beef stock, 1 pint guinness stout, 4 medium potatoes(1 lb. peeled). 2 tablespoons parsley, large "manly" sweet carrots.
Instructions: Heat butter in skillet. Brown the beef in batches.Set beef aside.2.cook onion in hot fat for 3 minutes-until just softened. Return meat to pan. Add bouquet garni, salt, pepper, stock and stout and bring the mixture to a boil. Cook stew uncovered in preheated

350 degree oven for about one hour add potatoes and bake for 45 minutes till all is tender. Add salt and pepper to taste. Thicken sauce with butter and flour. Garnish with parsley.

Limerick Ham

A great flavor and easy to make. Great for a festive meal.
Ingredients:
One ham-cured and cooked- not a salted country ham.
1/4 cup juniper berries (if dried soak until soft) If you can't get them soak ham in 3-4 cups gin for longer.
1 1/2 cups French style mustard (country style coarse if possible)
1 cup Gin
1 cup brown sugar
Instructions
Score the ham to a depth of 1/2 inch on all sides.
Rub juniper berries into the cuts all over (if no berries just use more gin)
Mix the gin, brown sugar and mustard. Soak ham in this mixture for 48 hours.
Cover the ham with the mixture. Bake in a hot oven covered
with foil until heated through. Remove foil and bake until
skin is crisp. From time to time baste with liquid from bottom of pan.

The Best Irish Soda Bread!

6 cups all purpose flour
2 teaspoons baking soda
2 teaspoons baking powder
3 tablespoons cornstarch
2 teaspoons sugar
1 teaspoon salt
2 1/2 cups buttermilk
Highly traditional and recommended option: Two tablespoons caraway seeds. Add them to the dry ingredients and sprinkle some on the top when ready for oven
Preheat oven to 375

Instructions: Do everything very quickly
Add all the dry ingredients in a large bowl and mix very well. Pour in all of the buttermilk into the bowl at once and stir. Stir only until the dough barely holds together. I mean barely! Do this quickly too!
Divide the dough into two portions. Shape each quickly into a round. Quickly!
Cut a cross 2/3 down into the top of each loaf so that you can see the cut.
-The loaf should come apart about 1/2 inch. Paint the loaf over with buttermilk being sure to get the bottom of the cross cut wet with it. Give the surface of the loaf a bit of texture by cutting into it with a knife or fork if it is too round and smooth. Let loafs rest for about ten minutes . Put into the oven- The baking takes about 30-40 minutes.
The loaf is done when the buttermilk in the bottom of the cross is dry to the touch. Do not

handle or cut hot soda bread! Let it cool down on a rack if possible. Wrap in newspaper to keep lightly warm.

Guinness Cake

Ingredients:
1 cup butter or margarine,1 cup brown sugar, 1 1/4 cups Guinness,1 1/2 cups raisins, 1 1/2 cups currants, 1 1/2 cups golden raisins, 3/4 cup mixed candied citrus peel, 5 cups flour, 1/2 tsp. baking soda,1 tsp. mixed spice, 1 tsp. nutmeg, 3 eggs.
Instructions:
Butter and line a 9 inch cake pan with wax paper. Place the butter, sugar and the Guinness in a pan and bring slowly to the boil, stirring all the time until the sugar and butter have melted. Mix in the dried fruit and peel and bring mixture back to the boil. Simmer for 5 minutes. Remove from heat and leave until cold. Sift flour, spices and baking soda into a large mixing bowl. Stir in cooled fruit mixture and beaten eggs. Turn into cake pan and bake in center of preheated oven at 325 degrees for 2 hours, or until done. Test with a skewer. When done cool in pan before turning out.

Strawberry Scones

Ingredients:
1 cup strawberries,2 1/4 cups all purpose flour,3 tablespoons sugar,2 teaspoons baking powder,1/4 teaspoon salt,6 tablespoons butter or margarine,2/3 cup milk.
Instructions:
Preheat oven to 425 degrees. Hull strawberries, cut into 1/2 inch pieces, set aside. In large bowl mix together flour and sugar baking powder and salt. Add butter. With pastry blender cut butter in until mixture resembles coarse crumbs. Stir in reserved strawberries. Toss well to coat. Add milk all at once. With fork lightly toss together until mixture holds together. With floured hands gently form into ball. On floured board with floured rolling pin roll out dough 1/2 inch thick. Cut dough into 2 1/2 inc h circles with floured biscuit cutter. Place on greased cookie sheet. Bake until golden, about 12 minutes. Serve warm. Makes 12 scones.

Queen of Puddings

Ingredients:
4 oz white bread without crusts,1/2 pint cream,1/2 pint of milk,2 oz unsalted butter, 3 eggs separated,grated zest of one lemon,5 oz caster sugar,4 tablespoons homemade jam.
Instructions:
Preheat a moderate 350 degree oven. Generously butter a 2-pint baking dish. Cut up the bread into small cubes or make into course crumbs and scatter in to the baking dish. Warm the milk and butter until the butter melts, then blend in the beaten egg yolks, grated lemon zest and 3 oz of the sugar. Pour this custard over the bread and bake in the preheated oven for 20 minutes or until set. Whisk the egg whites until stiff and fold in the remaining sugar. Remove the pudding from the oven, spread with the jam and pile the meringue mixture on

top. Return to the oven and cook for another 10 minutes or until the top is lightly browned and crisp. Serve hot with chilled cream..

The Irish Wedding Cake

Ingredients

Makes one

Currants 1 lb. 12 oz./800g.	Flour 1lb 3oz. 525 g.	Black treacle 2 tbsp.
Sultanas (Golden Raisins) 1lb./450g.	Salt 1 teaspoon	Orange and Lemon zest 1 1/2 tsp. each
Raisins 9 oz./25 oz 250 g.	Mixed Spice 2 1/2 tsp.	Eggs 8 large
Shredded Almonds 7 oz./200g.	Butter 1lb.450g.	Vanilla essence 1 1/2 tsp.
Glace Cherries 7oz/200g.	Rich Dark sugar 1lb.450g.	Brandy 4 tbsp.
Peel,cut,mixed 7oz/200g.		12"/30cm. tin

Cooking time: 4 1/2-5 1/2 hours

Instructions

1. Grease tin and line it with three layers of greaseproof paper, extending about 2" above the top of the tin.
2. Tie a thick band of folded newspaper around the outside of the tin to protect the edge of the cake from over cooking.
3. Have a suitable sized piece of brown paper to put over the cake if it is in danger of overbrowning.
4. Cake will be cooked when a skewer put into the center comes out clean.
5. Sort the fruit and remove any stalks or irregular pieces.
6. Mix fruit with halved cherries, peel and a tablespoon or two of the flour.
7. Sift flour, salt and the spices.
8. Cream the butter and sugar until light and fluffy.
9. To the butter add the treacle, zests, and essences. Beat well.
10. Add the eggs, one by one with a tablespoon full of flour with each-beat well. Fold in the fruit and remaining flour plus the brandy. Mix well.
11. Turn mixture into the prepared tin and smooth down with tablespoon making a slight hollow in the center.
12. You may leave the cake over night or till ready to bake.
13. Pre heat oven to 300 degrees F., 150 degrees C, Gas mark 2 . Bake cake in center of the oven for 1-1/2 hours.
14. Reduce heat to 275 degrees F, 140 degrees C, Gas mark 1 for the remaining baking time or until the top of cake feels firm to the touch and skewer comes out clean and dry.
15. Watch cake as it bakes. Cover if it looks like it might overbrown.
16. Cool cooked cake in tin. Then remove paper and turn upside down onto a board. Make small holes into the cake with skewers and pour on some extra brandy.
17. When brandy is absorbed wrap cakes in double layer of greaseproof paper and then a layer of foil. Seal and store in airtight container and place in a cool place for at least a month. You should finish the cake about a fortnight before the wedding.
18. Cover with white Irish Royal Icing or Fondant Icing

Love is like stirabout.. It must be made fresh every day. -Old Irish Saying.

The Customs of the Strawboys

This is a wonderful custom, which is well worthy of revival and is great fun.
From: Luba Kaftannikoff :

We had entered a countryside which was still steeped in the old traditions and customs, closely followed, although their origins were often lost. The young people could not say why they danced on the great slabs covering the dolmens-those tombs of kings who lived, perhaps, four thousand years ago when the Megalithic culture of the Mediterranean countries existed also in Ireland--but dance there they did, each Midsummer's Eve, having brought with them offerings of flowers. For eons, these dolmens were centers of fertility rites, perhaps because of some dim but universal belief that where death and decay had been, birth and growth might spring...
So on an April day Nancy and Frank got married, and the Strawboys came and danced at their wedding.
"What did they look like?" I asked, when a week later I made my way up the long bourheen to see the bride.
"They had high caps on them made of straw, pointed like," said Nancy. "And masks, and straw capes round their shoulders. They'd straw tied up in the front of their legs as well. They came at sundown-about eight o'clock, new time--and stayed half an hour. They danced with all, but they never spoke." "If they spoke' would break the spell," the bridegroom interjected. "They take no refreshment either." "And it's to bring good luck?" I asked. "Tis," Nancy said, as a long intimate look passed between husband and wife and I thought of the ancient fertility rites, which always seem so near and credible in this countryside.
"Do you know where the Strawboys came from?" I asked.
"Somewhere back in the hills," Nancy said. "But Frank thought a couple of them might have been comrades of his. "'Tis years and years since the strawboys were seen in these parts, and there was a great cheer when we seen them coming high up across the crags, just as the sun went down."(18th c. Source)

Strawboy Costume
(Source: Evans,1957)

Strawboy Mask
-(Source:Evans1957)

	It is said that the Strawboy custom originated as cattle rustlers hiding in a wedding reception. Called: "sopers" also a way of getting into a wedding house "strawing it". Although this explanation may fit Evens (1957) points out that the custom has many cross cultural parallels which involve persons dressing in straw who perform ritual acts.

Readings, Sayings, Stories, Blessings- Getting them Talking!

The Irish, like many traditional cultures, love a good story or saying. Often, however, those attending do not bring stories with them or the ones they have brought along are not appropriate. There is a way to fix this, which is easy and results in much fun and entertainment. I have included traditional wedding blessings. Stories and sayings are very important. They help people forget their differences, get to know each other, and escape the world around them. And of course the toasts help the Irish to drink.

There is of course not really one Irish Blessing or wedding reading. There are however, a large number of stories, tales, sayings and prayers and of course there is the body of the tradition to guide you in the creation of your own unique masterpiece. I would encourage your creativity.

The Solution to People without Stories:
Prior to the wedding assemble a collection of short Irish Traditional Stories, Sayings, and Toasts.Xerox them and place one or more of each on a large card. Then when the guests arrive, hand each a different card. You can provide instructions on one side of the card or make an announcement. Instruct the guests to read over the stories so that they can tell them in their own words. Instruct them to study the toasts and sayings and to chime in when appropriate during the celebration. Instantly you will have a wedding filled with Irish stories, lore and wisdom. Guests will enjoy sharing their stories across the room and the toasts will animate the celebration. This is a great way to share the culture.

Below you will find a treasure of 20 traditional stories. This should be enough for a large party. Hand one set to the bride's side and one set to the groom's side and let the story exchange begin. This should get things moving along, and there's more where that came from.
Here are some sources for this material:

Cross,Tom,Peete and Clark H. Slover.,Ancient Irish Tales., Figgis,Dublin,1969.
Murphy,Gerard.,Early Irish Lyrics., Oxford.,1970.
O'Sullivan,Sean.,Folktales of Ireland., U. Of Chicago Press,1966.
Glassie,Henry(Ed.)., Irish Folk Tales., Penguin,1987.
Jackson,Kenneth,H. A Celtic Miscellany., Penguin, 1975.
Myer,Kuno, Ancient Irish Poetry.,"Triads of Ireland".,Constable,London,1911.
Chronicle Books., Irish Toasts.,Chronicle Books,San Fransisco,1987.

The Stories

A few Saint's Tales:

From Cogitosus's Life of St Brigid

Of Brigid and the Dead wood which grew

Once Brigid's parents wanted to marry her to a man as is the custom. Brigid, being inspired by God and wishing to become a chaste virgin to God, went to the bishop Mac Caille. The bishop saw her desire motivated by heaven and noted her great love of chastity and placed the white veil and white garment on to her head. Brigid kneeled humbly in front of the bishop and God and touched the wooden base on which the altar sat. The wood grew fresh and green and continues to grow to this day as if it had never been cut down. The wood now heals the faithful of all diseases and afflictions.

Of the Cooked Bacon given to a dog and later found Intact

Brigid was cooking bacon in a cauldron. Her guests had already arrived. A fawning and begging dog came in to the kitchen. Brigid took pity on the dog and gave it a piece of the bacon. When it came time to serve her guests Brigid took the bacon out of the cauldron, but despite having given a piece to the dog the original amount was found intact in the pot. All who witnessed this were amazed.

Of the Garment thrown over a Sunbeam

While Brigid was grazing her sheep while she was working as a shepherdess on a flat grassy plain a rain storm came up and drenched her with a heavy downpour. She went back to her house. Her clothes were soaking wet. A ray of sunshine came into the house through an opening. Brigid's eyes were dazzled by the sun. As a result she thought that the sunbeam was a tree growing on a slant. She then put her wet clothes on it. Her clothes hung on the sunbeam even though it was in fact only filmy and was not transformed into a large solid tree. This miracle dumbfounded both the people in the house and the neighbors. They then praised Brigid.

Of the Bacon she let go with the Dog

Brigid was once meditating on heavenly things (something she did regularly). Not paying attention she let a dog go off with a large piece of bacon. Once it was found to be missing a search was made for it. The bacon was found whole even though it had been missing for a month. It was found in a place where the dog used to stay. The dog had been held in check by divine power and could not eat something which belonged to the holy virgin. The dog was a patient guardian and was completely tame.

Of the Portion of Meat thrown into her Cloak

A poor person needed food and asked her for some. Brigid then went right off to people who were cooking meat to see if she could get some food for the poor person. Then "one very obtuse servant among them who was cooking the meat stupidly transferred a piece of meat not yet cooked into the white receptacle of her upfolded mantle". Brigid carried the meat in this way to the poor person. However, her mantle remained white and unstained

Of the Untamed Fox given to the King in Return

One day an uneducated man saw a fox. The fox was walking through the palace of the king. The man thought that the fox was wild. His senses were blinded. He did not know that the fox was tame and a pet of the king trained to do tricks. The fox was agile and very intelligent. The king and his friends and visitors found the trained fox to be very entertaining. The man killed it in front of a crowd of people who were in the palace. The man was then denounced and shackled by the witnesses. He was then brought before the king. The king was enraged when he learned what had been done. The king ordered the man to be killed unless he could find a similar fox to replace the one, which he had killed. The fox would have to do all the tricks, which the other fox had been able to do. The man's wife and sons were made slaves. All of the man's possessions were seized by the king. Brigid heard of all that had occurred. She "grieved in her inmost heart." Brigid prayed to the Lord for the man who had been unjustly sentenced. Brigid was moved and called for her chariot to be yoked. Brigid drove across the flat wide plain to the king's palace. The Lord heard Brigid's ceaseless prayers. He told a wild fox to come to her. The fox ran quickly across the plains to Brigid's chariot. It jumped nimbly up into the chariot and sat quietly under her cloak. Brigid then came to the king. She asked that the ignorant man be freed. The king refused to listen to her. He demanded that the dead fox be replaced with one, which was just as clever and tame. Brigid then brought out the fox which had been sent to her. The fox was just like the one, which had been killed. It performed all of the same tricks. The king and all of his dignitaries were pleased with the fox and there was "tumultuous applause." The man was freed Brigid then returned home. As she was traveling home the fox weaved through the crowds, outwitted many horsemen and dogs and fled across the open plains and escaped unharmed to the wild desert places where his den was located. All wondered at what had occurred. Brigid was venerated

A Story of Saint Kevin

One day in spring before the blossoms were on the trees, a young man grievously afflicted with the falling sickness fancied that an apple would cure him, and the dickens an apple tree at all was about the place. But what mattered that to the Saint! He ordered a score of fine yellow pippins to grow upon a willow, and the boy gathered and ate and was cured.

The Saint was one day going up Derrybawn, and he meets a woman that carried five loaves in her apron. "What have ye there, good woman?" says the Saint. "I have five stones" says she "If they are stones," says he, "I pray that they may be bread. And if they are bread," says he, "I pray that they may be stones." So, with that, the woman lets them fall, and sure enough, stones they were, and are to this day.

The Saint managed to get from King O' Toole a grant of the land upon which he built his churches. The king was old and weak in himself, and took a mighty liking to a goose, a live goose,. And in course of time the goose was like the master, old and weak. So O'Toole sent for his Holiness. And his Holiness went to see what would the pagan—for King O'Toole was a heathen--want with him. "God save ye," says the Saint. "God save ye kindly," says the king. "A better answer than I expected," says the Saint, "Will ye make my goose young?" says the king. "What'll ye give me? Says the Saint. "What'll ye ask? Says the king. "All I'll ask will be as much of the valley as he'll fly over." Says the Saint. "Done," says the king. So with that Saint Kevin stoops down, takes up the goose, and flings him up, and away he goes over the lake and all round the Glen, which in course was the Saint's hereditary property from that day out.

A Basket full of Traditional Tales
As told by Conrad Bladey

Two Stories of Daniel O'Connell

Daniel O' Connell and the Trickster

There was a man living at Carhan, near Caherciveen, in the time of Daniel O' Connell. He was poor and he had a large family. One day he was selling two pigs, a white one and a black one, at Tralee fair. A buyer asked him how much he wanted for the white one, along with the black one. The poor man thought, and no wonder that the buyer wanted only the white pigs; so he named the price. The buyer immediately marked both pigs and took from his pocket only that which had been asked for the white one. " What do you mean?" asked the poor man. "You only inquired about the white pig" "That's a lie!" said the buyer. "Didn 't I ask you how much you wanted for the white one along with the black one?" The poor man could do nothing but give him the two pigs for the price of one. He returned home and told his story to his wife and to all the neighbors. It wasn't long till it spread all over the district, and everybody was sorry for the poor man. He told his story to Daniel O'Connell, who had great sympathy for him. "We'll get our own back on that buyer later on," said O'Connell. "Are you willing to cut off the lobe of your right ear?" "I am ," said he. O'Connell cut of the lobe of the man's right ear, put it into an envelope, and took it home. He asked the poor man to accompany him to Tralee next day to play a trick on the buyer. "He has a tobacco shop in Tralee," said O'Connell; "and we'll call into him. After a while, you must take out your pipe and take a whiff or two from it. I will then pass the remark that you don't smoke very much, and you must reply that you would smoke seven times as much, if you had the tobacco. I will then say that I'll give you all the tobacco you want." The following day, they both went to Tralee and went into the tobacco shop. The poor man pulled out his pipe, reddened it, drew a few whiffs, and put it back into his pocket. "You don't smoke very much," said O'Connell to him. "I'd smoke seven times as much, if I had it," said the poor man.
"Well, I'll give you plenty of tobacco," said O'Connell. He ordered the buyer to give the poor man as much tobacco as would reach from his toe to the lobe of his right ear and asked how much it would cost. "Eight shillings" said the buyer. "That's agreed" said O'Connell . The buyer then began to measure the length from the man's toe to the lobe of his right ear, but when he reached the ear, he found that the lobe was missing. He pretended nothing. "We have caught you!" said O'Connell. "That's not the lobe of his right ear. It is back in Carhan, if you know where that place is. So you must measure from his toe to Carhan!" The buyer was dumbfounded. He could say nothing. The O'Connell ordered him to pay the man for the black pig, and he would not insist on the tobacco at all. The buyer paid the money, and even something extra, and went off to his kitchen covered with shame. And no wonder!

The Smell of Money for the Smell of Food

There were six young fellows visiting a town one day. One of them suggested that they go and eat some food. They had some drinks before that. The went into an hotel, and one of them ordered a meal for them all. Each was to pay his own share. A pound of meat was placed in front of each of them. One of the fellows told the woman to take away his own meat, as he wasn't going to eat it at all. "I won't," she said. "It was ordered and you can eat it or leave it." He ate a small bit of bread and took a cup of soup or tea, whichever it was. Tea wasn't very plentiful at that time. After the meal, each of them went to pay his share, but this fellow wanted to pay only for the bread and the soup or tea. As they were about to leave, the woman snatched this fellow's hat at the doorway. He asked her to give it back to him, but it was no use. They started to argue about it, but she remained firm.

Daniel O'Connell was walking along the street when he heard the argument and saw the young fellow bareheaded. He stopped and asked what was the trouble. "This is the trouble," said the fellow. "Five others and myself came to this woman to get a meal. One of us ordered a pound of meat for each. When she put the meat in front of me, I said I wouldn't have any and wouldn't eat it. She told me to eat it or leave it. I didn't taste the meat at all; so I didn't want to pay for it." "If this fellow didn't eat the meat," said O'Connell, "'tis strange that he should have to pay for it. Give him back his hat." "He didn't have to eat it," said the woman. "The smell of my meat filled his belly." "You may be right in that," said O'Connell. "I have always herd that all a woman needs to do to get an excuse is to glance over her shoulder." O'Connell took off his own hat, put his hand into his trousers' pocket, and threw a fistful of silver into the hat. "Come over here now," said he to the woman. "Place your nose over this money and take your time smelling it. Fill your belly well with it." She was taken aback by that.

"Does that satisfy you?" asked O'Connell. She was covered with shame and made no reply. "Give him his hat quickly," said O' Connell. "You have got as good a bargain as you gave." That ended the matter. The fellow got his hat and went off.-

The Fox and the Eagle

There came a very bad year one time. One day the fox was near the shore of the Lakes of Killarney, and he couldn't find a bird or anything else to eat. Then he spied three ducks a bit out from the shore and thought to himself that if he could catch hold of them, he would have a fine meal. There was some water parsnip with very large leaves growing by the shore, and he swam out to it and cut off two big leaves of it with his teeth. He held one of them at each side of his mouth and swam toward the ducks. The never felt anything until he had taken one of them off with him. Very satisfied with himself, he brought her ashore, laid her down, and decided to try and catch the other two as well- 'tis seldom they would be an offer! He caught a second duck by the same trick and left her dead near the first. Then out he swam for the third and brought her in. But, if he did, there was no trace of the other two where he had left them. "May god help me!" said he. "I have only the one by my day's work. What'll I do? I wonder who is playing tricks on me." He looked all around but couldn't see an enemy anywhere. Then he looked toward the cliff that was nearby, and what did he spy but the nest of an eagle high up on it. "No one ever took my two ducks but the eagle," said he. "As good as I am at thieving, there's a bigger thief above my head." He didn't know how to get at the eagle. Then he saw a fire smoldering not far away, where men had been working at a quarry a few days before. They had a fire and it was still burning slowly under the surface of the ground. He dragged the duck to the fire and pulled her hither and thither through the embers. Then he left her down on the grass and hid. The eagle must have been watching out for the third duck too, for down he swooped and snatched her up to his nest. No sooner did the dead duck's body touch the dry nest than the nest caught fire---there were live embers stuck in the duck's feathers. Down fell the blazing nest with the three dead ducks as well as the eagle's three young ones inside it, so the fox had six birds for his supper. Didn't he get his own back well on the eagle?

The Cat and the Dog

Long ago the dog used to be out in the wet and the cold, while the cat remained inside near the fire.

One day, when he was "drowned wet," the dog said to the cat, "You have a comfortable place, but you won't have it any longer. I'm going to find out whether I have to be outside every wet day, while you are inside." The man of the house overheard the argument between the two and thought that it would be right to settle the matter. "Tomorrow," said he, "I will start a race between ye five miles from the house, and whichever of ye comes into the house first will have the right to stay inside from then on. The other can look after the place outside."

Next day, the two got themselves ready for the race. As they ran toward the house, the dog was a half -mile ahead of the cat. Then he met a beggar man. When the beggar man saw the dog running toward him with his mouth open, he thought he was running to bite him. He had a stick in his hand and he struck the dog as he ran by. The dog was hurt and started to bark at the beggar man and tried to bite him for satisfaction. Meanwhile the cat ran toward the house, and she was licking herself near the fire and resting after the race when the dog arrived. "Now," said the cat when the dog ran in, "the race is won, and I have the inside of the house for ever more. "

The Man who swallowed the Mouse

There was a man in Rinnard one time. He felt very thirsty one evening after a day's mowing; so he took a bowl of thick milk to drink. The kitchen was half dark, as lamps and lights were scarce at that time. He swallowed the milk, and what was in it but a mouse! He never felt anything until he had swallowed the milk, mouse and all. Every day from that day on, especially when he would lie down, he could feel the mouse running about and dancing inside of him. At that time, the doctors were not as good as they are now, and no doctor or anybody else could help him. He told all of his friends about the mouse, for he knew that they wouldn't wish anything to be wrong with him. One woman came to see how he was, and she said that the best thing to do was to put a piece of roasted bacon and a piece of mutton on a plate on both sides of his mouth when he lay down in bed. The cat should be kept in the room too. When the mouse would smell the roasted meat, she would come out taste it.

The man tried this remedy for three nights. On the third night didn't the mouse come out and start to eat the meat ! She hadn't eaten much before the cat killed her. The man lived to a great age after that happened. That story is as true as any I ever heard!

The Uglier Foot

There was a tailor in Ballyvourney a long time ago. He had very big ankles, and the nickname the people had on him was "Tadhg of the Ankles" . At that time, tradesmen traveled from house to house, and the people used to gather in for sport and fun with them. One night Tadhg was sewing away, sitting on the table, and he had one of his legs stretched out from him. The woman of the house was sitting at the head of the table, between Tadhg and the fire. She noticed Tadhg's big ankle. "Upon my conscience, that's an ugly foot," said she. One or two people laughed at this. "Upon my conscience," said Tadhg, "there's a still uglier foot than it in the house."

The woman of the house must have had badly shaped feet herself, and she thought that Tadhg was hinting at her. "There isn't an uglier foot than it in the whole world, " said she "Would you lay a bet on that?" asked Tadhg "I would," said she. "I'll bet you a quart of whiskey that there's an uglier foot than it is in this house," said Tadhg. " I'll take that bet," said the woman.

At that, Tadhg pulled his other foot from under him. "Now," said he, "which is the uglier, the first foot or the second one?" "Upon my word, the second is a lot uglier," said the woman. "Very well," said Tadhg. "Send out for a quart of whiskey for me." "I will, indeed," said the woman.

The Swine of the Gods

A few years ago a friend of mine told me of something that happened to him when he was a young man and out drilling with some Connacht Fenians. They were but a car-full, and drove along a hillside until they came to a quiet place. The left the car and went further up the hill with their rifles, and drilled for a while. As they were coming down again they saw a very thin, long legged pig of the old Irish sort, and the pig began to follow them. One of them cried out as a joke that it was a fairy pig, and they all began to run to keep up the joke. The pig ran too, and presently, how nobody knew, this mock terror became real terror, and they ran as for their lives. When they got to the car they made the horse gallop as fast as possible, but the pig still followed. Then one of them put up his rifle to fire, but when he looked along the barrel he could see nothing. Presently they turned a corner and came to a village. The told the people of the village what had happened, and the people of the village took pitchforks and spades and the like, and went along the road with them to drive the pig away. When they turned the corner they could not find anything.

The Heather Beer

People say that the Danes were able to make the sweetest of beer from the tops of the heather. But the Irish people could not get the secret of it from them, although they tried their best. When they were routing the Danes out of Ireland, they killed most of them until there were only two left alive, a father and son. The Irish made up their minds to try to get the secret of the beer from these two, or it would be lost for ever. So they said to the pair that were left that whoever of them would give up the secret would be let go free. Then the father spoke, and he said, "If that's the way things are and if only one of us will be let go alive, let ye kill the boy, and I will tell you how my people make the beer from the heather." The son was put to death, and then the father was asked to tell the secret. "Well," said he, " I asked ye to kill the boy first, because I was afraid that ye would get the secret out of him, if I died before him. Since he's dead now, I want to tell ye that ye won't get from me the secret ye at trying so hard to get. Ye'll never get it from me. Do what ye wish with me." The father was put to death, and the secret was never found since.

Willie Brennan

Brennan was born in Kilmurry, near Kilworth. He listed in the army and then he deserted out of it. They were hunting him around the country day and night. One day outside at Leary's Bridge, Brennan met the Pedlar Bawn. I never heard him called by another name. The Pedlar was traveling for a firm in Cork, going about the country selling different kinds of things. Brennan put the blunderbuss up to him and made him hand out what he had watch and chain and all. Then the Pedlar asked him to give him some token to show to the people of the firm in Cork that he had met him. "Tell them that you met Brennan the Highwayman." "Give me some token that you met me, or I'll be put to jail," said the Pedlar. "What have I to do for you?" asked Brennan. "Fire a shot through this side of my old coat," said the Pedlar. He did. "Fire another through this side now," said the Pedlar. So he did. "Here! Said the Pedlar. "Fire another through my old hat." Brennan did. "Come!" said the Pedlar. "Fire another through my old cravat." "I have no more ammunition," said Brennan. The Pedlar then drew a pistol, whenever he had it hid. "Come! Said he. "Deliver!" Brennan had to deliver, quick and lively too! "You're a smarter man than me," said he. "All I ever went through, I robbed army, men and lords, and you beat me. Will you make a comrade for me?" The Pedlar only flung his pack over the ditch. "I will," said he. "I'll stand a loyal comrade until my dying day." And so he was, a loyal comrade. "We'll go along to County Tipperary, " said Brennan. "Tis a wealthy county. There's agents and landlords and there going around the country gathering the rent in the houses, and we'll whip them going back in the evening." So the two of them went along to the County Tipperary. Brennan went in to a widow there one morning. The poor woman was crying and lamenting. He asked her what was the matter with her. "What good is it for me to tell you, my good man?" Said she. She didn't know but he was a tramp. "How do you know? " said he. "The agent is coming here by and by, and I haven't a halfpenny to give him for the rent, "said she. "Well, what would you say to the man who'd give it to you?" said Brennan. He asked her how much it was, and she told him --five or six pounds, I suppose. He counted it out to her. "Tell me now," said he, "the road he goes home in the evening." She told him the road he'd take after giving the day gathering around. He made her go down on her knew then and swear to God and to him that she would never tell anyone that she saw him, or mention that anyone gave her the money. Himself and the Pedlar met the agent going home with the money and whipped the whole lot that he had gathered that day . Brennan is buried over in Kilcrumper near the old church wall.

The Black Art

A man and his wife were living in Malinmore long ago, and they had an only daughter, a young girl. As with every couple of that kind, the daughter was the apple of their eye. One day the father was cutting turf at Rossmore. When dinnertime came, the mother sent the girl with food, consisting of some broth in a wooden dish, to her father. There were only wooden vessels at that time. The father sat down at the edge of the bog to take his meal. It was a fine day, and the two of them were looking out over the s ea. It wasn't long until a large sailing ship came into view, making for the mouth of the river. "Isn't that a fine large ship?" said the little girl to her father. "It is, indeed! " said he. "I wonder--where is she going to?" said the girl. "I'd say she was making for Killybegs."
"Well, if I wished so now, she would never reach there, big and all as she is," said the girl. "Shut up, you little fool!" said the father. "What could you do to a ship that's out on the sea? Have sense in what you say." The girl made no reply and waited until her father had finished his meal. Then she took the dish to wash it in the pool of water in the bog. When she had done that, she started to play tricks with the dish in the water. The father was lighting his pipe and took no notice of what she was doing; he thought she was only washing the vessel. Soon she spoke to him. "Look now, father, and see what I can do with that ship," said she. The father looked out to sea and saw that ship, which should have been making for the river mouth, was coming straight for the cliffs below them. "Who taught you how to do that?" he asked. "My mother," said she "And what are you going to do to the ship when you get her near the shore?" he asked. "As soon as I get her near enough to the rocks, I can turn this dish upside down and the same will happen to the ship on the sea," said she. "I see," said the father. "And you tell me that it was your mother who taught you this?" "She did, indeed," said the girl.
At any rate, the girl let the ship go free, and it floated out to the open sea again. The little girl took the dish home, and her father passed no remark on whether what she had learned from her mother as good or bad. That night, when he returned from the bog, he cleaned and washed himself well and put on his best suit of clothes. He left the house that night, and wherever he went, his wife and daughter never saw him again for the rest of their lives. He was angry to learn that he had married a woman who practiced the black art. Had she not taught some of it to her daughter, he would never have found out. But the girl had let the cat out of the bag, and that left her without seeing her father any more. Wasn't it strange, whatever place he went to, that he was never seen again?

The Cow that Ate the Piper

There were three spalpeens coming home to Kerry from Limerick one time after working there, on their way, they met a piper on the road. "I'll go along with ye," said the piper. "All right," they said. The night was very cold, freezing hard, and they were going to perish. They saw a dead man on the road with a new pair of shoes on his feet. "By heavens! " said the piper. "I haven't a stitch of shoes on me. Give me that spade to see can I cut off his legs." "Twas the only way he could take off the shoes. They were held on by the frost. So he took hold of the spade and cut off the two feet at the ankles. He took them along with him. They got lodgings at a house where three cows were tied in the kitchen. "Keep away from that gray cow," said the servant girl, "or we'll eat your coats. Keep out from her." They all went to sleep. The three spalpeens and the piper stretched down near the fire. The piper heated the shoes and the dead man's feet at the fire and got the shoes off. He put on the shoes and threw the feet near the gray cow's head. Early next morning he left the house wearing his new pair of shoes. When the servant girl got up, she looked at the door. It was bolted, and the three spalpeens were asleep near the fire. "My God!" she cried. "There were four of ye last night, and now there are only three. Where did the other man go?" "We don't know," they said. "How would we know where he went?" She went to the gray cow's head and fond the two feet. "Oh my! She cried. "He was eaten by her." She called the man of the house."The gray cow has eaten one of the men,"
said she. "What's that you're saying?" asked the farmer. "I'm telling the truth " she said "There's only his feet left. The rest of him is eaten." The farmer got up. "There were four of ye there last night, men," said he. "There were," said one of the spalpeens, "and our comrade has been eaten by the cow."
"Don't cause any trouble about it," said the farmer. "Here's five pounds for ye. Eat your breakfast and be off. Don't say a word." They left when they had the breakfast eaten. And they met the piper some distance from the house, and he dancing on the road. Such a thing could happen!

The Four leafed Shamrock and the Cock

There was a great fair being held in Dingle one day long ago. Tis a good many years ago, I think. All of the people were gathered there as usual. Whoever else was there, there was a showman there, and the trick that he had was a cock walking down the street ahead of him drawing a big, heavy beam tied to his leg. At least, all the people thought that it was a beam, and everyone was running after him, and as he went from street to street, the crowd was getting bigger all the time . Each new person who saw the cock and the beam joined in the procession. Then there came up the street a small old man carrying a load of rushes on his back. He wondered what all the people were looking at. All that he could see was a wisp of straw being dragged along by a cock. The thought that everybody had gone mad, and he asked them why they were following the cock like that. Some of them answered him, "Don't you see the great wonder?" they said. "That great beam of wood being dragged after him by that cock, and he's able to pull it through every street he travels and it tied to his leg?"

"All that he's pulling is a wisp of straw," replied the old man. The showman overheard him saying this. Over to him he went, and he asked him how much he wanted for the load of rushes he had on his back. The old man named some figure--to tell the truth, I can't say how much he wanted for the load of rushes he had on his back--but whatever it was, the showman gave it to him. He would have given him twice as much. As soon as the showman took the load of rushes off the old man's back, the old man followed after the crowd, but all that he could see was the cock pulling a heavy beam tied to his leg. He followed him all over Dingle. What happened was that the old man had a four leafed shamrock, unknown to himself, tied up in the load of rushes. That's what made what he saw different from what the people saw, and that's why the showman paid him three times the value for the rushes. He told the people, and they gave up the chase. I heard that story among the people, and it could be true, because the four-leafed shamrock has that power.

The Three Questions

It was this codger and he was hired as a heardsboy to a bishop. Things were bad in Ireland at the time: the enemy had come and conquered the country and took the land and was killing before them, priest and people. So this evening the heardsboy come home and he seen the bishop walking up and down and looking very down-in-the-mouth. "My Lord Bishop," says the herdsboy, "what ails you? You look very downhearted?" "I'm to die in the morning," says the bishop. "How is that?" says the herdsboy. "I'm to lose me head," says the bishop. "The chief that took over this country" he says, "sent for me this morning and give me three questions to answer by the morra morning and if I'm not fit he's to take the head off me. "What's the three questions, my lord?" says the herdsboy. "I might be fit to help." "You could not, " says the bishop. "You might only lose your own head as well." Anyway he got the bishop to tell him, and the herdsboy said that he would go in place of the bishop next morning and to leave all to him. "You'll only lose your head, too" says the bishop. Morning come and the herdsboy set off and meets this big fellow and stands before him. "How are you?" says he. "I'm

herdsboy to the Lord Bishop," says he. "Why didn't he come himself?" says he. "The Lord Bishop didn't think it worth his while," says he, "to come himself to answer three simple questions." "Then if you're not fit to answer them you 'll lose your head," says this big fellow. "Fair enough," says the herdsboy. "Here's my first question then," says the big fellow. "What's the first thing I think of in the morning when I rise?" "What you'll eat," says the herdsboy. "That's right," says he. "Now here's me second question: How many loads of sand are there round the shores of Ireland?" "One," says the herdsboy, "if you had a cart big enough to hold it." "Right, says the big fellow. "And now

here's my third and last question: How much am I worth?" "Twenty-nine pieces of silver," says the herdsboy. "How do you make that out?" "Well, our Lord God Himself was sold for thirty pieces," says the herdsboy, "and you can't be as good as Him." And he got him and the bishop off.

The Air Ship

One day the monks of Clonmacnoise were holding a meeting on the floor of the church, and as they were at their deliberations there they saw a ship sailing over them in the air, going as if it were on the sea. When the crew of the ship saw the meeting and the inhabited place below them, they dropped anchor, and the anchor came right down on to the floor of the church, and the priests seized it. A man came down out of the ship after the anchor, and he was swimming as if he were in the water, till he reached the anchor; and they were dragging him down then. "For God's sake let me go!" said he, "for you are drowning me." Then he left them, swimming in the air as before, taking his anchor with him.

A good Source for Prayers:

Daily Readings from Prayers & Praises in the Celtic Tradition., Ed. A.M. Allchin and Esther de Waal, Templegate Publishers, Springfield Illinois,1986.

Irish Blessing for Weddings

May the road rise to meet you.
May the wind be always at your back.
May the sunshine warm upon your face,
The rains fall soft upon the fields.

May the light of friendship guide your paths together.
May the laughter of children grace the halls of your home.
May the joy of living for one another trip a smile from your lips,
A twinkle from your eye.

And when eternity beckons,
at the end of a life heaped high with love,
May the good Lord embrace you
with the arms that have nurtured you
the whole length of your joy-filled days.
May the gracious God hold you both
in the palm of His hands.

And, today, may the Spirit of Love
find a dwelling place in your hearts. Amen

Length of life and sunny days,
And may your soul not go homewards
'Til your own child falls in love!

May God go with you and bless you,
May you see your children's children,
May you be poor in misfortune and rich in blessings,
May you know nothing but happiness from this day forward.
-Traditional

Sayings:

Proverb:
Marriages are all happy. Its having breakfast together that causes all the trouble.

Sayings:
A growing moon and a flowing tide are lucky times to marry in.

Never make a toil of pleasure, as the man said when he dug his wife's grave only three feet deep.
Marriage at the dung heap and the godparents far away.
Woe to him who does not heed a good wife's counsel.
It's why women marry--the creatures, God bless them, are too shy to say no.
There was never an old slipper but there was an old stocking to match it.
A young man is bothered till he's married, after that he's bothered entirely .
There's only one thing in the world better than a good wife....no wife .
The dowry falls over the cliff; but the protruding lip remains on the wife.
A bad wife takes advice from everyone but her husband.
He breaks his wife's head and then buys a plaster for it.
There are no trials till marriage.
The carefree mother's daughter makes a bad wife.
It's a lonesome washing that there's not a (man's) shirt in.
Marry a mountainy woman and you'll marry the mountain.
She's a good woman, but she didn't take off her boots yet.
The day you marry your wife you marry your children .
The blanket is the warmer of being doubled .
She burnt her coal and did not warm herself .
He married money and got a woman with it.
Marry in haste and be sorry at your leisure.
When you go forth to find a wife leave your eyes at home, but take both ears with you.
It's the last suitor that wins the maid.
The beak of the goose is no longer than that of the gander.
Wait till you're eighteen to marry and don't be spoiling your growth.
It's a lonesome washing that there's not a man's shirt in it.
Before the age of fifty-five there is no such thing as a confirmed bachelor only an obstinate one.
The best test of a man is his choice of a wife.
Three with the lightest hearts: a student after reading his psalms, a young lad who has left off his boy's clothes for good and a maid who has been made a woman.
Every thrush thinks her mate sings the sweetest.
A man is a man when his woman is a woman.
May God give you luck and put a good man in your way, and if he is not good, may the wedding whiskey be drunk at his wake.

Triad:
Three cohabitations that do not pay a marriage-portion:taking her by force, outraging her without her knowledge through drunkenness, her being violated by a king.

Games

Games have always been important for all Irish Traditional gatherings but often they are the most neglected aspect. They are great for after dinner! These were for children as well as adults. They are quite wild and filled with energy. Be sure to have materials on hand which are clean and safe. You may have to make some substitutions! While this collection is for Wakes such games are interchangeable with all occasions.

-O'Suilleabhain,Sean, <u>Irish Wake Amusements</u>.,Mercier,Dublin,1976.

Here are a few. Enjoy!

Lifting the Corpse

A very large man would lie down on his back on the floor. The legs must be kept straight and rigid. Four men then tried to lift him off the floor with their thumbs placed under the shoulders right and left and on the calf of the legs right and left. Each lifter used only one of his thumbs. If the man was lifted places were exchanged. If they failed they would have their heads bashed against the floor (especially if they dropped the man!)

Pulling the Stick- Sweet Draughts

Two men sat facing each other on the floor. Legs were extended so that the soles of their shoes touched. A strong stick, a handle of a spade or pitchfork, was laid across the tops of their shoes. Both gripped the stick, one hand inside and one outside and each tried while holding his legs rigid to lift his opponent off the floor even as much as an inch. After three pulls places were exchanged and the test continued similarly. Sometimes a man who was to be lifted off the floor would make his foot slip from the opponent's shoe. Friends would stand on the coat tails of the person they
did not wish lifted.

Lifting a Chair

A chair was gripped at the base of one of the legs by each contestant in turn in an attempt to raise it above his head. It was by no means an easy thing to do, as the old chairs were quite heavy.

Breaking an Egg

An egg was held between the contestant's two hands with the pointed ends against the palms. He then tried to crush the egg, and generally failed.

The Stronger Hand

Two men stood facing each other, with their right hands raised against each other. Pressure was then exerted by each in an attempt to force down his opponent's hand.

Wrestling

A man would enter the house dressed in a suit of straw and challenge all present to wrestle the Connachtman.
A. A man gripped a stick with his hands at either end and tried to jump over it, without breaking his hold. An open razor edge upwards was used instead of a stick.

B. 12 men faced each other in two lines, six in each row. The men in each line stood about two feet apart from their neighbors. Each player extended his two arms and gripped the hands of the man facing him. Other active men at the wake then tried in turn to jump over each pair of hands in turn, down between the lines without stopping. This was a very difficult feat to perform.

C. Two men stood with a spade handle or other stick resting on their shoulders. Two others then tried to excel each other in performing acrobatic tricks on the stick, like circus performers.

D. Two men competed to do somersaults on the floor returning to a standing position. Driving the Pigs across the Bridge. Those who arrived late at the wake house were the pigs. They are scolded for not having arrived earlier and then someone would shout "We must drive the pigs across the bridge" The bridge consisted of a number of men, who stood in line behind one another, with their shoulders bent forward. The "pigs" were then forced with blows to mount like riders, on the backs of the others; when all had mounted, they were suddenly thrown on the floor in a heap on the floor.

Riding the Wild Ass

A rope with a noose at one end was thrown over one of the rafters of the house. The man who wished to show his agility then grasped the other end of the rope and put one of his feet into the noose. He then pulled on the free end of the rope and tried to raise himself high enough to enable him to kick against another rafter or couple with his free foot. The difficulty and danger of the trick came from the fact that one part of his body (the hands) was pulling against another (the foot) and he might easily fall on to the floor and injure his head or back.

Stealing the Goats

The player grabbed two sods of turf, one in either hand, and faced the floor with his hands and legs extended; only the turf sods and the toes of his shoes were allowed to touch the floor. The player's objective was a potato, which lay on the floor below his face. He had to pick this up with his mouth without allowing his stomach to touch the floor or bending his arms or legs. This was difficult enough to do while uninterrupted, but it became more so when he had to reply to questions during the attempt:

Questioner: Where are you going now?
Reply: Stealing the goats from Hell.
Questioner: Swear that you are.
Reply: I swear that I am.

Lifting a horseshoe

The shoe was placed three or four inches out from the foot of the kitchen wall. The person who tried to pick it up took his stand about three feet from the wall, and h ad to pick up the shoe without bending his knees. Whenever he bent forward in making the attempt, his head would touch the wall, and he was not allowed to use his hands to help straighten himself again.

Going around Under a Table

The player would lie face downwards on a table, catching the edges with both hands. He then was required to bring his body around under the table, between its legs, and return to his starting point without touching the floor. His main difficulty was to keep the table from overturning in the process.

Walking on the legs of a Stool

A fairly long stool would be laid on the floor, legs upwards. The contestant had to mount the stool, placing his two hands on the front legs and his two feet on the back ones. To do the trick he had to walk around on the stool legs with his hands and feet until he returned to his original position.

The Donkeys and Baskets

A man lay face down on the wake house floor. Two others sat facing each other at either side of him and extended their legs across his back toward each other. Each took hold of the other's legs. The prone man was now the donkey and the other two the baskets. His task was to rise up as a real donkey would raising the baskets on his back. Two groups of three often took part in this test each striving to be the first in completing it.

Spinning the Tin Box

Each of the male players was given an even number while each female got an odd number. The players sat here and there in the kitchen while a tin box was spun in the center of the floor by the man in charge of the game. As the box spun around he would call out the number of some player whose duty it then was to rush forward and catch the box before it ceased to spin. A player who failed to do so was given some penalty.

The Mock Court or The Police Game

Eight or so of the players remained in the kitchen, while everybody else went outside the door. Those who were inside then divided themselves up according to their duties in the game; one would act as judge, two as lawyers; one as court-clerk, and three or four as policemen. The police would then go outside and drag in somebody as prisoner, while the others pressed in also to hear the case being tried. The judge took his seat, and the clerk read out the name and address of the prisoner, as well as the offense with which he was being charged. The trial then proceeded as it would in a legal court, one lawyer prosecuting, the other defending. The main source of the fun, apart from the charge itself, was to be found in the sly references made by both counsel to the private affairs of some of those present, who were dragged into the case. These mischievous, though irrelevant, hints caused great laughter, as they were understood by all. Having heard the evidence, the judge announced his verdict, which was witty and light or severe, according to how he regarded the defendant. The police had then the task of seeing that the verdict was carried out; if guilty, the defendant might be handled roughly as punishment or even doused nine or ten times in a tub of water. If the first trial produced a good deal of amusement, as second or third would follow, until all were tired of the game.

A somewhat similar game, which involved a court-case, was the following. A man lay down on the floor, feigning illness and a doctor would be sent for. The doctor arrived into the kitchen on horseback, the horse being two fellows clad in straw to resemble an animal. The horse would be a very wild one and, in the course of prancing around the kitchen, the doctor would be thrown down on top of the sick man on the floor. When examined, it would be found that both the patient and the doctor were dead, and the two who played the part of the horse would be tried for causing their deaths.

Building the Ship

John L. Prim has provided a garbled account of the way in which this game was played at wakes in Kilkenny over a hundred years ago. He mentions how the keel was first laid, followed by the prow and stern of the ship; then a woman, who was taking part in the game, would raise the mast with "some gesture" and speech that convinced Prim that the game had its origin in pagan times. His account is so unclear that it would be difficult, for want of additional details, to imagine how the game was really played. Henry Morris has noted that his uncle had seen a similar game played about one hundred years ago in Co. Monaghan. It was a lively game, with lots of activities going on, he said; the only part he could remember was the tarring of the ship (soot being smeared on somebody). Morris said that the game died out in Farney, Co. Monaghan, before the year 1880.

A Co. Galway man has described the game, as he saw it played there. Three men sat down astride a stool, one behind the other, all facing in the same direction. The man in front was the prow of the ship; the man in the middle, the body of the ship; and the third man the stern. A fourth player stood on the floor beside them; he was the builder of the ship. He would ask the company for a hammer or sledge, which he needed for the work, and he got it-a hard sod of turf, a piece of turnip, or something like that. Having got the implement, he would walk around the stool, talking loudly to himself about his accomplishments as a ship-builder. He would then insert the right hand of the center man under the right armpit of the man in front, and continue to walk around the ship, striking hard blows with his hammer on the three, as he went. He would next put the left hand of the center man under the left arm-pit of the first man, striking blows all the time to make things firm. He then placed the legs of the hind pair around the body of the person in front of each, hammering away to keep the timbers from splitting. The trio would then have to lie back, as far as they could, and the builder would start to raise the mast. This part of the game was often obscene. Another game is mentioned by Prim called Drawing the Ship Out of the Mud, but it is not described.

Building the Bridge

Twelve men or so stood out on the floor and formed into two lines of six each, facing one another. Each man took hold of the two hands of the man opposite, thus forming the bridge from which the game took its name. The bridge had now to be tested for strength. Another player mounted on the crossed hands and walked to and fro along them. Finding no apparent fault with its construction, he dismounted. Somebody would then suggest that the bridge be tested to see if it would take a flood of water through its eye. This would be done by some rogue who sluiced the legs and feet of the players with a bucketful of dirty water.

Making the Poteen

This game is both imitative and a booby-trap. Somebody who had not seen it played previously would be asked to sit on a chair or stool in the center of the floor. He would be, as it were the still. The man who was working the still would walk fussily around him, getting ready for the work, while some others remained outside the house to keep an eye out for the police or "Revenue men". As the busy preparations were at their height within, the watchers would rush in to say that the police were coming. Speedy action was now necessary; the first thing to be done was to hide the still outside in the dark. The stiller gave this order to his helpers, and they set to work with a will. Pity the poor still! The innocent fellow who simulated that was dragged out into the darkness and flung headlong into the cesspool of the dung -hill or some equally unpleasant hiding-place from which he had to extricate himself without light or help.

Coining the Money
Another booby-trap! Counterfeit money was to be coined, as it were, and some innocent fellow was got to sit in the middle of the floor to represent the mint. The players circled around him chanting "Coin the money! Coin the money!" until somebody rushed in from outside to say that the police were approaching. The mint had now to be hidden as quickly and as disagreeably as the still in the preceding game.

Sledging
A man who had no experience of the game was asked to sit in the center of the floor to represent the anvil. As soon as the victim was seated, the master, and his apprentices began to thump him with their fists, as hammers Booby-trap again! The master smith and his helpers announced that they had to make some plough-"socks", or horseshoes or something like that., chanting in time with the blows:
"Strike him strike, strike together!
Strike, strike, all together!
Having pummeled the anvil well for a time, one of the apprentices would suddenly shout that the anvil was on fire! It had to be taken out quickly lest the forge be burned. The poor anvil was taken hold of by three or four strong fellows and dumped into the cess-pool outside, or else was douched with buckets of water.

The Kiln on Fire
In this game, players simulated a miller and his men drying corn. The floor represented the kiln. The miller would order his men to bring in sacks of corn to put into the kiln. Each man went outside and came back with a man on his back; this process went on until some twenty men, as sacks, were lying in a heap on the floor. The were left there for a while to dry, as it were, and were then turned, those underneath being placed on top. When this had been done, and the process of drying the corn was progressing well, one of the workmen would suddenly should that the kiln was on fire. The miller and his helpers would rush to pour buckets of water on the sacks, drenching all who were heaped on the floor, especially those on top. In some areas, only two players took part, the miller and his daughter.

The Deaf Miller
A player (the miller) sat on the floor, mixing soot and water in a dish with a stick. As he worked, he carried on a conversation with himself, his remarks causing great laughter among the audience. One of his mill-hands would enter carrying another player, as a sack of corn, on his back, would tell the miller that the sack was to be ground. The miller would pretend not to be able to hear him, owing to the noise of the   mill, and would finally order the helper to lay the sack down behind him. When five or six sacks had thus been deposited behind the miller, who all the continued to mix the soot and water (to simulate grinding) and keep up his remarks in a loud voice, the helper would shout that the mill was on fireThe miller would have no trouble in hearing this and would throw the sooty water over his shoulder on top of the sacks behind his back to quench the blaze.

Lifting the Old Nag

A heavily-built man would hobble into the kitchen, pretending to be an old foundered horse, and throw himself down on the floor, grunting and complaining. Some players would gather about him, and he would ask them to raise him to his feet. Two or three would attempt this and would fail; others would come to their assistance, but even nine or ten would not be able to lift the nag. The leader of the game would then order them to remove their coats. They did so, throwing aside the coats here and there, and started to lift again, straining every muscle, but to no avail. The nag was too heavy. The leader would then order them to remove other garments, and when they had finally got rid of their socks, they would succeed in their task. At this point, some mischievous fellow would quench all the lights in the wake-house; the others would let the nag collapse on the floor and, in the darkness, set about finding their clothes, which would have been hidden away by members of the audience. Rough-and-tumble searching went on until the lights were restored, and the game was over.

Cutting the Timber

A man lay down across the threshold of the kitchen feet outside, head within. He was to represent the saw. Two players now took hold of his feet outside, while two others caught his head and shoulders in the kitchen. They pulled against one another, forward and backwards, as if they were sawing wood, until one pair proved too strong for the other.

Get everyone involved! There are many more of these games. You can use them for all of the gatherings related to the wedding festivities and planning. Make up your own! No one should ever be bored! Games also help bridge the generations and help everyone get acquainted.

Selecting The Date

Taking Care to be Safe and Special

In Ireland weddings have a few general ground rules:

- The last day of the old year is thought especially lucky for weddings. Childermas Day or Holy Innocents (Dec. 28) is, on the contrary, a very unlucky one.
- It is advisable that Luck Money- be given by the groom to parents of the bride for good house fortune. This should be a significant amount.
- If a bridegroom unbuttons one button of his britches at the right knee the little people cannot harm him.
- A green wedding gown is a temptation to the fairies to steal the bride.
- After the ceremony have young girls give the bride horseshoes made of silver paper looped with white ribbons. The shoe must be turned up.
- Have young men carry bogwood torches to light the bride on her journey home after the wedding.
- Shower bride and groom with flower petals for good luck
- The Bride should never take her feet off the floor lest the fairies obtain power.
  -Traditional-Source-Danaher,1972, Haggerty,1999.

To and from the wedding there must be some special events:
- At Bride's house bride and groom are given oatmeal and salt. If each take three mouthfuls they are protected from the "evil eye".
- In County Galway neighbors light small bonfires along the road traveled by bridal party for good luck, warmth and children.
- You must have a procession of all after the wedding: "the wedding drag"

- It is said that the Bride's mother-in-law must break piece of wedding cake on Bride's head when entering the house so that there will be friendship between mother in law and bride for life.
- On the first night going to the new home to live with the husband and a group from the husband's home meets a group from the wife's home. Both groups stay with the wife. When she is inside the house the mother-in-law of the wife stands in front of here in the middle of the floor, removes the wife's cloak and holding both hands she says: "Wisha - husband's last name- welcome to you, a welcome and forty to you and all and may the young pair have seven sons"- Traditional in:Conchúr Ó Siocháin, The Man from Cape Clear.

When you select a date which is special in Irish History or perhaps a Saint's Day there can be loads of benefits. The date selected can contribute to a theme and it will surely be easier remembered. Be careful in Ireland as some important dates are also local or national holidays and little else can be arranged. Some Saint's days are *pattern* days when in certain areas everything stops and special events are held. There is however, a distinct benefit when someone, somewhere celebrates the date of your wedding! A good source of important dates in Irish history is: A Chronology of Irish History Since 1500., J.E. Doherty and D.J. Hickey, Barnes and Noble,1990. Below is a list of Irish Saint's days, which might help. Take a moment to read the stories of the saint. Who knows what interesting aspects you might turn up which are just right for wedding themes.

Saints Days

The list below is not complete. I have seen one list containing 1714 of them. (Many were only of Irish descent and gained fame elsewhere.)   If you wish to have a longer list please consult the primary reference work The Martyrology of Donegal.

Date Saint, Title,Town/CountyType of feast

3 Jan St Mainchin, Bp Limerick Feast
15 Jan St Ita, V Limerick Opt Mem
30 Jan St Adian, Bp Ferns Feast

1 Feb St Brigid, V National Feast
7 Feb St Mel, Bp Ardagh & Clon Feast
17 Feb St Fintan, Ab Leighlin Opt Mem

5 Mar St Kieran, Bp Ossory Feast
8 Mar St Senan, Bp Killaloe Opt Mem
17 Mar St Patrick, Bp National Feast (Obligatory)

15 May St Carthage, Bp Lismore Feast
16 May St Brendan, Ab Kerry, Clonfert Feast

4 Jun St Kevin, Ab Dublin Feast
6 Jun St Jarlath, Bp Tuam Feast
7 Jun St Colman, Bp Dromore Feast
9 Jun St Colum Cille, Ab National Feast

8 Jul St Kilian, Bp, Mar Kilmore Opt Mem
10 Jul St Oliver Plunkett, Bp, Mar National Memorial
24 Jul St Declan, Bp Lismore Opt Mem

9 Aug St Nathy, Bp Achonry Feast
9 Aug St Felim, Bp Kilmore Feast
12 Aug St Attracta, V Achonry Memorial
12 Aug St Lelia, V Limerick Opt Mem
12 Aug St Muredach, Bp Kilalla Feast
14 Aug St Fachanan, Bp Ross Feast
15 Aug Assumption of Our Lady National Solemnity (Obligatory)
23 Aug St Eugene, Bp Derry Feast
30 Aug St Fiacra, Monk Ossory Opt Mem

4 Sep St Mac Nissi, Bp Connor Feast
9 Sep St Ciaran, Ab Ardagh & Clon Feast
12 Sep St Ailbe, Bp Cashel & Emly Feast
23 Sep St Eunan, Ab Raphoe Feast
25 Sep St Finbarr, Bp Cork Feast

11 Oct St Canice, Ab Kilkenny Solemnity
16 Oct St Gall, Ab Down & Connor Opt Mem
25 Oct Bl Thaddeus McCarthy, Bp Cork, Cloyne Memoria
27 Oct St Otteran, Monk Waterford Feast
29 Oct St Colman Kilmacduagh Feast

3 Nov St Malachy Ardagh, Down Feast
6 Nov All Saints of Ireland National Feast
14 Nov St Laurence O'Toole, Bp Dublin Feast
23 Nov St Columbanus, Ab National Feast
24 Nov St Colman Cloyne Feast
27 Nov St Fergal, Bp Ossory Opt Mem

6 Dec St Nicholas, Bp Galway Solemnity
12 Dec St Finnian, Bp Meath Feast
18 Dec St Flannan, Bp Killaloe Feast
20 Dec St Fachanan, Bp Kilfenora Feast

Sayings about Dates

Then even if you follow all of the guidelines carefully other things may just come up out of nowhere and you must guard against even the elements of weather!

- A fine day=good luck
- Sun shines on Bride=good luck
- Rain=hardship
- Saturday=not lucky
- Harvest=those married would always be gathering

- The first wish of good luck to bride should come from a man
- Hearing a cuckoo or seeing three magpies on wedding morning= good luck
- Meeting a funeral on the road=bad luck
- Taking the longest road home from the church=good luck
- Breaking a glass or cup=bad luck
- Shoe thrown over bride on way out of church= good luck
- Bride and groom wash hands at same time in one sink = bad luck
- Marry during a growing moon/flowing tide= good luck
- Meeting a man on their way home from the church=good luck

(Traditional- Source-Danaher,1972, Haggerty, 1999)

Then even after the wedding you must be careful to make sure you follow through with even more ritual:

- Have friends dip pieces of cloth in a holy well and make a wish for those married. Then tie the cloths to a tree near the well: "Clootie"

- You must take care to observe "Bride's Sunday," The first Sunday after the wedding. Friends who attended the wedding go with the couple to church then to tea or dinner at the bridesmaid's house.

- A bride should be careful not enter her old home for thirty days after the wedding.

- On May day following the wedding a May tree is cut, placed in front of the house of the newlyweds and decorated. May day festivities are performed around it.
  (Traditional- source- Danaher, 1972, Haggerty, 1999)

Now that all has been taken care of carefully and in detail…

Where?

Three Rooms

In Ireland a house with three contiguous compartments is selected for a wedding; the reason of this is to preserve a distinction between the classes of company expected. The best apartment is reserved for the bride and bridegroom, the priest and piper, and the more opulent and respectable guests, as the landlord, his family, and the neighbouring gentry, who are always invited, and generally attend on these occasions. The second apartment is appropriated for the neighbours in general ; and the third, or an outhouse, is devoted to the reception of buckhaughs, shulers, and other beggars To this same custom of inviting all the community to be present can be referred the origin of our church appeal to the congregation upon giving out the banns of marriage for the ascertainment of any just cause or impediment against the marriage.

-Gome, Laurence, George, Folk-Lore Relics of Early Village Life, 1883. P. 213.

The Day Itself-

What is it like? At an Irish Wedding…
?

Getting there! And Back.

In the south west of Ireland the bridal party would board horse-traps or side cars at the house of the bride and depart in the early morning. Before there were carts brides were carried by the men on horseback. On the way to the church she would be carried by her father and on the way back by her new husband. The bride and her parents would go first. Behind would follow the relatives and guests of both bride and groom. The groom himself would become a part of the procession at some point and

The Wedding Party (Hall, 1841-3)

would bring up the rear. His chance to ride in the front would come after the wedding when he and his bride returned from the wedding. The bridesmaid and groomsman would ride with them in the first vehicle of the procession. Sometimes things were not so formal. It was common to see smaller groups of the wedding party going to the church by themselves. Sometimes a fiddler played tunes such as *Haste to the Wedding* or *Your Bargain is Made* as he lead the immediate wedding party on the way back from the church. In addition to the wedding procession simultaneously the young men of the community would have horse races from place to place. The riders competed for bottles of liquor. The race was called "the race for the bottle." These races had a reputation for being dangerous and during at least one a rider was killed.

In East Munster and Leinster where farmers were prosperous the groom was given a container of coins when he left the church with the bride. The groom would throw these up into the air for those in the crowd to catch. This was a way weddings could aid in the re distribution of wealth and a method by which people of all status and class could benefit from the event. It is no wonder that the community looked forward to them with such great interest.

Often weddings were not held at the church but took place at the house. A record book was kept of the proceedings, which was signed by the most important guests who served as witnesses. The names of others in attendance were not always recorded.

Next stop: The home of the Bride's Parents

On the way from the church to the house of the parents of the Bride boys would often stop the party by placing a rope across the road in front of it. No one could pass until they were given money with which safe passage could be purchased.

Even when safely at home the Bride had one last trial. Her mother was to break a small cake over her head so that luck and prosperity would be delivered.

Even today processions help to give an air of public celebration to the wedding. The sight of a wedding party processing in full wedding dress down the main street unites the family with the community and is symbolic of the ancient importance of the wedding as that catalyst which provided for the renewal and expansion of the civilized world on the edge of the frontier of ancient Ireland.

Take a moment to arrange for a procession for a few blocks from the church to your waiting transportation. Provide for candy and coins to be thrown out to onlookers and you will have created an event of memory which is steeped in tradition!

Let the fun begin!

I have provided a few descriptions of traditional Irish weddings below, for your inspiration! Let's sneak into the wedding house to see what is going on!

The following account of an Irish country wedding is taken from the well-known and excellent work of Mr. And Mrs. S.C. Hall:--

We had scarcely passed the tunnel, and entered the county of Kerry, when we encountered a group that interested us greatly ; on enquiry we learned that a wedding had taken place at a cottage pointed out to us, in a little glen among the mountains, and that the husband was bringing home his bride. She was mounted on a white pony, guided by as smart looking and well dressed a youth as we had seen in the country ; his face was absolutely radiant with joy ; the parents of the bride and bridegroom followed ; and a little girl clung to the dress of a staid and sober matron—whom we at once knew to be the mother of the bride, for her aspect was pensive, almost to sorrow ; her daughter was quitting for another home the cottage in which she had been reared—to become a wife. We made a hasty sketch of the party ; and a clever artist, Mr. Timbrell, has rendered to it more than justice.

We may take advantage of the occasion to describe the ceremonies and formalities connected with an Irish wedding ; presuming, however, that a very essential part of them—the drinking to intoxication " for the honour of the bride,"—has been, of late, essentially abridged.

When the match is made, it becomes necessary for the bridegroom to obtain a certificate from his parish priest that he is to contract marriage cum quavis similiter soluta (it is always written in Latin) with any woman equally free from canonical bonds or impediments; to this a fee is always attached, we believe five shillings. He must also procure from the bishop or vicar-general, a license to marry, to which also a fee is attached of seven shillings and sixpence. This being done, he repairs with his bride to the house of her parish priest, accompanied by his and her friends, as many as they can muster; and before he is married, pays down to the priest the marriage fee according to his circumstances. The friends of both parties are also called upon to pay down something, and between their reluctance to meet the demand and the priest's refusal to marry them till he is satisfied, a scene, sometimes humorous and sometimes discreditable, often arises. If the bride's father or brother be a "strong" farmer, who can afford to furnish a good dinner, the marriage takes place at the bride's house, the bridegroom bringing with him as many of his friends as choose to accompany him. The same process as to money takes place here, and it is not uncommon for the collection to amount of twenty or thirty pounds. The time most in favor for celebrating weddings is just before Lent.

The guests are always numerous, and consist of all ranks, from the lord and the lady of the manor, through the intermediate grades of gentlemen, "squireens," farmers, down to the common laborer--wives, of course, included. Perfect equality prevails on this occasion, and yet, the natural courtesy of the Irish character prevents any disturbance of social order-every one keeps his place, while at the same time, the utmost freedom reigns. The dinner is usually at the expense of the Bride's family; and as nothing is spared in procuring the materials, and the neighboring gentry allow their cooks etc.. to assist, and lend dinner services etc... it is always "got up" in the best style. The priests sits at the head of the table; near him the bride and bridegroom, the coadjutors of the clergyman, and the more respectable guests; the other guests occupy the remainder of the table, which extends the whole length of the barn- in which the dinner generally takes place.

Immediately on the cloth being removed, the priest marries the young couple, and then the bridecake is brought in and placed before the priest who, putting on his stole, blesses it, and cuts it up into small slices which are handed round on a large dish among the guests, generally by one of the coadjutors. Each guest takes a slice of the cake, and lays down in place of it a donation for the priest, consisting of pounds, crowns, or shillings, according to the ability of the donor. After that, wine and punch go round, as at any ordinary dinner party. In the course of an hour or so, part of the range of tables is removed, and the musicians (consisting usually of a piper and a fiddler) who, during the dinner, had been playing some of the more slow and plaintive of the national airs, now strike up, and the dance immediately commences."

First single parties dance reels, jigs, and doubles*. Country-dances now succeed, in which, as in the single dances, priest and laic, old and young, rich and poor, the master and his maid, the landlord and his tenant's daughter, as well as the landlord's daughter and his tenant's son—all join together without distinction. Yet it is pleasing to observe how the poor peasants return, on such occasions, the condescension of their superiors with additional respect. During the intervals of the dance, drinking is, or rather was, resumed ; and though on these occasions it was often carried to excess, we never knew, nor ever met any one who knew, of anything like a quarrel taking place at a country wedding. Indeed, we have seen people who, as the saying goes, were " wicked in their licker," get intoxicated at these joyous festivals without manifesting ill-temper—on the contrary, they have been remarkably entertaining, as if the general harmony had expelled the demon of discord. Songs are also sung both in English and Irish.

The Irish words of one of them were given to us by a friend, accom-

• This last is a speeies of dance very difficult to deseribe— it is, however, the male partner who "shows off" in it : the best idea we can give of it is that it consists in striking the ground very rapidly with the heel and toe, or with the toes of each foot alternately. The perfection of this motion consists, besides its rapidity, in the furor with which it is performed. A stranger, not hearing the music and seeing only tho dancer, would be likely to imagine he was killing a rat ; nor would it bo very safe to have this dance performed by a stout fellow on a crazy loft.

panied by a literal translation ; we have endeavoured to return them to verse ; they are sung to the well-known air " Shule Aroon."

Oil, have you seen my Norah Fay?
She's left me all the sad long day,
Alone to sing a weary lay ;

Go dhi mo vourneen, slaun ;
Shule, shule, shule, aroon ;
Shule go sochir, agus shule go cuue,
Shule go theev dorris agus eilig lume,
As' go dhi mo vourneen slaun.*

You'll know her by her raven hair,
Her deep blue eye, her forehead fair,
Her step and laugh that banish eare ;

As' go dhi mo vourneen, slaun.
In form you may her semblance find,
But none like her, of womankind,
If you ean see her heart and mind ;

As' go dhi mo vourneen slaun.
Oh, bring to me my Norah Fay,
For hours are days when she's away ;
The sun looks dark, and sweet birds say,

Go dhi mo vourneen, slaun,
Shule, shule, shule aroon ;
Shule go sochir, agus shule go cune,
Shule go theev dorris agus eilig lume,
As' go dhi mo vourneen, slaun.

In the course of the night a collection is made for " the music," and
another for the poor. The dancing generally continues till morning,
when the first intimation of breaking up is the dancing of the figure called
" Sir Roger De Coverly." As soon as that dance is over, all the more timid
part of the female guests slip out of the barn to avoid the finale, which is as
follows :—The music striking up the quadrille air called " Voulez-vous danser,"
a " gentleman " goes round with a handkerchief, which he throws round the
neck of any " lady " he chooses, falls on his knees, gently pulls her down and
kisses her ; then giving her the handkerchief, continues a kind of trot round
the barn ; the lady does the same with any gentleman she likes, and giving him
the handkerchief, catches the first gentleman by the skirts of the coat and trots
after him around the barn. This is done alternately by all present, until all
the young men and women are trotting round catching hold of each other as

Come, come, come, my love,
Come quietly, come—come stealingly
Beside the door and away with me,
And may my love come safe.

in the play of " Chickens, come cluck." They then form a ring around the
last person who has the handkerchief, who selects a lady or gentleman, as the
case may be, and after another salutation leads his or her partner to a seat.
This is done until the whole circle is broken up; and thus terminates a country
wedding*.

Our readers will bear in mind, however, that we are describing a picture
as exhibited in the cottage of a small farmer, where there is comparative
abundance ; and on such occasions the national hospitality is never bounded
even by prudence : far less merry, and infinitely less plentiful of good cheer,
is the scene enacted within one of the common cabins of the hard-handed
labourer, where, not unfrequently, the marriage feast is little more than a dish
of potatoes and a jug of sweet-milk.

Yet, amid the want so often attendant upon the young and thoughtless
marriages of the Irish peasantry, it is wonderful to note how closely heart
clings to heart. Poverty, the most severe and prolonged, rarely creates dis
union, and still more rarely separation. The fidelity of the Irish wife is
proverbial ; she will endure labour, hunger, and even ill usage, to an almost
incredible extent, rather than break the marriage vow ; we have known cases
in abundance.

" He beat me," said a pretty weeping girl, not nineteen, who had married

from the service of an old friend,—" He beat me, ma'am, long ago ; but I never thought more of it since ; and yet that didn't hurt me half so much as he's saying that maybe little Ned wasn't his; that's breaking the heart in me intirely, though I know he didn't mane it, and that it was the temper that spoke in him—the weary on it for temper !—I've known nothing but hardship since I married him; but I didn't complain of that; we both expected nothing else ; and I don't mind a hasty stroke, for it's hard on him to see us wanting a potato, and he wet and weary—an ould man before his time with the slavery —and though I put little Neddy to bed early to sleep off the hunger, yet often it's too teazing on the poor child, and wakes him in spite of me, and I know the little hungry face of the darlint aggravates his father. I know all that ; but he ought to know that I'd follow him faithful through the gates of death, if that would save him an hour's pain ; he ought to know it—and he does know it—I'm sure he does ; and he kissed me this morning on his fasting

*On the first May-day after the wedding, it was customary for the young men and maidens of the parish to go to the wood and cut down the tallest tree, which they dressed up with ribbons, placing in the centre a large ball, decorated with variously coloured paper and gilt. This they carried in procession to the bride's house, and setting it up before the door, commenced a dance round it, which lasted throughout the day. They were " th rated " liberally by the bride on such occasions. The custom, which appears to have been a relic of Druidism, is now nearly obsolete.

breath, leaving the handful of potatoes for me, and saying the masther, where he gives his strength for eight-pence a day, ordered him a breakfast, which I'm sure ain't the truth. The love's in his heart as strong as ever ; but the misery, ma'am, often hardens the man while it softens the woman ; he didn't mane it, and he knows it's not true, but it's hard to listen to such a word as that. He was my first love, and he'll be my List. None of us can tell what's before us, but I'd go all my trouble over again if it would do him any sarvice ! "

It is also worthy of remark that second marriages are very rare among the peasantry, and, we may perhaps add, comparatively, among the higher classes. This affords a strong proof of the depth of their attachment, for it is very improbable that prudence can restrain in the second instance those who take so little of her counsel in the first. They do not hold it strictly right for either man or woman to marry again ; and if a woman does so, she prefaces it with an apology :—" It's a father I was foreed to put over his children, because I had no way for them, God help me ! and this man, ye see, says, ' Mary,' he says, ' I have full and plenty for them, and the Lord above he knows it's justice I'll do them, and never hinder yer prayers for the man ye lost, or any thing in rason, or out of rason either ; ' an' troth he has kep his word wonderful." And the neighbours of the married widower apologise for him after this fashion :—" Well, to be sure ! we must consider he had a whole houseful of soft children, and no one to turn round on the flure or do a hand's turn for them; so it's small blame to him after all." Or they condemn— " Yarra huish ! to see an old struckawn like that set himself up with a young wife, and grown up daughters in his house. To think of the hardness of him —passing the churchyard, where the poor heart that loved him, and put up with him, and slaved for him and his children, is powdering into dust—passing

*the grave where the grass isn't yet long, with a slip of a girleen in the place
of her with the thoughtful head and the ready hand. Oh, bedad ! she'll punish
him I'll engage ; and I'm glad of it." They are more angry with a woman
for a second marriage than with a man, and certainly never consider a second
union as holy as a first*.*

*The following is a striking and creditable instance of attachment to tie memory of a wife. We once remarked
to a very respectable old man , and of very prepossessing appearance, that he must have been a great favourite
with the fair sex in his youth. " Listen to me," said he, "and the divil a word of a lie I'm tellin' you, for I can't
be far from my end now. Sometime afther the death o' my wife, a rich widow, and a handsome one, fell in
love with me, and offered to marry mc. Faith, it was a temptin' offer—my manes were small, and the family
were large and helpless. But when I went home and Iook'd at the poor childher,
and thought of her that was gone— oh, I could never bear to bring another in her place—for she was a good
woman, and a lovin' woman, and a sensible woman, (here his voice began to grow tremulous with emotion,
but by an effort he added) and a likely woman!" He burst into tears. This man's wife had been dead

*It is not a little strange that a people so indifferent to consequences as the
Irish certainly are, should, when they have anything to bestow in the way of
a marriage portion on their children, frequently drive the hardest and most
heartless bargains. If two young people form an attachment for each other,
and have hardly enough between them to pay the priest his dues, the only
parental observation is, " Well, sure !—We did the same thing ourselves."
—" They can't be worse off than they are ; "—" It's asy to halve the potato
where there's love."—" It's an ould saying, marriages are made in heaven ;"
and so on. But if a farmer can bestow a cow with his daughter, he will insist
on a horse, or an equivalent in pigs, ' slips,' or full-grown. We have known
a match broken off, without the question ever being asked whether the young
people's affections were engaged or not, only because the girl's father would
not bestow a feather-bed on the young couple as a set-off against the " twoyear-old" heifer
which the boy's parent proposed to give. " See now, I wouldn't be putting betwixt them,"
said old Dennis ; " but sorra a taste of your whisky shall pass my lips, barrin' ye' consint to
put the bed agin the heifer ; and only I have a grate regard for you and yours, Mr. Barney,
Sir, it isn't only that I'd be asking. Johnny's a nate boy—not that I've a word to say
against Nancy—but he's the sort of boy to have the pick of the fair." " I'm
not denying it, Misther Dennis, he's a clever likely boy, though a little
inclined to be foxy ; but as to the bed, its clane out of the question. I don't
say but if we're lucky with the ould pig that I won't halve the bonneens* with
them. Mary's a fine sonsy girl, with eyes to see, and a tongue in her head
that would win the birds off the bushes." " She's been a good while batin'
the bush then," rejoins Dennis, who is a regular ' hard man,' and in no hurry
to marry his son. " Mary's purty hardy **, but that's neither here nor there ;
I've nothing to say agin the dacent girl, only in regard of the two-year-ould*

nearly thirty years.

 We may link with this an aneedote of one of the other sex. We know a widow, who
is now about fifty years old ; she had two daughters well provided for, and two sons who " help to keep the
cabin over her." She was as susceptible as most of her countrywomen, and in her youth had a sweetheart.
He waa not, however, the choice of her parents, who married her to another—the ugliest man in the parish.
We were once present when somebody asked her whether she was not crying the whole night of her marriage?
The question brought out her natural eloquence.—" I was," she said, " I'm not ashamed to own it now ; I

was giving myself up to a man T didn't like, and I fond of another at the time. He was the ordinaryest man in the county ; but I won't wrong him ; he was a good husband to me, and nobody can pay I wasn't a good wife to him, thank God ! He was sickly for eleven years before he died ; and all that time I didn't lay my side on a bed for three hours together, day nor night, besides having a family of four children to look after. He left me without the means of helping them, except by the work of these two hands. I brought them up, thank God, decently; nobody can say I didn't, and never asked a meal for them from any christian 1 didn't carn it from."

* Give half the litter of pigs—bonneens—bonevcens—bonnifs—young pigs.

** Advanced in years.

beautiful heifer, it's small price I set upon her to be evenin' her to a bit of a feather bed ! "—" Well, some people's unconscionable, but there's no harrum clone ; " &c, &c. And thus one cunning old fellow endeavours to outwit the other, without, as we have said, cither consulting the affections of his child.

-From: Ireland its Scenery, Character &c. Vol. 1, Mr. &Mrs. S.C. Hall, 1841.

-From: The Knot Tied, Marriage Ceremonies of all Nations, William Tegg, Omnigraphics,Detroit 1989, original 1877.

From: **Knocknagow, or the Homes of Tipperary**, by: Charles J. Kickham, pp.215-212, James Duffy and Co., Ltd. Dublin, 1887-

"I am curious to know," said he, "who that old gentleman is?"
As he spoke, his curiosity was further excited by seeing a little boy come into a room and place a green bag on the old man's knees. "That's the celebrated Irish piper," she replied. "I am surprised to see him here. I did not think he attended country weddings."
"I suppose he goes round among the nobility and gentry, as we are told the harpers used to do."

"He does., and he has a beautiful little pony the countess gave him. But I suppose he's stopping at present with the priests, and Father Hannigan has brought him with him."
As he uncovered his pipes their splendor quite took Mr. Lowe by suprise. The keys were of silver, and the bag covered with crimson velvet fringed; while the little bellows was quite a work of art, so beautifully was it carved and ornamented with silver and ivory. Having tied an oval piece of velvet with a ribbon attached to each and above his knee, he adjusted his instrument, and after moving his arm, to which the bellows was attached by a ribbon, till the crimson velvet bag was inflated, he touched the keys, and catching up the chanter quickly in both hands began to play... the musician soon seemed to forget all mere human concerns. He threw back his head, as if communing with invisible spirits in the air above him; or bent down over his instrument as if the spirits had suddenly flown into it, and he wanted to catch their whispering there, too.

The audience to some extent, shared in the musician's ecstasy; particularly Father Hannigan, from whose eyes tears were actually falling as the delicious melody ceased, and the old man raised his sightless eyes and listened, as it were, for the echo of his strains from the skies...

The wedding guests had been silently dropping into the room, which was now pretty well filled. Mat Donovan occasionally seized a bottle or decanter, and filled out a glass of wine, of whiskey, or "cordial" for some of them....There was a hustling heard at the door, and Ned Brophy himself was seen pushing two blind pipers into the parlor with a degree of violence and expression of countenance that led Mr. Lowe to imagine he must have caught them in the act of attempting to rob him or something of the kind. The two pipers were tall and gaunt and yellow- a striking contrast in every way to Mr. Flaherty. One was arrayed in a soldier's gray watch-coat, with the number of the regiment stamped in white figures on the back, and the other wore a coarse blue body-coat with what appeared to be the sleeves of another old gray watch-coat, sewed to it between the shoulders and the elbow. Both wore well patched corduroy knee-breeches and bluish worsted stockings, with brogues of unusual thickness of sole, well paved with heavy nails. Their rude brass mounted instruments were in keeping with their garments. The sheepskin bag of one had no covering whatever, while that of the other was covered with faded plaid, cross barred with green and yellow. They dropped into two chairs near the door, thrusting their old "caubeens" under them, and sat bolt upright like a pair of mummies or figures at a wax work exhibition.

"Play that tune that the angels sang again, Mr. Flaherty," said Father Hannigan.
Mr. Flaherty complied, and the noise and hum of voices were once hushed.
" Have you that?" the piper in the watch coat asked his companion in a whisper, at the same time beginning to work with his elbow.

"I have," replied the other, beginning to work with his elbow, too.
A sound like snoring followed for a moment, and Mr. Flaherty jerked up his head suddenly, and looked disturbed-as if an evil sprit had intruded among his delicate Ariels. But as the noise was not repeated, his countenance resumed its wonted placidity, and he bent over his instrument again.

"I think I could do it better myself," said he of the blue bodycoat, holding his big knotty fingers over the holes of the chanter. "He didn't shake enough."
"So could I," replied the gray watch coat, giving a squeeze to his bag which was followed by a faint squeak.

"Turn him out! " shouted Mr. Flaherty, as he started to his feet, his eyes rolling with indignation.

There was great astonishment among the company; and Miss Lloyd jumped up in her chair and starred wildly about her, with a vague notion that Wat Murphy's bulldog--of which interesting animal she entertained the profoundest dread--had got into the room and seized Mr. Flaherty by the calf of the leg.

"Come Seumas," said Father Hannigan, "this is no place for you. Come, Thade, be off with you." And Father Hannigan expelled the grumbling minstrels form the parlor; but in so doing he gave each a nudge in the ribs and slipped a shilling into his fist, which had the effect of changing their scowl into a broad grin, as they jostled out of the kitchen.

Accounts of Irish Weddngs

An Account by William Carleton

From:" The Three Tasks"
Traits and Stories of the Irish Peasantry, William Carleton, Vol. 1,1864.

At last he began to look about him for a wife,
and the only one in that part of the country that would be at
all fit for him, was the Honourable Miss Bandbox, the daughter of a
nobleman in the neighbourhood. She indeed flogged all the world for
beauty; but it was said that she was proud and fond of wealth, though,
God, he knows, she had, enough of that any how. , Jack, however, saw
none of this, for she was cunning enough to smile, and simper, and , look,
pleasant, whenever he'd come to her father's. Well, begad, from, one
thing, and one word, to another, Jack thought it was best to make up to
her at wanst, and try if she'd accept of him for a husband ; accordingly
he put the word to her like a man, and she, making as if she was blushing,
put her fan before her face and made no answer Jack, however,
wasn't to be daunted; for he knew two things worth knowing, when a
man goes to look for a wife : the first is—that "faint heart never won
fair lady,' and the second—that "silence gives consint; he, therefore,
spoke up to her in fine English, for it's he that knew how to speak now,
and, after a little more fanning and blushing, by jingo, she consinted.
Jack then broke the matter to her father, who was as fond of money as
the daughter, and only wanted to grab at him for the wealth.
"When the match was a making, says ould Bandbox to Jack, "Mr.
Magennis,' says he, (for nobody called him Jack now but his mother)—
" these two things you must comply with, if you marry my daughter,
Miss Gripsy :—you must send away your mother from about you, and
pull down the cabin in which you and she used to live; Gripsy says that
they would jog her memory consarning your low birth and former poverty;

* Such is the popular opinion.

she's nervous and high-spirited, Mr. , Magennis, and, declares upon her
honour, that she couldn't bear the thoughts of having the dilicacy of her,
feeling offinded by these things."
"'Good morning to you both, says Jack, like an honest fellow as he
was, "if she doesn't marry me except on these conditions, give her my
compliments, and tell her our courtship is at an end."
"But it wasn't long till they soon came out with another story, for
before a week passed, they were very glad to get him on his own conditions.

Jack was now as happy as the day was long—all things appointed for the
wedding, and nothing a wanting to make everything to his heart's con
tent but the wife, and her he was to have in less than no time. For a
day or two before the wedding, there never was seen such grand preparations:
bullocks, and hogs, and sheep were roasted whole—kegs of
whisky, both Roscrea and Innishowen, barrels of ale and beer, were there
in dozens. All descriptions of niceties and wild-fowl, and fish from the
say; , and the dearest wine that could be bought with money, was got for
the gentry and grand folks. Fiddlers, and pipers, and harpers, in short,
all kinds of music and musicianers, played in shoals. Lords and ladies,
and squares of high degree were present—and, to crown the thing, there
was open house to all comers.

"At length the wedding-day arrived; there was nothing but roasting
and boiling; servants dressed in rich liveries ran about with joy and
delight in their countenances, and white gloves and wedding favours on
their hats and hands. To make a long story short, they were all seated
in Jack's castle at the wedding breakfast, ready for the priest to marry
them when they'd be done; for in them times people were never married
until they had laid in a good foundation to carry them through the
ceremony. Well, they were all seated round the table, the men dressed
in the best of broadcloth, and the ladies rustling in their silks and satins
—their heads, necks, and arms hung round with jewels both rich and
rare : but of all that were there that day, there wasn't the likes of the
bride and bridegroom. As for him, nobody could think, at all at all,
that he was ever any thing else than a born gintleman; and what was
more to his credit, he had his kind ould mother sitting beside the bride,
to tache her that an honest person, though poorly born, is company for
the king. As soon as the breakfast was served up, they all set to, and
maybe the vaarious kinds of eatables did not pay for it; and amongst all
this cutting and thrusting, no doubt but it was remarked, that the bride
herself was behindhand wid none of them—that she took her dalin-trick
without flinching, and made nothing less than a right fog meal of it:
and small blame to her for that same, you persave.

"When the breakfast was over, up gets Father Flannagan—out with his
book, and on with his stole, to marry them. The bride and bridegroom
went up to the end of the room, attended by their friends, and the rest of
the company stood on each side of it, for you see they were too high bred,
and knew their manners too well, to stand in a crowd like spalpeens.
For all that, there was many a sly look from the ladies to their bachelors,
and many a titter among them, grand as they were; for, to tell the truth,
the best of them likes to see fun in the way, particularly of that sort.

The priest himself was in as great a glee as any of them, only he kept it
under, and well he might, for sure enough this marriage was nothing less
than a rale windfall to him and the parson that was to marry them after
him—bekase you persave a Protestant and Catholic must be married by
both, otherwise it does not hould good in law. The parson was as grave

as a mustard-pot, and Father Flannagan called the bride and bride
groom his childher, which was a big bounce for him to say the likes of,
more betoken that neither of them was a drop's blood to him.
"However, he pulled out the book, and was just beginning to buckle
them, when in comes Jack's ould acquaintance, the smoking cur, as grave
as ever. The priest had just got through two or three words of Latin,
when the dog gives him a pluck by the sleeve; Father Flannagan, of
coorse, turned round to see who it was that nudged him: 'Behave your
self,' says the dog to him, just as he peeped over his shoulder—'behave
yourself,' says he ; and with that he sat him down on his hunkers beside
the priest, and pulling a cigar instead of a pipe out of his pocket, he put
it in his mouth, and began to smoke for the bare life of him. And, by my
own word, it's he that could smoke : at times he would shoot the smoke
in a slender stream like a knitting-needle, with a round curl at the one end
it, ever so far out of the right side of his mouth ; then he would shoot it
out of the left, and sometimes make it swirl out so beautiful from the
middle of his lips'—why, then, it's he that must have been the well-bred
puppy all out, as far as smoking went. Father Flannagan and they all
were tundherstruck.

"'In the name of St. Anthony, and of that holy nun, St. Teresa," said
his Reverence to him, "who and what are you, at all at all ?"
"'Never mind that,' says the dog, taking the cigar for a minute between
his claws; "but if you wish particularly to know, I'm a thirty
second cousin of your own by the mother's side."
"' I command you in the name of all the saints,' says Father Flan
nagan, believing him to be the devil, 'to disappear from among us, and
never become visible to any one in this house again."
"'The sorra a budge, at the present time, will I budge,' says the dog
to him , "until , I , see all , sides rightified, and the rogues disappointed.'

"Now one would be apt to think, the appearance of a spaking dog
might be after fright'ning the ladies; but doesn't all the world, know that
spaking puppies are their greatest favourites? Instead of that, you see,
there was half a dozen fierce-looking whiskered fellows, and three or four
half-pay officers, that were nearer making off than the ladies. But,
besides the cigar, the dog had his beautiful eye-glass, and through it,
while he was spaking to Father Flannagan, he ogled all the ladies, one
after another, and when his eye would light upon any that pleased him, he
would kiss his paw to her and wag his tail with the greatest politeness.
"'John,' says Father Flannagan, to one of the servants, "bring me
salt and water, till I consecrate them.* to banish the divil, for he has
appeared to us all during broad daylight in the shape of a dog.'
"'You had better behave yourself, I say again,' says the dog, " or if

* Salt and water consecrated by a particular form is Holy Water.

you make me speak, by my honour as a gintleman I'll expose you : I
say, you won't marry the same two, neither this nor any other day, and

I'll give you my rasons presently ; but I repate it, Father Flannagan, if you compel me to speak, I'll make you look nine ways at once.'
"'I defy you, Satan," says the priest; and if you don't take yourself away before the holy wather's made, I'll send you off in a flame of fire.'
"'Oh! yes, I'm trimbling,' says the dog: 'plenty of spirits you laid in your day, but it was in a place that's nearer to us than the Red Sea, you did it: listen to me though, for I don't wish to expose you, as I said;' so he gets on his hind legs, puts his nose to the priest's ear, and whispers something that none of the rest could hear—all before the priest had time to know where he was. At any rate, whatever he said seemed make his Reverence look double, though, faix, that wasn't hard to do, for he was as big as two common men. When the dog was done speaking, and had put his cigar in his mouth, the priest seemed tundherstruck, crossed himself, and was, no doubt of it, in great perplexity.

"'I say it's false,' says Father Flannagan, plucking up his courage;
"but you know you're a liar, and the father of liars.'
"'As thrue as gospel, this bout, I tell you,' says the dog.
"'Wait till I make my holy wather,' says the priest, and if I don't cork you in a thumb-bottle for this,* I'm not here.'
"Just at this minute, the whole company sees agintleman galloping for the bare life of him, up to the hall-door, and he dressed like an officer. In three jiffeys he was down off his horse, and in among the company. The dog, as soon as he made his appearance, laid his claw as usual on his nose, and gave the bridegroom a wink, as much as to say, 'watch what'll happen.'

"Now it was very odd that Jack, during all this time, remembered the dog very well, but could never once think of the darling that did so much for him. As soon, however, as the officer made his appearance, the bride seemed as if she would sink outright; and when he walked up to her, to ax what was the meaning of what he saw, why, down she drops at once—fainted clane. The gintleman then went up to Jack, and says, 'Sir, was this lady about to be married to you?"
"'Sartinly, says Jack, "we were going to be yoked in the blessed and holy tackle of mathrimony; or some high-flown words of that kind.
"'Well, Sir," says the other back to him, 'I can only say that she is most solemniously sworn never to marry another man but me at a time; that oath she tuck when I was joining my regiment before it went abroad; and if the ceremony of your marriage be performed, you will sleep with a perjured bride."

"Begad, he did, plump before all their faces. Jack, of coorse, was struck, all, of a, hape at this; but as he had the bride in his arms, giving her a little sup of whisky to bring her to, you persare, he, couldn't make him an answer. However, she soon came to herself, and, on opening her eyes, 'Oh, hide me, hide me,' says she, "for I can't bear to look on him "
"'He says you are his sworn bride, my darling, says Jack.

* According to the superstitious belief of the Irish, a priest, when banishing a spirit, puts it into a thumb-bottle, which he either buries deep in the earth, or in some lake.

"'I am—I am,' says she, covering her eyes, and crying away at the rate of a wedding: "I can't deny it ; and, by tare-an-ounty ' says she, "I'm unworthy to be either his wife or yours; for, except I marry you both, I dunna how to settle this affair between you, at all;-oh, murther sheery! but I'm the misfortunate crathur, entirely.'

"'Well, says Jack to the officer, "nobody can do more than be sorry for a wrong turn; small blame to her for taking a fancy to your humble servant, Mr. Officer,'—and he stood as tall as possible to show himself off: "you see the fair lady is sorrowful for her folly, so as it's not yet too late, and as you came in the nick of time, in the name of Providence take my place, and let the marriage go an.'

"'No,' says she, "never; I'm not worthy of him, at all at all : tun dher-an-age, but I'm the unlucky thief!'

"While this was going forward, the officer looked closely at Jack, and seeing him such a fine, handsome fellow, and having heard before of his riches, he began to think that, all things considhered, she wasn't so much to be blempt. Then, when he saw how sorry she was for having forgot him, he steps forrid.

feel 'Well,' says he, "I'm-still willing to marry you, particularly as you feel contritiom

"He should have said contrition, confession, and satisfaction," observed father Peter.

"Pether, will you keep your theology to yourself," replied Father Ned, "and let us come to the plot without interruption."

"Plot l" exclaimed Father Peter, "I'm sure it's no rebellion that there should be a plot in it, any way !"

" Tace," said Father Ned—"tace and that's Latin for a candle."

"I deny that," said, the curate; "tace , is the imperative mood from taceo, to keep silent. Taceo, taces, tacui, tacere, tacendi, tacendo, tac—",

"Ned, go on with your story, and never mind that deep larning of his—he's almost cracked with it," said the superior : "go on, and never mind him."

"'Well,' says he, "I'm still willing to marry you, particularly as you feel conthrition for what you were going to do. So, with this, they all gother about her, and as the officer was a fine fellow himself, prevailed upon her to let the marriage be performed, and they were according spliced as fast as his Reverence could make them.

"'Now, Jack,' says the dog, "I want to spake with you for a minute —it's a word for your own ear; so up he stands on his two hind legs, and purtinded to be whispring something to him; but what do you think?—he gives him the slightest touch on the lips with his paw, and that instant Jack remimbered the lady and every thing that happened betune them.

"Tell me, this instant,' says Jack, seizing him by the throath, "where's the darling, at all, at all, or by this an by that you'll hang on the next tree l'

"Jack spoke finer nor this, to be sure, but as I can't give his tall
English, the sorra one of me will bother myself striving to do it.
"'Behave yourself, says the dog, "just say nothing, only follow me.'
"Accordingly, Jack went out with the dog, and in a few minutes
comes in again, leading along with him, on the one side, the loveliest lady
that ever eye beheld, and the dog, that was her brother, now metamur
phied into a beautiful, illegant gintleman, on the other.
"'Father Flannagan,' says Jack, "you thought a while ago you'd
have no marriage, but instead of that you'll have a brace of them ;' up
and telling the company, at the same time, all that had happened him,
and how the beautiful crathur that he brought in with him had done so
much for him.
"Whin the gintlemen heard this, as they were all Irishmen, you may
be sure there was nothing but huzzaing and throwing up of hats from
them, and waving of hankerchers from the ladies. Well, my dear, the
wedding dinner was ate in great style; the nobleman, proved himself no
disgrace to his rank at the trencher; and so, to make a long story short,
such faisting and banquetteering was never seen since or before. At last,
night came and, among ourselves, not a doubt of it, but Jack thought
himself a happy man; and maybe if all was known, the bride was much
of the same opinion : be that as it may, night came—the bride, all blushing,
beautiful, and modest as your own sweetheart, was getting tired after
the dancing; Jack, too, though much stouter, wished for a trifle of repose,
and many thought it was near time to throw the stocking, as is proper,
of coorse, on every occasion of the kind. Well, he was just on his way
up stairs, and had reached the first landing, when he, hears a voice at his
ear, shouting, 'Jack—Jack—Jack Magennis", Jack could have spitted
anybody for coming, to disturb him, at such a criticality. "Jack Magennis'
says the voice., Jack looked about to see who it was that called, ,
him, and there he found himself lying on the green Rath, a little above
his mother's cabin, of a fine calm summer's evening, in the month of June.

His mother was stooping over him, with her mouth at his ear, striving
to waken him, by shouting and shaking him out of his sleep.

"'Oh! by this and by that, mother,' says Jack, "what did you
waken me for ?"
"'Jack, a-vourmeen," says the mother, "sure and you war lying
grunting, and groaning, and snifthering there, for all the world as if you
had the cholic, and I only nudged you for fraid you war in pain."
"'I wouldn't for a thousand guineas,' says Jack, 'that ever you
wakened me, at all, at all; but whisht mother, go into the house, and
I'll be afther you in less than no time.'
"The mother went in, and the first thing, Jack did was to try the
rock; and, sure enough, there he found as much money as made him the,
richest man that ever was in the country and what was to his credit,
when he did grow rich, he wouldn't let his cabin be thrown down, but
built a fine castle on a spot near it, where he could always have it under
his eye, to prevent him from getting proud. In the coorse of time, a

harper, hearing the story, composed a tune upon it, which everybody knows is called the 'Little House under the Hill" to this day, beginning with th * Hi for it, ho for it, hi for it still ;

Och, and whoo ! your sowl—hi for the little house under the hill!"

"So you see that was the way the great Magennisses first came by their wealth, and all because Jack was industrious, and an obadient, dutiful, and tindher son, to his helpless ould mother, and well he deserved what he got, ershi misha." Your healths Father Ned—Father Pether— all kinds of happiness to us; and there's my story."

"Well," said Father Peter, "I think that dog was nothing more or less than a downright cur, that deserved the lash nine times a day, if it was only for his want of respect to the clergy; if he had given me such insolence, I solemnly declare I would have bate the devil out of him with a hazel cudgel, if I failed to exorcise him with a prayer."

Father Ned looked at the simple and credulous curate with an expression of humour and astonishment.

"Paddy," said he to the servant, "will you let us know what the night's doing?"

Paddy looked out. "Why, your Rev'rence, it's a fine night, all out, and cleared up it is bravely."

At this moment the stranger awoke.

"Sir," said Father Ned, "you missed an amusing story, in consequence of your somnolency."

"Though I missed the story," replied the stranger, "I was happy enough to hear your friend's critique upon the dog."

Father Ned seemed embarrassed; the curate, on the contrary, exclaimed with triumph—"but wasn't I right, sir?"

"Perfectly," said the stranger; "the moral you applied was excellent."

"Good night, boys," said Father Ned—"good night, Mr. Longinus *Polysyllabus Alexandrinus !"*

* Say I.

Shane Fadh's Wedding.

<u>Traits and Stories of the Irish Peasantry</u>, William Carleton, Vol. 1,1864. Fiction

On the following evening, the neighbors were soon assembled about Ned's hearth in the same manner as on the night preceding:—And we may observe, by the way, that though there was a due admixture of opposite creeds and conflicting principles, yet even then, and the time is not so far back, such was their cordiality of heart and simplicity of manners when contrasted with the bitter and rancorous spirit of the present day that the very remembrance of the harmony in which they lived is at once pleasing and melancholy.

After some preliminary chat, "Well Shane," said Andy Morrow, addressing Shane Fadh, "will you give us an account of your wedding? I'm tould it was the greatest let-out that ever was in the country, before or since."

"And you may say that, Mr. Morrow," said Shane, "I was at many a wedding myself, but never at the likes of my own, barring Tim Lannigan's, that married Father Corrigan's niece."

"I believe," said Andy, "that, too, was a dashing one; however, it's your own we want. Come, Nancy, fill these measures again, and let us be comfortable, at all events, and give Shane a double one, for talking's druthy work:—I'll stand this round."

When the liquor was got in, Shane, after taking a draught, laid down his pint, pulled out his steel tobacco-box, and, after twisting off a chew between his teeth, closed the box, and commenced the story of his wedding.

"When I was a Brine-Oge," * said Shane, "I was as wild as an unbroken cowlt—no divilment was too hard for me; and so sign's on it, for there wasn't a piece of mischief done in the parish, but was laid at my door—and the dear knows I had enough of my own to answer for, let alone to be set down for that of other people; but, any way, there was many a thing done in my name, when I knew neither act nor part about it. One of them I'll mintion: Dick Cuillenan, father to Paddy, that lives at the crass-roads, beyant Gunpowdher Lodge, was over head and ears in love with Jemmy Finigan's eldest daughter, Mary, then, sure enough, as purty a girl as you'd meet in a fair—indeed, I think I'm looking at her, with her fair flaxen ringlets hanging over her shoulders, as she used to pass our house, going to mass of a Sunday. God rest her sowl, she's now in glory—that was before she was my wife. Many a happy day we passed together; and I could take it to my death, that an ill word, let alone to rise our hands to one another, never passed between us—only one day, that a word or two happened about the dinner, in the middle of Lent, being a little too late, so that the horses were kept nigh half an hour out of the plough; and I wouldn't have valued that so much, only that it was Beal Cam** Doherty that joined*** me in ploughing that year—and I was vexed not to take all I could out of him, for he was a raal Turk himself.

* A young man full of fun and frolic. The word literally signifies Young Brian. Such phrases originate thus:—A young man remarkable for one or more qualities of a particular nature becomes so famous for them that his name, in the course of time, is applied to others, as conveying the same character.

** Crooked mouth.

***In Ireland, small farmers who cannot afford to keep more than one horse are in the habit of "joining," as it is termed—that is, of putting their horses together so as to form a yoke, when they plough each other's farms, working alternately, sometimes, by the week, half-week, or day; that is, I plough this day, or this week, and you the next day, or week, until our crops are got down. In this case, each is anxious to take as much out of the horses as he can, especially where the farms are unequal. For instance, where one farm is larger than another the difference must be paid by the owner of the larger one in horse-labor, man-labor, or money; but that he may have as little to pay as possible, he ploughs as much for himself, by the day, as he can, and often strives to get the other to do as little per day, on the other side, in order to diminish what will remain due to his partner. There is, consequently, a ludicrous undercurrent of petty jealousy running between them, which explains the passage in question.

"I disremember now what passed between us as to words—but I know I had a duck-egg in my hand, and when she spoke, I raised my arm, and nailed—poor Larry Tracy, our servant boy, between the two eyes with it, although the crathur was ating his dinner quietly fornent me, not saying a word.

"Well, as I tould you, Dick was ever after her, although her father and mother would rather see her under boord* than joined to any of that connection; and as for herself, she couldn't bear the sight of him, he was sich an upsetting, conceited puppy, that thought himself too good for every girl. At any rate, he tried often and often, in fair and market, to get striking up with her; and both coming from and going to mass, 'twas the same way, for ever after and about her, till the state he was in spread over the parish like wild fire. Still, all he could do was of no use; except to bid him the time of day, she never entered into discoorse with him at all at all. But there was no putting the likes of him off; so he got a quart of spirits in his pocket, one night, and without saying a word to mortal, off he sets full speed to her father's, in order to brake the thing to the family.

* In that part of the country where the scene of Shane Fadh's Wedding is laid, the bodies of those who die are not stretched out on a bed, and the face exposed; on the contrary, they are placed generally on the ground, or in a bed, but with a board resting upon two stools or chairs over them. This is covered with a clean sheet, generally borrowed from some wealthier neighbor; so that the person of the deceased is altogether concealed. Over the sheet upon the board, are placed plates of cut tobacco, pipes, snuff, &c. This is what is meant by being "undher boord."

"Mary might be about seventeen at this time, and her mother looked almost as young and fresh as if she hadn't been married at all. When Dick came in, you may be sure they were all surprised at the sight of him; but they were civil people—and the mother wiped a chair, and put it over near the fire for him to sit down upon, waiting to hear what he'd say, or what he wanted, although, they could give a purty good guess as to that!—but they only wished to put him off with as little offince as possible. When Dick sot a while, talking about what the price of hay and oats would be in the following summer, and other subjects that he thought would show his knowledge of farming and cattle, he pulls out his bottle, encouraged to by their civil way of talking—and telling the ould couple, that as he came over on his kailyee,* he had brought a drop in his pocket to sweeten the discoorse, axing Susy Finigan, the mother, for a glass to send it round with—at the same time drawing over his chair close to Mary who was knitting her stocken up beside her little brother Michael, and chatting to the gorsoon, for fraid that Cuillenan might think she paid him any attention.

* Kailyee—a friendly evening visit.

When Dick got alongside of her, he began of coorse, to pull out her needles and spoil her knitting, as is customary before the young people come to close spaking. Mary, howsomever, had no welcome for him; so, says she, 'You ought to know, Dick Cuillenan, who you spake to, before you make the freedom you do'

"'But you don't know, says Dick, 'that I'm a great hand at spoiling the girls' knitting,—it's a fashion I've got,' says he.

"'It's a fashion, then,' says Mary, 'that'll be apt to get you a broken mouth, sometime'.*

* It is no unusual thing in Ireland for a country girl to
repulse a fellow whom she thinks beneath her, if not by a
flat at least by a flattening refusal; nor is it seldom that
the "argumentum fistycuffum" resorted to on such occasions.
I have more than once seen a disagreeable lover receive,
from that fair hand which he sought, so masterly a blow,
that a bleeding nose rewarded his ambition, and silenced for
a time his importunity.

"'Then,' says Dick, 'whoever does that must marry me.'

"'And them that gets you, will have a prize to brag of,' says she; 'stop yourself, Cuillenan—-single your freedom, and double your distance, if you plase; I'll cut my coat off no such cloth.'

"'Well, Mary,' says he, 'maybe, if *you*, don't, as good will; but you won't be so cruel as all that comes to—the worst side of you is out, I think.'

"He was now beginning to make greater freedom; but Mary rises from her seat, and whisks away with herself, her cheek as red as a rose with vexation at the fellow's imperance. 'Very well,' says Dick, 'off you go; but there's as good fish in the say as ever was catched.—I'm sorry to see, Susy,' says he to her mother, 'that Mary's no friend of mine, and I'd be mighty glad to find it otherwise; for, to tell the truth, I'd wish to become connected with the family. In the mane time, hadn't you better get us a glass, till we drink one bottle on the head of it, anyway.'

"'Why, then, Dick Cuillenan,' says the mother, 'I don't wish you anything else than good luck and happiness; but, as to Mary, She's not for you herself, nor would it be a good match between the families at all. Mary is to have her grandfather's sixty guineas; and the two *moulleens** that her uncle Jack left her four years ago has brought her a good stock for any farm. Now if she married you, Dick, where's the farm to bring her to?—surely it's not upon them seven acres of stone and bent, upon the long Esker,** that I'd let my daughter go to live. So, Dick, put up your bottle, and in the name of God, go home, boy, and mind your business; but, above all, when you want a wife, go to them that you may have a right to expect, and not to a girl like Mary Finigan, that could lay down guineas where you could hardly find shillings.'

* Cows without horns.

** Esker; a high ridge of land, generally barren and
unproductive, when upon a small scale. It is also a ridgy
height that runs for many miles through a country.

"'Very well, Susy,' says Dick, nettled enough, as he well might, 'I say to you, just as I say to your daughter, if you be proud there's no force.'"

"But what has this to do with you, Shane?" asked Andy Morrow; "sure we wanted to hear an account of your wedding, but instead of that, it's Dick Cuillenan's history you're giving us."

"That's just it," said Shane; "sure, only for this same Dick, I'd never got Mary Finigan for a wife. Dick took Susy's advice, bekase, after all, the undacent drop was in him? or he'd never have brought the bottle out of the house at all; but, faith he riz up, put the whiskey in his pocket, and went home with a face on him as black as my hat with venom. Well, things passed on till the Christmas following, when one night, after the Finigans had all gone to bed, there comes a crowd of fellows to the door, thumping at it with great violence, and swearing that if the people within wouldn't open it immediately, it would be smashed into smithereens. The family, of coorse, were all alarmed; but somehow or other, Susy herself got suspicious that it might be something about Mary, so up she gets, and sends the daughter to her own bed, and lies down herself in the daughter's.

"In the mane time, Finigan got up, and after lighting a candle, opened the door at once. 'Come, Finigan,' says a strange voice, 'put out the candle, except you wish us to make a candlestick of the thatch,' says he—'or to give you a prod of a bagnet under the ribs,' says he.

"It was a folly for one man to go to bell-the-cat with a whole crowd; so he blew the candle out, and next minute they rushed in, and went as straight as a rule to Mary's bed. The mother all the time lay close, and never said a word. At any rate, what could be expected, only that, do what she could, at the long-run she must go? So according, after a very hard battle on her side, being a powerful woman, she was obliged to travel—but not till she had left many of them marks to remimber her by; among the rest, Dick himself got his nose split on his face, with the stroke of a churn-staff, so that he carried half a nose on each cheek till the day of his death. Still there was very little spoke, for they didn't wish to betray themselves on any side. The only thing that Finigan could hear, was my name repeated several times, as if the whole thing was going on under my direction; for Dick thought, that if there was any one in the parish likely to be set down for it, it was me.

"When Susy found they were for putting her behind one of them, on a horse, she rebelled again, and it took near a dozen of boys to hoist her up; but one vagabone of them, that had a rusty broad-sword in his hand, gave her a skelp with the flat side of it, that subdued her at once, and off they went. Now, above all nights in the year, who should be dead but my own full cousin, Denis Fadh—God be good to him!—and I, and Jack, and Dan, his brothers, while bringing; home whiskey for the wake and berrin, met them on the road. At first we thought them distant relations coming to the wake, but when I saw only one woman among the set, and she mounted on a horse, I began to suspect that all wasn't right. I accordingly turned back a bit, and walked near enough without their seeing me to hear the discoorse, and discover the whole business. In less than no time I was back at the wake-house, so I up and tould them what I saw, and off we set, about forty of us, with good cudgels, scythe-sneds, and flails, fully bent to bring her back from them, come or go what would. And troth, sure enough, we did it; and I was the man myself, that rode afore the mother on the same horse that carried her off.

"From this out, when and wherever I got an opportunity, I whispered the soft nonsense, Nancy, into poor Mary's ear, until I put my *comedher** on her, and she couldn't live at all without me. But I was something for a woman to look at then, any how, standing six feet two in my stocking soles, which, you know, made them call me Shane *Fadh*.** At that time I had a dacent farm of fourteen acres in Crocknagooran—the same that my son, Ned, has at the present time; and though, as to wealth, by no manner of manes fit to compare with the Finigans, yet, upon the whole, she might have made a worse match. The father, however, wasn't for me; but the mother was: so after drinking a bottle or two with the mother, Sarah Traynor, her cousin, and Mary, along with Jack Donnellan, on my part, in their own barn, unknown to the father, we agreed to make, a runaway match of it, and appointed my uncle Brian Slevin's as the house we'd go to. The next Sunday was the day appointed; so I had my uncle's family prepared, and sent two gallons of whiskey, to be there before us, knowing that neither the Finigans nor my own friends liked stinginess.

* Comedher—come hither—alluding to the burden of an old
   love-charm which is still used by the young of both sexes on
   May-morning. It is a literal translation of the Irish word
   "gutsho."

** Fadh is tall, or long

"Well, well, after all, the world is a strange thing—it's myself hardly knows what to make of it. It's I that did doat night and day upon that girl; and indeed there was them that could have seen me in Jimmaiky for her sake, for she was the beauty of the country, not to say of the parish, for a girl in her station. For my part, I could neither ate nor sleep, for thinking that she was so soon to be my own married wife, and to live under my roof. And when I'd think of it, how my heart would bounce to my throat, with downright joy and delight! The mother had made us promise not to meet till Sunday, for fraid of the father becoming suspicious: but if I was to be shot for it, I couldn't hinder myself from going every night to the great flowering whitethorn that was behind their garden; and although she knew I hadn't promised to come, yet there she still was; something, she said, tould her I would come.

"The next Sunday we met at *Althadhawan* wood, and I'll never forget what I felt when I was going to the green at St. Patrick's Chair, where the boys and girls meet on Sunday; but there she was—the bright eyes dancing: with joy in her head to see me. We spent the evening in the wood, till it was dusk—I bating them all leaping, dancing, and throwing the stone; for, by my song, I thought I had the action of ten men in me; she looking on, and smiling like an angel, when I'd lave them miles behind me. As it grew dusk, they all went home, except herself and me, and a few more who, maybe, had something of the same kind on hands.

"'Well Mary,' says I, 'acushla machree, it's dark enough for us to go; and, in the name of God, let us be off.'"

"The crathur looked into my face, and got pale—for she was very young then: 'Shane,' says she, and she thrimbled like an aspen lafe, 'I'm going to trust myself with—you for ever—for ever, Shane, avourueen,—and her sweet voice broke into purty murmurs as she spoke; 'whether for happiness or sorrow God he only knows. I can bear poverty and distress, sickness and want will' you, but I can't bear to think that you should ever forget to love me as you do now, or your heart should ever cool to me: but I'm sure,' says she, 'you'll never forget this night—and the solemn promises you made me, before God and the blessed skies above us.'

"We were sitting at the time under the shade of a rowan-tree, and I had only one answer to make—I pulled her to my breast, where she laid her head and cried like a child with her cheek against mine. My own eyes weren't dry, although I felt no sorrow, but—but—I never forgot that night—and I never will."

He now paused a few minutes, being too much affected to proceed.

"Poor Shane," said Nancy, in a whisper to Andy Morrow, "night and day he's thinking about that woman; she's now dead going on a year, and you would think by him, although he bears up very well before company that she died only yestherday—but indeed it's he that was always the kind-hearted, affectionate man; and a better husband never broke bread."

"Well," said Shane, resuming the story, and clearing his voice, "it's great consolation to me, now that she's gone, to think that I never broke the promise I made her that night; for as I tould you, except in regard to the duck-egg, a bitther word never passed between us. I was in a passion then, for a wonder, and bent upon showing her that I was a dangerous man to provoke; so just to give her a *spice* of what I could do, I made *Larry* feel it—and may God forgive me for raising my hand even then to her. But sure he would be a brute that would beat such a woman except by proxy. When it was clear dark we set off, and after crossing the country for two miles, reached my uncle's, where a great many of my friends were expecting us. As soon as we came to the door I struck it two or three times, for that was the sign, and my aunt came out, and taking Mary in her arms, kissed her, and, with a thousand welcomes, brought us both in.

"You all know that the best of aiting and dhrinking is provided when a runaway couple is expected; and indeed there was galore of both there. My uncle and all that were within welcomed us again; and many a good song and hearty jug of punch was sent round that night. The next morning my uncle went to her father's, and broke the business to him at once: indeed it wasn't very hard to do, for I believe it reached him afore he saw my uncle at all; so she was brought home* that day, and, on the Thursday night after, I, my father, uncle, and several other friends, went there and made the match. She had sixty guineas, that her grandfather left her, thirteen head of cattle, two feather- and two chaff-beds, with sheeting, quilts, and blankets; three pieces of bleached linen, and a flock of geese of her own rearing—upon the whole, among ourselves, it wasn't aisy to get such a fortune.

* One-half, at least, of the marriages in a great portion of Ireland are effected in this manner. They are termed "runaway matches," and are attended with no disgrace. When the parents of the girl come to understand that she has "gone off," they bring her home in a day or two; the friends of the parties then meet, and the arrangements for the marriage are made as described in the tale.

"Well, the match was made, and the wedding day appointed; but there was one thing still to be managed, and that was how to get over *standing* at mass on Sunday, to make satisfaction for the scandal we gave the church by running away with one another—but that's all stuff, for who cares a pin about standing, when three halves of the parish are married in the same way! The only thing that vexed me was, that it would keep back the wedding-day. However, her father and my uncle went to the priest, and spoke to him, trying, of coorse, to get us off it, but he knew we were fat geese, and was in for giving us a plucking.—Hut, tut!—he wouldn't hear of it at all, not he; for although he would ride fifty miles to sarve either of us, he couldn't break the new orders that he had got only a few days before that from the bishop. No; we must *stand**—for it would be setting a bad example to the parish; and if he would let us pass, how could he punish the rest of his flock, when they'd be guilty of the same thing?

* Matches made in this manner are discountenanced by the Roman Catholic clergy, as being liable to abuse; and, for this reason, the parties, by way of punishment, are sometimes, but not always, made to stand up at mass for one or three Sundays; but, as Shane expresses it, the punishment is so common that it completely loses its effect. To "stand," in the sense meant here, is this: the priest, when the whole congregation are on their knees, calls the young man and woman by name, who stand up and remain under the gaze of the congregation, whilst he rebukes them for the scandal they gave to the church, after which they kneel down. In general it is looked upon more in fun than punishment. Sometimes, however, the wealthier class compromise this matter with the priest, as described above.

"'Well, well, your Reverence,' says my uncle, winking at her father, 'if that's the case, it can't be helped, any how—they must only stand, as many a dacent father and mother's child has done before them, and will again, plase God—your Reverence is right in doing your duty.'

"'True for you, Brian,' says his Reverence, 'and yet, God knows, there's no man in the parish would be sorrier to see such a dacent, comely young couple put upon a level with all the scrubs of the parish; and I know, Jemmy Finigan, it would go hard with your young, bashful daughter to get through with it, having the eyes of the whole congregation staring on her.'

"'Why, then, your Reverence, as to that,' says my uncle, who was just as stiff as the other was stout, 'the bashfulest of them will do more nor that to get a husband.'

"'But you tell me,' says the priest, 'that the wedding-day is fixed upon; how will you manage there?'

"'Why, put it off for three Sundays longer, to be sure,' says the uncle.

"'But you forget this, Brian,' says the priest, 'that good luck or prosperity never attends the putting off of a wedding.'

"Now here, you see, is where the priest had them; for they knew that as well as his Reverence himself—so they were in a puzzle again.

"'It's a disagreeable business,' says the priest, 'but the truth is, I could get them off with the bishop, only for one thing—I owe him five guineas of altar-money, and I am so far back in dues that I'm not able to pay him. If I could inclose this to him in a letter, I would get them off at once, although it would be bringing myself into trouble with the parish afterwards; but, at all events,' says he, 'I wouldn't make every one of you both—so, to prove that I wish to sarve you, I'll sell the best cow in my byre, and pay him myself, rather than their wedding day should be put off, poor things, or themselves brought to any bad luck—the Lord keep them from it!'

"While he was speaking, he stamped his foot two or three times on the flure, and the housekeeper came in.—'Katty,' says he, 'bring us in a bottle of whiskey; at all events, I can't let you away,' says he, 'without tasting something, and drinking luck to the young folks.'

"'In troth,' says Jemmy Finigan, 'and begging your Reverence's pardon, the sorra cow you'll sell this bout, any how, on account of me or my childhre, bekase I'll lay down on the nail what'll clear you wid the bishop; and in the name of goodness, as the day is fixed and all, let the crathurs not be disappointed.'

"'Jemmy,' says my uncle, 'if you go to that, you'll pay but your share, for I insist upon laying down one-half, at laste.'

"At any rate they came down with the cash, and after drinking a bottle between them, went home in choice spirits entirely at their good luck in so aisily getting us off. When they had left the house a bit, the priest sent after them—'Jemmy,' says he to Finigan, 'I forgot a circumstance, and that is, to tell you that I will go and marry them at your own house, and bring Father James, my curate with me.' 'Oh, wurrah, no,' said both, 'don't mention that, your Reverence, except you wish to break their hearts, out and out! why, that would be a thousand times worse nor making them stand to do penance: doesn't your Reverence know that if they hadn't the pleasure of running for the bottle, the whole wedding wouldn't be worth three half-pence?' 'Indeed, I forgot that, Jemmy.' 'But sure,' says my uncle, 'your Reverence and Father James must be at it, whether or not—for that we intended from the first.' 'Tell them I'll run for the bottle, too,' says the priest, laughing, 'and will make some of them look sharp, never fear.'

"Well, by my song, so far all was right; and may be it's we that weren't glad—maning Mary and myself—that there was nothing more in the way to put off the wedding-day. So, as the bridegroom's share of the expense always is to provide the whiskey, I'm sure, for the honor and glory of taking the blooming young crathur from the great lot of bachelors that were all breaking their hearts about her, I couldn't do less nor finish the thing dacintly; knowing, besides, the high doings that the Finigans would have of it—for they were always looked upon as a family that never had their heart in a trifle, when it would come to the push. So, you see, I and my brother Mickey, my cousin Tom, and Dom'nick Nulty, went up into the mountains to Tim Cassidy's still-house, where we spent a glorious day, and bought fifteen gallons of stuff, that one drop of it would bring the tear, if possible, to a young widdy's eye that had berrid a bad husband. Indeed, this was at my father's bidding, who wasn't a bit behindhand with any of them in cutting a dash. 'Shane,' says he to me, 'you know the Finigans of ould, that they won't be contint with what would do another, and that, except they go beyant the thing, entirely, they won't be satisfied. They'll have the whole countryside at the wadding, and we must let them see that we have a spirit and a faction of our own,' says he, 'that we needn't be ashamed of. They've got all kinds of ateables in cart-loads, and as we're to get the drinkables, we must see and give as good as they'll bring. I myself, and your mother, will go round and invite all we can think of, and let you and Mickey go up the hills to Tim Cassidy, and get fifteen gallons of whiskey, for I don't think less will do us.'

"This we accordingly complied with, as I said, and surely better stuff never went down the red lane (* Humorous periphrasis for throat) than the same whiskey; for the people knew nothing about watering it then, at all at all. The next thing I did was to get a fine shop cloth coat, a pair of top-boots, and buckskin breeches fit for a squire; along with a new Caroline hat that would throw off the wet like a duck. Mat Kavanagh, the schoolmaster from Findramore bridge, lent me his watch for the occasion, after my spending near two days learning from him to know what o'clock it was. At last, somehow, I masthered that point so well that, in a quarter of an hour at least, I could give a dacent guess at the time upon it.

"Well, at last the day came. The wedding morning, or the bride's part of it,* as they say, was beautiful. It was then the month of July. The evening before my father" * and my brother went over to Jemmy Finigan's, to make the regulations for the wedding. We, that is my party, were to be at the bride's house about ten o'clock, and we were then to proceed, all on horseback, to the priest's, to be married. We were then, after drinking something at Tom Hance's public-house, to come back as far as the Dumbhill, where we were to start and run for the bottle. That morning we were all up at the shriek of day. From six o'clock my own faction, friends and neighbors, began to come, all mounted; and about eight o'clock there was a whole regiment of them, some on horses, some on mules, others on raheries** and asses; and, by my word, I believe little Dick Snudaghan, the tailor's apprentice, that had a hand in making my wedding-clothes, was mounted upon a buck goat, with a bridle of salvages tied to his horns. Anything at all to keep their feet from the ground; for nobody would be allowed to go with the wedding that hadn't some animal between them and the earth.

> * The morning or early part of the day, on which an Irish
> couple are married, up until noon, is called the bride's
> part, which, if the fortunes of the pair are to be happy, is
> expected to be fair—rain or storm being considered
> indicative of future calamity.
>
> ** A small, shaggy pony, so called from being found in great
> numbers on the Island of that name.

"To make a long story short, so large a bridegroom's party was never seen in that country before, save and except Tim Lannigans, that I mentioned just now. It would make you split your face laughing to see the figure they cut; some of them had saddles and bridles—others had saddles and halthers; some had back-suggawns of straw, with hay Stirrups to them, but good bridles; others sacks filled up as like saddles as they could make them, girthed with hay-ropes five or six times tied round the horse's body. When one or two of the horses wouldn't carry double, except the hind rider sat stride-ways, the women had to be put foremost, and the men behind them. Some had dacent pillions enough, but most of them had none at all, and the women were obliged to sit where the pillion ought to be—and a hard card they had to play to keep their seats even when the horses walked asy, so what must it be when they came to a gallop! but that same was nothing at all to a trot.

"From the time they began to come that morning, you may be sartain that the glass was no cripple, any how—although, for fear of accidents, we took care not to go too deep. At eight o'clock we sat down to a rousing breakfast, for we thought it best to eat a trifle at home, lest they might think that what we were to get at the bride's breakfast might be thought any novelty. As for my part, I was in such a state, that I couldn't let a morsel cross my throat, nor did I know what end of me was uppermost. After breakfast they all got their cattle, and I my hat and whip, and was ready to mount, when my uncle whispered to me that I must kneel down and ax my father and mother's blessing, and forgiveness for all my disobedience and offinces towards them—and also to requist the blessing of my brothers and sisters. Well, in a short time I was down; and my goodness! such a hullabaloo of crying as there was in a minute's time! 'Oh, Shane Fadh—Shane Fadh, acushla machree!' says my poor mother in Irish, 'you're going to break up the ring about your father's hearth and mine—going to lave us, avourneen, for ever, and we to hear your light foot and sweet voice, morning, noon, and night, no more! Oh!' says she, 'it's you that was the good son all out; and the good brother, too: kind and cheerful was your voice, and full of love and affection was your heart! Shane, avourneen dheelish, if ever I was harsh to you, forgive your poor mother, that will never see you more on her flure as one of her own family.'

"Even my father, that wasn't much given to crying', couldn't speak, but went over to a corner and cried till the neighbors stopped him. As for my brothers and sisters, they were all in an uproar; and I myself cried like a Trojan, merely bekase I see them at it. My father and mother both kissed me, and gave me their blessing; and my brothers and sisters did the same, while you'd think all their hearts would break. 'Come, come,' says my uncle, 'I'll have none of this: what a hubbub you make, and your son going to be well married—going to be joined to a girl that your betters would be proud to get into connection with. You should have more sense, Rose Campbell—you ought to thank God that he had the luck to come acrass such a colleen for a wife; and that it's not going to his grave, instead of into the arms of a purty girl— and what's better, a good girl. So quit your blubbering, Rose; and you, Jack,' says he to my father, 'that ought to have more sense, stop this instant. Clear off, every one of you, out of this, and let the young boy go to his horse. Clear out, I say, or by the powers I'll—look at them three stags of huzzies; by the hand of my body they're blubbering bekase it's not their own story this blessed day. Move—bounce!—and you, Rose Oge, if you're not behind Dudley Pulton in less than no time, by the hole of my coat, I'll marry a wife myself, and then where will the twenty guineas be that I'm to lave you?'

"God rest his soul, and yet there was a tear in his eye all the while—even in spite of his joking!

"Any how, it's easy knowing that there wasn't sorrow at the bottom of their grief: for they were all now laughing at my uncle's jokes, even while their eyes were red with the tears: my mother herself couldn't but be in a good humor, and join her smile with the rest.

"My uncle now drove us all out before him; not, however, till my mother had sprinkled a drop of holy water on each of us, and given me and my brothers and sisters a small taste of blessed candle, to prevent us from sudden death and accidents.* My father and she didn't come with as then, but they went over to the bride's while we were all gone to the priest's house. At last we set off in great style and spirits—I well mounted on a good horse of my own, and my brother (On one that he had borrowed from Peter Dannellon), fully bent on winning the bottle. I would have borrowed him myself, but I thought it dacenter to ride my own horse manfully, even though he never won a side of mutton or a saddle, like Dannellon's. But the man that was most likely to come in for the bottle was little Billy Cormick, the tailor, who rode a blood-racer that young-John Little had wickedly lent him for the special purpose; he was a tall bay animal, with long small legs, a switch tail, and didn't know how to trot. Maybe we didn't cut a dash—and might have taken a town before us. Out we set about nine o'clock, and went acrass the country: but I'll not stop to mintion what happened some of them, even before we got to the bride's house. It's enough to say here, that sometimes one in crassing a stile or ditch would drop into the shough;** sometimes another would find himself head foremost on the ground; a woman would be capsized here in crassing a ridgy field, bringing

Finigans axed here for the sake of her decent son-in-law, who ran away with her daughter Betty, that was the great beauty some years ago: her breath's not good, Shane, and many a strange thing's said of her. Well, maybe, I know more about that nor I'm not going to mintion, any how: more betoken that it's not for nothing the white hare haunts the shrubbery behind her house.'

"'But what harm could she do me, Sonsy Mary?' says I—for she was called Sonsy—'we have often sarved her one way or other.'

"'Ax me no questions about her, Shane,' says she, 'don't I know what she did to Ned Donnelly, that was to be pitied, if ever a man was to be pitied, for as good as seven months after his marriage, until I relieved him; was gone to a thread he was, and didn't they pay me decently for my throuble!'

"'Well, and what am I to do, Mary?' says I, knowing very well that what she sed was thrue enough, although I didn't wish her to see that I was afeard.

"'Why,' says she, 'you must first exchange money with me, and then, if you do as I bid you you may lave the rest to myself.'

"'I then took out, begad, a daicent lot of silver—say a crown or so—for my blood was up and the money was flush—and gave it to her for which I got a cronagh-bawn* half-penny in exchange.

* So-called from Cronebane, in the county of Wicklow, where
there is a copper mine.

"'Now,' says she, 'Shane, you must keep this in your company, and for your life and sowl, don't part wid it for nine days after your marriage; but there's more to be done,' says she—'hould out your right knee;' so with this she unbuttoned three buttons of my buckskins, and made me loose the knot of my garther on the right leg. 'Now,' says she, 'if you keep them loose till after the priest says the words, and won't let the money I gave you go out of your company for nine days, along with something else I'll do that you're to know nothing about, there's no fear of all their pisthroges.'* She then pulled off her right shoe, and threw it after us for luck.

* Charms of an evil nature. These are ceremonies used by
such women, and believed to be of efficacy by the people. It
is an undoubted fact that the woman here named—and truly
named—was called in by honest Ned Donnelly, who, I believe,
is alive,and could confirm the truth of it. I remember her
well, as I do the occasion on which she was called in by Ned
or his friends. I also remember that a neighbor of ours, a
tailor named Cormick M'Elroy—father, by the way, to little
Billy Cormick, who figures so conspicuously at the wedding—
called her in to cure, by the force of charms, some cows he
had that were sick.

"We were now all in motion once more—the bride riding behind my man, and the bridesmaid behind myself—a fine bouncing girl she was, but not to be mintioned in the one year with my own darlin'—in troth, it wouldn't be aisy getting such a couple as we were the same day, though it's myself that says it. Mary, dressed in a black castor hat, like a man's, a white muslin coat, with a scarlet silk handkercher about her neck, with a silver buckle and a blue ribbon, for luck, round her waist; her fine hair wasn't turned up, at all at all, but hung down in beautiful curls on her shoulders; her eyes, you would think, were all light; her lips as plump and as ripe as cherries—and maybe it's myself that wasn't to that time o' day without tasting them, any how; and her teeth, so even, and as white as a burned bone. The day bate all for beauty; I don't know whether it was from the lightness of my own spirit it came, but, I think, that such a day I never saw from that to this; indeed, I thought everything was dancing and smiling about me, and sartinly every one said, that such a couple hadn't been married, nor such a wedding seen in the parish for many a long year before.

"All the time, as we went along, we had the music; but then at first we were mightily puzzled what to do with the fiddler. To put him as a hind rider it would prevent him from playing, bekase how could he keep the fiddle before him and another so close to him? To put him foremost was as bad, for he couldn't play and hould the bridle together; so at last my uncle proposed that he should get behind himself, turn his face to the horse's tail, and saw away like a Trojan.

"It might be about four miles or so to the priest's house, and, as the day was fine, we' got on gloriously. One thing, however, became troublesome; you see there was a cursed set of ups and downs on the road, and as the riding coutrements were so bad with a great many of the weddiners, those that had no saddles, going down steep places, would work onward bit by bit, in spite of all they could do, till they'd be fairly on the horse's neck, and the women behind them would be on the animal's shoulders; and it required nice managing to balance themselves, for they might as well sit on the edge of a dale board. Many of them got tosses this way, though it all passed in good humor. But no two among the whole set were more puzzled by this than my uncle and the fiddler—I think I see my uncle this minute with his knees sticking into the horse's shoulders, and his two hands upon his neck, keeping himself back, with a *cruiht** upon him, and the fiddler with his heels away, towards the horse's tail, and he stretched back against my uncle, for all the world like two bricks laid against one another, and one of them falling. 'Twas the same thing going up a hill; whoever was behind, would be hanging over the horse's tail, with the arm about the fore-rider's neck or body, and the other houlding the baste by the mane, to keep them both from sliding off backwards. Many a come-down there was among them—but, as I said, it was all in good humor; and, accordingly, as regularly as they fell, they were sure to get a cheer.

* The hump, which constitutes a round-shouldered man. If the
reader has ever seen Hogarth's Illustrations of Hudibras,
and remembers the redoubtable hero as he sits on horseback,
he will be at no loss in comprehending what a cruiht means.
Cruiht is the Irish for harp, and the simile is taken from
the projection between the shoulders of the harper which was
caused by carrying that instrument.

"When we got to the priest's house, there was a hearty welcome for us all. The bride and I, with our next kindred and friends, went into the parlor; along with these, there was a set of young fellows, who had been bachelors of the bride's, that got in with an intention of getting the first kiss* and, in coorse, of bating myself out of it. I got a whisper of this; so by my song, I was determined to cut them all out in that, as well as I did in getting herself; but you know, I couldn't be angry, even if they had got the foreway of me in it, bekase it's an ould custom. While the priest was going over the business, I kept my eye about me, and sure enough, there were seven or eight fellows all waiting to snap at her. When the ceremony drew near a close, I got up on one leg, so that I could bounce to my feet like lightning, and when it was finished, I got her in my arm, before you could say Jack Robinson, and swinging her behind the priest, gave her the husband's first kiss. The next minute there was a rush after her; but, as I had got the first, it was but fair that they should come in according as they could, I thought, bekase, you know, it was all in the coorse of practice; but, hould, there were two words to be said to that, for what does Father Dollard do but shoves them off, and a fine stout shoulder he had—shoves them off, like childre, and getting his arms about Mary, gives her half a dozen smacks at least—oh, consuming to the one less—that mine was only a cracker** to. The rest, then, all kissed her, one after another, according as they could come in to get one. We then went straight to his Reverence's barn, which had been cleared out for us the day before, by his own directions, where we danced for an hour or two, his Reverence and his Curate along with us.

* There is always a struggle for this at an Irish wedding, where every man is at liberty—even the priest himself—to anticipate the bridegroom if he can.
** Cracker is the small, hard cord which is tied to a rustic whip, in order to make it crack. When a man is considered to be inferior to another in anything, the people say, "he wouldn't make a cracker to his whip."

"When this was over we mounted again, the fiddler taking his ould situation behind my uncle. You know it is usual, after getting the knot tied, to go to a public-house or shebeen, to get some refreshment after the journey; so, accordingly, we went to little lame Larry Spooney's—grandfather to him that was transported the other day for staling Bob Beaty's sheep; he was called Spooney himself, for his sheep-stealing, ever since Paddy Keenan made the song upon him, ending with 'his house never wants a good ram-horn spoon;' so that let people say what they will, these things run in the blood—well, we went to his shebeen house, but the tithe of us couldn't get into it; so we sot on the green before the door, and, by my song, we took (* drank) dacently with him, any how; and, only for my uncle, it's odds but we would have been all fuddled.

"It was now that I began to notish a kind of coolness between my party and the bride's, and for some time I didn't know what to make of it—I wasn't long so, however; for my uncle, who still had his eye about him, comes over to me, and says, 'Shane, I doubt there will be bad work amongst these people, particularly betwixt the Dorans and the Flannagans—the truth is, that the old business of the law-shoot will break out, except they're kept from drink, take my word for it, there will be blood spilled. The running for the bottle will be a good excuse,' says he, 'so I think we had better move home before they go too far in the drink.'

"Well, any way, there was truth in this; so, accordingly, the reckoning was ped, and, as this was the thrate of the weddiners to the bride and bridegroom, every one of the men clubbed his share, but neither I nor the girls anything. Ha—ha—ha! Am I alive at all? I never—ha—ha—ha—!—I never laughed so much in one day as I did in that, today I can't help laughing at it yet. Well, well! when we all got on the top of our horses, and sich other iligant cattle as we had—the crowning of a king was nothing to it. We were now purty well I thank you, as to liquor; and, as the knot was tied, and all safe, there was no end to our good spirits; so, when we took the road, the men were in high blood, particularly Billy Cormick, the tailor, who had a pair of long cavalry spurs upon him, that he was scarcely able to walk in—and he not more nor four feet high. The women, too, were in blood, having faces upon them, with the hate of the day and the liquor, as full as trumpeters.

"There was now a great jealousy among thim that were bint for winning the bottle; and when one horseman would cross another, striving to have the whip hand of him when they'd set off, why you see, his horse would get a cut of the whip itself for his pains. My uncle and I, however, did all we could to pacify them; and their own bad horsemanship, and the screeching of the women, prevented any strokes at that time. Some of them were ripping up ould sores against one another as they went along; others, particularly the youngsters, with their sweethearts behind them, coorting away for the life of them, and some might be heard miles off, singing and laughing; and you may be sure the fiddler behind my uncle wasn't idle, no more nor another. In this way we dashed on gloriously, till we came in sight of the Dumb-hill, where we were to start for the bottle. And now you might see the men themselves on their saddles, sacks and suggans; and the women tying kerchiefs and shawls about their caps and bonnets, to keep them from flying off, and then gripping their fore-riders hard and fast by the bosoms. When we got to the Dumb-hill, there were five or six fellows that didn't come with us to the priest's, but met us with cudgels in their hands, to prevent any of them from starting before the others, and to show fair play.

"Well, when they were all in a lump,—horses, mules, raheries, and asses—some, as I said, with saddles, some with none; and all jist as I tould you before;—the word was given and off they scoured, myself along with the rest; and divil be off me, if ever I saw such another sight but itself before or since. Off they skelped through thick and thin, in a cloud of dust like a mist about us; but it was a mercy that the life wasn't trampled out of some of us; for before we had gone fifty perches, the one-third of them were sprawling a-top of one another on the road. As for the women, they went down right and left—sometimes bringing the horsemen with them; and many of the boys getting black eyes and bloody noses on the stones. Some of them, being half blind with the motion of the whiskey, turned off the wrong way, and galloped on, thinking they had completely distanced the crowd; and it wasn't until they cooled a bit that they found out their mistake.

" HOW HE KEPT HIS SATE NO LOSS HAS PUZZLED ME FROM THAT DAY TO THIS."—Shane Fadh's Wedding, p. 000, I. and S. of the I. P.

"But the best sport of all was, when they came to the Lazy Corner, just at Jack Gallagher's flush,* where the water came out a good way acrass the road; being in such a flight, they either forgot or didn't know how to turn the angle properly, and plash went above thirty of them, coming down right on the top of one another, souse in the pool. By this time there was about a dozen of the best horsemen a good distance before the rest, cutting one another up for the bottle: among these were the Dorans and Flanagans; but they, you see, wisely enough, dropped their women at the beginning, and only rode single. I myself didn't mind the bottle, but kept close to Mary, for fraid that among sich a divil's pack of half-mad fellows, anything might happen her. At any rate, I was next the first batch: but where do you think the tailor was all this time? Why away off like lightning, miles before them— flying like a swallow: and how he kept his sate so long has puzzled me from that day to this; but, any how, truth's best—there he was topping the hill ever so far before them. After all, the unlucky crathur nearly missed the bottle; for when he turned to the bride's house, instead of pulling up as he ought to do—why, to show his horsemanship to the crowd that was out looking at them, he should begin to cut up the horse right and left, until he made him take the garden ditch in full flight, landing him among the cabbages. About four yards or five from the spot where the horse lodged himself was a well, and a purty deep one, by my word; but not a sowl present could tell what become of the tailor, until Owen Smith chanced to look into the well, and saw his long spurs just above the water; so he was pulled up in a purty pickle, not worth the washing; but what did he care? although he had a small body, the sorra one of him but had a sowl big enough for Golias or Sampson the Great.

* Flush is a pool of water that spreads nearly across a
     road. It is usually fed by a small mountain stream, and in
     consequence of rising and falling rapidly, it is called
     "Flash."

"As soon as he got his eyes clear, right or wrong, he insisted on getting the bottle: but he was late, poor fellow, for before he got out of the garden, two of them comes up—Paddy Doran and Peter Flanagan—cutting one another to pieces, and not the length of your nail between them. Well, well, that was a terrible day, sure enough. In the twinkling of an eye they were both off the horses, the blood streaming from their bare heads, struggling to take the bottle from my father, who didn't know which of them to give it to. He knew if he'd hand it to one, the other would take offince, and then he was in a great puzzle, striving to raison with them; but long Paddy Doran caught it while he was spaking to Flanagan, and the next instant Flanagan measured him with a heavy loaded whip, and left, him stretched upon the stones.—And now the work began: for by this time the friends of both parties came up and joined them. Such knocking down, such roaring among the men, and screeching and clapping of hands and wiping of heads among the women, when a brother, or a son, or a husband would get his gruel! Indeed, out of a fair, I never saw anything to come up to it. But during all this work, the busiest man among the whole set was the tailor, and what was worst of all for the poor creature, he should single himself out against both parties, bekase you see he thought they were cutting him out of his right to the bottle.

"They had now broken up the garden gate for weapons, all except one of the posts, and fought into the garden; when nothing should sarve Billy, but to take up the large heavy post, as if he could destroy the whole faction on each side. Accordingly he came up to big Matthew Flanagan, and was rising it just as if he'd fell him, when Matt, catching him by the nape of the neck, and the waistband of the breeches, went over very quietly, and dropped him a second

151

time, heels up, into the well; where he might have been yet, only for my mother-in-law, who dragged him out with a great deal to do: for the well was too narrow to give him room to turn.

"As for myself and all my friends, as it happened to be my own wedding, and at our own place, we couldn't take part with either of them; but we endeavored all in our power to red (* Pacify or separate) them, and a tough task we had of it, until we saw a pair of whips going hard and fast among them, belonging to Father Corrigan and Father James, his curate. Well, its wonderful how soon a priest can clear up a quarrel! In five minutes there wasn't a hand up—instead of that they were ready to run into mice-holes:—

"'What, you murderers,' says his Reverence, 'are you bint to have each other's blood upon your heads; ye vile infidels, ye cursed unchristian Anthemtarians?* are ye going to get yourself hanged like sheep-stalers? down with your sticks, I command you: do you know—will you give yourselves time to see who's spaking to you—you bloodthirsty set of Episcopalians? I command you, in the name of the Catholic Church and the Blessed Virgin Mary, to stop this instant, if you don't wish me,' says he, 'to turn you into stocks and stones where you stand, and make world's wonders of you as long as you live.—Doran, if you rise your hand more, I'll strike it dead on your body, and to your mouth you'll never carry it while you have breath in your carcass,' says he.—'Clear off, you Flanagans, you butchers you—or by St. Domnick I'll turn the heads round upon your bodies, in the twinkling of an eye, so that you'll not be able to look a quiet Christian in the face again. Pretty respect you have for the decent couple at whose house you have kicked up such a hubbub. Is this the way people are to be deprived of their dinners on your accounts, you fungaleering thieves!'

* Antitrinitarians; the peasantry are often extremely fond
  of hard and long words, which they call tall English.

"'Why then, plase your Riverence, by the—hem—I say Father Corrigan, it wasn't my fault, but that villain Flanagan's, for he knows I fairly won the bottle—and would have distanced him, only that when I was far before him, the vagabone, he galloped across me on the way, thinking to thrip up the horse.'

"'You lying scoundrel,' says the priest, 'how dare you tell me a falsity,' says he, 'to my face? how could he gallop acrass you if you were far before him? Not a word more, or I'll leave you without a mouth to your face, which will be a double share of provision and bacon saved any way. And, Flanagan, you were as much to blame as he, and must be chastised for your raggamuffianly conduct,' says he, 'and so must you both, and all your party, particularly you and be, as the ringleaders. Right well I know it's the grudge upon the lawsuit you had and not the bottle, that occasioned it: but by St. Peter, to Loughderg both of you must tramp for this.'

"'Ay, and by St. Pether, they both desarve it as well as a thief does the gallows,' said a little blustering voice belonging to the tailor, who came forward in a terrible passion, looking for all the world like a drowned rat. 'Ho, by St. Pether, they do, the vagabones; for it was myself that won the bottle, your Reverence; and by this and by that,' says he, 'the bottle I'll have, or some of their crowns, will crack for it: blood or whiskey I'll have, your Reverence, and I hope that you'll assist me.

"'Why, Billy, are you here?' says Father Corrigan, smiling down upon the figure the little fellow cut, with his long spurs and his big whip; 'what in the world tempted you to get on horseback, Billy?'

151

"'By the powers, I was miles before them,' says Billy; 'and after this day, your Reverence, let no man say that I couldn't ride a steeplechase across Crocknagooran.'

"'Why, Billy, how did you stick on at all, at all?' says his Reverence.

"'How do I know how I stuck on?' says Billy, 'nor whether I stuck on at all or not; all I know is, that I was on horseback leaving the Dumb-hill, and that I found them pulling me by the heels out of the well in the corner of the garden—and that, your Reverence, when the first was only topping the hill there below, as Lanty Magowran tells me who was looking on.'

"'Well, Billy,' says Father Corrigan, 'you must get the bottle; and as for you Dorans and Flanagans, I'll make examples of you for this day's work—that you may reckon on. You are a disgrace to the parish, and, what's more, a disgrace to your priest. How can luck or grace attind the marriage of any young couple that there's such work at? Before you leave this, you must all shake hands, and promise never to quarrel with each other while grass grows or water runs; and if you don't, by the blessed St. Domnick, I'll exkimnicate* ye both, and all belonging to you into the bargain; so that ye'll be the pitiful examples and shows to all that look upon you.'

* Excommunicate. It is generally pronounced as above by the people.

"'Well, well, your Reverence,' says my father-in-law, 'let all by-gones be by-gones; and please God, they will, before they go, be better friends than ever they were. Go now an' clane yourselves, take the blood from about your faces, for the dinner's ready an hour agone; but if you all respect the place you're in, you'll show it, in regard of the young crathurs that's going, in the name of God, to face the world together, and of coorse wishes that this day at laste should pass in pace and quietness: little did I think there was any friend or neighbor here that would make so little of the place or people, as was done for nothing at all, in the face of the country.'

"'God he sees,' says my mother-in-law, 'that there's them here this day we didn't desarve this from, to rise such a *norration*, as if the house was a shebeen or a public-house! It's myself didn't think either me or my poor coolleen here, not to mention the dacent people she's joined to, would be made so little of, as to have our place turned into a play-acthur—for a play-acthur couldn't be worse.'

"'Well,' says my uncle, 'there's no help for spilt milk, I tell you, nor for spilt blood either; tare-an-ounty, sure we're all Irishmen, relations, and Catholics through other, and we oughtn't to be this way. Come away to the dinner—by the powers, we'll duck the first man that says a loud word for the remainder of the day. Come, Father Corrigan, and carve the goose, or the geese, for us—for, by my sannies, I bleeve there's a baker's dozen of them; but we've plenty of Latin for them, and your Reverence and Father James here understands that langidge, any how—larned enough there, I think, gintlemen.'

"'That's right, Brian,' shouts the tailor—'that's right; there must be no fighting: by the powers, the first man attempts it, I'll brain him—fell him to the earth like an ox, if all belonging to him was in my way.'

"This threat from the tailor went farther, I think, in putting them into good humor nor even what the priest said. They then washed and claned themselves, and accordingly went to their dinners.—Billy himself marched with his terrible whip in his hand, and his long cavalry spurs sticking near ten inches behind him, draggled to the tail like a bantling cock after a shower.

But, maybe, there was more draggled tails and bloody noses nor poor Billy's, or even nor was occasioned by the fight; for after Father Corrigan had come, several of them dodged up, some with broken shins and heads and wet clothes, that they'd got on the way by the mischances of the race, particularly at the Flush. But I don't know how it was; somehow the people in them days didn't value these things a straw. They were far hardier then nor they are now, and never went to law at all at all. Why, I've often known skulls to be broken, and the people to die afterwards, and there would be nothing more about it, except to brake another skull or two for it; but neither crowner's quest, nor judge, nor jury, was ever troubled at all about it. And so sign's on it, people were then innocent, and not up to law and counsellors as they are now. If a person happened to be killed in a fight at a fair or market, why he had only to appear after his death to one of his friends, and get a number of masses offered up for his sowl, and all was right; but now the times are clane altered, and there's nothing but hanging and transporting for such things; although that won't bring the people to life again."

"I suppose," said Andy Morrow, "you had a famous dinner, Shane?"

"'Tis you that may say that, Mr. Morrow," replied Shane: "but the house, you see, wasn't able to hould one-half of us; so there was a dozen or two tables borrowed from the neighbors and laid one after another in two rows, on the green, beside the river that ran along the garden-hedge, side by side. At one end Father Corrigan sat, with Mary and myself, and Father James at the other. There were three five-gallon kegs of whiskey, and I ordered my brother to take charge of them; and there he sat beside them, and filled the bottles as they were wanted—bekase, if he had left that job to strangers, many a spalpeen there would make away with lots of it. Mavrone, such a sight as the dinner was! I didn't lay my eye on the fellow of it since, sure enough, and I'm now an ould man, though I was then a young one. Why there was a pudding boiled in the end of a sack; and troth it was a thumper, only for the straws—for you see, when they were making it, they had to draw long straws acrass in order to keep, it from falling asunder—a fine plan it is, too. Jack M'Kenna, the carpenther, carved it with a hand-saw, and if he didn't curse the same straws, I'm not here. 'Draw them out, Jack,' said Father Corrigan—'draw them out.—It's asy known, Jack, you never ate a polite dinner, you poor awkward spalpeen, or you'd have pulled out the straws the first thing you did, man alive.'

"Such lashins of corned beef, and rounds of beef, and legs of mutton, and bacon—turkeys and geese, and barn-door fowls, young and fat. They may talk as they will, but commend me to a piece of good ould bacon, ate with crock butther, and phaties, and cabbage. Sure enough, they leathered away at everything, but this and the pudding were the favorites. Father Corrigan gave up the carving in less than no time, for it would take him half a day to sarve them all, and he wanted to provide for number one. After helping himself, he set my uncle to it, and maybe he didn't slash away right and left. There was half a dozen gorsoons carrying about the beer in cans, with froth upon it like barm—but that was beer in airnest, Nancy—I'll say no more."

"When the dinner was over, you would think there was as much left as would sarve a regiment; and sure enough, a right hungry ragged regiment was there to take care of it—though, to tell the truth, there was as much taken into Finigan's as would be sure to give us all a rousing supper. Why, there was such a troop of beggars—men, women, and childher, sitting over on the sunny side of the ditch, as would make short work of the whole dinner, had they got it. Along with Father Corrigan and me, was my father and mother, and Mary's parents; my uncle, cousins, and nearest relations on both sides. Oh, it's Father Corrigan, God rest his sowl, he's now in glory, and so he was then, also—how he did crow and laugh! 'Well, Matthew Finigan,' says-he, 'I can't say but I'm happy that your Colleen Bawn here has lit upon a husband that's no discredit to the family—and it is herself didn't drive her pigs to a bad market,' says he. 'Why, in troth, Father avourneen,' says my mother-in law, 'they'd be hard to plase that couldn't be satisfied with them she got; not saying but she had her pick and choice of many a good offer, and might have got richer matches; but Shane Fadh M'Cawell although you're sitting there beside my daughter, I'm prouder to see you on my own flure, the husband of my child, nor if she'd got a man with four times your substance.'

"'Never heed the girls for knowing where to choose,' says his Reverence, slyly enough: 'but, upon my word, only she gave us all the slip, to tell the truth, I had another husband than Shane in my eye for her, and that was my own nevvy, Father James's brother here.'

"'And I'd be proud of the connection,' says my father-in-law, 'but you see, these girls won't look much to what you or I'll say, in choosin' a husband for themselves. How-and-iver, not making little of your nevvy, Father Michael, I say he's not to be compared with that same bouchal sitting beside Mary there.'

"'No, nor by the powdhers-o-war, never will,' says Billy M'Cormick the tailor, who had come over and slipped in on the other side betune Father Corrigan and the bride—'by the powdhers-o' war, he'll never be fit to be compared with me, I tell you, till yesterday comes back again.'

"'Why, Billy,' says the priest, 'you're every place.' 'But where I ought to be!' says Billy; 'and that's hard and fast tackled to Mary Bane, the bride here, instead of that steeple of a fellow she has got,' says the little cock.

"'Billy, I thought you were married,' said Father Corrigan.

"'Not I, your Reverence,' says Billy;' but I'll soon do something, Father Michael—I have been threatening this longtime, but I'll do it at last'

"'He's not exactly married, Sir, says my uncle 'but there's a colleen present' (looking at the bridesmaid) 'that will soon have his name upon her.'

"'Very good, Billy,' says the priest, 'I hope you will give us a rousing wedding-equal, at least, to Shane Fadh's.'

"'Why then, your Reverence, except I get sich a darling as Molly Bane, here—and by this and that, it's you that is the darling Molly asthore—what come over me, at all at all, that I didn't think of you,' says the little man, drawing close to her, and poor Mary smiling good-naturedly at his spirit.

"'Well, and what if you did get such a darling as Molly Bane, there?' says his Reverence.

"'Why, except I get the likes of her for a wife—upon second thoughts, I don't like marriage, any way,' said Billy, winking against the priest—'I lade such a life as your Reverence; and by the powdhers, it's a thousand pities that I wasn't made into a priest, instead of a tailor. For, you see, if I had' says he, giving a verse of an old song—

'For you see, if I had,
It's I'd be the lad
That would show all my people such larning;
And when they'd do wrong,
Why, instead of a song,
I'd give them a lump of a sarmin.'

"'Billy,' says my father-in-law, 'why don't you make a hearty dinner, man alive? go back to your sate and finish your male—you're aiting nothing to signify.' 'Me!' says Billy—'why, I'd scorn to ate a hearty dinner; and, I'd have you to know, Matt Finigan, that it wasn't for the sake of your dinner I came here, but in regard to your family, and bekase I wished him well that's sitting beside your daughter: and it ill becomes your father's son to cast up your dinner in my face, or any one of my family; but a blessed minute longer I'll not stay among you. Give me your hand, Shane Fadh, and you, Mary—may goodness grant you pace and happiness every night and day you both rise out of your beds. I made that coat your husband has on his back beside you—and a, betther fit was never made; but I didn't think it would come to my turn to have my dinner cast up this a-way, as if I was aiting it for charity.'

"'Hut, Billy,' says I, 'sure it was all out of kindness; he didn't mane to offind you.'

"'It's no matter,' says Billy, beginning to cry, 'he did offend me; and it's, low days with me to bear an affront from him, or the likes of him; but by the powdhers-o'-war,' says he, getting into a great rage, 'I won't bear it,—only as you're an old man yourself, I'll not rise my hand to you; but, let any man now that has the heart to take up your quarrel, come out and stand before me on the sod here.'

"Well, by this time, you'd tie all that were present with three straws, to see Billy stripping himself, and his two wrists not thicker than drumsticks. While the tailor was raging, for he was pretty well up with what he had taken, another person made his appearance at the far end of the boreen* that led to the green where we sot. He was mounted upon the top of a sack that was upon the top of a sober-looking baste enough—God knows; he jogging along at his ase, his legs dangling down from the sack on each side, and the long skirts of his coat hanging down behind him. Billy was now getting pacified, bekase they gave way to him a little; so the fun went round, and they sang, roared, danced, and coorted, right and left.

    * A small pathway or bridle road leading to a farm-house.

"When the stranger came as far as the skirt of the green, he turned the horse over quite nathural to the wedding; and, sure enough, when he jogged up, it was Friar Rooney himself, with a sack of oats, for he had been *questin*.* Well, sure the ould people couldn't do less nor all go over to put the *failtah*** on him. 'Why, then,' says my father and mother-in-law, "tis yourself, Friar Rooney, that's as welcome as the flowers of May; and see who's here before you—Father Corrigan, and Father Dollard.'

    * Questin—When an Irish priest or friar collects corn or
      money from the people in a gratuitous manner, the act is
      called "questin."

    ** Welcome.

"'Thank you, thank you, Molshy—thank you, Matthew—troth, I know that 'tis I am welcome.'

"'Ay, and you're welcome again, Father Rooney,' said my father, going down and shaking hands with him, 'and I'm proud to see you here. Sit down, your Reverence—here's everything that's good, and plinty of it, and if you don't make much of yourself, never say an ill fellow dealt with you.'

"The friar stood while my father was speaking, with a pleasant, contented face upon him, only a little roguish and droll.

"'Hah! Shane Fadh,' says he, smiling dryly at me, 'you did them all, I see. You have her there, the flower of the parish, blooming beside you; but I knew as much six months ago, ever since I saw you bid her good-night at the hawthorn. Who looked back so often, Mary, eh? Ay, laugh and blush—do—throth, 'twas I that caught you, but you didn't see me, though. Well, a colleen, and if you did, too, you needn't be ashamed of your bargain, any how. You see, the way I came to persave yez that evening was this—but I'll tell it, by and by. In the mane time,' says he, sitting down and attacking a fine piece of corn-beef and greens, 'I'll take care of a certain acquaintance of mine,' says he. 'How are you, reverend gintlemen of the Secularily? You'll permit a poor friar to sit and ate his dinner, in your presence, I humbly hope.'

"'Frank,' says Father Corrigan, 'lay your hand upon your conscience, or upon your stomach, which is the same thing, and tell us honestly, how many dinners you eat on your travels among my parishioners this day.'

"'As I'm a sinner, Michael, this is the only thing to be called a dinner I eat this day;—Shane Fadh—Mary, both your healths, and God grant you all kinds of luck and happiness, both here and hereafter! All your healths in gineral! gintlemen seculars!'

"'Thank you, Frank,' said Father Corrigan; how did you speed to-day?'

"'How can any man speed, that comes after you?' says the Friar; 'I'm after travelling the half of the parish for that poor bag of oats that you see standing against the ditch.'

"'In other words, Frank,' says the Priest, 'you took Allhadhawan in your way, and in about half a dozen houses filled your sack, and then turned your horse's head towards the good cheer, by way of accident only.'

"'And was it by way of accident, Mr. Secular, that I got you and that illoquent young gintleman, your curate, here before me? Do you feel that, man of the world? Father James, your health, though—you're a good young man as far as saying nothing goes; but it's better to sit still than to rise up and fall, so I commend you for your discretion,' says he; 'but I'm afeared your master there won't make you much fitter for the kingdom of heaven any how.'

"'I believe, Father Corrigan,' says my uncle, who loved to see the priest and the friar at it, 'that you've met with your match—I think Father Rooney's able for you.'

"'Oh, sure,' says Father Corrigan, he was joker to the college of the Sorebones (* Sorbonne) in Paris; he got as much education as enabled him to say mass in Latin, and to beg oats in English, for his jokes.'

"'Troth, and,' says the friar, 'if you were to get your larning on the same terms, you'd be guilty of very little knowledge; why, Michael, I never knew you to attempt a joke but once, and I was near shedding tears, there was something so very sorrowful in it.'

"This brought the laugh against the priest—'Your health, Molshy,' says he, winking at my mother-in-law, and then giving my uncle, who sat beside him, a nudge; 'I believe, Brian, I'm giving it to him.' "Tis yourself that is,' says my uncle; 'give him a wipe or two more.' 'Wait till he answers the last,' says the friar.

"'He's always joking,' says Father James, 'when he thinks he'll make any thing by it.'

"'Ah!' says the friar, 'then God help you both if you were left to your jokes for your feeding; for a poorer pair of gentlemen wouldn't be found in Christendom.'

"'And I believe,' says Father Corrigan, 'if you depinded for your feeding upon your divinity instead of your jokes, you'd be as poor as a man in the last stage of a consumption.'

"This drew the laugh against the friar, who smiled himself; but he was a dry man that never laughed much.

"'Sure,' says the friar, who was seldom at a loss, 'I have yourself and your nephew for examples that it's possible to live and be well fed without divinity.'

"'At any rate,' says my uncle, putting in his tongue, 'I think you're both very well able to make divinity a joke betune you,' says he.

"'Well done, Brian,' says the friar, 'and so they are, for I believe it is the only subject they can joke upon! and I beg your pardon, Michael, for not excepting it before; on that subject I allow you to be humorsome.'

"'If that be the case, then,' says Father Corrigan, 'I must give up your company, Frank, in order to avoid the force of bad example; for you're so much in the habit of joking on everything else, that you're not able to accept even divinity itself.'

"'You may aisily give me up,' says the friar, 'but how will you be able to forget Father Corrigan? I'm afeard you'll find his acquaintance as great a detriment to yourself, as it is to others in that respect.'

"'What makes you say,' says Father James, who was more in airnest than the rest, 'that my uncle won't make me fit for the kingdom of heaven?'

"'I had a pair of rasons for it, Jemmy,' says the friar; 'one is, that he doesn't understand the subject himself; another is, that you haven't capacity for it, even if he did. You've a want of natural parts—a *whackuuum* here' pointing to his forehead.

"'I beg your pardon, Frank,' says Father James 'I deny your premises, and I'll now argue in Latin with you, if you wish, upon any subject you please.'

"'Come, then,' says the friar,—'Kid eat ivy mare eat hay.'

"'Kid—what?' says the other.

"'Kid eat ivy mare eat hay,' answers the friar.

"'I don't know what you're at,' says Father James, 'but I'll argue in Latin with you as long as you wish.'

"'Tut man,' says Father Rooney, 'Latin's for school-boys; but come, now, I'll take you in another language—I'll try you in Greek—*In-mud-eel-is in-clay-none-is in-fir-tar-is in-oak-no ne-is*.'

"The curate looked at him, amazed, not knowing what answer to make. At last says he, 'I don't profess to know Greek, bekase I never larned it—but stick to the Latin, and I'm not afeard of you.'

"'Well, then,' says the friar, 'I'll give you a trial at that—Afflat te canis ter—Forte dux fel flat in guttur.'

"'A flat tay-canisther—Forty ducks fell flat in the gutthers!' says Father James,—'why that's English!'

"'English!' says the friar, 'oh, good-bye to you, Mr. Secular; 'if that's your knowledge of Latin, you're an honor to your tachers and to your cloth.'

"Father Corrigan now laughed heartily at the puzzling the friar gave Father James. 'James,' says he, 'never heed him; he's only pestering you with bog-Latin; but, at any rate to do him justice, he's not a bad Scholar, I can tell you that.... Your health, Prank, you droll crathur—your health. I have only one fault to find with you, and that is, that you fast and mortify yourself too much. Your fasting has reduced you from being formerly a friar of very genteel dimensions to a cut of corpulency that smacks strongly of penance—fifteen stone at least.

"'Why,' says the friar, looking down quite plased, entirely, at the cut of his own waist, Uch, among ourselves, was no trifle, and giving a growl of a laugh—the most he ever gave, 'if what you pray here benefits you in the *next life* as much as what *I fast* does for me *in this*, it will be well for the world in general Michael.'

"'How can you say, Frank,' says Father 'with such a carkage as that, you're a poor friar? Upon my credit, when you die, I think the angels will have a job of it in wafting you upwards.''

"'Jemmy, man, was it *you* that said it?—why, my light's beginning to shine upon you, or you never could have got out so much,' says Father Rooney, putting his hands over his brows, and looking up toardst him; 'but if you ever read scripthur, which I suppose you're not overburdened with, you would know that it says, "Blessed are the poor in spirit," but not blessed are the poor in flesh—now, mine is spiritual poverty.'

"'Very true, Frank,' says Father Corrigan, 'I believe there's a great dearth and poverty of spirituality about you, sure enough. But of all kinds of poverty, commend me to a friar's. Voluntary poverty's something, but it's the divil entirely for a man to be poor against his will. You friars boast of this voluntary poverty; but if there's a fat bit in any part of the parish, we, that are the lawful clargy, can't eat it, but you're sure to drop in, just in the nick of time, with your voluntary poverty.'

"'I'm sure, if we do,' says the friar, 'it's nothing out of your pocket, Michael. I declare I believe you begrudge us the air we breathe. But don't you know very well that our ordhers are apostolic, and that, of coorse, we have a more primitive appearance than you have.'

"'No such thing,' says the other; 'you, and the parsons, and the fat bishops, are too far from the right place—the only difference between you is, that you are fat and lazy by toleration, whereas the others are fat and lazy by authority. You are fat and lazy on your ould horses, jogging about from house to house, and stuffing yourselves either at the table of other people's parishioners, or in your own convents in Dublin and elsewhere. They are rich, bloated gluttons, going about in their coaches, and wallying in wealth. Now, we are the golden mean, Frank, that live upon a little, and work hard for it.'

"'Why, you cormorant,' says the friar, a little nettled, for the dhrop was beginning to get up into his head, 'sure if we're fat by toleration, we're only tolerably fat, my worthy secular!'

"'You see,' says the friar, in a whisper to my uncle, 'how I sobered them in the larning, and they are good scholars for all that, but not near so deep read as myself.' 'Michael,' says he, 'now that I think on it—sure I'm to be at Denis O'Flaherty's Month's mind on Thursday next.'

"'Indeed I would not doubt you,' says Father Corrigan; 'you wouldn't be apt to miss it.'

"'Why, the widdy Flaherty asked me yesterday, and I think that's proof enough that I'm not going unsent for.'

"By this time the company was hard and fast at the punch, the songs, and the dancing. The dinner had been cleared off, except what was before the friar, who held out wonderfully, and

159

the beggars and shulers were clawing and scoulding one another about the divide. The dacentest of us went into the house for a while, taking the fiddler with us, and the rest, with the piper, staid on the green to dance, where they were soon joined by lots of the counthry people, so that in a short time there was a large number entirely. After sitting for some time within, Mary and I began, you may be sure, to get unasy, sitting palavering among a parcel of ould sober folks; so, at last, out we slipped, and the few other dacent young people that were with us, to join the dance, and shake our toe along with the rest of them. When we made our appearance, the flure was instantly cleared for us, and then she and I danced the *Humors of Glin*.

"Well, it's no matter—it's all past now, and she lies low; but I may say that it wasn't very often danced in better style since, I'd wager. Lord, bless us, what a drame the world is! The darling of my heart you war, avourneen machree. I think I see her with the modest smile upon her face, straight, and fair, and beautiful, and—hem—and when the dance was over, how she stood leaning upon me, and my heart within melting to her, and the look she'd give into my eyes and my heart, too, as much as to say, 'This is the happy day with me;' and the blush still would fly acrass her face, when I'd press her, unknownst to the bystanders, against my beating heart. A *suilish machree*, (* Light of my heart.) she is now gone from me—lies low, and it all appears like a drame to me; but—hem—God's will be done!—sure she's happy—och, och!!

"Many a shake hands did I get from the neighbors' sons, wishing me joy; and I'm sure I couldn't do less than thrate them to a glass, you know; and 'twas the same way with Mary: many a neighbors' daughter, that she didn't do more nor know by eyesight, maybe, would come up and wish her happiness in the same manner, and she would say to me, 'Shane, avourneen, that's such a man's daughter—they're a dacent friendly people, and we can't do less nor give her a glass.' I, of coorse, would go down and bring them over, after a little pulling—making, you see, as if they wouldn't come—to where my brother was handing out the native.

"In this way we passed the time till the evening came on, except that Mary and the bridesmaid were sent for to dance with the priests, who were within at the punch, in all their glory,—Friar Rooney along with them as jolly as a prince. I and my man, on seeing this, were for staying with the company; but my mother, who 'twas that came for them, says, 'Never mind the boys, Shane, come in with the girls, I say. You're just wanted at the present time, both of you, follow me for an hour or two, till their Reverences within have a bit of a dance with the girls, in the back room; we don't want to gother a crowd about them.' Well, we went in, sure enough, for awhile; but, I don't know how it was, I didn't at all feel comfortable with the priests; for, you see, I'd rather sport my day figure with the boys and girls upon the green: so I gives Jack *the hard word** and in we went, when, behold you, there was Father Corrigan planted upon the side of a settle, Mary along with him, waiting till they'd have the fling of a dance together, whilst the Curate was capering on the flure before the bridesmaid, who was a purty dark-haired girl, to the tune of 'Kiss my lady;' and the friar planted between my mother and my mother-in-law, one of his legs stretched out on a chair, he singing some funny song or other, that brought the tears to their eyes with laughing.

* A pass-word, sign, or brief intimation, touching something
of which a man is ignorant, that he may act accordingly.

"Whilst Father James was dancing with the bridesmaid, I gave Mary the wink to! come away from Father Corrigan, wishing, as I tould you, to get out amongst the youngsters once more; and Mary, herself, to tell the truth, although he was the priest, was very willing to do so. I went over to her, and says, 'Mary, asthore, there's a friend without that wishes to spake to you.'

"'Well,' says Father Corrigan, 'tell that friend that she's better employed, and that they must wait, whoever they are. I'm giving your wife, Shane,' says he, 'a little good advice that she won't be the worse for, and she can't go now.'

"Mary, in the meantime, had got up, and was coming away, when his Reverence wanted her to stay till they'd finished their dance. 'Father Corrigan,' says she, 'let me go now, sir, if you plase, for they would think it bad threatment of me not to go out to them.'

"'Troth, and you'll do no such thing, acushla,' says he, spaking so sweet to her; 'let them come in if they want you. Shane, says his Reverence, winking at me, and spiking in a whisper, 'stay here, you and the girls, till we take a hate at the dancing—don't you know that the ould women here, and me will have to talk over some things about the fortune; you'll maybe get more nor you expect. Here, Molshy,' says he to my mother-in-law, 'don't let the youngsters out of this.''

"'Musha, Shane, ahagur,' say's the ould woman 'why will yez go and lave the place; sure you needn't be dashed before them—they'll dance themselves.'

"Accordingly we stayed in the room; but just on the word, Mary gives one spring away, leaving his Reverence by himself on the *settle*. 'Come away,' says she, 'lave them there, and let us go to where I can have a dance with yourself, Shane.'

"Well, I always loved Mary, but at that minute, if it would save her, I think I could spill my heart's blood for her. 'Mary,' says I full to the throat, 'Mary, acushla agus asthore machree,* I could lose my life for you.'

*The very pulse and delight of my heart.

"She looked in my face, and the tears came into her—yes—'Shane, achora,' says she, 'amn't I your happy girl, at last?' She was leaning over against my breast; and what answer do you think I made?—I pressed her to my heart: I did more—I took off my hat, and looking up to God, I thanked him with tears in my eyes, for giving me such a treasure. 'Well, come now,' says she, 'to the green;' so we went—and it's she that was the girl, when she did go among them, that threw them all into the dark for beauty and figure; as fair as a lily itself did she look—so tall and illegant, that you wouldn't think she was a farmer's daughter at all; so we left the priests dancing away, for we could do no good before them.

"When we had danced an hour or so, them that the family had the greatest regard for were brought in unknown to the rest, to drink tay. Mary planted herself beside me, and would sit nowhere else; but the friar got beside the bridesmaid, and I surely observed that many a time she'd look over, likely to split, at Mary, and it's Mary herself that gave her many's a wink, to come to the other side; but, you know, out of manners, she was obliged to sit quietly, though among ourselves it's she that was like a hen on a hot griddle, beside the ould chap. It was now that the bride-cake was got. Ould Sonsy Mary marched over, and putting the bride on her feet, got up on a chair and broke it over her head, giving round a *fadge** of it to every young person in the house, and they again to their acquaintances: but, lo and behold you, who should insist on getting a whang of it but the friar, which he rolled up in a piece of paper, and put it in his pocket. 'I'll have good fun,' says he, 'dividing this to-morrow among the colleens when

I'm collecting my oats—the sorra one of me but I'll make them give me the worth of it of something, if it was only a fat hen or a square of bacon.'

* A liberal portion torn off a thick cake.

"After tay the ould folk got full of talk; the youngsters danced round them; the friar sung like a thrush,and told many a droll story. The tailor had got drunk a little too early, and had to be put to bed, but he was now as fresh as ever, and able to dance a hornpipe, which he did on a door. The Dorans and the Flanagans had got quite thick after drubbing one another—Ned Doran began his courtship with Alley Flanagan on that day, and they were married soon after, so that the two factions joined, and never had another battle until the day of her berrial, when they were at it as fresh as ever. Several of those that were at the wedding were lying drunk about the ditches, or roaring, and swaggering, and singing about the place. The night falling, those that were dancing on the green removed to the barn. Father Corrigan and Father James weren't ill off; but as for the friar, although he was as pleasant as a lark, there was hardly any such thing as making him tipsy. Father Corrigan wanted him to dance—'What!' says he, 'would you have me to bring on an earthquake, Michael?—but who ever heard of a follower of St. Domnick, bound by his vow to voluntary poverty and mortification——young couple, your health—will anybody tell mo who mixed this, for they've knowledge worth a folio of the fathers——poverty and mortification, going to shake his heel? By the bones of St. Domnick, I'd desarve to be suspinded if I did. Will no one tell me who mixed this, I say, for they had a jewel of a hand at it?—Och—

    'Let parsons prache and pray—
    Let priests to pray and prache, sir;
    What's the rason they
    Don't practise what they tache, sir?
    Forral, orral, loll,
    Forral, orral, laddy—

Sho da slainthah ma collenee agus ma bouchalee. Hoigh, oigh, oigh, healths all! gintlemen seculars! Molshy,' says the friar to my mother-in-law, 'send that bocaun* to bed—poor fellow, he's almost off—rouse yourself, James! It's aisy to see that he's but young at it yet—that's right—he's sound asleep—just toss him into bed, and in an hour or so he'll be as fresh as a daisy.

* A soft, unsophisticated youth.

Let parsons prache and pray—
    ——-Forral, orral, loll.'

"For dear's sake, Father Rooney,' says my uncle, running in, in a great hurry, 'keep yourself quiet a little; here's the Squire and Mister Francis coming over to fulfil their promise; he would have come up airlier, he says, but that he was away all day at the 'sizes.'

"'Very well,' says the friar, 'let him come—who's afeard—mind yourself, Michael.'

"In a minute or two they came in, and we all rose up of course to welcome them. The Squire shuck hands with the ould people, and afterwards with Mary and myself, wishing us all happiness, then with the two clergymen, and introduced Master Frank to them; and the friar made the young chap sit beside him. The masther then took a sate himself, and looked on while they were dancing, with a smile of good-humor on his face—while they, all the time, would give new touches and trebles, to show off all their steps before him. He was landlord both to my father and father-in-law; and it's he that was the good man, and the gintleman every inch of him. They may all talk as they will, but commend me, Mr. Morrow, to some of the ould squires of former times for a landlord. The priests, with all their larning, were nothing to him for good breeding—he appeared so free, and so much at his ase, and even so respectful, that I don't think there was one in the house but would put their two hands under his feet to do him a sarvice.

"When he sat a while, my mother-in-law came over with a glass of nice punch that she had mixed, at least equal to what the friar praised so well, and making a low curtshy, begged pardon for using such freedom with his honor, but hoped that he would just taste a little to the happiness of the young couple. He then drank our healths, and shuck hands with us both a second time, saying—although I can't, at all at all, give it in anything like his own words— 'I am glad,' says he, to Mary's parents, 'that your daughter has made such a good choice;'— throth he did—the Lord be merciful to his sowl—God forgive me for what I was going to say, and he a Protestant;—but if ever one of yez went to heaven, Mr. Morrow, he did;—' such a prudent choice; and I congr—con—grathu-late you,' says he to my father, 'on your connection with so industrious and respectable a family. You are now beginning the world for yourselves,' says he to Mary and me, 'and I cannot propose a better example to you both than that of your respective parents. From this forrid,' says he, 'I'm to considher you my tenants; and I wish to take this opportunity of informing you both, that should you act up to the opinion I entertain of you, by an attentive coorse of industry and good management, you will find in me an encouraging and indulgent landlord. I know, Shane,' says he to me, smiling a little, knowingly enough too, 'that you have been a little wild or so, but that's past, I trust. You have now sarious duties to perform, which you cannot neglect—but you will not neglect them; and be assured, I say again, that I shall feel pleasure in rendhering you every assistance in my power in the cultivation and improvement of your farm.'—'Go over, both of you,' says my father, 'and thank his honor, and promise to do everything he says.' Accordingly, we did so; I made my scrape as well as I could, and Mary blushed to the eyes, and dropp'd her curtshy.

"'Ah!' says the friar, 'see what it is to have a good landlord and a Christian gintleman to dale with. This is the feeling which should always bind a landlord and his tenants together. If I know your character, Squire Whitethorn, I believe you're not the man that would put a Protestant tenant over the head of a Catholic one, which shows, sir, your own good sense; for what is a difference of religion, when people do what they ought to do? Nothing but the name. I trust, sir, we shall meet in a better place than this—both Protestant and Catholic'

"'I am happy, sir,' says the Squire, 'to hear such principles from a man who I thought was bound to hould different opinions.'

"'Ah, sir!' says the friar, 'you little know who you're talking to, if you think so. I happened to be collecting a taste of oats, with the permission of my friend Doctor Corrigan here, for I'm but a poor friar, sir, and dropped in *by mere accident*; but, you know the hospitality of our country, Squire; and that's enough—go they would not allow me, and I was mintioning to this young gintleman, your son, how we collected the oats, and he insisted on my calling— a generous, noble child! I hope, sir, you have got proper instructors for him?'

"'Yes,' said the Squire; 'I'm taking care of that point.'

"What do you think, sir, but he insists on my calling over to-morrow, that he may give me his share of oats, as I told him that I was a friar, and that he was a little parishioner of mine: but I added, that that wasn't right of him, without his papa's consent.'

"'Well, sir,' says the Squire, 'as he has promised, I will support him; so if you'll ride over to-morrow, you shall have a sack of oats—at all events I shall send you a sack in the course of the day.'

"'I humbly thank you, sir,' says Father Rooney and I thank my noble little parishioner for his generosity to the poor old friar—God mark you to grace, my dear; and wherever you go, take the ould man's blessing along with you.'

"They then bid us good-night, and we rose and saw them to the door.

"Father Corrigan now appeared to be getting sleepy. While this was going on, I looked about me, but couldn't see Mary. The tailor was just beginning to get a little hearty once more. Supper waa talked of, but there was no one that could ate anything; even the friar, was against it. The clergy now got their horses, the friar laving his oats behind him; for we promised to send them home, and something more along with them the next day. Father James was roused up, but could hardly stir with a *heddick*. Father Corrigan was correct enough; but when the friar got up, he ran a little to the one side, upsetting Sonsy Mary that sat a little beyond him. He then called over my mother-in-law to the dresser, and after some collogin (* whispering) she slipped two fat fowl, that had never been touched, into one of his coat pockets, that was big enough to hould a leg of mutton. My father then called me over and said, 'Shane,' says he, 'hadn't you better slip Father Rooney a bottle or two of that whiskey; there's plenty of it there that wasn't touched, and you won't be a bit the poorer of it, may be, this day twelve months.' I accordingly dropped two bottles of it into the other pocket, so that his Reverence was well balanced any how.

"'Now,' said he, 'before I go, kneel down both of you, till I give you my benediction.'

"We accordingly knelt down, and he gave us his blessing in Latin before he bid us good-night!

"After they went, Mary threw the stocking—all the unmarried folks coming in the dark, to see who it would hit. Bless my sowl, but she was the droll Mary—for what did she do, only put a big brogue of her father's into it, that was near two pounds weight; and who should it hit on the bare sconce, but Billy Cormick, the tailor—who thought he was fairly shot, for it levelled the crathur at once; though that wasn't hard to do any how.

"This was the last ceremony: and Billy was well contintted to get the knock, for you all know, whoever the stocking strikes upon is to be married first. After this, my mother and mother-in-law set them to the dancing—and 'twas themselves that kept it up till long after daylight the next morning—but first they called me into the next room where Mary was; and—and—so ends my wedding; by the same token that I'm as dry as a stick."

"Come, Nancy," says Andy Morrow, "replenish again for us all, with a double measure for Shane Fadh—because he well desarves it."

"Why, Shane," observed Alick, "you must have a terrible memory of your own, or you couldn't tell it all so exact."

"There's not a man in the four provinces has sich a memory," replied Shane. "I never hard that story yet, but I could repate it in fifty years afterwards. I could walk up any town in the kingdom, and let me look at the signs and I would give them to you agin jist exactly as they stood."

Thus ended the account of Shane Fadh's wedding; and, after finishing the porter, they all returned home, with an understanding that they were to meet the next night in the same place.

"The Wedding At Connevoe". From: <u>The Catholic World,</u> Vol. XXXVII, 1883.

The prevalent English or American impression in regard to the characteristics of an Irish country wedding is that it would be a scene of uproarious mirth and rude horse-play, in which the shouting and rioting guests would for the most part get drunk, and which would probably end in a friendly fight. - This impression, like a good many others regarding the Irish people, is derived from the dull slanders of cockney writers who never saw Ireland, and have merely kept up the tradition of the Teagues, that represented the monsters of ignorance and absurdity created by the prejudices of the first English dramatists. Much has been done in later years to banish this absurd and ridiculous caricature, which is about as true to nature as the English admiral in top-boots whom Thackeray saw on the stage of the theatre of the Porte St. Martin ; and the faithful pictures by native writers and the closer observations by visitors have shown that the type of the Irish peasant is not a blundering blockhead whose supreme idea of festivity is that of a drunken riot. But old prejudices are hard to dispel, and it is quite probable that the " Wedding of Ballyporeen " is still taken as a characteristic type of the Irish marriage festival, although any one who knows any thing about the country would discover that it was a vulgar cockney fraud in the first half-dozen lines :

" First, book in hand, came Father Quipes

And the bride's dadda, the baillie, O.

" Father " Quipes " is about as felicitous an appellation as " Lor' Beef" in the French melodrama, and the "baillie " is a functionary of the Goosedubs and not of Kilballyowen. But the whole ballad is beneath contempt, and as false as it is vulgar and dull ; nor would it be worth mention, except, as has been said, its spirit is so often taken as the characteristic of an Irish country wedding.

It may be said that there has been of late years a diminution in the joviality manifested at Irish weddings, as in many others of the ancient customs of the people, produced by the change in manners and by the cloud of misfortune that has darkened down upon the land since the famine years, and that half a century ago they would be much less subdued and quiet than they are to-day. This is quite true ; and however authentic 1883 for its time was the picture of the prolonged festivity, with its accompaniments of racing for the bottle and other extravagant features, given by Carleton in his sketch of Shane Fadh's Wedding, it would be almost impossible to find its counterpart in modern life. But at no time were there any such scenes of drunkenness and rioting as caricatured by English writers and accepted as national characteristics. An Irish country wedding contains much that is peculiar, but little or nothing that is extravagant, and its peculiar characteristics are simply the national or local habits and participants, and the dialect and humor of the people.

One day, during a visit to the doctor in charge of a dispensary district in the west of Ire land, I had been sitting in the surgery during the hours for the attendance of patients able to come to the office for their relief, and had been deeply moved and interested in the cases of real want and suffering, as well as amused by some of the imaginary complaints of the most unheard-of and complicated disorders, that were presented with a wealth of lamentation and eloquence that would have moved the hardest heart, if it had not been apparent that they were ingenious figments intended to procure an order for meal and meat from the relieving officer, or simply from the impulse to get attention and a bottle of medicine, because they were free. Most of the cases, indeed, were only too genuine, in which the patients, whose pinched and pallid faces showed that they suffered from want as well as from disease, had come for miles, with weary limbs and feeble steps, from the bed of straw on the earthen floor of some lonely cabin in the mountains, for the relief of pains that were the direct result of their miserable habitations and unhealthy and insufficient food ; and even the impostors had temptation enough in their wretched condition. To treat the genuine sufferers with a real and gentle sympathy and such relief as was possible, and to confound the frauds with a blatherskite blarney as ingenious as their own in its learned and authoritative phraseology, to the effect that their distressing symptoms were merely the exaggerated evidences of robust health, were the easy transitions of the doctor's management, and finally the large number of patients was reduced to one. This was a little, wizened old man with a complexion of a dirty white, either from his distress or from his customary seclusion from the rays of the sun, and apparently, from the appearance of his hands, the cobbler of the village. He approached with his hands locked in front of his apron, and, in response to an inquiry as to his ailment, ejaculated : " O doctor ! the wind of the world is in my stomach." " Well, have you a bottle? I thought not. You never have a bottle except for whiskey. Take a spoonful of this every hour until you feel better; and, mind you, don't eat so much cold cabbage, or you may find yourself turned into a balloon, and the last we see of you is your coat-tails as you are blown on a sou'west gale to America." " Ach, hach ! Long life to your honor, but you're funny with the old man. A spoonful every hour. I'll mind" (anglici, remember). " Be sure you don't break the bottle, or your life will not be worth an hour's purchase. What's the news in Clogher, Mickle?" " Not much, your honor, except the hard times, and sure that's no news. There's a daughter of Long John Rafferty's, Maurya, the second eldest, married to Willy McGrath—whose father has the Connevoe farm—this day ; and it will be a good wedding, for both families has strong ' backs ' " (a large number of relatives). " There, thou second Captain Cook, is a chance to see a genuine Irish wedding. We must go." " Oh ! but will you come, doctor dear? " " To be sure, you supralaprarian vagabond ! " " And will Mister Captain Yankee come, too ? ' " Don't dare to doubt it. And now get out and cure yourself, so that you can be on hand and sing us the '

Cobbler's Lament ' this evening." I had no reason to doubt of the heartiness of my welcome at the gathering, even if I had entered it with no other sesame than that of being an American, however singular it would have appeared in other regions for a stranger to make himself a guest at so peculiar and intimate a family party as that assembled at a wedding ; for the abounding hospitality and kindliness of the people toward a representative of a country which afforded an asylum to so many of their friends had been too often exhibited to leave any room for question. But the doctor was the friend of the family, as of everybody in the district, and was entitled to bring any number of friends with the assurance of a hearty and familiar welcome.

The marriage ceremony had already taken place, as usual, in the forenoon, that portion of the day being called the " bride's day " and presaging from its sunshine or storm the complexion of her married life. Happily, so far as this proverb goes, the promise of Maurya McGrath's felicity had been an unclouded one, which is rare enough in the change able skies of an Irish winter. After tea the jaunting-car was brought around to the halldoor, and, when we had bestowed ourselves comfortably dos-h-dos, the gossoon gave an encouraging " whup " to the mare, and we jolted down the avenue and into the broad highroad. As we passed through the single street of the village of Clogher the moon was rising and shedding a yellow light on the thatched roofs of the contiguous rows of cabins, the blue smoke from whose peat-fires rose softly wreathing upward in the calm evening air. The hospitable light was shining, through the open halfdoor of the hostel over the way, on a diminutive donkey and cart hitched to a ring in the jamb, and the plump figure of " Peggy Margaret," dearest and rosiest of landladies, came to the door at the sound of the wheels to wish us a cheery " good-night." In a moment or two we were past the dark church and its field of white headstones, had rumbled across the stone bridge over the stream, and were swaying along the quiet country road between the hedgerows. It was a warm night in the early winter, and the cattle were lying out in the fields, which were illumined by the mellow moonlight. Here and there twinkled the light of a cabin on the neighboring hillside, or was clearly marked by its white walls against the dark green of the fields. The outline of the distant mountain that dominated the landscape was drawn clear against the sky, and the light of a cabin near the summit shone like a tiny star. Our road lay up a long valley that seemed to shut us in closer and closer and with steeper hills as we proceeded toward its head.

At first the wayfarers were few, but as we approached our destination we passed several parties of young fellows and girls proceeding with chatter and laughter to the wedding, and more than one old man and his vanithee {anglice, old woman) walking with more deliberation and sobriety to the same festival. Every one of them had a kindly response for the hearty salutation of the doctor, and it was apparent that he was an object of general good-will and regard. One belated beggar, known as " Briney with the Bag," who was making the best of the speed that his crippled limbs would permit in order to get a share of the feast, had his anxious heart consoled with a sixpence and an intimation that his approach should be made known, so that his ration might not be stinted. How many miles he had travelled in order to partake of the wedding hospitality was quite uncertain ; but the gentry of the staff and scrip scent such an affair from an incredible distance, and the wedding at a house of , substance which had not a dozen or more of these unbidden but ungrudgingly-received guests would be considered to have something unlucky as well as extraordinary about it. Connevoe farm was at the very head of the valley, which shut it all around with such steep hillsides that it would seem as though its fields could not be pastured by anything but goats or ploughed except with horses whose legs were shorter on one side than the other. That the farmer managed to get good crops from them, however, was apparent in the size and number of the stacks in the " haggard " and the general air of substance and comfort about the house and steading. The house was of stone and substantially built, although low, with its thatched roof newly laid, and other signs of neatness and thrift not always to be seen about the houses of even substantial farmers. How it happened that the tenant was thus able to live in the careless display of comfort was doubtless due to the fortunate accident of a long lease or an exceptionably reasonable landlord. Altogether the establishment looked very snug and cosy in its sheltered nook, and was a welcome contrast to the appearance of hopeless struggle, if not distress, very common among the farming population of the district. The windows and the wide-open door streamed with light, and the number of jaunting-cars in the yard indicated the importance of a portion of the guests. Half a dozen hands were ready to take the bridle of the doctor's mare as we drove up to the door, and there was a general welcome from the people about as we entered the doorway, where the broad and jovial countenance of the farmer met us and our knuckles almost cracked in the heartiness of his grasp.

The lady of the house, just behind, greeted us with hardly less cordiality of welcome, while from behind her skirts ran out the youngest daughter of the family, a chubby lass of five or six, who had made the acquaintance of the doctor before, and, in spite of his cruelty in wounding her arm for vaccination, was deeply enamored of his smiles and his candy. With this young lady in the doctor's arms we were ushered into the low parlor, where the bride and bridegroom sat doing penance in their new clothes and under the burden of their unaccustomed honors, amid their nearest relations and the more substantial portion of the company, who apparently did not quite succeed in feeling the proper degree of unconstraint suitable for the occasion. The company were ranged around the room, in whose centre was a long table bearing the bride-cake and a decanter and glasses, both for ceremonial observance rather than for substantial eating and drinking, but which were by no means to be slighted in wishing good health and prosperity to the happy pair in a sip of negus and in the carrying away a piece of the bride-cake to dream on. The company in the parlor consisted of the relatives of the bride and bridegroom and the well-to-do neighbors, dressed in their best, and a trifle subdued and formal under the influence of the ceremonial occasion, except as the stiffness was invaded by the irrepressible younger fry, who made noisy fun among themselves in spite of the occasional reproving whisper and the restraint of lap or arm. The priest who had performed the ceremony was not present, having been summoned away by other duties, and there was a lack of his cordial influence in setting the neighbors to talk and inciting the cheerful merriment of the occasion. The bride, a comely and rosy girl, and the bridegroom, a stout, healthy young fellow, were silent and embarrassed with the novelty and dignity of their position, and could hardly reply to the occasional good-humored jest at their condition. By far the most notable figure in the room was that of the aged grandmother, apparently so old as to have reached the visible fading of vitality into passive quietude and immobility, who sat in her straw chair on one side of the turf fire and smiled upon the scene with the tranquil aspect of serene old age. Her abundant, snowy hair was crowned with a white lace cap, and her yet beautiful dark eyes illumined a face of tranquil benignity which, although perfectly pale and colorless, was firm in contour and showed none of the wreck of feebleness in its features. She was neatly dressed, with a white handkerchief drawn across her shoulders, and as she sat with her arms folded in her lap she made a beautiful picture of happy old age enjoying the retrospect of memory and yet warmed and comforted by the happiness of the present hour. It was not long before the room was invaded by the volunteer helpers, who had been preparing the wedding-feast in the kitchen, from which potent smells and the steam of abundance had pervaded the house and whetted the appetites of the waiting guests of the scrip and bag outside the door. The table was cleared of its cake and negus, and speedily laid with an abundant supply of boiled mutton, fowls, and pigs' heads, all embedded in masses of white cabbage, with white bread and tea, and every body was invited to fall to by a hearty summons from the head of the house. In the kitchen there was a similar feast going on, with much more noise and clatter of dishes and noggins for the home-brewed beer which took the place of tea in that less aristocratic quarter, and the guests outside were soon supplied with an abundance. It was rather a difficulty to struggle with the abundance with which the hearty hospitality insisted upon piling the plate, and to which it would have been a discourtesy not to do full justice ; but there is an end to all things, even to an Irish wedding-supper, and at last the time came to adjourn to the ball room, which in this instance, as generally, was the barn, which had been duly swept and garnished, the holes in its earthen floor filled with fresh clay and moistened and beaten to give smoothness and solidity. The barns in Ireland are not the large buildings, familiar in the United States, in which the hay and grain are protected from the weather, but merely shelters for the cattle. This one, like the most, was built of rough stones set in earth, with low walls and a thatched roof. Within it was lighted with dozens of candles stuck up against the walls with lumps of clay. At one end on a temporary plat form were a couple of fiddlers and a piper, the two former assiduously tuning their strings and rosining their bows, while the latter, with his bellows under his arm, was squeezing it to a subdued groan or two and fingering his pipes in the preliminary salute of the melody. This piper was a notable performer, one of the last and best of the ancient race of pipers, whose instruments are disappearing before the foreign fiddle and the cockney concertina. He was called " White Phelim," being an albino, and had a deficiency of vision, although it did not amount to the absolute blindness which is the usual badge of his profession. He was famous for his skill over a wide district, and no wedding or merry-making could be considered to have met all its requirements without his attendance, and he was frequently invited to give his performances of the native airs in the drawing-rooms of the gentry. His pipes had been used a generation before him, and the keyholes were worn into deep hollows by the continuous tapping of hardened fingers, and the skin of the bag was patched in many places. They were, however, a set of noble proportions, and, as we had the opportunity of ascertaining, their tone and quality had lost nothing by age, even if they had not been improved like those of a Stradivarius violin. The assemblage in the barn, which included the guests of both parlor and kitchen, filled its proportions to the utmost consistent with giving room for a couple of reel sets, one on each side of the row of posts supporting the roof-tree ; and many of the young ladies were obliged, without any apparent evidence of reluctance, to occupy the laps of the lads, and there was a great deal of laughing over the squeezing and adjustment. The elders " took a draw at the pipe " and passed it around in token of friendship and good- ' will, as they were prepared to approve or to criticise the dancers, and the children snuggled themselves into every vantage-ground of observance. The first dance belongs by right to the bridal couple and their partners, and their places were supplied by a younger brother of the one and a sister of the other. The fiddles supplied the music, the piper's contribution to the entertainment being, as we found, more in the nature of an independent concert, although he did condescend to " put the wind under " some favorite jigs, which were duly honored by the heels of the most accomplished dancers, before the night was over. The first dance was rather a tame affair, the performers being weighted down by the sense of ceremony and the uneasiness of being under the particular gaze of the assembly, and did not reach the proper spirit and energy of an Irish dance ; nor did the fiddlers, although anxious to do their best for the honor of their patrons, reach the full inspiration and vigor which came afterward from elbow-joints limbered by frequent liquid refreshment and the enthusiasm generated when the ball was in full fling. Still, the dancers did not do discredit to their race in the skill and accuracy with which they executed the steps, but there was an evident sense of relief when this decorous opening of the ball was over, and its conclusion gave room for the spirit of more genuine festivity and the dancing that was its own delight. As soon as the dance of ceremony was over there was a speedy filling of the floor by other performers, and the real spirit of the dance began. The fiddlers, having taken a refresher from the ready tumblers of punch that were furnished them, wiped their mouths and commenced to put the life into that most inspiring of tunes, " The Wind that shakes the Barley," and the patter of steps and the lively grace of movement that are natural to every native-born Irishman and Irishwoman to accompany the vivacious notes. The perfection and charm of an Irish girl's dancing has been the admiration of every one who has had the good fortune to see it, and been the theme for many poets and prose writers, native and foreign. It well deserves its praise, and has a distinctive grace peculiarly its own. There are many forms of native and national charm in the dance ; the fiery amativeness of the Spanish woman in the bolero, the languid and sensuous grace of the Italian, the fire of the gipsy, and the meretricious vivacity to be seen in the promiscuous ball-rooms of Paris—all have their admirers and their peculiar types of excellence. But the modesty combined with the hearty spirit of enjoyment, the healthful vigor, the easy precision and natural skill of the Irish girl, under the inspiration of the vigorous and spirited native airs, carry off the palm. Although they may step heavily in the common walk, and their frames and limbs seem almost too robust for light movement, there is scarce one of them who does not move with equal grace and vigor in the dance, and to whom the perfection of precision in accenting the rapid and complicated measure does not seem to be the gift of nature. And when the beauty and grace of budding womanhood, the light and erect carriage of perfect health, the lovely face, the modest eyes and abundant tresses, characteristic of Irish beauty, set off by a neat and ap propriate costume, appear upon the floor, it is a figure long to be remembered. There was more than one such at the wedding at Connevoe. To see one of them with her dress pinned behind to show the gay petticoat, the handkerchief drawn across the shoulders, and the whole trim figure alert with life and vigor, while the feet in the buckled shoes pattered in perfect time, and the rosy cheeks grew rosier still with the exercise, and the eyes sparkled with modest pleasure, was to realize the truth of the portrait of Allingham's " Lovely Mary Donnelly " and to feel that there was no sort of extravagance in the expression that "The music nearly killed itself To listen to her feet," or in the many eloquent metaphors in which Irish swains have confessed the conquering power of beauty in the dance, to the most beautiful and expressive of all, " Dance light, for my heart lies under your feet, love." Nothing but poetry can create the proper apotheosis of the theme, and any humbler inspiration must fail. The floor was not allowed to be monopolized by the younger dancers. The elders took their share with as much vigor and spirit, if not with as much perseverance ; and more than one com fortable dame, the mother of many children, stepped out as gaily and lightly as her daughter amid the smiles and applause of the company. Even venerable old men, who might have been grandfathers, caught the inspiration of their youth and took a turn on the floor with a temporary energy in their action not to be expected from their ordinary rheumatic gait, and sometimes with a skill and variety in their steps that more than rivalled the younger dancers. Such exhibitions always excited a great deal of interest and applause, and were accompanied with frequent exhortations to hold out and dance each other down. The fiddlers were unwearied, only requiring periodical refreshment in a liquid form, which stimulated their activity without injuring their precision, and the fun grew flaming and hearty without becoming boisterous. The doctor had figured on the floor with credit to his assiduous course of study and to the admiration of the assembly, when, instigated, as I believe, by his wicked suggestion, a comely young damsel appeared before me with a courtesy and a smile that would have secured obedience from a graven image. There was nothing for it but to step out, and, desperately swallowing my fears, I did the best I could with such recollections of "hoe-downs" in my youth and such improvisations as necessity compelled, and have reason to believe that I acquitted myself without entire ignominy, although I must admit that the encomium which I received was to be attributed more to good-nature than to merit, and was even unkindly ironical on the part of the doctor. Nevertheless it was something to get rid of the infectious uneasiness in the heels, under the inspiration of the music, by actual exercise, even if I had not felt properly flattered by the compliment. It was not all dancing, however. White Phelim with his pipes was not there for nothing, and, although the enthusiasm of the dance gave no signs of subsidence, he was called upon to take his turn at the entertainment. It was the first time I had heard the Irish pipes in perfection, and although the scene was not altogether congenial to the spirit of some of the finest airs of the melancholy or martial kind, which need the solitude of the lonely rath or the breadth of the broad hillside to have them speak with full power to the heart, their noble strength and the natural interpretation of the music were fully perceptible. The features of the piper were naturally rather heavy and commonplace, and he had somewhat of that dazed and uncertain look which accompanies imperfection of vision ; but when he had taken the seat of honor on the platform vacated by the fiddlers, and blown up his bag with a squeeze or two of his elbow, and his fingers tried the notes of the reed resting on the pad of leather on his knee, his features assumed a vivified and inspired expression, and he doubtless felt the power and command of the accomplished artist. There was a hush upon the company in deference to his dignity or in gratified ex pectation, and, perhaps with a desire to express as strong a con trast as possible to the light flippancy of the dance music, he gave out with strong force and power the finely martial strain of "Brian Boroimhe's March." The magic of the pipes to the sensitive ear is in the complete appropriateness of the instrument to the spirit of the music, the simplicity of the sounds by which the meaning is accented, and the historic associations, which are an actual power in music as in other forms of art. There are some Irish airs which cannot be interpreted with full effect even by the violin, while their spirit is almost completely lost in the artificial sharpness of the pianoforte, and can only be fully expressed by the peculiar melody of the bagpipe, for which they were composed. The drone and the treble, rude as they may seem, are thoroughly adapted to the motive and emphasize the spirit and meaning by their very simplicity. As there are certain martial airs that never reach their full effect and make the " heart-strings dumb," except with the beat of the drum and the shrill accent of the fife, around which the spirit of historic ap propriateness also clings, so in a still stronger way the pipes are necessary for the adequate interpretation of the music which was composed for their peculiar capacities, and which carry with them the power of a moving tradition. I am by no means pre pared to enter into a disquisition upon the antiquity of the Irish bagpipes, but I am confident that many of the old Irish airs, both grave and gay, which are so ancient as to be without knowledge of their origin, were composed for the pipes, and this from their inherent characteristics and prevailing motive. The instrument evidently dominated the audience and commanded an attention which was not given to the violins for themselves. The piper played several airs, favorites of his own or by request, and the whole gamut of Irish melody was evidently at his fingers' ends. The deep spirit of melancholy that pervades the sweetness of some of the Irish airs finds its most appropriate interpretation in the pipes, and not even the wider capacity and more delicate power of the violin can give their essence and effect like the drone and the chanter. But the spirit of the occasion was one of merriment, and after " The old Head of Dennis " and " My Lodging is on the cold Ground," the piper struck up with lively fingers " Miss McLeod's Reel," and in a moment the dancers were in their places " welting it out upon the flure." The exercise was also pretermitted at times for a vocal entertainment. There were several favorite singers in the company, and it would have been improper not to allow their talents an opportunity for display. After the conclusion of a jig there was a knocking for silence, and an admonitory " whish" passed it around. Then a voice was heard soaring up in the indescribable, long-drawn intonation in which the Irish country ballads are sung, and which is at once utterly laughable and lugubrious. The singer was a "jock," whose meaning is precisely as spelled— that is, half a jockey, a sort of rough rider and breaker of gentle men's colts, but not possessing the skill or the genius necessary for the course. This one wore a coarse imitation of the regular jockey garb—a jacket, dirty knee-breeches of corduroy, and leggings—and was evidently a prime favorite with the girls from his impudence and other accomplishments. He had pulled his cap over his eyes, and, fixing his eyes on the wooden noggin half full of beer in his hand, he was " rising " the song to its full key, slightly oscillating his body to the rhythm. There was no air to the song or ballad, except the inimitable melancholy cadence and intonation peculiar to the street ballad, and its substance was the performances of a famous racing mare, " Nancy Till," and her rider, John Clancy. At pauses in the song there were expressions of encouragement and approval, and at the end of the concluding apostrophe " More power to John Clancy and sweet Nancy Till," there was quite an outburst of applause, which the singer received with becoming modesty, and, stealing his arm once more around his partner's waist, he slowly elevated his noggin until its bottom pointed toward the roof-tree. Then the host was persuaded without much entreaty, the false modesty of more fashionable society being entirely alien to the spirit of the occasion, to give his favorite, " The Little Brown Jug," which he sang with a mellow heartiness quite infectious, and in whose jolly chorus everybody joined. Several other ballads followed, and among the singers a little old plough man, with a face of weatherbeaten bloom and merry blue eyes, achieved a great success by his rendering of the " *Drimin dhu dheelish,*" with a comic emphasis of melancholy that would have made his fortune on the variety stage, if he could have been transferred there, but which no imitation could at all equal in its unconscious humor. A stout young woman gave us " The Pretty Girl milking her Cow " in the original Irish, and two charming young girls, sisters, one with a natural soprano and the other with an alto, and an exquisite, untaught harmony and feeling, sang modestly yet bravely a sweetly pathetic ballad whose title I could not learn. I afterward induced one of them to repeat it for a transcript, and, as I have never seen it in print, I venture to give it, although its simple pathos needs the voices that gave it for its full effect: '*

'Twas early spring; the year was warm;
The flowers they bloomed and the birds they sang;
 Not a bird was happier than I
When my loved sailor-boy was nigh. "
The evening star was shining still;
 The twilight peeped o'er the distant hill;
The sailor-boy and I, his bride,
Were walking by the ocean side. "
Scarce six months since we were wed;
 But, ah! how quickly the moments fled.
Since we must part at the dawning day:
The proud bark bears my love away.
" Time's long past. He comes no more

To his weeping friends on the silent shore.
The ship went down in the howling storm,
 The seas engulfed his lifeless form. "
 I wish that I was sleeping, too,
Beneath the waves of the ocean blue,
My soul to God, and my body in the sea,
The broad waves rolling over me."

It was a touch of pathos which the finest art could not reach. When the dancing began again we felt that we had had our full share of the merriment, and did not wait for the throwing of the stocking or the break-up of the festivity, at whatever hour of the night or morning that took place. Much to the discontent of the gossoon, who was in the height of enjoyment, the car was ordered round, and, after our good wishes to the bride and bridegroom, and many warm handshakings, we mounted the car amid a volley of " good-nights " and " safe-homes " ; we took our seats, and in a moment were rolling home on the silent highway, the dewy freshness of the night air blowing gratefully upon our cheeks, and the moon, riding high in cloud-racked sky, illuming the calm fields and solemn hills.

The Accounts of Edward J. Wood, 1869,

THE WEDDING DAY

CHAPTER II. Irish Marriages — Wife-seizing—The Agreement Bottle — Casting Darts—Horsing and Goaling—Changing Wives— Lending Wedding Rings—Scotch Marriages—Gretna Green — Banns Superstition — Unlucky Wedding Days — The Threshold—Money and Shoe throwing—Winning the Kail— Creeling the Bridegroom—The Deasuil—Highland Weddings — Bedding the Bride—Penny Weddings—Wedding Presents — Handfasting—Under the Apron String—St. Andrew and Marriages—Orcadian Marriages—Manx Marriages

 In early times in Ireland no marriage ceremony was performed without the parties consulting the Druidess and her Purin. A certain divination was practised with small stones, which were thrown up and caught on the back of the hand. Upon the success of the cast by the sorceress depended the happiness of the proposed match. The ancient custom of seizing wives and carrying them off by force was practised in Ireland, and even so late as 1767 an instance of this usage occurred in Kilkenny. A desperate lover, with a party of armed men, besieged the house of his rival, and in the contest one of the fathers-in- law was shot dead, and several of the besiegers were mortally wounded. The attacking party was forced to retire without the maiden. Sampson, writing in 1802 of weddings in the mountainous districts of Ireland, says: " However suitable the match, it is but a lame exploit, and even an affront, if the groom does not first run away with the bride. After a few days' carousal among the groom's friends, the weddingers move towards the bride's country, on which occasion not only every relative, but every poor fellow who aspires to be the well-wisher of either party, doth bring with him a bottle of whiskey, or the price of a bottle, to the rendezvous. After this second edition of matrimonial hilarity, the bride and groom proceed quietly to their designed home, and, forgetting all at once their romantic frolic, settle quietly down to the ordinary occupations of life." Piers, in his " Description of West Meath," about 1682, says that in Irish marriages, " especially in those countries where cattle abound, the parents and friends on each side meet on the side of a hill, or, if the weather be cold, in some place of shelter, about midway between both dwellings. If agreement ensue, they drink the agreement bottle, as they call it, which is a bottle of good usquebaugh, and this goes merrily round. For payment of the portion, which is generally a determinate number of cows, little care is taken. The father or next of kin to the bride sends to his neighbours and friends *sub mutuce vicissitudinis obtentu*, and every one gives his cow or heifer, which is all one in the case, and thus the portion is quickly paid. Nevertheless, caution is taken from the bridegroom on the day of delivery for restitution of the cattle, in case the bride die childless within a certain day limited by agreement; and, in this case, every man's own beast is restored. Thus, care is taken that no man shall grow rich by frequent marriages. On the day of bringing home, the bridegroom and his friends ride out and meet the bride and her friends at the place of meeting. Being come near each other, the custom was of old to cast short darts at the company that attended the bride, but at such distance that seldom any hurt ensued. Yet it is not out of the memory of man that the Lord of Hoath on such an occasion lost an eye. This custom of casting darts is now obsolete." The following was an ancient custom in Ireland among the poor people. The country folks settled among themselves that a certain young woman ought to be married, and they also agreed together that a particular young man ought to be her husband. This being determined, on some subsequent Sunday she was "horsed," that is, carried upon the backs of men, whom she had to provide with liquor. After she had been "horsed," a hurling match was played, in which her selected swain joined. If he happened to be the conqueror he married her, but if another man was the victor, she became his wife. These games were not always finished on the "horsing " Sunday, but were continued on two or three subsequent Sundays. The common expression in reference to the match was that the girl was "goaled." In former days marriages were very irregularly performed in Ireland, and the custom of men changing their wives with each other was very common. Separations were frequent and easily effected. The Irish living in the mountains married their daughters at a very early age— generally at twelve or thirteen years. A usual gift from a woman to her betrothed husband was a pair of bracelets made of her own hair. It has been suggested that this, custom arose from a superstition that a lock of hair had a peculiar charm, and also that the gift was a symbol of possession, or, as lawyers say, seizin. In the present century it is not an uncommon event for marriages to be solemnised within the ruined churches of Ireland. The Irish peasantry have a general impression that a marriage without the use of a gold ring is not legal. At a town in the south-east of Ireland a person kept a few gold wedding rings for hire, and when parties who were too poor to purchase a ring of the necessary precious metal were about to be married, they obtained the loan of one, and paid a small fee for the same, the ring being returned to the owner immediately after the ceremony. In some places in Ireland it is common for the same ring to be used for many marriage ceremonies, which ring remains in the custody of the priest. Among the fishermen inhabiting the Claddagh at Galway the wedding rings are of the old clasped-hands pattern, and are heirlooms in the family. They are regularly transferred from the mothers to the daughters who are first married, and from them the rings pass to their descendants. Many of the nuptial rings still worn on the western coast are very old, and show traces of still older design. It was customary in Scotland for marriages to take place when the parties were at a very early age. An Act of Assembly in 1600 endeavoured to stop untimely unions by interdicting men from marrying under the age of fourteen years, and women under the age of twelve years; but there are several recorded instances of marriage in Scotland, in the seventeenth century, by persons at the ages of eleven and thirteen years. There are two forms of marriage in use in this country—one regular, the other irregular. The former is preceded by the publication of banns in the kirk of the parish where one of the parties resides, and the union is afterwards registered in the kirk. The irregular marriage is contracted without any religious or other formalities, and simply by the parties acknowledging themselves to be husband and wife before a witness, or by living together as such permanently. This latter kind of marriage was that performed by the celebrated blacksmith and other persons at Gretna, over the border, who assisted runaway couples into matrimony merely by witnessing their avowal that they were husband and wife. The necessity for witnesses in the case of irregular marriages is exemplified by an argument used in a Scotch court of law; namely, that if two persons came before the thirteen judges of the Session in Scotland, and acknowledged themselves to be husband and wife, and if, before they got downstairs, twelve of the thirteen judges died, the evidence' of the remaining one would not be sufficient to substantiate that marriage. Usually marriages are solemnised in the kirk after publication of banns, and substantially the ceremony is after the manner of the Church of England, with the exception of the use of the ring, which is deemed to be a relic of popery. It certainly is a remnant of paganism, for we find that the sacramental ring witnessed the vows of the rude Celtic races, and rings have frequently been found in cists, and under memorial cairns in Scotland. Such rings, when taken from barrows of female burial, may undoubtedly be regarded as either espousal or wedding pledges. In the kirk at the present time the parties join their right hands and give their mutual consent to marry in the presence of the minister, who delivers prayers. The banns are generally proclaimed before divine service on three successive Sundays, as with us under our Marriage Act; but on payment of an additional fee at the registry couples can be " cried " three times at once on one Sunday. There is a superstition in Scotland that it is unlucky for a woman to attend in the kirk when the banns are " put up." A similar notion obtains in Worcestershire, where it is thought that if a woman were to attend at the church on either of the three Sundays on which her intended wedding is proclaimed, all her offspring would be born deaf and dumb. A sense of modesty perhaps helps to keep this custom alive. The upper classes in Scotland are generally married on Monday, and the middle and lower classes on Tuesday or Friday; but at Forglen, in Banffshire, Friday is accounted an unlucky day for marriage. Another peculiarity with the Scotch people is that they much favour the last day of the year for celebrating marriages. There are more weddings on that day in Scotland than in. any week of the year, except, of course, the week in which that day occurs. The months of January and May are considered to be particularly objectionable for marriages; the superstition as to the latter having been taken from the Romans probably. It is also not proper to have the banns published at the end of one quarter of a year, and to marry at the beginning of the next quarter. At Logierait, in Perthshire, and the neighbourhood, that day of the week upon which the 14th of May fell was deemed to be unlucky all through the remainder of the year, and no person would marry upon it. At Kirkwall and St. Ola it was considered an unhappy omen if a couple were disappointed in getting married on the day which they had fixed for the purpose. In Scotland a bride is generally lifted over the threshold of her new home, a custom which is probably derived from the Romans. The threshold is considered to be a sort of sacred limit, and is the subject of much superstition. It is customary for the mother, or some other near female relative of the bridegroom, to attend at his house to receive the newly-married pair. She meets them at the door with a currant bun, which she breaks over the head of the bride before entering the house. It is considered very unlucky if the bun by mistake should be broken over the head of any person other than the bride. The distribution of money at marriages is still observed in Scotland. About the time when the couple are about to leave the house of the bride's father, either for the wedding trip or the bridegroom's home, the boys and girls of the neighbourhood assemble in front of the house and cry out, " Bell money, bell money!" When the door is opened, the shouts are redoubled, and they do not cease until some one of the wedding party throws a shower of copper and small silver coins among the crowd. The departing bride and bridegroom are generally saluted with a volley of old slippers and shoes, for luck. The Scotch had a superstition about happy and unhappy feet. Thus, at Porglen, it was formerly the custom to wish brides and bridegrooms a happy foot. In some remote districts of Scotland the friends of the bridegroom assemble at his residence, and proceed with him to that of the bride, where a clergyman meets them and performs the marriage ceremony. All then go in procession, preceded by a fiddler, to the future residence of the couple. The young men of the party start off at full speed on foot or horseback, and the one who first reaches the house and announces the wedding is said to have won the broose or kail, and is entitled to salute the bride with a kiss on her arrival. He was formerly also entitled to some refreshment out of the kailpot prepared for the approaching party, a dish of spiced broth, or a cake. On the arrival of the bride a farle of oatcake, that is, a quarter of a circle into which the cake is generally cut, is broken over her head, and she is presented with a pair of tongs, as a symbol of her future right to rule the household. The custom of riding for the kail is referred to in the " Collier's Wedding," by Chicken, in 1764, as follows: " Pour rustic fellows wait the while To kiss the bride at the church-style; Then vig'rous mount their f elter'd steeds, With heavy heels, and clumsy heads; So scourge them going, head and tail— To win what country call the kail." Sampson, writing in 1802, says: "At the Scotch weddings the groom and his party vie with the other youngsters who shall gallop first to the house of the bride. Nor is this feat of gallantry always without danger; for in. every village through which they are expected they are received with shots of pistols and guns. These discharges, intended to honour the parties, sometimes promote their disgrace, if to be tumbled in the dirt on such an occasion can be called a dishonour. At the bride's house is prepared a bowl of broth, to be the reward of the victor in the race, which race is therefore called the running for the brose." The "Courier," of the 16th of January, 1813, in recording a wedding in the preceding month at Mauchline, says: "Immediately after the marriage, four men of the bride's company started for the brose, from Mauchline to Whitehill, a distance of thirteen miles, and when one of them was sure of the prize, a young lady, who had started after they were a quarter of a mile off, outstripped them all, and, notwithstanding the interruption of getting a shoe fastened on her mare at a smithy on the road, she gained the prize, to the astonishment of both parties." Sinclair, writing in 1792, says that at Galston, in Ayrshire, the custom was when a young man wished to pay his addresses to a girl, not for him to go to her father's house and profess his passion, but to go to a public-house; and he having let the landlady into the secret, the girl was sent for. She seldom refused to come under such circumstances, and when she arrived she was entertained with ale and spirits, and the marriage was agreed on. Another custom formerly in use in Scotland was called creeling the bridegroom. On the day after the wedding, when the marriage feast was continued, the bridegroom had a creel or basket filled with stones firmly fastened upon his back ; and with this incumbrance he was compelled to run about the neighbourhood, followed by his friends, who would not allow him to remove it until his wife came after him, and either kissed him or unfastened the creel. This she did in token that she was no longer a maiden; and sometimes it happened that, as the relief depended upon her, the husband had not to run far; but when she was either very bashful or very sportive, he had to carry his load a considerable distance. The custom was very strictly enforced, for the friend who was last creeled had charge of the ceremony, and he was generally anxious that the new bridegroom should not escape. Pennant, in his "Tour in Scotland," relates that among the Highlanders it was the custom for the bride immediately after her marriage to walk round the church alone. In some places all the company after leaving the church walked round it, keeping the walls always upon their right hands. Another custom in the Highlands, and particularly at Logierait, was to unloose every knot about a newly-married couple before the celebration of the ceremony, for fear of barrenness; but the knots were retied before the parties walked round the church. A similar usage as to the unloosing of the knots prevailed in France and elsewhere. The walk round the church was called the Deasuil, and is of Celtic origin. Among the Highlanders great care was taken that dogs did not pass between a couple on their way to be married; and particular attention was paid to leaving the bridegroom's left shoe without a buckle or latchet, in order to prevent the secret influence of witches on the wedding night.

A Highland wedding early in the present century was generally conducted as follows. When a couple of young people had agreed to get married, the nearest relations of both parties met to ratify the contract, which was generally done by the consumption of a quart or two of whiskey, as in Ireland. This proceeding was called the booking. Some Tuesday or Thursday in the growth of the moon was appointed for the celebration of the nuptials. Meanwhile, two trustworthy persons were selected, one being a man, to protect the bride from being stolen, which in olden times most likely she would have been; and the other being a woman, who acted as the bed-chamber custodian on the wedding day. A few days before the wedding the parties, attended by their friends, perambulated the country to invite the guests. On the bridal morning some lady friend was appointed mistress of the ceremonies for the day, and she decked the bride in her best clothes. The bridegroom also was, made as smart as possible, and adorned with wedding favours. Volleys of musketry welcomed the guests to a substantial breakfast, after which the company had a dance. At the proper hour the bride was mounted on horseback behind an experienced rider, and with musketry and bagpipes she proceeded with her friends to the appointed place. The bridegroom and his party followed, and allowed the bride and her friends to enter the meeting-house first. After the nuptial ceremony all the company adjourned to the nearest inn or the house of some relation of the bride, it being considered unlucky for her new home to be the first which she entered after her marriage. All parties then returned to the bridegroom's house, where they were received with gun-shots. At the door the bride was welcomed with a basket of bridal bread and cheese. The couple were then seated at the upper end of a banquet, after which followed dancing and deep drinking. Late at night came the "bedding of the bride," who was put to bed in the presence of all the company. Her left stocking was then flung over the shoulder of some person, and the one upon whom it fell was reckoned to be the individual who would next get married. The bridegroom was then led in and put to bed, and while there he drank the company's health. The festivities lasted all the next day; and this continued mirthful celebration of the affair was called " backing the wedding." A pennie brydal, or penny wedding, was a common event in Scotland in the last century. The expense of the marriage entertainment was defrayed, not by the couple or their friends, but by the guests, all of whom paid something. Sometimes as many as two hundred guests assembled, usually at a tavern, and their contributions often amounted to a good sum, which greatly assisted the couple upon their outset in life. In Aberdeenshire this kind of wedding was called the siller marriage. The penny weddings were in olden times reprobated by respectable people : is leading to disorder and licentiousness; but it was found to be impossible to suppress them. All that could be done was to place restrictions upon the amount allowed to be given, and five shillings was the limit. An act of the General Assembly, in 1645, endeavoured to abolish pennie brydals, without success. The records of the parish which includes the most northern burgh on the mainland of Scotland, show that in the last century those persons who had been fined by the Kirk Session were not entitled to " get the benefit of marriage" until the fines were paid. These fines had been imposed principally for " Sabbath-daye enormities." In 1709 the Session, "considering the great abuses committed by the confluence of people who frequent contracts" (betrothals), appointed " that none contract till they come to the minister, and find caution that there be no dancing or music at the contracts." In 1711 it was enacted that, for the better preservation of the sanctity of the Sabbath, "there be no marriages hereafter upon Monday." Persons "contracted " or publicly betrothed were fined WL Scots by the Session if they afterwards refused to " implement the contract;" and persons intending marriage were, after the change of currency, obliged to " consign" 10s. in the clerk's hands before publication of the banns. It is recorded that the Session " sat upon an elder for going and courting here and there several women," for which he was "sharplie reproved." At Caithness, early in the present century, when a man wished to be married and could not repeat the shorter catechism, the Session required him to produce two " cautioners " to the amount of 121. Scots, that he would acquire it within six months after his marriage. The custom of assembling many persons together, and spending several days in drinking, feasting, and dancing, at weddings, was very common in all parts of Scotland; and usually the greater part of the provisions was provided by the many guests who assembled on the occasions. Douglas's " Virgil" tells us, " There was a custom in the Highlands and north of Scotland, where newly-married persons had no great stock, or others low in their fortune, brought carts and horses with, them to the houses of their relations and friends, and received from them corn, meal, wool, or whatever else they could get." Ramsay's " Poems," in 1721, tell us that it was the custom in Scotland for the friends to assemble at a newly-married couple's house, before they had risen from bed, and to throw presents upon the bedclothes: " As fou's the house cou'd pang, To see the young f ouk or they raise, Gossips came in ding dang, And wi' a BOSS aboon the claiths Ilk ane their gifts down flang." At a village near Glasgow was a little round isolated mount called a Mote, and in recent times it was the custom, after the celebration of a marriage in the neighbourhood, for the wedded pair, with their friends, to assemble and dance on the flat top of the Mote. The penalty for a neglect of this usage was sterility in the couple. In early times the Scottish lairds and barons regulated the marriages of their vassals, and had the right to sleep with the wife of any of them on the first night after marriage. This privilege was in later days waived upon the payment of a sum of money by the husband. " It was said that Eugenius III., king of Scotland, did wickedly ordain that the lord or master should have the first night's lodging with every woman married to his tenant or bondman, which ordinance was afterwards abrogated by King Malcolme III., who ordained that the bridegroom should have the sole use of his own wife, and therefore should pay to the lord a piece of money called Marca." In early times there were few churches on the borders of Scotland, hence a priest used to visit the forlorn regions once a year for the purpose of solemnising marriages and baptisms. This, says Scott, gave rise to a custom called hand-fasting, by which a couple, who were too impatient to wait the arrival of the priest, consented to live as husband and wife in the interim. Each had the privilege, without loss of character, to draw back from the engagement if he or she were not disposed to legitimatise the cohabitation by the rites of the church. But the party retiring was obliged to maintain the issue of the union, if any. This custom of hand-fasting, or hand-fisting, was in use in the last century, when, at an annual fair, the unmarried persons of both sexes chose companions for the ensuing year, with whom they lived until the next fair. If they mutually suited at the end of the twelve months they got married, and if otherwise, they separated. Sinclair, writing at the end of the last century, suggested that as this custom obtained at a place situated near a Roman encampment, possibly it was based upon the Roman marriage by use, by which, if a woman lived with a man for a year without being absent three nights, she became his wife. The hand-fasting kind of marriage contract is said to have been in use among the ancient Danes, who called it hand-festing, and upon which followed the freedom, without the actual ceremony, of marriage. A writer in 1543 says : " Every man lyke- wyse must esteme the parson to whom he is hand-fasted, none otherwyse than for his owne spouse, though as yet it be not done in the church After the hand-fastynge and makyng of the contracte, the churchgoying and weddyng shuld not be differred to longe. . . At the hande- fasting there is made a greate feaste and superfluous bancket, and even the same night are the two hand-fasted personnes brought and layed together, yea, certan wekes afore they go to the chyrch." Brand, writing early in the present century, says that the system of full probation before marriage was practised on Portland Island, and that traces of the hand- fasting system might be found in many parts of England. According to the Scotch law, the marriage of the father and mother legitimatises all children previously born, however old they may be. An old saying is that all children under the mother's girdle or apron-string at the time of her marriage are legitimate. In very early days children born before wedlock used to perform a part in the marriage ceremony, by being placed under the veil or mantle of the bride or the pallium of the altar, in which position they received the nuptial benediction. And instances have occurred in more modern times where premature offspring have been put under their mother's apron, and had the string tied over them during her marriage. In the last century the purchase of silver teaspoons always preceded nuptials in Scotland. They were as much a necessary part of the wedding gear as the household furniture, and they were as regularly bought. The country folks resorted for these spoons to the Parliament Close, in Edinburgh, where all the goldsmiths were located. Sometimes a bridal party in Scotland takes a pleasure sail upon the water, but when they do they always go up the river. It is considered very unlucky to go down the water; and if the party should do so, either the bride, bridegroom, or one of the bridesmaids will be drowned. On the eve of the day of St. Andrew, the patron saint of Scotland, maidens, in pursuance of an old and wide-spread custom, sought to learn what kind of husbands they were to have by praying in these words: "Oh, St. Andrew! cause that I obtain a good pious husband. Tonight show me the figure of the man who will take me to wife." There was an ancient superstition that, in order to ensure good fortune to a bride, it was necessary that she should enter her house under two drawn swords placed in the form of St. Andrew's cross. In certain districts of the Orkneys the people marry only when the moon is growing, believing that the waning moon is fruitless ; a superstition which recalls the words of Theseus in the " Midsummer Night's Dream:" " Chanting faint hymns to the cold fruitless moon." Some couples even wish for a flowing tide at their nuptials. Thursday is also esteemed the luckiest day iu the week for marriage by the.

Orcadians. Possibly this respect for Thor's day is a remnant of Scandinavian paganism. (Vide vol. i. p. 229.) Near the Loch of Stennis, in the Orkneys, are certain standing stones, which are relics of two large circles, called respectively the Circle of the Moon, and the Circle of the Sun. As recently as one hundred years since these two enclosures were made to fulfil a matrimonial duty. A maiden who wished to be married performed alone a circuit round the stones dedicated to the moon, and her intended husband used to do the same in solitude round those devoted to the sun. This ceremony completed, the pair met at the stone of Odin, through the centre of which was a hole of capacious size. They took their stand on either side, joined their hands through the hole, pledged their troth, and thus became husband and wife. At any time afterwards, when the match became mutually irksome, the couple met in the evening in the church of Stennis, each departed through a different door, and thus a divorce was completely effected. In other parts of the Orkneys the contracting parties joined their hands through a perforation or ring in a stone pillar at the ceremony of marriage. In the Scilly Isles marriages were performed without banns or licence. The nuptials were celebrated with dancing and music, and they concluded with the bride's dance at night. In the Isle of Man a superstition prevails that it is very lucky to carry salt in the pocket, therefore the natives always do so when they marry. Train, in his history of this island, says, " On the bridegroom leaving his house it was customary to throw an old shoe after him, and, in like manner, an old shoe after the bride on leaving her home to proceed to church, in order to ensure good luck to each respectively; and if by stratagem either of the bride's shoes could be taken off by any spectator on her way from church, it had to be ransomed by the bridegroom." Waldron, writing of a Manx wedding, says: " They have bridemen and bridesmaids who lead the young couple, as in England, only with this difference, that the former have osier wands in their hands, as an emblem of superiority." The same author tells us that at the marriages of the inhabitants of the Isle of Man they were preceded to church by musicians, " who play all the while before them the tune, The Black and the Grey, and no other is ever used at weddings.' He adds that, " when they arrived at the church yard they walk three times round the church before they enter it." And, in reference to a wedding feast, he says: " Notice is given to all the friends and relations on both sides, though they live ever so far distant. Not one of these, unless detained by sickness, fails coming, and bringing something towards the feast; the nearest of kin, if they are able, commonly contribute the most, so that they have vast quantities of fowls of all sorts ; I have seen a dozen of capons in one platter, and six or eight fat geese in another; sheep and hogs roasted whole, and oxen divided, but into quarters."

-The Wedding Day in all Ages and Countries, Edward J. Wood, 1869, pp. 560-79.

The Account of Archibald M'Sparran

The Irish Legend; Or, M'Donnell, and the Norman De Borgos: A Biographical Tale, Archibald M'Sparran, A.Gross, 1846.

Either good or evil fortune cast me upon your hospitable shore title which I think I may very well use. —At this M'Quillan turned away his head, as if unwilling to hear that part of it. I saw said he, your lovely daughter, and seeing her she caused me to forget my danger, my toils, my parents, kinsmen, and almost my country , if therefore a mistake has happened, and if the honour of my family, which I am certain you will admit, can make amends for it I am at your will, and you have nought to do but command me ; no I say that is not even necessary, for I maun confess that the attachment which has been formed with Aveline M'Quillan has rendered me more happy, than if I were seated in Hollyrood, having the royal diadem of Scotland placed on my brows; 'tis herself alone, and no other object 1 am fond of; but I entreat you in the name of my ancestors, say nothing severe against me, or any thing that would wound my feelings, for language of this kind I am not able to bear, and on the other hand to be angry with you is more than I ever can ; so otherwise you may talk to me as you like.

Such an open avowal softened the heart of M'Quillan, and he did not say any thing more, save some little to them for misconduct, and M'Donnel; with the consent of both, appointed the following week for repeating the ceremony of their nuptials. On this important day the clans were all invited to the castle and in front of the barrack were casks of liquor set forth for the use of the garrison and tenantry or any other that came to Dunluce during that week. The noble family of Clanbuoy were also invited, and all their friends as far as a messenger could ride in one day, so that such a bustle and throng scarcely ever was witnessed on the shores of Dalriadagh before.

The Highlanders were not hindmost to dip deep in the strong Falernian, and after an immersion in this fluid, it seemed to have the power of the waters of Styx, rendering them invulnerable all over. The bagpipes both Irish and Scottish, were all blown up, and the dance on the green before the barrack door never ceased, sometimes two different sets performing at the same time ; 'twas here that the peasantry with their sons and daughters from sincere hearts, showed their attachment to the family of De Borgo and every young Hibernian vied with another in leading out whether to the dance* or rustic sport his *callien dhas,* decked in all the finery that either the season or the village shop could bestow ; and it is not to be doubted but the fire of bright eyes that week subdued more hearts than Sir Coll M'Donnel's.

The marriage was celebrated in the great hall in presence of all the friends of the house of De Borgo, who acknowledged that Aveline on the occasion shone with more than ordinary beauty being arrayed in nearly the same dress which she wore the same night Sir Coll M'Donnel had the happiness of seeing her: and one part of it, that is, the royal necklace, she did not forget to assume on that day.

The venerable chaplain belonging to the family, with all that solemnity which was truly characteristic of his holy function, united them, and imploring a blessing on them and their posterity, with many injunctions regarding their future conduct, and chiefly in bringing up and educating their children, he departed, leaving them to all the hilarity usually attendant on like occasions. As marriages whether of a high or low order are seldom celebrated without murmuring on one side or other, there was a family living at a small distance who were nearly allied to the house of De Borgo, and as they expected to become inheritors of the estates of Dunluce, should the brothers not return, which was doubtful, they shewed much envy and uneasiness at this alliance, not deigning to attend on the day of invitation with other friends and acquaintances who were asked.

Old Daniel M'Quillan shewed himself remarkably happy on

the night of his daughter's nuptials, drank to former cronnies, and
often renewed the stories of his boyish days, till at length a

* Dancing on the green was formerly customary in Ireland, but chiefly on May-eve, when a
branch was cut down, whether of the thorn or birch, the one that was more clothed in verdure
they usually choose, and this being pretty tall was planted in the centre of the village green. A
rural queen was then choosen, and always the prettiest girl in the assembly, having decked her
out with such flowers as the season produced, they left it to her own option to choose a king, and
thls being done, the others taking hands around the May-pole, danced about with the royal pair
in the middle. In my opinion this was the only way of thanking providence for a return of the
season.

retrospective view brought the idea of his scattered children to
his mind, and admitting this sensation he returned to himself
with a sigh.

In Ireland wherever a marriage was heard of, and in such a
family as M'Quillan's, the minstrels and wandering bards came
from all quarters in. search of it, as here an unbounded scope was
given to revelling and Irish conviviality, and although there was
an open door to every stranger, none was so acceptable to them
as the minstrels : nor indeed had the affair of a marriage been
even unpublished in the country was it possible that a traveller
could pass Dunluce ignorant of the scenes that were going forward
within ; for a person was stationed at the outer "gate to
proclaim the event to every passenger, and also to bring all in,
even to the poorest mendicant, so that it is no wonder if in other
countries the name of an Irish wedding has been proverbial : and
to the present day I can well attest the extraordinary efforts made
by the descendants of that hospitable people on the like occasion;
their best rag is clean and on, with the most respectable side out,
the cabin is swept up from front to rear, and a large turf fire
being kindled without regard to the heat of the weather, when
from the farther end of the dwelling the master of the ceremonies
walks forth armed with a bottle in the one hand, and a glass in
the other, and seating himself at the head of the company, if I
may be allowed the expression, like the son of an Irish king, pours
out first to himself a flowing bumper of this strong water of life,
in the juice of which he quaffs the kead a miel a faultie to them
all round, filling out to them as they chance to sit next him, until
all are pretty well: the exercise then commences in leaping,
wrestling, throwing the stone, and frequently boxing, in all
which it is indispensably necessary that the groom be foremost,
otherwise he can never expect to be so dear to his enchanting
fair one.

If straying from the leading subject in local descriptions be a
fault, I have certainly often transgressed, but the matter which
has induced me thus to err being so nearly connected with my
lale, I have considered it only as a fuller explanation of the fact
in question ; and besides this, it saves the interruption of inserting
notes which are often nothing more than a continuation of
the theme.

The marriage festivities being concluded, and the different friends having retired to their places of abode, M'Donnel now began to find himself among the happiest of mankind, possessed as he was of the only treasure that ever gave him the least un easiness—he had nothing to concern his thoughts farther than to make her happy, and as to Aveline her heart never received an impression before she saw Sir Coll M'Donnel.

Like most ladies of that age, she thought she could entertain a tender affection for no other man breathing ; and in regard of a husband, we must suppose she was at the end of her wishes. She now turned her thoughts wholly toward private economy, and with the assistance of her maids and some old women followers of her father's house, was busy every day in laying plans for her approaching family; and nothing was so much longed for at that time as a visit to the islands where she might see her husband's connexions with their families, of whom she had heard so many wonderful tales.

And for Mating....

Under the Couvade: A most peculiar custom that has existed among peoples in various parts of the world is the couvade. This provides that at the time of childbirth, the husband takes to his bed and simulates the pains that the wife actually undergoes. Following the birth of the child, he keeps to his bed and receives all the attentions commonly bestowed upon the mother......

...The couvade has also been described by explorers and missionaries among some of the aborigines of North, Central and South America. It appears in Celtic legend and is bound up by certain elements of witchcraft, with the forceful transference of pain to the father by nurse or midwife, as noted in Scotland and Ireland..."

-From: Strange Customs of Courtship and Marriage, by William J. Fielding, New Home Library, New York.

In Wexford if a couple is said to be "mighty coonagh" if they were going strong or walking out. (Traditional)

Marriage of Widows....

A girl was engaged to a widower at Blessington in Ireland, and the village boys followed her wherever she went serenading her with harsh discordant instruments. This was called a"horning," and was always done in the case of remarriage of widows or widowers.

Marriage Law

Due to popular demand I have included a section on Irish Marriage Law. Please be sure to contact the authorities directly as laws do change. This section will give you an idea of how Ireland and the Province of Northern Ireland regard marriage.

"Until the Eighteenth century, the Marriage law of Ireland was nearly identical with that of England, and followed by nearly the same consequences; that is, marriages were for the most part regular, but irregular marriages and pre-contracts were tolerated, and not infrequent. It was not till 1818 that pre-contracts were deprived of their efficacy; and it was not necessary until 1844 that even marriages celebrated by the established clergy should be protected by forms analogous to those prescribed by the English law as settled in 1823 and 1835. But he distinctive peculiarity of the Irish Marriage Law has long been its sectarian character, that it regulates the conditions of the contract according to religious distinctions. For, while the clergy of the Establishment were permitted to marry persons without any reference to their religious faith, the Roman Catholic clergy were restricted to persons of their own creed; and it was enacted by a well-known statute that "every marriage between a Papist, and any other person who hath been or hath professed him or herself to be a Protestant, at any time within 12 calendar months before the celebration of such marriage, or between two Protestants, by a Popish priest, shall be null and void without any judgment, process, or sentence of law." Roman Catholic priests had, however, full liberty to marry persons of their own faith as they pleased, in any irregular or clandestine way, the discipline of their Church, however, rendering this practice sufficiently uncommon. At the same time the ministers of Protestant Nonconformist congregations were permitted only to marry persons professing Protestant Nonconformity.

In consequence of a marriage solemnized by a Presbyterian clergyman between a person of his own creed and an Episcopal Protestant having been declared null in 1844, the Irish Marriage Law was again reformed. The leading principle of the new code was to transfer to Ireland, in case of marriages in the Established Church, the rules in force in England, with some modifications, to give Irish Protestant Nonconformist ministers power to celebrate marriages as in England, throughout the intervention of civil registrars, and with formalities very analogous-- a peculiar exception being, however, made as to one class of Nonconformist ministers--to imitate the English Law in the cases of marriage without any religious ceremony, and of the marriages of Jews and Quakers, to create a system of general registration for all marriages, but to leave untouched the principles relating to marriages solemnized by the Roman Catholic clergy. Since the disestablishment of the Irish Church, power has been given by Act of Parliament to its Archbishops and Bishops, and to the heads of the different Protestant bodies in Ireland to grant special licenses.

In the News

The Act of the Irish Government giving the rights of marriage is known as- *An tAcht um Pósadh* In 2015 it gave full marriage rights to same sex couples.

-Arbuthnot, Sharon, "The Language of Marriage", In: <u>Marriage and the Irish,</u> Salvador Ryan, Ed., 2019, p. 1.

Marriage Regulations

The Republic of Ireland

The information below is provided for information only and should not be considered to be the law. You should always consult the relevant churches and offices prior to making any plans.

Update 2010

Legal requirements for marriage

- <u>Introduction</u>
- <u>Rules</u>
- <u>Further information</u>

Introduction

Marriage is a legally binding contract that will affect both parties (and, to a certain extent, their children) for all of their lives. There are a number of strict rules and regulations governing marriage. The first set of rules specifies who may and may not marry each other and in what circumstances.

Once you have fulfilled these conditions and are sure that you are entitled to marry, you should consider how you wish to marry. There are <u>several different ways (religious, secular and civil) of solemnising a marriage</u> so that it is legally binding.

Please note that this document deals only with the legal requirements for the capacity to marry. If you are marrying through a religious or secular ceremony, you should discuss their requirements with the celebrant of your marriage.

Rules

For a marriage to be legally valid in Ireland the parties to the marriage must:

- Have the capacity to marry each other

- Freely consent to the marriage. Free consent may be absent if, at the time of the marriage, a person is suffering from intoxication, brain damage, mental disability, mental instability or insanity to the extent that they are not able to understand the implications of marriage. Additionally, if someone agrees to marry because of threats or intimidation, their apparent consent may also be invalid and the marriage may be void.

- Observe the necessary formalities

Capacity to marry

To be legally entitled to marry, both of you must fulfil all of the following requirements at the time the marriage takes place. Both parties must:

- Be over 18 years of age.

- Have given the Registrar 3 months' notification of the marriage (or have a Court Exemption Order if this is not the case) and have been issued by the Registrar with a Marriage Registration Form. A couple whose civil partnership was registered in Ireland do not have to give the 3 months' notice.

- Be either single, widowed, divorced, a former civil partner of a civil partnership that ended through death or dissolution, or have had a civil annulment of a marriage or civil partnership or a valid foreign divorce or dissolution. (If you are marrying your civil partner you do not need to have your civil partnership dissolved before marrying. It will be automatically dissolved when you marry.)

- Have the mental capacity to understand the nature of marriage

- Not be related by blood or marriage to a degree that prohibits you in law from marrying each other. If you are related to your proposed spouse by blood or by marriage, you should contact a solicitor to ensure that you do not fall within the prohibited degree of relationship. (See "Further information" below on prohibited degrees.

If either party doesn't fulfil even one of the above requirements, any subsequent marriage ceremony is legally void.

Age requirement

If you are ordinarily resident in the State, the minimum age at which you may marry is 18 years. This is the case even if you marry outside of Ireland. Even if you are not ordinarily resident in the State, you must be over 18 years of age if you wish to marry someone in Ireland.

There is no requirement for parental consent to a marriage, irrespective of the ages of the parties concerned.

A foreign divorce

Not all foreign divorces are recognised under Irish law. Under the <u>Domicile and Recognition of Foreign Divorces Act 1986</u>, a foreign divorce will only be recognised in Ireland if at least one spouse was *domiciled* in the state that granted the divorce when the proceedings started. You may have to provide good evidence that this was the case and, therefore, that the divorce is valid under Irish law. Under <u>EU Regulation 2201/2003 ("the Brussels II bis")</u> it is the spouse's habitual residence that determines a court's right to grant a divorce.

Where the divorce comes within EU regulations, it is sufficient to confirm that both parties to the divorce were notified of the proceedings and had an opportunity to give evidence to the court which granted the divorce.

Where EU regulations do not apply, certain information as to place of birth, countries of residence and other relevant facts must be supplied on a questionnaire provided by the Registrar. The information is then forwarded to the <u>General Register Office</u>, whose consent is required before the marriage ceremony can take place.

If the General Registrar is of the opinion that the foreign divorce is valid, then the new marriage can go ahead. If not, you can provide additional information to prove validity or else you can apply for a hearing before the Circuit Court. The Court's decision on the validity of a foreign divorce in Irish law is final and binding, although you may appeal to a higher court. If the Court decides that your foreign divorce is not binding, your only option if you wish to remarry in Ireland may be to get a divorce under Irish law.

A foreign dissolution

If a legal dissolution of a civil partnership is granted outside Ireland, it will be recognised under Irish law if the Minister of Justice and Equality has made an order recognising the appropriate class of legal relationship in the country in which the dissolution was granted.

Further information

Prohibited degrees of relationship

Prohibitions apply to marriage between certain people related by blood or marriage. A couple who fall within the prohibited degrees of relationship cannot marry. These prohibitions are based on:

- Consanguinity – blood relationship including half blood (half blood means having one parent in common, for example, a half-brother)

- Affinity – relationship by marriage

The prohibited degrees apply to a wide range of family relationships and include marital and non-marital offspring.

An adopted child is within the prohibited degrees in relation to its natural family and adoptive parents. However, it would appear an adopted child can marry the child of their adoptive parents.

You can marry your deceased spouse's sister or brother. This also applies if your marriage ends due to a divorce rather than a death.

There is no legal restriction on the marriage of first cousins.

Consanguinity – blood relationships

You may not marry your:

- Grandmother or grandfather

- Mother or father

- Father's sister (aunt) or brother (uncle)

- Mother's sister (aunt) or brother (uncle)

- Sister or brother

- Father's daughter (half sister) or son (half brother)

- Mother's daughter (half sister) or son (half brother)

- Daughter or son

- Son's daughter (granddaughter) or son (grandson)

- Daughter's daughter (granddaughter) or son (grandson)

- Brother's daughter (niece) or son (nephew)

- Sister's daughter (niece) or son (nephew)

Affinity – relationship by marriage

You may not marry your:

- Grandfather's or grandmother's spouse (step-grandmother or step-grandfather)

- Father's or mother's spouse (stepmother or stepfather)
- Father's brother's or sister's spouse
- Mother's brother's or sister's spouse
- Son's or daughter's spouse
- Son's son's or daughter's spouse
- Daughter's son's or daughter's spouse
- Brother's son's or daughter's spouse
- Sister's son's or daughter's spouse
- Spouse's grandmother (grandmother-in-law) or grandfather (grandfather-in-law)
- Spouse's mother (mother-in-law) or father (father-in-law)
- Spouse's father's sister or brother
- Spouse's mother's sister or brother
- Spouse's daughter (stepdaughter) or son (stepson)
- Spouse's son's son or daughter
- Spouse's daughter's son or daughter
- Spouse's brother's son or daughter
- Spouse's sister's son or daughter

---

https://www.citizensinformation.ie/en/birth_family_relationships/getting_married/legal_prerequisites_for_marriage.html

The Regulations 1996

" For a marriage to be valid, the proper formalities must be observed. The man and woman must be free to marry, they must have the required physical and psychological ability to "enter into and sustain a normal marital relationship" and they must marry voluntarily. There are however other legal restrictions relating to age, notice, residency or other requirements. If these are not followed the marriage may be invalidated.

As of August 1st 1996, both individuals involved in a civil marriage must be over 18 years old on the marriage date. They also have to have given three month's prior written notification to the registrar for the district in which the marriage is to be held . The courts may exempt a couple from either of these requirements, but a written exemption order must be obtained before the event.

The Family Law Act 1995, was passed requiring the minimum age of marriage to be 18. Until 1972, the minimum age for marriage in the Republic was 14 years for boys and 12 years for girls. In 1972, the Government raised the minimum marriage age to 16 for boys and girls. At that time anyone between the ages of 16 and 21 had to have their parents' written consent to marry. One third of all applications for exemption to this regulation were refused.

Under the 1995 Act, any marriage - whether civil or religious - must comply with the new rules to be registered as a valid civil marriage. Anyone who knows that they have performed a marriage ceremony for a person under 18 is guilty of a criminal offence and is therefore liable to a fine of £500 if convicted. The law applies to all marriages within the Republic of Ireland. This age requirement
also applies to marriages in any other country if any of the parties is normally resident in Ireland.

If a 17-year-old who normally lives in the Republic goes to Northern Ireland to marry, the marriage will not be valid in the Republic. It will be valid in Northern Ireland.

There are two ways to give the notification of marriage:

1 The parties may write jointly or separately to the (Catholic or civil)
registrar of the district in which they will be married. They must provide the names and addresses of both parties, along with the name of the church or place where the ceremony will take place, the date of the marriage and must confirm the age of the couple or
2.a form may be provided to the local (both parties must sign it.) If both parties write jointly, they must both sign the letter. If they write separately, the required three months runs from the receipt of the last letter received. A full three months is required (so, for example, April 1st prior to July 1st.)

The registrar will then issue an official receipt of the application, which must be
provided on request to the person solemnising the marriage.

The Circuit Family Court or the High Court can grant an
exemption from the age limits or the notification requirements if both applicants
show that the exemption is justified by serious reasons. It must be in the couple's best interests.

If a parish straddles the border with Northern Ireland, for example, a priest who marries a 17-year-old parishioner in her own parish church would - depending on which side of the border she lived - could be contracting a valid and lawful marriage blessed by the British State or committing a criminal offence subject to a £500 fine in the Republic!

Catholic priests have claimed that the new law interferes with the Catholic
Church's right to marry, and some priests do not see themselves able to follow
the new civil statutes.
The Diocese of Cashel and Emly gave its priests new guidelines on marriages. Priests have been asked to comply with the statutory three month's notice to the registrars. But if a court exemption could not be obtained for couples wishing to marry immediately, the priests should proceed with the marriage, which was still valid for the Catholic Church. Later the couple would give three months' notice and have a civil ceremony at a register office.

By the end of August 1996, at least 10 couples had been married in the eyes of the Catholic Church, but not in the eyes of the State, because they had not given the required three months' notice to civil registrars.

If those couples do not marry in a later civil ceremony, they remain unmarried under the law. This condition restricts both parties from making use of the marital legislation which applies only to married couples. For example any children will be "non-marital" and they will not be able to divorce because, under the law, they are not married. The 1995 Act lets either party to ask the court to rule such a marriage null and void - it may not be necessary to make an application.

The new regulations extend existing regulations. Anyone who marries by violating these regulations will find that their marriage is invalid.There are two formalities of marriage which relate to the two elements of marriage: civil and religious. For civil registration of a marriage, Catholics are treated differently from non-Catholics. Their marriages are registered under a different Act.

Catholics who pursue a Catholic Church marriage are required to provide a notice of their intended marriage to the local Superintendent Registrar of Births, Deaths and (Catholic) Marriages. (divorced Catholics must apply to the Registrar General.) Non-Catholics and anyone planning only a civil ceremony must notify their local district registrar. Districts are often/not always - divided by county.

Every marriage has to take place in a registered, certified or licensed building.. Churches of the Church of Ireland are licensed for marriage by the Bishops of the Church.
The Minister for Health must approve. Presbyterian churches are certified by the Ministers with a registeration by the Registrar General. Anyone who wishes to be married in, for example, a hotel or other ordinary building , must have a civil ceremony in an approved building first and then proceed to a ceremony or blessing in the unapproved building . For Baptists holding a wedding in a Baptist chapel, at least one of the parties must be a Baptist.

The following religions have buildings which have been registered for marriages: :the Catholic Church, Church of Ireland, Presbyterians, Methodists, Baptists, Greek Orthodox, Jews, Congregationalists, Quakers, Lutherans, Christian Brethren, Jehovah's Witnesses and Mormons. Mosques are not registered for marriages because of the issue of polygamy.

Marriage regulations are of six distinct types:

    1.Catholics,
    2.Church of Ireland,
    3.Presbyterian,
    4.other Christians,
    5.Quakers and Jews and
    6.civil marriages.

As follows:

Catholic

Episcopal dispensation: Catholic Church rules apply.

Publication of banns and special licence: don't apply.

Ordinary licence requires seven days' notice. One party must be a Catholic. The licence is granted by the Bishop's representative. A copy must be sent to the parish where the couple attend church.

Registrar's certificate: in a mixed marriage. The registrar must be notified in the local district, and be given name, age, status and home parish. This is entered into the marriage notice book.

Copies are then sent to both the churches they attend and the parish/church where they will marry.

A certificate will be issued 21 days later which the couple provide to the priest who will be marrying them.

Solemnisation must be in public, in a Catholic church, with two witnesses present . The husband has to register the marriage. In People v Ballins 1964, the judge said: "The decree of the Council of Trent has been promulgated in Ireland. It is applicable to and controls Roman Catholic marriages and makes the presence of two witnesses necessary. A ceremony not in accordance with its requirements as to the presence of a priest and two witnesses is null and void."

Church of Ireland

Episcopal dispensation, registrar's certificate and registrar's licence: not applicable.

Publication by banns: done according to the Canons of the Church of Ireland and the rubrics of the Prayerbook. Both individuals must be Protestant Episcopalians.

Ordinary licence: issued by the Bishop's representatives, in specific districts. The licence authorises marriage in any church licensed in the Licenser's district. At least one individual must be a Protestant Episcopalian. One party must reside in the district of the church where the marriage is to take place for seven days before the granting of the licence and seven days after.

One of the parties must appear before the Licenser and swear an oath or declaration that there are no lawful impediments to the marriage. The Licenser then enters a copy of the notice in the marriage notice book, which is open to the public at all reasonable times. The cleric must register the marriage.

Special licence: by any Church of Ireland Bishop. One individual must be a Protestant Episcopalian. The individuals involved must provide a certificate, signed by the couple, two witnesses and the clergyman, to the district registrar. The husband has three days to register the marriage.

Solemnisation: done publicly, in the presence of a cleric and two witnesses.

Presbyterians

Episcopal dispensation, registrar's certificate and registrar's licence:not applicable.

Publication of banns: not used .

Ordinary license: one or both participants must be members of the Presbyterian Church in Ireland. Special appointed ministers grant the license. The licence takes seven days to be issued and each of the parties must obtain a certificate from their own Minister stating that a notice of the marriage was entered in the congregation book. One of the participants must have resided in the Presbytery for 15 days. An affirmation must be given that there are no impediments. The Minister must enter the information in a notice book open at all reasonable times. A caveat to the issue of the licence may be entered by anyone. The marriage must take place within one month of the date of the licence (or three months of the entry in the marriage notice book), otherwise, both notice and licence are void. Disputes regarding the caveat will cause it to be referred to the Presbytery of the Church.

Special licence: by the Moderator of the General Assembly. One individual must be a member of the Presbyterian Church in Ireland. A solemn declaration has to be completed before a Justice of the Peace or a Peace Commissioner. A certificate of marriage by special licence has to be sent to the Registrar General within three days of the marriage, it must be complete, and signed by the parties, two witnesses and the officiating minister.

Solemnisation: in public, in the presence of a minister and two or more witnesses. The marriage has to be registered and entered in duplicate in the marriage registration book provided by the Registrar General. The husband has to register the marriage.

Other Christians

Episcopal dispensation, publication of banns and ordinary licence: not applicable.

Special licence: the appropriate officials (the Secretary of the Methodist Conference, the Chairman of the Congregational Union and the Moderator of the Reformed Presbyterian Church) may issue special licences.

Registrar's certificate: As for Catholics. Notice must be given by the parties with all relevant details. The registrar files the notice. He then sends a copy to the place of worship and enters it in the marriage notice book which is open to the public at all reasonable times. The certificate is issued in 21 days.

Registrar's licence: the registrar must be informed, in writing that there are no impediments to the marriage. Requirements concerning age, parental consent and residency will apply. The registrar files the notice, enters it in the marriage notice book, notifies the church attended and the church in which the couple intend to be married. The licence is issued in seven days and must be given to the cleric celebrating the marriage.

Solemnisation: in registered building in the presence of the relevant minister of religion of the creed of one or both parties and in the presence of two or more witnesses.
The cleric must to register the marriage in duplicate.

Quakers and Jews

Episcopal dispensation, publication of banns, registrar's licence and ordinary licence: not applicable.

Special licence: both parties have to be Jews or Quakers.
The Chief Rabbi or the Clerk to the yearly meeting issues the license.

Registrar's certificate: as for "other Christians". The certificate is conveyed to the synagogue or meeting house. One individual must be a non-Jew or non Quaker.
Solemnisation: In keeping with the beliefs of the parties, in public and with presence of two or more witnesses. The person performing the ceremony must register the marriage.

Civil ceremony

Episcopal dispensation, publication of banns, ordinary licence and special licence: not applicable.

Registrar's certificate: both individuals must establish seven full days' residence in their districts (Ireland or the UK) and must be married in one of those districts. They must then give notice to their respective district registrars. The ceremony may occur 22 days later.

Registrar's licence: When both parties are resident in a district, they can marry eight days after providing notice. If both are not resident in a district, one party must establish 15 full days' residence in the district and then give notice to the appropriate registrar. The other party can give notice the same day if they are resident in the same district for seven full days (or by giving notice to their local registrar, if resident in Ireland). The marriage may occur eight days later.

(Notice and notification must be fulfilled before the marriage can take place. "Notice" means attending at the office of the registrar for him to fill in a notice of marriage form and declaration of freedom to marry form . Residency requirements must be complied with in advance. "Notification", which relates to the written three months' notice required under the 1995 Act, is not connected with residency.)

If either party to a civil marriage has been divorced, a certified copy of the decree absolute is required at the time of serving notice, along with the birth certificates of both parties to the divorce if they were born outside the State. The divorced individual must complete two questionnaires, one concerning each of the divorced spouses. The documents are examined by the Registrar General. This may take five weeks or more.

The Domicile and Recognition of Foreign Divorces Act 1986 recognises UK divorces where either spouse is resident in the UK. Where neither spouse is resident in Ireland, a foreign divorce will be recognized here if it is recognized in the country where either spouse is resident.

Where either party is widowed, a certified copy of the death certificate and the original marriage certificate must be produced at the time of serving notice.

If either party has been granted a civil nullity decree, a certified copy of the decree must be provided when serving notice, with a statement from the Supreme Court that no appeal has been lodged against the decree. If a couple aged 18 or over wish to marry outside Ireland they must ensure that they fulfil the legal requirements of marriage in that country. The embassy for the particular country should be able to provide details and explain how to qualify for a marriage certificate. Such marriages are not registered in Ireland.

Some countries require a certificate of freedom to marry. The certificate states that a person has not already been married, can be obtained from the Department of Foreign Affairs in Dublin.

If a couple wish to know if their own marriage conformed with the necessary formalities, they should contact a family law solicitor."

Source: (Note: you should be sure to consult the relevant churches and offices prior to making any plans in the event that this information has changed.)

--Divorce in Ireland, The options, the issues and the law. By Kieron Wood BL and Paul O'Shea, Solr.

Below you will find the currently required by form FLA. 1.98. Please note that this is provided as an example only. Be sure to inquire concerning the requirements in effect when you begin your own process. The information below is not the form itself but simply a listing of instructions provided and information called for by the form.

Notification to the Registrar of Marriages of Intention to Marry

Form FLA.1.98 - To be used to give notification to the appropriate Registrar of a person's intention to marry.

General Information: Each party to a marriage taking place in the State either by civil or religious ceremony, must give at least three months written notification to the Registrar of Marriages for the District in which the marriage is to take place. Certain exempmtions may apply where either the High Court or Circuit Family Court has granted its approval in accordance with Section 33 of the Family Law Act 1995. An explanatory leaflet detailing the requirements in civil law to have a valid marriage registered is available from the Registrar. The three months notification person commences on the date the notification of intention to marry is received by the relevant Registrar and the onus is on the parties to an intended marriage to ensure that the notification is received in time and is valid in all other respects. Please see overleaf for details of how to locate the registrar to whom this form should be returned and a note on how to complete this form.

Please use block capitals. Notifications must be signed by both parties to the intended marriage. All sections should be completed in as much detail as possible. Please enter the details of the first party to the proposed marriage in this section:
Surname(s):
Forename(s):
Home Address:
Have you been previously married :

(If YES, full details should be supplied incle. Divorce Decrees/Orders)

Daytime Telephone No.:

Date of Birth (or confirmation of being over eighteen years of age):

Please enter the details of the second party to the proposed marriage in this section:

Surname(s):

Forename(s):

Home Address:

Have you been previously married :

(If YES, full details should be supplied incle. Divorce Decrees/Orders)

Daytime Telephone No.:

Date of Birth (or confirmation of being over eighteen years of age):

General Details:

Please state the exact pace and/or building in which the proposed marriage will be solemnised

Please state the (religious) denomination or form of the proposed ceremony:

Please state the (religious) denomination or form of the proposed ceremony:

Please state the name of the person solemnising the marriage, if known:

Date of intended marriage:

Signature of both parties (to the proposed marriage):

1.

2.

Notifications should NOT be sent to the General Register Office

They should be sent to the Registrar of Marriages for the district in which the marriage will take place.

DO NOT WRITE BELOW THIS LINE OR IN THE BOX BELOW

FOR OFFICE USE ONLY:

Date of Receipt:

District:

Received By:

Rank (Int/Asst Registrar):

Receipt issued by:

Date Receipt Issued:

MNB Ref No.:

Notes:

Instructions provided with the form are as follows:

"To avoid any difficulty in the processing of your notification of intention to marry it is very important that the form be completed as clearly and accurately as possible. Block capitals should be used in the body of the form with original signatures entered at the foot of the document.

The home address entered on the form should be that at which you are ordinarily resident as this is the address to which the Official Receipt of Marriage Notification will be sent. The daytime telephone number entered will be used to contact you in a case where matters need to be clarified. Please do not enter your home telephone number is you will not be at that number during office hours (09:00 to 17:00 hours). You should answer "Yes" to the question "Have you been previously married?" if it is the case that you underwent a previous marriage ceremony in this country or abroad.

In the "General Details" section it is important that the location and form of the proposed ceremony be given, as this will be used to determine precisely who the appropriate Registrar of Marriages is.

In regard to the date of intended marriage it is not absolutely necessary that an exact date is given but where an exact date is known it should be quoted. If an exact date is not quoted it should be noted that at least threes months notification of an intention to marry must be given.

General Note: If you require further information please contact your local Health Board Registration Office, Civil Registrar's Office (as above) or the General Registrar Office, Joyce House, 8-11 Lombard Street East, Dublin 2, Tel. 01-635 4000."
+++

The Law in Northern Ireland

There is still one interesting benefit from being married in the Province of Northern Ireland. You will have to be married there to receive a congratulatory telegram on certain wedding anniversaries from the Queen!

Here are the rules:

"Telegrams can be sent for 60th, 65th, 70th and every following year. If you have the marriage
  certificate you can apply direct to Buckingham Palace on +44 (171) 930-4832. Alternatively,
  the ONS will verify the details and notify Buckingham Palace for you for a charge of £3.00.
  The couple must be re-nominated for each and every occasion. It is not automatic. You can
  get more information on +44 (151) 471-4256."-Source: The Office for National Statistics, part of the Government Statistical Service.
Legal Requirements in Northern Ireland

Forbidden Marriages

You can not be related to each other in a way that is forbidden by Law

Minimum Age

16 years old. In Northern Ireland the written consent of
the parents or Guardians is required for persons who are younger than 18 years old and have not been married before . If under 18 a birth certificate must be provided. All persons should produce such evidence.

Sex
In Northern Ireland (All the United Kingdom) one partner must have
been born a male and the other a female.

Update: In 2013, Parliament passed the Marriage (Same Sex Couples) Act, introducing same-sex marriage in England and Wales. Same-sex weddings began on 29 March 2014; however, the provisions of the Act came into force on 13 March 2014, meaning that existing same-sex marriages performed abroad were recognised from that date. Prior to this, Civil partnerships had been made available to same-sex couples in the United Kingdom in 2005, granting rights and responsibilities virtually identical to civil marriage.

Consent

Both partners must be acting by their own free will.

Sound Mind

Both must be of sound mind so that they can understand the nature of the marriage contract.

Second and subsequent marriages

There is no limit to the number of marriages you can enter into. You must, however, be free to do so. You must be widowed or have been divorced and granted a decree absolute. Evidence is required : i.e. original death certificate or divorce absolute certificate with the original court seal.(no photocopies)

Procedure

Northern Ireland was excluded from the Marrige Act 1994 which allowed venues authorised by the local authority to be used for weddings. A civil ceremony which must take place in a register office of the district where one of the partners lives.

Civil marriages may only take place in a register office. Religious marriages may take place anywhere at the discretion of the authorised person.

The legal formalities

Notice of marriage-Registrar's Licence

If both partners live in the same registrar's district, one must have lived there for at least fifteen days and the other for at least seven days prior to notice.. If the partners live in different districts then notice must be given to both districts and both partners must have lived in their respective districts for more than fifteen days notice.

The Registrar will issue the licence seven clear days after notice is received.

Registrar's Certificate

The residency requirements are seven days for both partners in the case of both partners living in same district or in different districts.

The certificate will be issued after 21 clear days.

So now with everything organized, and legal, you can move on to select the day.

Irish Weddings In The News

At the Hammersmith Police Court, on Tuesday, Eliza Welsh, ironer, living in Bolton-mews, Notting Hill, was charged with being drunk and assaulting her father and mother. The prisoner said her sister was married on Sunday, and they had been drunk ever since. Mr. Ingham said Irish wedding without a broken head was very extraordinary thing. was astonished that so little mischief had been done. He committed the prisoner for fourteen days, with bard labour. The prisoner, on being removed, fell on her knees and swore to do one of the witnesses an injury.

-Illustrated London News – Saturday, October 17,1874.

Rutland Echo and Leicestershire Advertiser - Saturday July 5, 1884

IRISH MARRIAGE. A case illustrative of the Irish custom of marrying and giving in marriage in the rural districts has been heard at the Limerick quarter sessions. The action was brought to recover £31 lent by the plaintiff, Mrs. Mary Ryan, of Templederry, John Hayes, tenant farmer, resident Doon. defendant, with two other men, went to Mrs. Ryan's house one evening in March, and an agreement was entered into that Hayes should marry Mrs. Ryan's daughter. He was to get marriage portion, £35O and the marriage was to take place the following Sunday. the interim defendant obtained £50 to cover the marriage expenses, but when the guests were assembled for the wedding breakfast, and the expected bridegroom arrived, he quarrelled about the money, broke off the match, and left suddenly. The guests, notwithstanding Forced with the wedding breakfast. A few days later married another girl with a larger marriage portion. He returned £19 of the £50 lent him by the plaintiff, and as a set-off to the claim now before the court put in a bill for entertainment which he gave for Mrs. Ryan, and some other statements of expenditure alleged to have been incurred on her behalf. The items included £13 for 16 of whisky and 30s. for port and sherry consumed by the ladies at the entertainment The last item was £10 "clergyman for intended marriage." which, as he stated, did not take place, anticipated, with the plaintiffs daughter. Judgment for the full amount was given.

Commentary

1748 From an Article on " Manners. Temperament, and Genius of the Irish Peasantry. ",1748, /. 462. P. 59, <u>The Gentleman's Magazine Library</u>: Manners and George Laurence Gomme, Frank Alexander Milne, A. C. Bickley, Alice Bertha Gomme Eliot Stock, 1883, <u>Great Britain.</u>

When a matrimonial compact is agreed, a cow and two sheep are generally the portion of the maid, and a little hut and potato-garden all the riches of the man. Here the woman always retains her maiden name, and never assumes the surname of her husband, as is generally practised in other countries. I have been informed, that this is owing to marrying for a custom they had among them, in ancient times, of year only, at the expiration of which term the couple might lawfully part, and engage elsewhere, unless they should choose to renew their agreement, for another year. By this means if there were any mutual liking at meeting both parties were continually upon their guard to oblige, each other that an inclination of living together might still be kept alive on both sides. The woman, therefore, who might, if she choose it have a new husband every year of her life always retained her, own name, because to assume, a new one with every husband would create infinite confusion; and this custom, as to the name, is retained to this very day. At their wedding they make, a great feast, which is the only time of their lives perhaps that they ever taste meat or any kind of strong liquors. Upon these occasions one of the sheep at least is consumed, and the other is sold to purchase a barrel of a kind of very bad ale, which, in their language, they call sheebeen, and a corn spirit called usquebaugh, or whisky, which very much resembles, in its taste and qualities, the worst London gin. With this they for once carouse, and make merry with their friends. They are, indeed, at all times great pretenders to hospitality as far as their abilities will permit; whence they have this universal custom amongst them, that in all kinds of weather when they sit down to their miserable meal, they constantly throw their doors open, as it were, to invite all strangers to partake of their repast ; and, in the midst of their poverty, cheerful content so constantly supplies the want of other enjoyments that I verily believe they are the happiest people in the world. In the very midst of very hard labour, and what, to an Englishman, would seem pinching necessity, they are ever cheerful and gay, continually telling stories, while at their work, of the ancient giants of that country, or some such simple tales, or singing songs in their own language; and in the wildness of their notes I have often found something irregularly charming. As these are always of their own composition I concluded they must be quite original in their thought and manner, as the authors are all illiterate, and understand no other language whence they might borrow either ; and I imagined it would be no bad way to discover the genius as well as abilities of the people, by observing what turn they gave their poetical performances. I was in some measure able to get over the difficulty of understanding their language by the assistance of a young lady, who understood the Irish tongue perfectly well; and she has often sung and translated for me some of their most popular ballads. The subject of these is always love ; and they seem to understand poetry to be designed for no other purpose than to stir up that passion in the mind. As you are a man of curiosity, I shall present you with one attempted in rhime as a specimen of their manner, which take as follows:

A translation of an Irish song beginning, " *Maville slane g'un oughth chegh khune*, etc."

" Blest were the days when in the lonely shade,
Join'd hand in hand my love and I have stray'd,
Where apple blossoms scent the fragrant air
I've snatched soft kisses from the wanton fair.

"Then did the feather'd choir in songs rejoice,
How soft the cuckoo tun'd her soothing voice,
The gentle thrush with pride display'd his throat,
Vying in sweetness with the blackbird's note.
" But now, my love, how wretched am I made,
My health exhausted and my bloom decay'd I
Pensive I roam the solitary grove—
The grove delights not—for I miss my love.
" Once more sweet maid, together let us stray,
And in soft dalliance waste the fleeting day ;
Through hazel groves, where clust'ring nuts invite,
And blushing apples charm the tempted sight.
"In awful charms secure, my lovely maid
May trust with me her beauty in the shade.
Oh ! how with sick'ning fond desire I pine,
Tiil my heart's wish, till you, my love, are mine.
" Hence with these virgin fears, this cold delay,
Let love advise, take courage and away.
Your confident swain for ever shall be true,
O'er all the plain, shall ne'er love" one, but you."

-The Garter at Marriage Ceremonies.
[1748,/. 462.]

CHAPTER XXVII.
Irish Marriage Customs.

" The face of my love has the changeful light
That gladdens the sparkling sky of Spring;
The voice of my love is a strange delight,
As when birds in the May-time sing.
Oh, hope of my heart! oh, light of my life!
Oh, come to me, darling, with peace and rest 1
Oh, come like the summer, my own sweet wife,
To your home in my longing breast! "

-Charles Gavan Duffy.

INNOCENT merriment is practised at Irish weddings, but nothing indecorous is ever allowed. The bride's and bridegroom's stockings were sometimes removed and thrown amongst young unmarried people. It was prognosticated, that the persons on whose heads those articles fell should be married before that day twelve months. So late as the seventeenth century, before an Irish marriage took place—especially in districts where cattle abounded—the parents and friends of the parties a boutto contract were accustomed to meet on a hill-side, or, if the weather were cold, at some sheltered place, midway between the dwellings of those parties concerned. If satisfactory arrangements ensued, the people there assembled drank what was called the bottle of agreement, which was filled with strong *usquebagh*, or whiskey. The marriage portion was usually a determinate number of kine. It was borrowed by the bride's father, or next kinsman, and from friends or neighbours in many cases. Each one of the latter lent a cow or heifer, security being taken from the bridegroom on the day of delivery, that the cattle he received should be restored, if his bride died childless within a certain time, limited by this agreement. In snch case, every man's own beast was restored. Thus, care was taken that, by frequent marriages, no man should grow over-rich. On the day of bringing home his bride, the bridegroom and his friends rode out and met herself and friends at the place of treaty. It was customary, in approaching each other, to cast darts at the bride's company; yet at such a distance, that no hurt usually ensued. Still, it was known to people living in 1682, that Lord Howth lost an eye on a similar occasion. In Sampson's Statistical Survey of Londonderry, published A.D. 1802, we are told, how at Scotch descendants' weddings in that county, the groom and his party view with other youngsters, as to the man who shall gallop first to the bride's house. Nor is this feat of gallantry always accomplished without danger; for in every village through which they are expected, pistol and gun shots salute them. These discharges are intended to honour the parties, yet often promote their disgrace, if a tumble in the dirt may be so considered. At the bride's house a bowl of broth is prepared. This was intended to be a reward for the victor in the race. Hence it was called running for the brose. In the mountainous districts especially, Irish wedding customs were somewhat different. There the groom must first affect to run away with the bride. After a few days' carousal among the groom's friends, the weddingers moved towards the bride's country. On this occasion, not only every relative, but every well-wisher of either party brought with him a bottle of whiskey, or the price of a bottle, to the place of rendezvous. After this hilarious matrimonial escapade, the bride and groom proceeded quietly to their designed home. Then, forgetting frolic, they settled down to their ordinary occupations .On coming home to her new dwelling, the bride must not step over the bridegroom's threshold, but her nearest relations were required to lift her over it, by locking their hands together, when she sat over their arms and leant upon their shoulders. This practice of carrying is known as the play of *sliougli-sollaghawn,* so merrily enjoyed by little Irish boys and girls, who thus coach one another about, until tired with the performance .Lavish expenditure and unlimited hospitality characterized marriage feasts in the olden time, especially within the houses of respectable farmers. Family pride and a natural generosity of disposition urged them to indulge in outlay for creature comforts and other objects, admittedly in excess of what the occasion and their social position naturally warranted. Not alone near and distant relations of the contracting parties, but even all neighbours and acquaintances, considered suitable as guests, had invitations to a real Irish country wedding. The humblest labourers or cottiers, and also strolling mendicants, who assembled there, were bountifully regaled; while to each comer was vouchsafed, not only the word, but also the look and feeling of welcome.

-O'Hanlon, John, <u>Irish folk Lore: traditions and superstitions of the country, with humorous tales </u>1870.

In Conclusion

I would like to wish each and every one of you the best of weddings. I am confident that you will be able to weave the scattered and fragmented flowers of the Irish traditions into a wonderful, memorable and exciting event. Feel free to let us know what you discover in your research and how we may have helped you.

And now a traditional Prayer:

Peace

The peace of God the peace of men
The peace of Columba kindly
Mary mild the loving
Christ king of tenderness
The peace of Christ king of tenderness
Be upon each window, upon each door
Upon each hole that lets in light
Upon the four corners of my house
Upon the four corners of my bed
Upon the four corners of my bed
Upon each thing my eye takes in
Upon each thing my mouth takes in
Upon my body that is of earth,
And upon my soul that came from on high
Upon my body that is of earth

And upon my soul that came from on high

Sources

Throughout the text you will find sources directly associated with relevant passages. Sources cited are from original works. Text published in later editions also cited may differ from the original. Here are a few other sources, which you may find to be useful.

Balard, Linda May, Forgetting Frolic.1998.

O'Clery, Michael, Compiler The Martyrology of Donegal, A Calendar of the Saints of Ireland, Trans. John O`Donovan,Dublin,The Irish Archaeological and Celtic Society, 1864.(Original:,Donegal, April 19,1630)

Connolly , Sean *"Cogitosus's Life of St. Brigit Content and Value",* in: The Journal of the Royal Society of Antiquaries of Ireland, ed: Michael Herity, Volume 117, 1987,pp.5-26.

Delaney, Mary Murray, Of Irish Ways, Dillon,1973.

Kelly, Eamon, In My Father's Time.Mercier,1976.

Ó Conchúr, Siocháin, The Man from Cape Clear, Mercier,1975.

Andersen, Jorgen,The Witch on the Wall, 1977.

Bluett, Anthony Ireland In Love. Mercier,1995.

Bluett, Anthony Things Irish., Mercier,1994.

Colum, Padraic, Treasury of Irish Folklore, Random House,1982.

Danaher, Kevin In Ireland Long Ago, Mercier,1964.

The Year in Ireland, Mercier,1972.

Delaney, Mary, Murray, Of Irish Ways.,Dillon,1973.

J.E. Doherty and D.J. Hickey, A Chronology of Irish History Since 1500, Barnes and Noble,1990

Evans, E. Estyn, Irish Folkways,1957.

Fielding, William J.Strange Customs of Courtship and Marriage.Omnigraphics,1995.

Guest, Edith, M.,"Irish Sheela-na-gigs", in: Journal of the Royal Society of Antiquaries of Ireland,1936,Vol.LXVI,pp. 107-129.

Haggerty, Briget, The Traditional Irish Wedding, Irish Books and Media, Minneapolis, 1999.

Hall, Mr. And Mrs. S.C. Ireland, Its Scenery and Character, London, 1841-3.

Joyce. P.W, English as We Speak it in Ireland.,Wolfhoiund Press.,1988.

Killen, John, <u>The Irish Christmas Book.</u>Blackstaff,1985.
McGuir, Kim, <u>The Irish Wedding Book</u>, Wolfehound Press 1994.
Morrissey, Martin <u>Land of My Cradle Days.</u>O'Brien,1990.
O'Farrell, Padric, <u>How The Irish Speak English,</u> Mercier,1993.
O'Lochlainn, Colm, <u>Irish Street Ballads.,</u> Three Candles, Dublin,1952.
Power, Patrick C. <u>Sex and Marriage in Ancient Ireland.,</u>Mercier,1993.
Ross, Anne. <u>Everyday Life of the Pagan Celts.,</u>Carousel, 1972.
Ryan, Salvadore, <u>Marriage and the Irish,2019.</u>

In this research work we have done our best to cite sources accurately. It it is found that a source is not accurately cited please bring this new information to the attention of the publisher and corrections will be made.

And a Grand Time will be Had by All!!!!!!!

Notes:

TheWake Which Knows No Sleeping

Being a Guide to Traditional Irish Funerary Customs

By Conrad Jay Bladey
Hutman Productions Linthicum, Maryland

Dedication

THE FAMINE IN IRELAND.— FUNERAL AT SKIBBEREEN.— FROM A SKETCH BY MR. H. SMITH, CORK.

At wake or at fair I would twirl my shillelagh, and trip through the jigs with my brogues bound with straw, and all the pretty maidens from the village, the valley Loved the bold Phelim Brady, the bard of Armagh.

We dedicate this publication to all those who by reason of the horrors of emigration, famine, the persecution by the Church or by other lapses of Irish Tradition have been denied a proper Irish send off on their journey to the next shore. It is hoped that this work might eliminate all other occurrences of this sad fate. (Image: Funeral at Skibbereen, Henry Smyth, Illustrated London News, January 30, 1847

The Bard of Armagh (Trad.)

Then Maggie O'Connor took up the job
"O Biddy," says she, "You're wrong, I'm sure"
Biddy she gave her a belt in the gob
And left her sprawlin' on the floor.
And then the war did soon engage
'Twas woman to woman and man to man,
Shillelagh law was all the rage
And a row and a ruction soon began. –

Finnegan's Wake (Trad)

Whack fol the darn O, dance to your partner
Whirl the floor, your trotters shake;
Wasn't it the truth I told you!
Lots of fun at Finnegan's wake

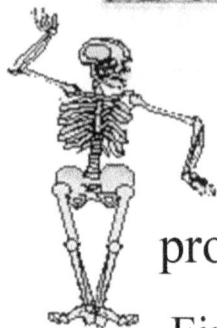

The Irish Wake or tórramn

An easy death and fine funeral-Irish proverb

First: Condolences in Irish Gaelic

Ar dheis Dé go raibh a anam

May he rest in peace

Ar dheis Dé go raibh a hanam

May she rest in peace

Ar dheis Dé go raibh a n-anamacha

May they rest in peace

The words uasal (noble) or dílis (faithful) can be used to provide emphasis:

Ar dheis Dé go raibh a anam uasal + dílis

Ar dheis Dé go raibh a hanam uasal + dílis

Ar dheis Dé go raibh a n-anamacha uaisle + dílse

Ní maith liom do thrioblóid

Sorry for your loss

Mo chomhbhrón ort agus ar do mhuintir

My condolences to you and your family

For a letter:

Comhbhrón ó chroí ort as bás do chéile ionúin agus is trua liom + linn do chás. Tá tú inár gcuid smaointe agus paidreacha. Ar dheis Dé go raibh a (h)anam uasal

Sincere condolences to you on the death of your beloved husband + wife and I am + we are sorry for your loss. You are in our thoughts and prayers. My (s)he rest in peace.

Glac mo chomhbhrón + ár gcomhbhrón le do thoil as chailliúint do mháthair + d'athair + do dheirfiúr + do dheartháir + do mhac + d'iníon.

Please accept my + our condolences for the loss of your mother + father + sister + brother + son + daughter

Why be Concerned with Wakes?

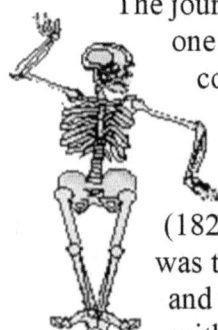

The journey that begins with death (In Irish Gaelic: *Bás*) has many travelers, only one of whom is the corpse itself. Death leaves a strange sort of void in a community. It is a wound like vortex through the living into which a life has disappeared. At the wake the people join hands across that deep chasm traveling round and round as far as they can travel with the corpse until the wound is repaired, sealed with the cold clay of mother earth. Croker (1824) noted that "to be decently put in the earth, along with his own people" was the most fervent and important wish of the Irish peasant. The social bond, and that with the locality, continued beyond the grave. Poor people would do without vital necessities when death approached so that the expenses of a proper wake or tórramh and funeral could be met. The wake must be "credible".

How can any people hope to survive without the healing power of the wake? How can one live on when one knows that there will not be the guarantee of the traditional send-off which has eased countless past generations as they have traveled, albeit for a short while, with death and with the corpses which have appeared amongst them? The Irish thought of purgatory as a "vast and dreary, extent, strewed with sharp stones and abounding in thorns and brambles"- (Croker 1824). The journey itself required careful preparation and equipment. Today we consider the traditional Irish wake so that we might all re-discover how to journey safely with death, prepare ourselves, and knit up our community literally caught within its wake.

Sure now.... that's well and good, but don't you know that life without a grand Irish wake now and then is as dry and tough as an old dry bone? - To be sure a good party now and again is a grand thing. It's not hard to tell all the grief we would suffer if it were not for death!

The Satchel; a repository of wit, whimsies, and what-not, Volume 9,1831.

To this we could possibly add: It's just the right thing to do!

The ancient traditions of the wake, some say, link Celtic Irish culture with that of India via common Indo-European Roots. These customs worked on many levels and served the living in many ways. To truly understand the Wake one must first understand the nature of the Celtic world. It is important to recognize that the divisions between life and death are not distant ones. The dead seem to reside just around the corner. At certain times of the year (Samhain around Halloween) the boundaries go away completely and the dead can wander around with us. For the Irish the transition from life to death is announced by signs. One must watch and prepare. So let us start at the beginning-

"The Banshee," T.Crofton Croker, Fairy Legends and Traditions of Ireland, 1862.

How do we know who will die and when a person will die?

When to expect Death?

The Irish believed that death brought you to a new dimension which was both nearby and accessible. It was strongly believed that the time of death could be known and determined. When should you expect death? Divinations are a reflection of the fierce loyalty of the Irish to their ancient ways which took precedence in many households over the views of the established church(es).

The force of the seasons was recognized as a way to explain and understand that which the church cloaked in mystery. Life therefore was looked upon with a unity with death, which could be understood and "lived with" on a daily basis. Divination allowed cultural adaptation to extend into the next dimension. Read on to find out when to expect death and in some cases how to avoid it......

"A child born on May Day.....almost certainly would die young"- p.125

"Among others it is thought right and proper to have the threshold swept clean on May-Eve. Ashes are then lightly sprinkled over it, and in the morning the print of a foot is looked for. If it turns inward a marriage is certain, but if outward then a death will happen in the family before the year is out."- p. 125.

"Any creature, human or animal, born at Whitsuntide was fated to cause death or die a violent death. A foal so born would throw a rider or trample or kick him to death, a bull or cow would gore somebody. Even smaller creatures were fated to cause evil; a dog or cat or fowl might bite or claw an infant. A human so born would either murder somebody or himself be hanged or killed in some startling fashion, or, worse than all, possess an evil eye of unusual virulence. Such a person or animal was known as a *cingciseach)* (*Cingcis*=Pentecost), and while still young must be protected from its fate by taking steps to nullify the evil. The simple way to do this was to make the infant creature kill something."

"People, especially children, who are ill, are more likely to die at this time (Whitsuntide) than at others. In parts of the midlands a counter-charm to this evil influence was the laying of a green sod on the head of the sufferer..." (a mimicry of burial) -p. 129.

215

A Traditional Samhain Divination:

"Four plates are put down on a table, water was poured into one, a ring placed on another, some clay in the third, and in the fourth was placed either some straw, salt, or meal.

 A person would then be blindfolded and led up to the table, and into whichever plate he or she placed their hand, so would their future turn out.

The water signified migration, the ring marriage, the clay death, and the fourth plate prosperity.

 On re-arranging the order of the plates, others would be blindfolded and led up in like manner."- p.219

R.H. Buchanan in Ulster Folklife, 1963, p.68 records another Samhain divination:

"Another Mourne custom, which was also recorded a century ago in Armagh, was to fill a thimble full of salt and turn it upside-down on a plate. "Stacks" of salt were made for each person, left overnight, and if one should have fallen by next morning the person so named would die within the next twelve months." p. 227 .

Mason in Parochial Survey notes that in Shruel parish, County Longford:

"A large candle is lighted on Christmas night, laid on a table, and suffered to burn out. If it should happen, by any means to be extinguished; or more particularly if it should (as has sometimes happened) go out without without visible cause, the untoward circumstance would be considered a prognostic of the death of the head of the family"- p.238.

On Epiphany....."over a considerable area of north Leinster, east Connaught and south Ulster...."

"A round cake of sufficient size was made of dough, or of ashes or clay, or even of dried cow dung, and in it were put standing a number of small candles, rushlights or bogdeal splinters, one for each member of the family, and each named for a particular individual. In the evening, when the whole household was assembled, these were lighted and then carefully observed and the order in which they burned out or quenched was regarded as an indication of the order in which the persons represented by them would die. This was usually a solemn occasion, and no levity was permitted. Indeed, this ceremony was almost always carried out during the family's evening devotions, when the saying of the rosary or other prayers...." was interrupted when one of the burning objects went out with a person saying the name of the person will be "the next to go."- p. 264.

- Danaher, Kevin. The Year in Ireland, Mercier Press, Irish Books and Media, Minneapolis, 1972.

"I recall with utter clarity
the first great shock of my life.
A scream came from the cottage
next door.
I rushed into the room,
as familiar as my own home. The
Larkin kids, Conor, Liam and Brigid
all hovered about the alcove in which
a mattress of bog fir bedded old Kilty.
They stood in gape-mouthed awe.
I stole up next to Conor.
"Grandfar is dead," he said.
Their ma, Finola, who was eight months
pregnant, knelt with her head pressed
against the old man's heart. It was my
very first sight of a dead person. He
was a waxy, bony specimen lying there
with his open mouth showing no teeth
at all and his glazed eyes staring up at
me and me staring back until I felt my
own ready to pop out of their sockets.... "

-Uris, Leon, Trinity, Doubleday, N.Y, 1976.
p. 5.

So now you have this dead body in the house......what do you do?

For those wondering- Yes! There is a way to attend to the preparation of the body
and burial at home in the traditional way without involving those outside the family.
A good source book is: The Natural Death Handbook, The Natural Death Center,
ISBN 0-948826-37-1. This is not essential, but it should be regarded as an
acceptable option. It would of course be traditional.

Ancient Origins- Cannibalism?

Cannibalism in Archeology
A Handbook of Irish pre-Christian Antiquities
W. G. WOOD -MARTIN, M.R.I. A.
1895

Accounts given by the Pagan writers, Strabo, Solinus, and
Diodorus, of the alleged cannibalism, of, the Irish or Scoti , of their
 day, are corroborated by St. Jerome,* who lived from about A.D. 346
 to 420. The passage occurs in a controversial book which was written
by him. Some writers, shocked at the narrative,
try to evade its force by observing that Caesar and
other standard authorities make no similar statement;
but if Jerome's assertion is false we might fairly expect
to find it contradicted at the time. Dr. O'Connor, in
his Prolegomena, goes so far as to assert that this Father
of the Church is, in the case in question, not worthy
of belief, as ' he was a man of very fervid temper.'
Classic writers are vituperated for reciting such tales,
whilst Keating, the 'father of apocryphal Irish history,'
who recounts a revolting story of a young girl being
reared upon human flesh, is allowed to escape criticism.
In the fourth century the principal food of the Irish
seems to have been ' stirabout,' and Jerome apparently

* Bede writes as follows :— 'In course of time, Britain, besides
the Britons and Picts, received a third nation, the Scoti, who,
issuing from Hibernia, under the leadership of Reuda, secured
for themselves, either by friendship or by the sword, settlements
among the Picts, which they still possess.'

had as great abhorrence of stirabout as of heresy, for
when writing against Celestine and his disciple,
Albinus, he describes the one as 'overfatted with
Scottish stirabout, and the other (Albinus), a huge and
corpulent dog—one better qualified to argue with
kicks than words— for he derives his origin from the
Scotic nation in the neighbourhood of Britain.' The
saint seems not to love the Scots {i.e. Irish) ; and in his
eyes the eating of stirabout is on a par with the eating
of human flesh, which he describes in emphatic
words :— ' What shall I say of other nations, when I
myself, when a youth in Gaul, saw the Scoti, a race of
Britons, eating human flesh ; and, although in the

forests they have herds of swine and herds of cattle,
they are accustomed *nates feminarumque papilas
abscindere solitos, et eas solas delicias arbitrari ? ' *
In connexion with this subject, O'Donovan remarks
that an ancient Scholiast on Horace's Odes states
that the ancient Britons used to eat their guests ; but
that Baxter asserts, in his edition of Horace, that the
poet meant not the Britons, but the Irish ! His words
may be translated thus: 'This is rather to be under
stood of the Irish. St. Jerome writes that he himself
saw two Scoti in Gaul feeding on a human carcase.' The

* W. K. , Sullivan, , in , his introduction , to O'Curry's Manners
and Customs of the Anc1ent Irish, , xxxi., , states that , St. , Jerome,
mentions , the, Atticotti in connexion with , the , Scoti, , and , alter
quoting the above passage, goes on to say that ' the picture which,
he , (Jerome) , paints of , both, was very unfavourable, , and , based,
rather on prejudice than accurate information." , A few of Jerome's
descriptions of the , ' manners and , customs ' of the Scoti are here
given :— ' *Scotorum , natio , uxores , proprias , non , habet, , et , quasi
Platonis , politiam , legerit , et , Catonis , sectetur , exemplum, , nulla
apud eos conjux propria est sed ut quique libitum , fuerit, , pecu, , , , ,
dum more lasciviunt.'*—*Advers. fovinian. , ' Scotorum et Atlieo, , , , , ,
torum ritu ac de Republica Platonis promiscuas uxores communes
liberos habeant.'*—*Epist. ad Acean,*

designation Scoti here means Irishmen, and on this subject
some curious mistakes have been made. Dempster,
when writing his *Menologium Sanctorum Seotorum*, took for
granted that Scotia meant Scotland, and he transferred
to Caledonia the greater part of that noble army of
confessors, of whom Erin is justly proud. For this
theft, Dempster was given the nickname of *Hagiokleptes*,
or the ' Saint-stealer.' Champion, who was in Ireland
in the year 1567,' remarks O'Donovan, 'and who was
not a rabid calumniator of the Irish people, like
Hanmer, and even Spenser, believes that the Pagan
Irish used to eat human flesh.'

Thomas Dinely, in a curious Journal which he kept
during his tour through Ireland in the reign of Charles
II., after describing the burial customs of the Irish,
concludes thus:— 'Several nations in Asia thought
themselves guilty of great impiety should they lett
their dead become a repast for worms. They outvyed the doctrines
of Pythagoras, ye philosopher maintaining only a Metempsychosis,
or the transmigration of soules into other bodies; whereas
these put in practice the transmigration of dead bodies into living ones.'
Thus, regarded from one point of view, the ancient

Scoti or Irish were possessed of no virtues, and from
the other point of view were innocent of crime ; yet,
when the past is examined, without regard to legendary
tales or poetic fiction, we find them, even in their
most brilliant periods, ' advanced only to an imperfect
civilization, a state which exhibits the most striking
instances both of the virtues and vices of humanity.'
If passages from classical authorities be compared
with statements made by modern travellers with regard
to the various customs at present prevalent amongst
savage tribes, they bear a great family likeness ; and in
trying to form a picture of human life in ages when
there were no written records, we ought carefully to
utilize the analogies presented by modern savage
custom for the elucidation of superstitions to be traced
in ignorant popular thought. Viewed thus, we find
many of these superstitions no longer inexplicable, for
we succeed very often in finding their probable parentage
in ancient thoughts and customs. 'Many of the passages'
—in classic writers—' have been bitterly assailed, but
it will do no good at this juncture to turn to questions
of textual criticism, or to evidences of personal credence
attachable to each authority. These will be met by
other methods : first, by the fact that the early recorded
evidences of savage practices in Britain do not supply
any customs but what are to be paralleled among
savage practices elsewhere than in Britain or in
Europe'; and it is impossible to believe that human
ingenuity could be charged with such a phenomenon,
as the invention, by different authors, at different times,
of customs which have their analogies in actual life.
Herodotus, when describing the customs of the Massagetae,

states that as soon as anyone amongst them ' becomes infirm
through age, his assembled relations
put him to death, boiling, along with the body, the
flesh of sheep and other animals, upon which they
feast, esteeming universally this mode of death the
happiest. Of those who die from any disease they
never eat ; they bury them in the earth and esteem
their fate a matter to be lamented, because they have
not lived to be sacrificed.'

Ideas and practices of races in a very low state of
culture are likely to present a faithful picture of the
ideas and practices of the earliest races of mankind.
When investigating the sites of Swiss lake-dwellings,
the anthropologist turns for parallels to Borneo and to
Africa; and when investigating the alleged cannibalism
of the primitive inhabitants of Erin, we necessarily
turn to the most uncultured savage races at present in
existence. The accusation of cannibalism relates not
alone to the Irish, but to all the ancient people of the
British Isles, though, at the time of the Roman conquest of England,
its inhabitants appear to have already
passed beyond the stage in which they eat their dead.
When the curtain is first raised on the drama of human
life in Ireland, the aborigines were entirely in the
hunting stage ; they lived on the produce of the chase,
and the spoils of the inland waters, and of the sea.
Later, the ox and the sheep became common, demonstrating
that the pastoral stage had been reached ; then
domesticated animals, such as the pig and goat, appear;
agriculture is the last and final stage in the ascending
scale of human amelioration. Of the primary inhabitants of Erin
we know comparatively nothing; they
may have been a remote swarm of colonists of cognate
race with the Lapps, Finns, and Esquimaux. The
scanty remains of their civilization are found in rude
sepulchral cists, in caves, and in water-drifts. Canon
Greenwell, who has explored numerous barrows of the
Stone Age—particularly in the north of England—is of
opinion that many of the human remains which they
enclose exhibited indications of cannibalism having
keen practised; whilst another specialist sees no difficulty in acceding
to the conclusions thus arrived at.
Human sacrifices and cannibalism, however, may have
co-existed with a comparatively high state of civilization, and
numerous instances could be mentioned—
the Aztecs in America will suffice. The practice of

eating the dead, whether captives in war or deceased
relatives, is known to have been prevalent in ancient
times, and modern travellers give so many instances
that only two typical cases need be cited, the one in
Africa—brought lately into such notoriety by Stanley—
and the description of a funeral feast amongst the
aborigines in Queensland, Australia, in the year 1870.
In the latter case we are told that a native having died, a
funeral procession was formed, and before a large fire, the
body was most scientifically skinned, and then dissevered

limb from limb, and the flesh removed from the bones.
After a short absence from the scene, the spectator
found, upon his unexpected return, great lumps of meat
roasting on the fire, and he significantly adds that the
natives ' abstain from kangaroo for several weeks after
a death.' In ancient days it was a belief that the physical, mental,
and moral qualities of man were intimately
connected with his food, and it is still a very prevalent
idea, amongst tribes in a rude state, that the flesh of
certain animals imparts, to some extent, the characteristics of
the animals eaten —the flesh of the fiercer beasts
of prey imparts courage; that of the stag, speed ; that
of the dove, gentleness; that of the hare,* timidity, for
which reason, perhaps, the ancient Irish did not eat the
hare. This train of thought may have tempted the

* It may appear strange that a creature apparently so
insignificant should have been looked on as sacred, but such appears the
case with the hare; at any rate in the British Isles, for we have the
authority of Caesar that, at the time of his invasion of Albion, the
hare was ' tabooed! ' They think it unlawful,' Caesar states, " to
feed upon hares, pullets, or , geese ; yet they breed sheep up for
their diversion and pleasure.', Even in the present day there is, in
some localities, a, ' prejudice against eating hares, on the part of,
some of the people, lest they should turn out, to be witches. A
cry would, however, be heard, I was informed, when the hare was,
being cut up.'—Folk Lore, vol. iv., p. 184.

aborigines of Erin to eat their deceased relatives, so
that the warlike or other virtues of the dead might be
perpetuated in the family or tribe. The custom still
surviving in Irish wakes of partaking of food, drink,
salt, tobacco,* or snuff in the presence of the dead
seems to be an amended form of the older practice of
consuming such things after they had been placed upon,
or near, the corpse or coffin ; and this in turn seems to
imply that the recipients would have transmitted to
them some of the qualities of the dead man ; so that
we have in the modern usage a fragmentary relic of the
savage feast, when the real body of the deceased was
consumed.

F W. K. Sullivan, in his introduction to O'Curry's
Manners and Customs of the Ancient Irish (cccxxiii.),
remarks that ' many of the funeral rites necessarily
survived the substitution of the burial of the body for

* Not many years ago there were deposited with the corpse, in
a graveyard in, Devonshire ' a candle, a penny and a bottle of
wine.' The candle was to give the deceased light, the money was,
to pay his fare over the river, of death, and the wine was to sustain,

him on his journey. It is alleged that, in the town of Cheltenham, a pipe and tobacco-pouch are sometimes placed in a coffin with the dead body.— The Cheltonian, No. clxxxv., 2nd Series, p. 39.

t Denis H. Kelly, writing to O'Donovan in 1858, thus describes this portion of the ceremony at an, Irish wake:— 'The corpse of, the deceased is dressed in clean white grave-clothes; , is stretched, on its back on a table in the middle of the room, with f1ve or seven candles round it, according to the circumstances of the defunct, the larger number being used by the wealthier. On the breast of the corpse is placed a plate of tobacco, cut in short lengths, and a plate of snuff. There are seats ranged round the wall, and immediately behind the corpse's head is the place of honour, where sit the chief mourners and most respected guests, amongst whom, in wakes of the higher classes, sits the keener.'
At these wakes certain games, or sports, were in use, which appear to have been essentially of Pagan origin, and of such a character that, although at first tolerated, yet, in more civilized days, they were suppressed.

cremation, and among them, no doubt, the lighting of torches with which the pyre was kindled, and which in after times were replaced by the candles put around the dead body. Hence, the kindling of torches or the lighting of candles, took the place of the lighting of the funeral pyre.'

In many localities throughout Ireland, mould taken from the reputed grave of a ' saint,' if mixed with water or boiled in milk, and swallowed by the recipient, is considered to be an infallible remedy for certain maladies. A small portion of the ' saint's' skull * is also regarded as a specific. Grose mentions that, in his time, in the graveyard of the Abbey of Clonthuskert, county Roscommon, a skull was shown ' in which milk was boiled and given to a man afflicted with epilepsy.'

In some localities, bodies when committed to the earth, do not decay in the ordinary way, and adipocere ** in large quantities has often been noticed when the ground was opened for fresh interments. In one graveyard the sexton had recently to gather up and carefully secrete this substance, as otherwise it would be carried off by people whose relations were afflicted with consumption: when melted, the adipocere was administered to the invalid as a certain cure for the malady. Here the real body of the deceased is consumed, as in the other instances noticed it is consumed figuratively.

* Portions of the skull of the poet Carolan were thus utilized by the peasantry. Small fragments broken oil were ground fine, put in water, and swallowed, as a cure for epilepsy. — Ulster Journal of, Archaeology, vol. i., p. 304.

** Adipocere is a soft, unctuous, or waxy substance, of a light brown colour into which the fat and , muscular fibre of bodies are converted by burial in soil of a peculiar nature.

According to Irish MS. authority many barbarities are to be met with in the tales relating to ancient warriors, who appear to have been addicted to an habitual savagery :— ' An Irish warrior, when he killed his enemy, broke his skull, extracted his brains, mixed up the mass well, and working the compound into a ball, he carefully dried it in the sun, and after wards produced it as a trophy of former valour and a presage of future victory. " Take out its brains there from," was Conall's speech to his gillie, who declared he could not carry Mesgegra's head, " and ply a sword upon it, and bear the brain with me, and mix lime therewith, and make a ball thereof." These trophies are described as being the object of pride and contention among the chiefs, and Mesgegra's brain being captured by Get from Conall, was hurled at Conchobar, and caused his death. Then we have the practice recorded, of cutting off the point of the tongue of every man they slew, and bringing it in their pouch. Carrying the heads of the slain at their girdle, first noted by Strabo and Diodorus Siculus, is clearly implied in the saga which Mr. Whitley Stokes has translated from a twelfth-century copy, called the " Siege of Howth." '* In the story of ' Echtra Nerai,' the hero is reputed to have beheld a heap of heads cut off by the warriors of the ' dun,' or fort, and this statement calls to mind the piles of heads described by travellers as often to be seen at the entrance to the residence of an African chief.

In the story of the death of Crimlhann and three other personages, as recorded in an old Irish manuscript, there occurs a passage which, according to O'Curry,

* Ethnology of Folk-lore, G. L. Gomme, pp. 146-7. The authorities for the statements are therein all quoted.

seems to prove 'not only the tradition in historic times of the practice of cremation of the dead in Ireland, but also that of putting persons to death at funerals. This important passage is as follows: —" Fiachra then

brought fifty hostages with him from Munster, and
he brought a great cain (i e. booty levied as legal fine),
and he went forth then on his way to Temar. When,
however, he reached Forud in Ui Mac Uais in Meath,
Fiachra died of his wounds there. His Leacht was
made, and his Fert was raised, and his Cluiche Caintcch
was ignited, and his Ogam name was written, and the
fifty hostages which he brought from the south were
buried alive around the Fert of Fiachra, that it might
be a reproach to the Momonians for ever, and that it
might be a trophy over them." The reproach which
this act was intended to cast on the men of Munster
consisted, no doubt, in treating the Munster hostages,
who were all of the highest birth, as if they were the
dependents and slaves of Fiachra. It may be, also,
that putting them to death in the way here described,
and burying them around him, as they would have sat
in fetters along the wall of his banqueting hall, consecrated them, as
it were, to perpetual hostageship even among the dead.'*
We read of the Curamas that, ' as soon as a relation
died, these people assembled, and ate him, roasted or
boiled according as he was thin or fat.'**Among
cannibals, the offering of human flesh to the dead is
inevitable. Human sacrifices at graves had originally
the purpose of supplying human flesh for the support of
the spirit of the deceased…

* Manners and Customs of the Ancient Irish, vol. i., pp. 320-1.
**The Principles of Sociology, Herbert Spencer, p. 102.

The Last Appearance of Teddy O'Rafferty, Robert Criukshank,1789-1856.

Wake Basics
May the heavens be his perch tonight!
-Popular Irish Expression of Grief.

(The Wake, Image: S. C. Hall, 1841)

The customs of the wake worked on many levels and served the living in many ways. A proper Irish Wake is worth the time and effort required returning to the old customs. It is hard to imagine a passing being complete without one! So now let's review the traditions.....

What is a Wake?

The wake is the period of time from death until the body is conveyed to the care of the church which is generally the evening before the day of burial.

The steps in the process of the Wake are provided below:

"Get to your ma.
I'll need her good hands
to help lay him out...
"Brigid had fallen to her knees
and was crossing herself at a furious pace.
"Off your knees and be
helping me, Brigid," Finola commanded,
for the corpse was a woman's work."

-- Uris op.cit.p.6.

"Little Brigid began to weep."Hush!" her ma said sharply."You'll not do any crying until Grandfar has been properly prepared. The house has been surrounded by fairies just waiting to pounce and your weeping will encourage them to break in and snatch his soul from us." Finola struggled to her feet, going into a flurry of activity. She flung open the windows and doors to let the evil spirits out and quickly covered the mirror to hide his image."

- Uris op.cit.p. 5-6.

1.Neighboring women experienced in laying out the body gather at the house of the deceased.
2. The body is washed
3. A habit is put on the body. The Shroud and burial dress were often obtained many years before death. (Even if you had to dress in rags you would keep your burial clothing unworn). Shoes were thought to be of great importance in the next world. While at times optional in life a good pair of shoes would be set aside for the corpse so that it could walk the long, wet and rough roads of the world to come. The face is left uncovered.
4. A bed is prepared for the body. Men are placed in the bed with their heads at the foot of the bead while women are placed in the usual position.
5. If a man who has shaved, the body is shaved before the habit is put on
6. A crucifix is placed on the breast and rosary beads are put in the fingers.
7. Sheets are hung over the bed and along two or three sides
8. Candles are lighted in candlesticks near the remains.

(The process takes about two hours)

The Wake by Nathania Grogan, early 19th Century

Keening and Crying

Vocalizations over the dead are very important.

Keen Tune, From: Hall, S.C., "Funeral Custroms of the Irish", p. 257, In: George Roberts, Roberts' Semi-Monthly Magazine, Vol.1, 1841.

The grief of the keen is no personal complaint for the death of one woman over eighty years, but it seems to contain the whole passionate rage that lurks somewhere in every native of the island. In this cry of pain the whole consciousness of the people seems to lay itself bare for an instant and to reveal the mood of beings who feel their isolation in the face of a universe that wars on them with wind and seas. They are usually silent, but in the presence of death all outward show of indifference or patience is forgotten; and they shriek with pitiable despair before the horror of the fate to which they are doomed- John Millinghton Synge, <u>The Aran Islands.</u>

How could anyone ever suggest the elimination of such an elemental aspect of cultural practice? All the more reason for it to be revived!

"The Irish funeral howl is notorious, and although this vociferous expression of grief is on the decline, there is still, in the less civilized parts of the country, a strong attachment to the custom, and many may yet be found who are keeners or mourners for the dead by profession."

-Croker p.173

Keening: What and Why?

Fear bruíne, bean chaointe ná garbhmhuilleoir,
Ní bhf aighidh sna Flaithis aon leaba go deo.

Three persons who will get no bed in Heaven: A quarrelsome man, a keening woman and a crude miller.

-O Súilleabháin, <u>Irish Wake Amusements</u>, p.142.

(Keening, Image :S.C. Hall 1841)

"Keen: a cry for the dead, according to certain loud and mournful notes, and verses, wherein the pedigree, land, property, generosity, and good actions of the deceased person, and his ancestors are diligently and harmoniously recounted, in order to excite pity and compassion in the hearers, and to make them sensible of their great loss in the death of the person whom they lament."

- Dr. O' Brien, <u>Irish Dictionary</u>, cdited by Croker (1824), p.173.

The dead could only be keened once the soul had a chance to leave the body. Early keening could wake the Devil's dogs which lay in wait for passing souls and might be awakened by the keening. The keening begins only when the body has been properly prepared and laid out at the wake. While many have interpreted keening as selfish lament, the relationship of the Irish themselves to the spirits of the dead may indicate that it is more communication than lamentation. The special sounds, tones and structures of keening may relate to an earlier "spiritual language" thought to be appropriate for such communication.

Most keening is impromptu and of the oral tradition. Relatives may mention the name of the dead one and ask: "Why did you die?" As Croker notes keening was often a way of communicating for the deceased especially those executed for crimes. Executions were postponed so that publishers could recover from illness so that they could take down the last words and speeches of the condemned. Later at the wake these words were read as a powerful tool of propaganda for the cause.

Men were more restrained than women in their crying. After keening had gone on for a while relatives helped the immediate family from the coffin and the wake proceeded. Crying and keening began again once the body was placed in the coffin and this kept up until the coffin was in the grave and was covered with earth. Sometimes local speakers were arranged to speak of the dead. Often poetry and genealogy were recited along with praise of the deceased lamenting the death. Virtues and interests of the deceased are noted. These recitations are punctuated by loud and piercing yet beautiful wails. At times professional keeners are hired. (Eugene O'Curry noted that the customary number of hired keeners was a minimum of four) The word keening is said to be derived from *Cáoine* which is pronounced keena. Croker (1824 p.173.) That the word was spelled Cine in Ancient Irish Gaelic and that it is remarkably the same as the Hebrew word *Cina* which has the same meaning.

One stood near the head of the bed or table on which the corpse was laid, one at the feet, who was charged with the care of the candles, and one or more at each side; the family and immediate friends of the deceased sat around near the table. The mourner at the head opened the dirge with the first note or part of the cry; she was followed by the one at the foot with a note or part of equal length, then the long or double part was sung by the two side mourners, after which the members of the family and friends of the deceased joined in the common chorus at the end of each stanza of the funeral ode or dirge, following as closely as they could the air or tune adopted by the professional mourners. Sometimes one or more, or even all the principal singers, were men.-sometimes harpers were employed

- O Súilleabháin, Irish Wake Amusements, p.136.

The paid keeners were given food and drink. It is said that the performance, which was better when louder, was much improved after the first glass of whiskey. Professional keeners would strive to better their professional standing by trying to outdo the competition of other keeners at the wake. This lead to fighting and clerical disapproval.

The Catholic Church acted frequently and harshly to persecute those practicing traditional cultural ways.

Such actions have changed forever the traditions of the Irish.

Caoinan: Of Some Account of the Antient Irish Lamentations, William Beauford, A. M.

Caoinan: ()f *fome account of tbe* Antient Irish
Lamentations. *By* William Beauford, *A. M.,1790. p.41.*
From: *The Transactions of the Royal Irish Academy*
Vol. 4 (1790 - 1792),

The modes of lamentation, and the epreffions of grief by
founds, geftures and' ceremonies, admit of an almoft infinite
variety: fo far as thefe are common to moil:' people, they
have very little to attract attention; but where they conftitute a
part of national character, they then become objects
of no incurious speculation.

The Irifh have been always remarkable for their funeral
lamentations, and this peculiarity has been noticed by almoft
every traveller who visited them, and it feerns derived from
their Celtic anceftors, the primeval inhabitants of this ifle,
Thefe were a timorous and unwarlike race, as their military
weapons, and every veftige of their cuftoms and manners
ftrongly indicate : their religion was fpiritual, and unftained with
human blood. Such a religion and fuch manners imply a
fufceptibility

 of tender impreflions, and feminine expreffions of
forrow. Grief quickly melted them into tears, and their
oppreffed hearts found relief in fhrieks and groans; and hence.

it has been * affirmed of the Irifh, that to cry was more
natural to them than to any other nation, and at length the
Irifh cry became proverbial.

The Belgic colonies, who fucceeded the Celtes, were a very
different race: of Scythic defcent, they indulged in all the
excefles of favage nature. Warfare was their paflime, and blood
was the cement of their folemn covenants. The day of interment,
among them, was occupied with feafting and fmging:
it was then they chaunted their rude fongs, the" joys of
Valhalla, and the happy lot of the brave.

The foregoing diftinctionss are fonded in fact, and antiquity gives
decifive evidence of their authenticity. Caefar in
t many places pointedly marks the .levity and ficklenefs of
the Gallic Celtcs: that they had a tt foftnefs which difqualilied them

231

from refifiing calamities, and Tacitus· §. informs us,
the Treveri and Nervii affected be thought of Germanic
origin, hoping thereby to avoid the difreputation attached to
the Celtic character,

,. *Williamfon. orat. in Iufcep. diad. Car. 2.
t Comment. lib. 2, 3, 4-
t Molles ac minirne reliflens ad cal.rmitares perferendas, mens Callorurn eft. eref. lib. 3.
§ De mor. Germ.

It was not before fome degree of civility was introduced
among us, that our rude poetry, mufic and lamentations,
affumed a regular form. Carnbrenfis, in the 12th century,
fays, the Irith then mufically exprefied their griefs, that is, they

applied the mufical art, - in which they * excelled all others,
to the orderly celebration of funeral obfequies, by dividing
the mourners into two bodies, each alternately finging their
part, and the whole, at times, joining in full chorus. This

antiphonial t finging was coeval with Chriftianity in this
ifle. It was then the funeral elegy rofe in poetic numbers,
and was fung in poetic accents to the found of mufical inftruments,
The body of the deceafed, drefled in grave-clothes, and ornamerited
with flowers, was placed on a bier or fame elevated fpot. The
relations and Keeners ranged themfelves in two divifions, one at the head and the other at
the feet of the corps. The bards and croteries had before prepared the funeral Caoinan. The
chief bard of the head chorus began, by finging the firft
flanza in a low doleful tone, which was foftly accompanied
by the harp: at the conclufion, the foot femi-chorus began
the lamentation or Ullaloo, from the final note' of the preceding ftanza, in which they Were
anfwered by the head femichorus; then both united in one general chorus. The chorus of the
firft ftanza being ended, the chief bard of the foot femi-chorus

* Walker's Irifh Bards. Append. p. 20.
t Walker, fupra,

chorus fung the fecond ftanza, the flrain of which was taken:
from the concluding note of the preceding chorus , which
ended, the head fcrni-chorus began the fecond Col or lamentation,
in which they were anfwered by that of the foot,· and, then, as before,
both united in the general full chorus. Thus alternately were the'
fong and chorufes performed during the night. The genealogy,
rank, poffeffions, the virtues and vices of the dead were rehearfed,
and a number of interrogations were addreffed to the deceafed: As,
Why did he die? If married, whether his wife was faithful to him,
his fons dutiful, or good hunters or warriors? If a woman,
whether her daughters were fair or chafte] If a young man,
whether he had been croffd in love? or if the blue-eyed maids of
Erin treated him with, fcorn ?

We are * told that each verficle of the Caoinan cqnfifted only
of four feet, and each foot was commonly of two fyllables:
that the three firft required no correfpondence, but the fourth
was to correfpond with the terminations of the other verficles.
This kind of artificial metre was much cultivated by the Irifh
bards, but, on the decline of that order, the Caoinan fell into the
hands of women, and became an extemporaneous performance.
Each province was .fuppofed to have different Caoinans, and
hence the Munfter cry" the Ulfter cry, &c. but they are only
imitations; of the different chorufes of the fame Caoinan independent
of provincial diftinctions. As the Caoinan was fang extempore,
there being no general. eftablifhed tune, each fet of

*Lhuyd, Archlcolog. Brit. p•. 309.

f Keeners varied the melody according to their tafte and
mufical abilities, carefully, however, prcferving the fubjet or
burden of the fong throughout, both in the vocal and inftrnmental
part, as begun by the leading Keener.

A:r prefent the Caoinan is much neglected, being only practired
in remote parts, fo that· this ancient cuftom will foon
finally ceefe, Englifh manners and the Eiiglifli language fupplanting .
thofe of the aboriinal natives; . The followg example bears
evident marks of bardic origin, bath in its verIification and language: it is probably
a production of the 15th century. The mufic of the. Go1 or chorufes is: the fame
-or nearly fo with· that played by the modern pipers, and by
them denominated the Irifh cries.' This. example, being an imitation. of
extreme 'and "Violent grief with broken lamentations,
is. wild and Irregular, and can have but little merit as a.mufical compofition.,
but may be of fome account, as preferving the laft remains of a. very ancient
 and univerfal cuftom.

Caoinan

Or IRISH FUNERAL SONG.

LARGO.

Œ muc Connal coidhuim baifaogh, Ruireach, rathmar, rachtmhar eachthach Crodha creachach.
O fon of Connal, why didft thou die? royal, noble, learned youth, valiant, active,

cathach ceadthagh Coidhuim baifaogh Ucha oionagh.
warlike, eloquent! Why didft thou die? Alas! awail-a-day!

First Semi-Chorus.

TERMANTE.

Ulla-lulla-lulla-lulla lù lù ucht o ong.

Second Semi-Chorus.

O ong ulla lulla lulla lulla lulla lulla lulla lu ucht o ong.

PEASANT FUNERAL IN THE MAM TURK MOUNTAINS OF CONNEMARA, IRELAND.—[See Page 234.]

Peasant Funeral in the Mam Turk Mountains of Connemara, Ireland. Harpers 1870

Full Chorus of Sighs and Groans.

Ucht o ong ucht o ong o ucht o ong ucht o ong o ong o o ong

ucht o ong o ong ucht o o ong o o o o o ong o

o ong ucht o ong ucht o ong o ong.

Uchta oin-nagh! boothach bear-tach Sli-ochd an Heber cath-ach coinnagh. A muc
Alas! alas! he who sprang from nobles of the race of Heber, warlike chief. O men

Con-nal each-agh earl--tach, Coidhinm baifaogh uchta o oin—nagh.
of Connal, noble youth, why didft thou die, alas! alas!

First Semi-Chorus.

Ul-la lulla lulla lulla lù li o ong.

Second

Second Semi-Chorus.

O ong ulla lulla lulla lulla lù lù ucht o ong.

Full Chorus.

Ucht o ong o ong o o ong ucht o ong o ong o ong

ucht o ong ucht o ong o ong ucht o ong o ong ucht o

ong o ong ucht o ong ucht o o o ong ucht

o ong ucht o ong o ong ucht o ong.

Full Chorus.

Ucht o ong ucht o ong ucht o ong o ong O ong o o ong o

ong o o o o ong o ong o o o o ong uch o ong uch o ucht

O o o ucht o ong ucht o ong o o ong ucht o ong o ong.

Ucht a oin—nagh coid-huim bai—faogh Amuc Connal roimhcreadh cloidh each doighbrach

Alas! alas! why didſt thou die, O ſon of Connal, before the ſpoils of victory by thy

gliadhach do—nal neitheach Sgaith le ſeanna ucht a oinnagh.

warlike arm was brought to the hall of the nobles, and thy ſhield with the ancient. Alas! alas!

Firſt

[51]

Firſt Semi-Chorus.

Ulla lulla lulla lulla   lù   lù   o   ong.

Second Semi-Chorus.

Ulla lulla lulla lulla   lulla lulla lù   lù   lul lù   ucht o ong.

Full Chorus.

Ucht   o   ong   o   ong   ucht o   ong   ucht   o   o   ong   o   ong ucht o   ong

ucht   o   o   ong ucht   o   o   o   o   o   o   o

ucht   o   ong   ong   o   ong.

[G 2]   AT

[5²]

At the conclusion of the Keenan, the body was conveyed to the place of interment, attended by the friends and relations of the deceased, and accompanied by the cries of women, who at certain intervals sung the *Gol* or Ullaloo.

In antient times, after the interment, the favourite bards of the family, seated on the grave or sepulchre, performed the *Connthal* or Elegy; which they repeated every new and full moon, for the first three months, and afterwards generally once every year, for persons of distinction. The Elegy was more regular than the Keenan, both in respect to its poetical composition and melodious cadence; though I have not been able to obtain any pieces of this kind, of a very antient date, nor the music appertaining to them. However, several families, both in Wales and this country, retained the custom to the close of the last century, and it is frequently alluded to in the Irish ballads and poetical romances.

The following is said to be the lamentations of Fin M'Comhal over his grandson Oscar, who is supposed to have been slain in the battle of Gabhra in the third century. It is taken from the poem on the death of Oscar, and the music is still preserved in Connaught and the Highlands of Scotland. I have chosen this passage from that poetical romance, as it is probable the poetry and music are coeval, having both originated in the bardic school of Errus, in the county of Mayo, towards the close of the fifteenth century: a fountain from whence flowed the greater part

of

of thofe Irifh ballads and romances which have, in thefe latter ages, become the foundation of the numerous ideal fuperftructures relative to the hiftory and antiquities of this ifland.

MARBH-RANN OSCAR.

Mo laoch fein u, laoch mo laoch. Leanabh mo leanabb, ghil cha--ömh
O my own youth, youth of my youth. Child of my child, gentle, valiant,

Mo chroidhe lium——nich mar long, Gulath bhrath cha n'ei——rich Of—car.
My heart cries like a blackbird's. For ever gone, never to rife, O Ofcar.

As the verfification of this poem is evidently bardic, if we could be certain of the mufic being the original air we might form fome idea of the ftate of that art among the Hibernian bards. One circumftance, however, feems in fome meafure to confirm its authenticity; the tune to which the fong of the death of Ofcar is fung, both in the weft of Ireland and Highlands of Scotland, is nearly the fame.

THE

The several poetic and musical compoutions of the Irish bards of the weft and north were introduced into the Highlands by the Erfe Boaaghta *or* Auiliaries retained by the Irish princes during the fifteenth, fixtcenth and feventeeath centuries.

Persecution Of Keening

Synod of Tuam (1631): Statue 3 ordered that thenceforth exaggerated crying and keening at wakes of the dead should cease.

Synod of Tuam 1660- The people were advised to discontinue the practice of employing female keeners at wakes and funerals.

Synod of Armagh 1660- This Synod forbade wailings and crying at funerals as an unchristian practice.

Synod of Dublin June 1670- This was a meeting of the archbishops and bishops of Ireland. Statute 5 ordered each priest in the country to make every effort in his power to bring to an end the wailings and screams of female keeners who accompanied the dead to the graveyard.

Synod of Armagh (August 1670): This Synod adopted the regulations laid down by the Dublin Synod two months before. It further announced that no priest would attend a wake or funeral at which female keeners cried and screamed. Any priest who neglected to endeavor to end such unseemly behavior would be removed from his parish.

Synod of Meath (1686): The bishops first condemned dancing, other amusements and drinking at wakes, and then went on to order the parish priests in their jurisdiction to continue their efforts to put an end to the customary keening at funerals.

Diocese of Leighlin (1748): Among the diocesan regulations adopted at a meeting presided over by Most Rev. Dr. Gallagher, was the following:

"Whereas likewise the heathenish customs of loud cries and howlings at wakes and burials are practiced amongst us, contrary to the express commandment of St. Paul in his Epist. to the Thess. forbidding such cries and immoderate grief for the dead, as if they were not to rise again, and to the great shame of our nation, since no such practice is found in any other Christian country; and Whereas in some parts of this Diocese some have the deplorable vanity in the very time of their humiliation and that God had visited them with the loss of a friend, not only to glory in the number of cries, but in order the more to feed their vanity and add fuel to their pride, do even send far and near to hire men and women to cry and compose vain fulsome rhymes in praise of their deceased friends. It is therefore (ordained) all Parish Priests and religious laymen of this Diocese are hereby strictly charged and commanded, in virtue of holy obedience, to use all possible means to banish from Christian burials such anti-Christian practices, by imposing arbitrary punishment of prayers, fasting, alms and such like wholesome injunctions on as many men and women as will loudly cry or howl at burials. But as to such men and women as we decree and declare that for the first crime of this kind they shall not be absolved by any but by the Ordinary or his representatives, and in case of a relapse (sic), the aforesaid criers or rhymes are to excluded from Mass and the Sacraments, and in case of perseverance in this detestable practice, they are to be excommunicated and denounced."

The practice of keening: "all unnatural screams and shrieks, and fictitious tuneful cries and elegies" was condemned as late as 1800 by Dr. Thomas Bray, Archbishop of Cashel.

-O Súilleabháin, Irish Wake Amusements., p.138-40.

Keening Observed

The practice of keening is described by a traveler in Kildare in 1683: *"as soon as the bearers have taken up the body, they begin their shrill cries and hideous hootings...and if there be not enough to make out a good cry they hire the best and deepest mouthed in all the country and so they proceed towards the church; this now may be heard two miles or more. When they come at the church-yard on this occasion, (and at other times also) perhaps 5, 10 or 20 years after their husband, friend or relation has been buried, they repair to their graves where they kneel over them, knocking and beating upon the grave and praising the party, repeating the former kindnesses have passed between them intreating that they would attend and give ear to them, then in an odd tone sorrowing and lamenting their loss and complain and tell them how they are misused and by whom injured and thereon pray their help to right them; and thus they continue commonly until some compassionating friend or neighbour come and lift them from the ground with expostulating language, so they return satisfied as having given an account to one that in time may redress their injuries, revenge or relieve them. The women are mostly inclined and observed to practice these things, and many the like a more anxious eye might discover amongst them"*

- O Súilleabháin, Irish Wake Amusements, p.135.

James Farewell in *The Irish Hudibras*, 1689, wrote of keening women:

They raise the cry, and so they fount him
Into a crate to howl about him;
Where, in one end, the parted brother
Was laid to rest, the cows in t'other
With all his followers and kin,
Who, far and near, come crowding in,
Wit hub-bub-boos, beside what cryers
For greater state his highness (sic) hires.

- O Súilleabháin, Irish Wake Amusements, p.135.

W. King wrote in the *Art of Cookery,* in 1776:

So at an Irish funeral appears
A train of drabs with mercenary tears;
Who, wringing of their hands with hideous moan,
Know not his name for whom they seem to groan,
While real grief with silent steps proceeds,
And love unfeigned with inward passion bleds

- O Súilleabháin, <u>Irish Wake Amusements,</u> p.136.

Keening is a pan-Celtic tradition also quite important in Scotland.

Some Folk Laments from Ireland

From Kerry:

Mo thaisce's mo ghamhain tu,
Mar bhuachaillín ceann-dubh,
Gur ghile liom thu ná an leamhnacht
'S ná uisce lae an tsamhraidh!
My treasure and my love,
My little dark-headed boy,
Whom I thought whiter than new milk
Or than water on a summer day!

From the Decies:

Érigh suas id' sheasamh,
A's gaibh do sheisreach capall!
Tóg fód chúig n-órdla ar treansnacht;
Féach ormsa, a thaisce,
'S gan tada 'gam mar thaca,
Ag dul ag baint ná ag gearradh!
Cé dhéanfaidh gnó an mharga?
Cé raghaidh go Cnoc an Aifrinn,
A's tusa sínte feasta? Och, ochón!

Rise and stand up,
And tackle your ploughing-team!
Plough a five-inch furrow;
Look at me, my treasure,
With nobody to help me
When I go reaping or cutting!
Who will do my business at the market?
Who will go to the Hill of the Mass,
As you lie stretched from now on? Och, ochón!

> *"O father, you have left us! Ochon!*
> *Why did you leave us? Ochon!*
> *Or what did we do to you? Ohon!*

That you went away from us? Ochon!
Tis you that had plenty! Ochon!
And why did you leave us? Ochon!
(all join in) Ochon! Ochon! Ochon!
Strong was your arm! Ochon!
Light was your step! Ochon!
Skilled were your hands! Ochon!
Poor we are without you! Ochon!
And why did you leave us? Ochon!
(all) Ochon, Ochon, Ullagon O!"

Traditional

Four keens from an elderly woman by the name of Harrington were collected by Crofton Croker (1824, p-173-184). This woman lead a wandering kind of life. Croker reports that she:

…began in a kind of whining recitative, but as she proceeded and as the composition required it, her voice assumed a variety of deep and fine tones, and the energy with which many passages were delivered, proved her perfect comprehension and strong feeling of the subject, but her eyes always continued shut, perhaps to prevent interruption to her thoughts, or her attention being engaged by any surrounding object.-p174.

Keens

1. On Sir Richard Cox d.1733

"My love and darling, though I never was in your kitchen, yet I have heard an exact account of it. The brown roast meat continually coming from the fire; the black boilers continually boiling; the cock of the beer-barrel for every running; and if even a score of men came in, no person would inquire their business; but they would give them a place at your table, and let them eat what they pleased, nor would they bring a bill in the morning to them."

"My love and friend, I dreamed through my morning slumbers, that your castle fell into decay, and that no person remained in it. The birds sung sweetly no longer nor were there leaves upon the bushes; all was silence and decay!—the dream told me that our beloved man was lost to us—that the noble horseman was gone! The renowned Squire Cox!"

"My love and darling, you were nearly related to the Lord of Clare, and to O'donovan of Bawnlehan; to Cox with the blue eyes and to Townsend of White Court. This is the appointed day for your funeral, and yet I see none of them coming to place even a green sod over you."

2. O'Donoghue of Affadown or Roaring Water, West County Cork for his three sons and son-in-law drowned

"It was on a rainy Monday; a fair gale blew, and my sons left the shore an half an hour before sun-rise to fish in the sea; my children were driven far away to be drowned. This year has been the year of my ruin for ever!"

"Cormick (Charles), my eldest child, he could kill with his gun every bird that flew in air,--the wild duck, and the partridge, and the grouse and black plover of the lonesome mountains!"

"Cormick, my dear!—flower of young men, who was mild and well educated, who was just and pure and good!—Oh! Glorious King of Heaven, if thou hadst but spared him to me!—It was the loss of him that broke my heart entirely; I might—I could have parted with the rest."

"Daniel, my dear Daniel, the youngest of my sons, it was this day fortnight he was washed on shore, without strength or life in his body. I saw him as he lay lifeless upon the shore, and my heart was cold and dumb and motionless at the sight!"

"Children, dear children, do you pity me? Do you see me? Look on me, your poor father crying and lamenting for the sunshine of his eyes; for the life of his life, for the soul of his soul; what is he now? –A poor broken hearted old man, weeping alone in the cold corner of a stranger's house!"

"Great is my grief and sorrow! Sadness and tears weigh heavy on my Christmas. To have my four young and stout men thrown on the will of the waves! If the great ocean, or the dark caves of the ocean would restore the three bodies that now lie in its depths, how beautifully they would be keened and lamented over in Affadown!"

"Great is my grief and sorrow that you did not all go from your father on board ship!—or if my sons had left me for a season, like the wild geese, to go to a foreign land, then might I have expected from my Maker the help of my four mild and clever young men at some future time."

3. On Morty Oge O' Sullivan of Beerhaven killed for having assassinated Mr. Puxley –West County Cork

Murty, my dear and loved master, you carried the sway for strength and generosity. It is my endless grief and sorrow—sorrow which admits of no comfort, that your white head should be gazed at as a shew upon a spike, and that your noble frame is without life."

"I have traveled with you, my dear and much loved master in foreign lands, and through various provinces and countries, and in the royal prince's army, when we moved with kings. But it is thought he means of Puxley that I am left in grief and confinement in Cork, locked in heavy irons, and without the hope of being released."

"The great God is good and merciful! I ask his grace and pardon, and his support, of I am to be hanged at the gallows tomorrow without doubt; the rope will squeeze my neck, and thousands will lament my fate, but may the Lord have mercy upon my master! It was for his sake that I am now in their power."

"Kerryonians, pray for us! Sweet and melodious is your voice, my blessing I give to you, but you will never see me again amongst you alive; our heads will be upon a spike as a shew, under the cold snow of the night, and the burning sun of the summer and every other change of weather."

"Oh! That I was ever born!—O! that I ever returned to Beerhaven! Mine was the best of master that Ireland could produce: may our souls be floating tomorrow in the rays of endless glory!"

"The lady his wife, heavy is her grief, and who may wonder at that, were her eyes even made of green stone: when he, her dear husband, was shot by that ball? If he had returned, our grief might have been lighter, but the brave man would not, for the pride of his country retreat."

"He has been in king's palaces, and in Spain he got a pension; the lady of Clare gave him robes bound with gold lace as a token of remembrance. He became a captain on the coast of France, and yet should he return to Ireland for us to loose him."

"There is a lady in London who expects him every day with his vessel"…

4.Smith's Keenan of Killavullian on the Blackwater

"Brother, dear brother! Your long absence from home did not raise you in this world, you left us, and you found a wife who knew not how to love you. No one here knows your family, you are in the midst of strangers; they only know that you were a smith, and son of a smith from the Blackwater's side!"

"Oh! If I had your cold limbs by the Blackwater's side, or on the banks of the small river or by the Bride; Mary and Kate and Julia would cry over you, and our mother would cry most sweetly for you; and I, oh! I would cry more than them all for you!"

"Oh! Brother, dear brother—I might have known that you were laid low, when I did not hear the sound of your forge, or of your sledges, striking strong and noisy!"

"Dear brother, and my darling brother, you have the marks of a wife that did not love you; she left my brother hungry in the winter, and dry in the summer; without a Sunday dress, and the sufferer from long fasting."

"You woman, his wife! My brother's wife, you woman with the dry eyes; you woman who are both dumb and deaf; go home! Go any where, leave your husband to me, and I will mourn for my brother."

"You woman above with the dry eyes! My brother's wife, come down, and I will keen you; you will get another husband if you are young enough; but I can never get a brother!"

The Priest:
"Hold your tongue, stubborn stranger, why will you provoke your brother's wife?"

She Answers:
"Hold you tongue stubborn priest! Read your Litany and Confiteor; earn your half-crown and be gone; I will keen my brother."

Literary Laments:

Lament written by Patrick Hegarty for his son:

Ochón, a Dhoncha, mo mhíle cogarthach, fén bhfód so sínte.
Fód an doichill 'na luí ar do cholainn bhig, mo lomasceimhle!
Dá mbeadh an codla so í gcill na Dromad ort nó i nuaigh san iarthar,
Mo bhrón do bhogfadh, cé gur mhór mo dhochar,'s ní bheinn id'dhiadh air.
Is feoidhte caithte tá na blátha scalpeadh ar do leaba chaoil-se;
Ba bhreá iad tamall, ach thréig a dtaitneamh; ní snas ná brí ionnta.
Tá an bláth bh ghile liom dár fhás in ithr riamh, ná d'fhásfaidh choíche,
Ag dreó sa talamh, a's go deó ní thacfaidh, ag cur éirí croí orm!

Ochón, my Donagh, my thousand loves, stretched under this sod-
This inhospitable sod which lies on your little breast, my bitter torture!
If you were thus asleep in Dromad churchyard or in some western grave,
My sorrow would soften, great though be my loss, and I would not grudge it!
Withered and spent are the blossoms which were laid on your narrow bed;

Fine they were once, but they faded; now they have neither colour nor life.

My own blossom, brighter than any that has ever grown or will grow,

Rotting away in the earth never again to return to raise my heart!

Irish Literature contains a wealth of laments in this style from all periods.

The women mix their cries, and clamour fills the fields. The warlike wakes continued all the night and funeral games were played at new returning light.—Dryden

THE FAMINE IN IRELAND.— FUNERAL AT SKIBEREEN— FROM A SKETCH BY MR. H. SMITH, CORK.

Wakes Observed and Commentary

"Wake" From: Castle Rackrent; an Hibernian Tale.., Maria Edgeworth,1733

Castle Rackrent; an Hibernian tale. taken from facts, and from the manners of the Irish squires, before the year 1733 by Maria Edgeworth, author of practical education, letters for literary ladies, the parent's assistant, &c. the fourth edition. London: printed for J. Johnson, St. Paul's church- yard By H. Bryer, Bridge-Street, Blackfriars.1804.
Wake—A wake, in England, means a festival held upon the anniversary of the Saint of the parish. At these wakes, rustic games, rustic conviviality, and rustic courtship, are pursued with all the ardor and all the appetite, which accompany such pleasures as occur but seldom.—In Ireland a wake is a midnight meeting, held professedly for the indulgence of holy sorrow, but usually it is converted into orgies of unholy joy. When an Irish man or woman of the lower order dies, the straw which composed his bed, whether it has been contained in a bag to form a mattress, or simply spread upon the. earthen floor, is immediately taken out of the house, and burned before the cabin door, the family at' the same time setting up the death howl. The ears and eyes of the neighbours being thus alarmed, they flock to the house of the deceased, and by their vociferous sympathy, excite and at the same time sooth the sorrows of the family. It is curious to observe how good and bad are mingled in human institutions. In countries which were thinly inhabited, this custom prevented private attempts against the lives of individuals, and formed a kind of coroner's inquest upon the body which had recently expired, and burning the straw upon which the sick man lay became a simple preservative against infection. At night the dead body is waked, that is to say, all the -friends and neighbours of the deceased collect in a barn or stable, where the corpse is laid upon some boards, or an unhinged door supported upon stools, the face exposed, the rest of the body covered with a white sheet .Round the body are stuck in brass candlesticks, which have been borrowed perhaps at five miles distance, as many candles as the poor person can beg or borrow, observing always to have an odd number. Pipes and tobacco are first distributed, and then, according to the ability of the deceased, cakes and ale, and sometimes whiskey, are, dealt to the company:

" Deal on, deal on, my merry men all,"
Deal on your cakes and your wine,"
For whatever is dealt at her funeral today.'?
Shall be dealt tomorrow - at mine. "

After a fit of universal sorrow, and the comfort of a universal dram, the scandal of the neighbourhood in higher circles, occupies the company. The young lads and lasses romp with one another, and when the fathers and mothers are at last overcome with sleep and whiskey,(*vino et somno*) the youth become more enterprising, and are frequently successful. It is said, that more matches are made at wakes than at weddings...

p. 149

Page 8.

Wil'aluh–Ullaloo, Gol, or la mentation over the dead— *"Magnoque ululante tumultu."* Vigil. " *Ululatibus omne Implevere ne mus*." Ovid. A full account of the Irish Gol, or Ullaloo, and of the Caoinan or Irish funeral song, with its first semichorus, second semichorus, full chorus of sighs and groans, together with the Irish words and music, may be found in the fourth volume of the transactions of the Royal Irish Academy. For the advantage of lazy readers, who would rather read a page than walk a yard, and from compassion, not to say sympathy with their infirmity, the Editor transcribes the following passages. "The Irish have been always remarkable for their funeral lamentations, and this peculiarity has been noticed by almost every traveller who visited them. And it seems derived from their Celtic ancestors, the primaeval in habitants of this isle. * * * *

"It has been affirmed of the Irish, that to cry was more natural to them than to any other nation, and at length the Irish cry became proverbial. * * * *

"Cambrensis in the twelfth century says, the Irish then musically expressed their griefs; that is, they applied the musical art, in which they excelled all others, to the orderly celebration of funeral obsequies, by dividing the . mourners into two bodies, each alternately singing their part, and the whole at times joining in full chorus. * * * * * *

The body of the deceased, dressed in grave clothes, and ornamented with flowers, was placed on a bier, or some elevated spot. The relations and keepers (singing mourners) ranged themselves in two divisions, one at the head, and the other at the feet of the corpse. The bards and croteries had before prepared the funeral Caoinan. The chief bard of the head chorus began by singing the first stanza in a low, doleful tone, which was softly ac companied by the harp: at the conclusion, the foot semichorus began the lamentation, or Ullaloo, from the final note of the preceding stanza, in which they were answered by the head semichorus; then both united in one ge neral chorus. The chorus of the first stanza being ended, the chief bard of the foot semi chorus began the second Gol or lamentation, in which he was answered by that of the head; and then, as before, both united in the general full chorus. Thus alternately were the song and choruses performed during the night. The genealogy, rank, possessions, the virtues and vices of the dead were rehearsed, and a number of interrogations were addressed to the deceased: as, Why did he die? If married, whether his wife was faithful to him, his sons dutiful, or good hunters or warriors? If a woman, whether her daughters were fair or chaste? If a young man, whether he had been crossed in love? or if the blue-eyed maids of Erin treated him with scorn?" We are told, that formerly the feet (the metrical feet) of the Caoiman were much at tended to ; but on the decline of the Irish bards, these feet were gradually neglected, and the Caoinan fell into a sort of slip-shod metre amongst women. Each province had different Caoinans, or at least different imitations of the original. There was the Munster cry, the Ulster cry, &c. It became an ex tempore performance, and every set of keepers varied the melody according to their own fancy. It is curious to observe how customs and ceremonies degenerate. The present Irish cry, or howl, cannot boast of such melody, mor is the funeral procession conducted with much dignity. The crowd of people who assemble at these funerals sometimes amounts to a thousand, often to four or five hundred. They gather as the bearers of the hearse proceed on their way, and when they pass through any village, or when they come near any houses, they begin to cry—Oh! Oh! Oh! Oh Oh! Aghſ Agh raising their notes from the first Oh! to the last Agh 1 in a kind of mournful howl. This gives notice to the inhabitants of the village that a funeral is passing, and immediately they flock out to follow it. In the province of Munster it is a common thing for the women to follow a funeral, to join in the universal cry with all their might and main for some time, and then to turn and ask—"Arrah who is it that's dead?—who is it we're crying for —Even the poorest people have their own burying places, that is, spots of ground in the church yards, where they say that their ancestors have been buried ever since the wars of Ireland: and if these burial-places are ten miles from the place where a man dies, his friends and neighbours take care to carry his corpse thither. Always one priest, often five or six priests, attend these funerals; each priest re peats a mass, for which he is paid sometimes a shilling, sometimes half-a-crown, sometimes half-a-guinea, or a guinea, according to their circumstances, or, as they say, according to the ability of the deceased. After the burial of any very poor man, who has left a widow or children, the priest makes what is called a collection for the widow; he goes round to every person present, and each contributes sixpence or a shilling, or what they please. The reader will find in the note upon the word Wake, p. 180, more particulars respecting the conclusion of the Irish funerals. Certain old women, who cry particularly loud and well, are in great request, and, as a man said to the Editor, "Every one would wish and be proud to have such at his funeral, or at that of his friends." The lower Irish are wonderfully eager to attend the funerals of their friends and relations, and they make their relationships branch out to a great extent. The proof that a poor man has been well beloved during his life, is his having a crowded funeral. To attend a neighbour's funeral is a cheap proof of humanity, but it does not, as some imagine, cost nothing. The time spent in attending funerals may be safely valued at half a million to the Irish nation: the Editor thinks, that double that sum would not be too high an estimate. The habits of profligacy and drunkenness, which are acquired at wakes, are here put out of the question. When a labourer, a carpenter, or a smith is not at his work, which frequently hap pens, ask where he is gone, and ten to one the answer is—"Oh faith, please your honour, he couldn't do a stroke to-day, for he's gone to the funeral." Even beggars, when they grow old, go about begging for their own funerals; that is, begging for money to buy a coffin, candles, pipes, and tobacco. For the use of the candles, pipes, and tobacco, see Wake. Those who value customs in proportion to their antiquity, and nations in proportion to their adherence to ancient customs, will doubt less admire the Irish Ullaloo, and the Irish nation, for persevering in this usage from time immemorial. The Editor, however, has observed some alarming symptoms, which seem to prognosticate the declining taste for the Ullaloo in Ireland. In a comic theatrical entertainment, represented not long since on the Dublin stage, a chorus of old women was introduced, who set up the Irish howl round the relics of a physician, who is supposed to have fallen under the wooden sword of Harlequin. After the old women have continued their Ullaloo for a decent time, with all the necessary accompaniments of wringing their hands, wiping or rubbing their eyes with the corners of their gowns or aprons, &c. one of the mourners suddenly suspends her lament able cries, and turning to her neighbour, asks . —"Arrah now, honey, who is it we're crying for P" , Page 9.

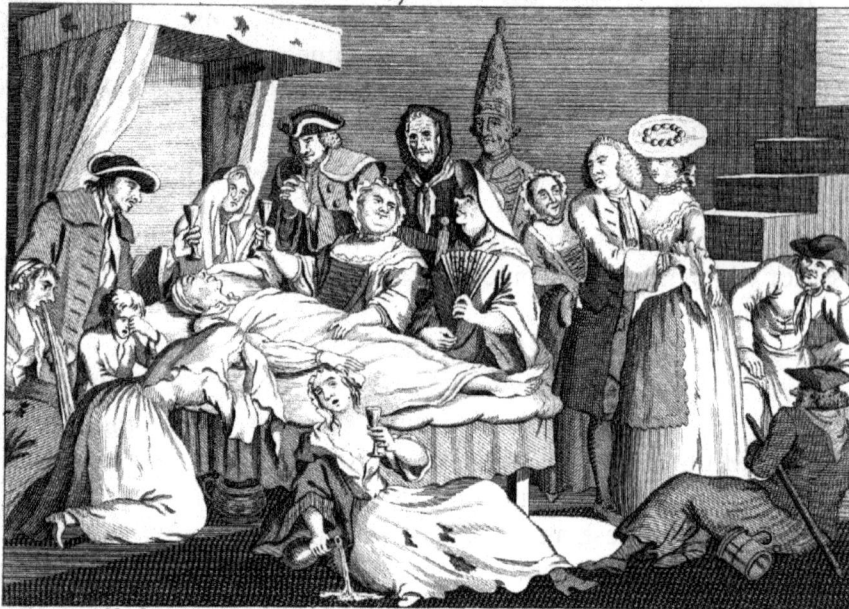

The Humors of an Irish Wake, 1770, Artist unknown

The Gentleman In No. 76., 1834

<u>Chambers Edinburgh Journal</u> No. 181. Saturday, August 2, 1834.

It is now several years since I was in Ireland. It was my first, and, in all human probability, will be my last visit. Not that I am one of those who despise the " Green Isle," as it is called; and not that I have any hatred of the Irish, God bless them! Far from it I liked the country well enough, considering that its lands, houses, and inhabitants, were so deplorably miserable in appearance. Still, I say, I trust I shall never set my foot within it again. But, my good fellow—someone will ask—why this horror of the pretty Emerald Isle? I am afraid you are under the influence of a stark raving prejudice. No; there you are wrong for once, at least, I answer. I am under no prejudice; I am only suffering from a nervish affection produced by a fright I got. What! did you see a ghost? inquires he again. No; certainly not a ghost; much won than a ghost. I am never afraid of these phantoms of the brain. It is ghosts of flesh and blood that I am alarmed about. But to stop all botheration, I shall tell you at once how the thing happened. Some four or five summers ago, I had occasion ….Every body knows that the Irish are a funny people ; that they have many funny customs, particularly at their deaths and burials. These consequently I kept my eye upon, for the purpose of noting down. When I saw a black painted hackney coach pass on the street, with the end of a coffin sticking out from a hole behind, down the circumstance went in my note-book. When I saw a oof fin disposed on the pavement in one of the bye streets, and a hat, or what was once a hat, standing upon it in the character of an " awmons dish," I always tacked towards it, and, in slewing past, dropped a few harps, for which of course I received a thousand blessings from the watching and weeping mourner. In this kind of way I passed my time for a few days, and at night I kept close to my apartment in the hotel, writing down and extending the result of my observations. During my stay at Holme's, I discovered that I had acquired the character of an orderly sort of person. One day on opening my room door I heard one attendant say to another, " Where are you going with that paper, Jem?" " Why," said the other, " it it to the gentleman in No. 76, that reads and writes such a dale." This was enough. I saw I was reckoned a studious personage, a character who, from not giving much trouble, is always sure to be well I was confirmed In my opinion. One… …. channel. I caught the view of a funeral procession on the point of moving from a door. Here was something to amuse me. What was now to hinder me from seeing the beginning, middle, and end of a regular Irish funeral? Nothing. I had the forenoon to spare. I therefore turned down the narrow alley or street, with a view to following at a respectful distance. The pageant, it was soon evident, was by no means "ilegant." A plain black deal coffin was tied obliquely across a species of low cart or car, which was drawn by a miserable half-starved pony with rope harness. What was wanting in " ilegance," was not obviously sup plied by the outward demonstration of sorrow. The mourners were of both sexes and divers ages, and all seemed fully to agree with the poet in the impropriety of donning the garments of woe— " To mimic sorrow when the heart's not sad" for all followed the car in the clothes and tatters In which their bodies must have been usually clad. It seemed, on the present occasion, that the deceased had had an extensive acquaintanceship. The procession moved down one lane, and tip another, collecting followers as it went, some with ragged greatcoats, and short stumpy black pipes in their mouths, others) with bottles of whisky in their hands, or peeping from their packets ; some with shoes, others without them. In short, there was a sample of all classes of the lower order of Irish. The pageant did not proceed to any of the town churchyards. It struck up a street which led to the country in a northerly direction, I all the time following it in its motions, but at a pretty good distance, to avoid being noticed or considered an intruder. And so, on and on the party went, and travelled, as the story-book says, I do not know how far. They kept the high road for several miles, stopping only now and them to apply to the bottles; and then, taking a crou path ever by a flat boggy region between two rising grounds, they next descended into a more secluded and wild part of the country. I cannot but own, that, in the course of the march, I began to think this was going to be rather a toil some and a tedious adventure. I had not calculated on proceeding above a mile from town ; but as an insatiable curiosity, or some indefinable sentiment, impelled me forward, and at I hated the idea of returning no wiser than I went, I continued to follow the car and its motley crew of attendants to the hub The march at length stopped. The party reached a rude-looking burying-ground, without any very distinct enclosure, and only distinguishable as a place or sepulture by a ruinous church, and a number of tomb stones and crosses. A decayed village, consisting of a dozen cabins, which sent forth a small addition to the group, was adjacent. The scene altogether was wild and solitary. The country was open, and unornamented by art; and a small sedgy stream pursued its way through the waste, draining in its course the peat-bog from whence the cottars most likely derived their only fuel. The scene was indeed appropriate to the melancholy purpose now before me. The funeral-car having been stopped, the coffin was un tied, and placed on the ground, preparatory to interment ; and while it was waked or howled over by a number of the female mourners, evidently under a strong excitement from repeated applications to the whisky, the male part of the assembly proceeded to measure and dig a grave for the body. In the course of making these observations, I had approached the rustic cemetery. But it was speedily quite apparent that my pretence was considered an intrusion. Side looks were cast at me as I loitered about the burial ground, and there was a good deal of mutteriug one with another, no doubt as to who I was, and what was my object in being there. I must say I did not like the aspect which affairs seemed to be taking. I re membered the stories told of blood and murder in Ireland, and well knew, that, if once aroused by pas ion and intoxication, the crew about the grave would think no more of sending me to my lung home, than they would of burying the man already dead. Every minute, things looked worse and worse. The women, I saw, were taken into consultation as to my intrusive visit, and one after another began to raise their voices in harsh objugatory exclamations. I now felt a tremor creep over me, which I had never experienced before, and triad to make up my mind to come rough treatment, if not to something worse. Yet I continued to affect an unconcern I did not feel. "1 commenced an examination of the picturesque ruined church,and seemed regardless of the hubbub which was fast fomenting. Sitting down on a projecting part of the outside of the ruin to rest myself, "I saw that I had placed myself in front of an upright monumental stone, which stood at the head of a grave, Into which a little wooden cross was stuck, and planted with a few flowers. Such an ornamental mound I had not expected to see in so rude a district, and it attracted my attention. While thus sitting in meditation, but still in a state of alarm, in dread of an attack, a stalwart personage, one of the leaders of the party, and whose flowing top-coat, and legs covered with twisted straw for stockings, not to speak of his brown physiognomy and high-seasoned brogue, lie spoke him a genuine son of Erin, came towards the place where I sat. The Irish have usually a tone of civility in all their opening addresses to strangers, but on this occasion there was no such demonstration. Paddy addressed me in a snappish, quick tone, evdently with the view of picking a quarrel, and there by opening the war. " That's a purty grave you're lookin' at, isn't it?" said he in a rude manner. Yes," I replied, " it seems recently made, and is neatly planted with flowers by some affectionate relation." " Och, and troth it is," he replied; " and what might you be afther wantin' wid that same purty grave—if it lookin' for daid bodies you're here, or what is it ?" " Indeed," I rejoined, in a mild good-humoured tone, " you are greatly mistaken, my friend, if you or any •ne else think that I am here for so base a purpose. I came for nothing else but curiosity to witness the form of burial in this country, being a total stranger in Ireland; and I am sorry that I have intruded where it seems my presence is felt to be troublesome." My self-defence was, however, no way regarded by tin' savage who stood before me. He waved his hand to his fellows, and the troop came down like a pack of yelling wolves. Amidst the unintelligible howling might be heard the words, "Och, murdther him, murdther him—down wid him and bury him in his clo'es—bury him in his clo'es—och, the ugly thaif that be is ; murdther him in a minit, and bury him ! " Fear ful as this onslaught of an enraged drunken mob was, till I preserved a degree of fortitude. Retreat was obviously useless, and reason prompted that it was Sow my best course to face out the danger, and in a peaceful attitude. As the crowd surrounded me, and yelled forth their menaces, I arose calmly and ad dressed them. I told them I was a harmless stranger, teeking no ill; that I might have done wrong in coming thither to see their ceremonies at the burial of their friend, but that I meant no wrong whatever. I concluded with saying, that if a few shillings to re fresh themselves in the village would do them any good, they were at their service. " Och, a thousand curses on you and your money, you ugly thaif you ; where is it you come from, you rascal you ?" burst from one of the gang. " Have a little patience," I answered, " and I shall tell you to your satisfaction. I am a Scotsman—I reside at Holme's hotel in Dulin—I am from Edinburgh; you know where that is : it is in Scotland." " The devil blister you then," roared out the monster, with the foam working from the corners of his mouth, " is it from that you come, you tbaiving scoundthrel you; and do you think we don't know that the Seotch come over and take away Our daid out of their graves, and cut them in paices, and don't give them their Christian burials at all. Och, you're a rectiouer, you ugly thaif ; and the lie Is in the tongue of you." This was received with a scream from echoing tongues. " That's thrue you say, Andy; you're the boy for the reckoners. Let us murdther him at once. Claivehis skull wid the spade; kuottk the pick into his brains. Down wid him, -and bury hun in his clo'es. Och, the ugly thaif that he is, fur to come afther talking' for the body o' the purty colleen." It was apparent that my minutes were numbered. I felt myself in the jaws of destruction; and seeing the uplifted slicks, spades, and mattocks, in the hands of those who pressed around me to be near enough for a stroke, I saw that death was to be my immedi\ate lot; and such a horrible death, too !—murdered by a gang of Irish desperadoes. " Gentlemen," cried I in desperation, "you may certainly murder me, for I am in your power ; hut both God and man will cry out for vengeance. You are about to commit a great, crime, in taking the life of an innocent fellow-creature." It occurred to me also to ask to speak to their priest; but they answered they had no priest present. I then earnestly begged to be conducted before a magistrate, or justice of peace; but this they laughed to scorn. In short, I tried every means to pacify them, without avail. Their wrath was working and lashing itself into madness. One of the wretches, to set an example to the rest, fetched a stroke at me with a stave torn from a fence on the road. This blow, which would certainly have felled me to the earth, I avoided by a smart jerk to one side; but stumbling as I moved, I was furced towards the upright grave-stone which I mentioned above. It was surely Heaven in its mercy which prompted this action.My eye caught one of the words at the bottom of the inscription on the monumental stone. It was the word IIalruddcey, cut in large uncouth characters. Why I had not seen this word before, I do not know. Now, however, an idea flashed through my brain. As the ruffian was rushing up to give a more certain blow, I called out, " Stop!—one moment for God's sake ! does any of you know Kitty Taddy, the mother of Mick Taddy, once of the mill of Balruddery." " Ay, sure we do," cried one of the women, ' and what of that; do you know Kitty ?" " Yes," said I ; the perspiration running down my face, and holding up my arm to avert the blows from my de voted head. " 1 know her a little. I saw her at Holme's hotel, where she now serves, and wrote a letter for her to her son Mirk, who is a soldier in the Royal Irish." " Och, he's a gentleman afther all !" cried a number of the females. But let us send acrass for Kitty; she's now at Molly Taddy' house down at the mill yondlher." An urchin in a ragged doublet was instantly sent off at a gallop to summon Kitty, who, I am glad to say, soon made her appearance on the scene. Kitty did not spend a minute in putting things to rights. She told in a moment that " he was a rael gentleman every inch of him. Sure, and he's the gentleman in No. 7C, that reads and writes such a tale. And didn't he write a letter to my son Mick, God bless his honour for that same!" This exclamation was received with a shout of approbation, and the short armistice that had taken place was turned into a lasting peace. The passions of the mob were directed instantaneously into an opposite channel. From being on the point of being murdered with blows, I now ran the risk of being smothered with kindness. I was invited by fifty tongues to stop and adjourn to drink "the dredgy,"* after the burial was over, in one of the cabins ; and 1 was assured, that, if I staid, I would be certain to taste some of the " rael Inishoue —none of your parliament Stuff." However, I took counsel with myself, and perceived that 1 had had a sufficient specimen of Irish manners. I had the discretion to feel, that, in the midst of the drinking fesivities that were to ensue, some of the original evil propensities of the crew might chance to ooze out, little to my Comfort; at least, that a regular row would be almost sure to be kicked up ; and that a stray bottle, or other missile, volant, might come in contact with my organs of vision. I therefore considered it better to be jogging on my way back to Dublin with " the scaith I had got," as we say in the north. So, turning to the multitude, I thanked them all generally, and the gentleman in the straw gaiters in particular, for the kind invitation ; but excusing myself by mentioning that I had very pressing business to execute in town before the evening, I politely took leave, slipping a sovereign into the hand of honest Kitty Taddy as I passed out of the burying-ground. My business was very speedily negotiated on my arrival in Dublin, and next morning I was on the wings of the wind homeward *dredgy. The ghost of a drowned person.

Funeral Ceremonies of the Irish, Mrs. S.C. Hall, 1841.

–From a new and splendidly illustrated work now in course of publication in London, entitled
Ireland, its scenery, character, &c.
By Mrs. S. C. Hall.,1841`

Thoughts of the Irish on Death—formalities over the corpse—description of the IRISH
WAKE accompanied with a sple N did illustration—lines of music giring the air usually
chaunted at Irish funerals—the lamentations—description of the KEE.NER, or *ban caoianthe,*
with a splendid lllustration—an Irish curse—*caoines,* or extempore compositions over the
dead, by the Keener (a.woman)—composition of "a fosterer" of Morty Oge Sullivan, the
chieftain of Bereharen, being eight verses translated from the original Irish by Mr. Callanan—
description of a funeral procession—party contests when two funerals meet at the same
ground—abhorrence at disinterring the dead- account of a touching and sad, though
interesting funeral—two widows at a grace yard, &c. &c.

The most anxious thoughts of the Irish peasant through life revert to his death; and he will
endure the extreme of poverty in order that he may scrape together the means of obtaining "a
fine wake" and a "decent funeral." He will, indeed, hoard for this purpose, though he will
economise for no other; and it is by no means rare to find among a family clothed with rags,
and living in entire wretchedness, a few untouched garments laid aside for the day of burial".
It is not for himself only that he cares; his continual and engrossing desire is, that his friends
may enjoy "full and plenty" at his wake; and however miserable his circumstances, "the
neighbors" are sure to have a merry meeting and an abundant treat after he is dead?. His first
care is, as his end approaches, to obtain the consolations of his religion; his next, to arrange
the order of the coming feast. To "die without the priest" is regarded as an awful calamity. We
have more than once heard a dying man exelaim in piteous accents, mingled with moans—
"Oh, for the Lord's sake, keep the life in me till the priest comes " In every serious case of
illness the priest is called in without delay, and it is a duty which he never omits; the most
urgent business, the most seductive pleasure, the severest weather, the most painful illness,
will fail in tempting him to neglect the most solemn and imperative of all his obligations—the
preparing a member of his flock to meet his Creator. When the Roman Catholic sacrament of
extreme unction has been administered, death has lost its terrors—the sufferer usually dies
with calmness, and even cheerfulness. He has still, however, some of the anxieties of earth;
and, unhappily, they are less given to the future destinies of his family, than to the ceremonies
and preparations for his approaching wake. The formalities commence almost immediately
after life has ceased; The corpse is at once laid* Only a month ago, we gave a poor woman, an
inmate of our parish workhouse, a few shillings. On asking her soon afterwards what she had
done with her money, she said she had purchased with it a fine calico under-garment, to be
kept for her shroud, that she might be buried decently.
The wake-feast of the present day, however, is confined to the use of tobacco and snuff. In
some cases, indeed, punch is distributed; more rarely still, tea and coffee. The practice, first
perhaps prompted by hospitality, was carried to injurious, and often ruinous excess.
Indeed, sometimes, that event is anticipated by the assembling of friends and neighbors. Mr.
Wakefield mentions the following circumstance, which occurred to him at a cottage where he

257

called to inquire after a poor man who was ill of consumption, but who, having a good constitution, seemed likely to live for some time. "I found," says he, "the kitchen full of men and women, all dressed in their Sunday clothes; I therefore, asked one of them what are they going to do, and the answer was, "We are waiting for the wake.' I inquired who was dead. "No one; but the man within is all but dead, and we are chatting a bit that we may help the widow to lift him when the breath goes out of his body.'"out, and the wake begins: the priest having been first summoned to say mass for the repose of the departed soul, which he generally does in the apartment in which the body reposes. It is regarded by the friends of the deceased as a sacred duty to watch by the corpse until laid in the grave; and only less sacred is the duty of attending it thither.

The ceremonies differ somewhat in various districts, but only in a few minor and unimportant particulars. The body, decently laid out on a table or bed, is covered with white linen, and, not unfrequently, adorned with black ribbons, if an adult; white if the party be unmarried; and flowers, if a child". Close by it, or upon it, are plates of tobacco and snuff; around it are lighted

candles. Usually a quantity of salt is laid upon it also ***The women of the household range themselves at either side, and the keen (*caoinet*) at once commences. They rise with one accord,

7

and moving their bodies with a slow motion to and fro, their arms apart, they continue to keep up a heart-rending cry. This cry is interrupted for a while to give the ban *caointhe* (the leading keener,) an opportunity of commencing. At the close of every stanza of the dirge, the cry is repeated, to fill up as it were, the pause, and then dropped; the woman then again proceeds with the dirge, and so on to the close. The only interruption which this manner of conducting a wake suffers, is from the entrance of some relative of the deceased, who, living remote, or from some other cause, may not have been in at the commencement. In this case, the ban caointhe ceases, all the women rise and begin the cry, which is continued until the new-comer has cried enough. During the pauses of the women's wailing, the men, seated in groups by the fire, or in the corners of the room, are indulging in jokes, exchanging repartees, and bantering each other, *some about their sweethearts, and some about their wives, or talking over the affairs of the day— prices and politics, priests and parsons, the all-engrossing subjects of Irish conversation. A very accurate idea of an Irish wake may be gathered from a verse of a rude song, with the singular title of "O'Reilly's Frolics," beginning—"When death at the bowlster approaches to summon me." We purchased it from a ballad vender in Limerick, who was bawling it through the streets in the voice of a stentor:—

"When my corpse will be laid on a table along the room,
With a white sheet on me down to my toes,
My lawful wife by me, and she crying most bitterly,
And my dear loving children making their moans !
The night of my wake long steamers of tobacco,
Cut on a plate, on my navel for fashion's sake,
Mould candles in rows, like torches, watching me,
And I cold in my coffin by the dawn of day."

It is needless to observe that the merriment is in ill keeping with the solemnity of the death chamber, and that very disgraceful scenes are or rather were, of frequent occurrence; the whiskey being always abundant, and the men and women nothing loath to partake of it to intoxication."The keener is usually paid for her services—the charge varying from a crown to a pound, according to the circumstances of the employer. They—

"live upon the dead,
By letting out their persons by the hour
To mimic sorrow when the heart's not sad."

It often happens, however, that the family has some friend or relation, rich in the gift of poetry; introduced the name or the custom, but that the Greeks were in Ireland might perhaps be proved from the Greek church at Trim, in the county of Meath, and also from the life of St Virgilius, Bishop of Saltzburg, where mention is made of Bishop Dobria, a Grecian, who followed St. Virgilius out of Ireland. Amongst the Romans there were women called *Praefic°*, who uttered conclamatio, and Virgil speaking of Dido's funeral says, *"Fat mineo ululatu tecta fremunt.*' "The analogy between the Roman and Irish funeral ceremony, before the government of the Decemviri, was amazingly striking. The Keenaghers or Keeners (for so the *Praeficae mulieres* are called by the Irish) are in the habit of beating their breasts, tearing their hair, and wringing their hands. Now we find the following law relative to Roman funerals, among those of the twelve tables—' *Mulier ne faciem car #. Mulieres genas ne radunto.*' The antiquity of this custom is thus established beyond doubt,and secures or the Irish peasantry the sanction of ages for a practice which a stranger might otherwise contemplate with horror."

* Two English Gentlemen, one an officer, visiting Killarney a few years ago, were exceedingly anxious to be present at a wake; and as their stay was to be very brief, they had some fear that their curiosity was not likely to be gratified. The carmen who drove them, overhearing their conversation, at once removed all dread on the subject, by information that "a dacent boy, a cousin of his, died suddenly that very morning;

and sure he was to be waked that night; only as his people lived far up the mountain, it would be troublesome
to bring him into the town." To oblige their honors, however, the thing was to he done. Of course the news was followed by a liberal donation; and a promise of whiskey enough to make the party merry. Evening came, and with it the two gentlemen. The body of "my poor cousin" was laid out in proper style; the empty bot tles were filled by contributions from the strangers; and an ample supply of pipes and tobacco was also procured. The evening commenced; one visitor after another dropt in; some expressing their astonishment and horror at finding "laid out" the hearty young man they walked and talked with yesterday. The affair was proceeding capitally; the Englishmen asking questions. and passing comments upon the novel and singular scene; until after some remark more than ordinarily lu icrous, the mouth of the corpse was observed to have a sudden twinge. One of the strangers noted the fact, and, starting up, exclaimed, "By Jove, the rascal is alive!" and at the same moment thrust a lighted cigar against his cheek. The dead man instantly started up., grave clothes and all, made a rush to the door, fortunately plunged through it, and ran along the road, pursued by the exasperated officer. The dead outran the living—or there might have been a wake in earnest. It is needless to add that the carman and his friends speedily vanished.

and who will for love of her kin give the unbought eulogy to the memory of the deceased. The Irish language, bold, forcible and comprehensive, full of the most striking epithets and idiomatic beauties, is peculiarly adapted for either praise or satire—its blessings are singularly touching an expressive, and its curses wonderfully strong, bitter and biting. The rapidity and ease with which both are uttered, and the epigrammatic force of each concluding stanza of the keen, generally bring tears to the eyes of the most indifferent spectator, or produce a state of terrible excitement.

The dramatic effect of the scene is very powerful: the darkness of the death chamber, illumined only by candles that glare upon the corpse, the manner of repetition or acknowledgement that runs round when the keener gives out a sentence, the deep, yet suppressed sobs of the nearer relatives, and the stormy, uncontrollable cry of the widow or bereaved husband, when allusion is made to the domestic virtues of the deceased—all heighten the effect of the keen; but in the open air, winding round some mountain pass, when a priest or person greatly beloved and respected, is carried to the grave, and the keen, swelled by a thousand voices, is borne upon the mountain echoes—it is then absolutely magnificent." The following affords an idea of the air to which it is usually chaunted.

This keen is very ancient, and there is a tradition that its origin is supernatural, as it is said to have been first sung by a chorus of invisible spirits in the air over the grave of one of the early kings of Ireland. The keener having finished a stanza of the keen, sets up the wail (indicated in the music by the semibrere at the conclusion) in which all the mourners join. Then a momentary silence ensues, when the keener commences again, and so on—each stanza ending in the wail. The1 teen usually consists in an address to the corpse, asking him, "Why did he die? &c., or a description of his person, qualifications, riches, &c."; it is altogether extemporaneous, and it is sometimes astonishing to observe with what facility the keener will put the verses together, and shape her poetical images to the case of the person before her."

This, of course, can only appear strongly to a person acquainted with the language, as any merit which these compositions possess is much obscured in a translation.

The lamentation is not always confined to the keener; any one present who has the "gift" of poetry may put in his or her verse: and this sometimes occurs. Thus the night wears away in alternations of lamentation and silence, the arrival of each new friend or relative of the deceased being, as already observed, the signal for renewing the keen. But we have witnessed the arrivals of persons who, instead of going over and sitting down by the corpse (which indicated an intention to join in the keen,) fell on their knees immediately on entering, and offered up a silent prayer for the repose of the departed soul. The intervals in the keen are not, however, always silent —they are often filled up by "small plays" on the part of the young, and on the part of the aged or more serious, by tales of farie and phantasie; nor is it uncommon to have the conversation varied by an argument on religion, for even in the most remote parts, so large an assemblage is seldom without a few straggling Protestants.

* Mr. Beauford, in a communication to the Royal Irish Academy, remarks, that "the modes of lamentation, and the expressions of grief by sounds, gestures, and ceremonies, admit of an almost infinite variety. So far as these are common to most people, they have very little to attract attention; but where they constitute a part of national character, they then become objects of no incurious speculation. The Irish," continues that gentle man, " have been always remarkable for their funeral lamentations, and this peculiarity has been noticedby almost every traveller who visited them ;" and he adds, "It has been affirmed of the Irish, that to cry was more natural to them than to any other nation; and at length the Irish cry became proverbial."

The facility of producing rhymes in Irish arises from this, that vocal rhymes are sufficient for poetry. Provided the closing vowels be the same, like consonants are unnecessary—contrary to the laws of rhyme in other tongues. *

The keener is almost invariably an aged woman; or if she be comparatively young, the habits of her life make her look old. We remember one, whom the artist has pictured from our description; we can never forget a scene in which she played a conspicuous part. A young man had been shot by the police as he was resisting a warrant for his arrest. He was of "decent people," and had a "fine wake." The woman, when we entered the apartment, was sitting on a low stool by the side of the corpse.

Her long black uncombed Her long black uncombed locks were hanging about her shoulders; her eyes were the deep set greys peculiar to the country, and which are capable of every expression, from the bitterest hatred and the direst revenge to the softest and warmest affection. Her large blue cloak was confined at her throat; but not so closely as to conceal the ontline of her figure, thin and gaunt, but exceedingly lithesome.—When she arose, as if by sudden inspiration, first holding out her hands over the body, and then tossing them wildly above her head, she continued her chaunt in a low monotonous tone, occasionally breaking into a style earnest and animated; and using every variety of attitude to give emphasis to her words, and enforce her description of the virtues and good qualities of the deceased: "Swift and sure was his foot," she said, "on hill and valley."

His shadow struck terror to his foes; he could look the sun in the face like an eagle; the whirl of his weapon through the air was fast and terrible as the lightning. There had been full and plenty in his father's house, and the traveller never left it empty; but the tyrants had taken all except his heart's blood—and that they took at last. The girls of the mountain may cry by the running streams, and weep for the flower of the country—but he would return no more. He was the last of his father's house; but his people were many both on hill and valley; and they would revenge his death " Then, kneeling, she clenched her hands together, and cursed bitter curses against whoever had aimed the fatal bullet—curses which illustrate but too forcibly the fervor of Irish hatred. "May the light fade from your eyes, so that you may never see what you love May the grass grow at your door May you fade into nothing like snow in summer May your own blood rise against ye, and the sweetest drink ye take be the bittherest cup of sorrow! May ye die without benefit of priest or clergy " To each of her curses there was a deep "Amen," which the ban caointhe paused to hear, and then resumed her maledictions. Akin to this is another keen, of which we have been favored with a translation —A keen, by a poor widow on her two sons, executed for treason, on the testimony of a perjured informer, whose name it appears was Hugh : translated as literally as the idiom of the English language will permit.

"My beloved, my faithful boys,
When yesterday your case was called,
Soon started up Hugh,
How many falsehoods did he not swear,
That would hang men a hundred and one.
Then shook the court to its foundations,
The earth shook, and the skies,
The bolt of heaven fell.
It blasted the bloom of the trees,
It stopped the song of the birds,
Alas! Alas! a thousand times,
That the bolt fell not on Hugh.
"Evil befal the grand jury, and the judge;
Evil befal the twelve who tried you.
"That did not look upon your brows,
To see the bloom of youth there,
And give arms to each upon his shoulders,
And send you beyond the waters far away;
For even then your mether would hope for you.
O, that she was not your judge or your jury |
She would spend days twenty and one
Without or food, or drink,
That she might save her boys."

The following is brief, but contains a volume of Irish history. A female member of the McCarthy More family dying in indigence, was carried to the grave on the shoulders of peasants: her coffin supported by poles. An old woman named Mary Riordan, celebrated in the south for her caoines, seeing her thus borne to her last home, pronounced the following lamentation:

"O mo cara thu as mo runcri, "O my love, my heart's love, "
A gaoil na prunci, Thou kin of princes,
As na Carhach coolmui, The yellow haired McCarthys—
A mead na diag a nun div, Of those who went not into exile,
As war vaag a thruliv, Or were not drowned in the waves,
Don clan do rug cunthis, The children whom a countess bore
D'iaria Muiscri, To the Earl of Muskerry.
Advreher da stumpin, Carried on two poor sticks
Thri do duhiv." Throughout thine own territory."

Another caone of this woman's has been preserved; she was known by the name of Maura

263

Vaan—"White Mary"—this being a distinctive title of her kindred, perhaps from the color of . their hair. An indigent stranger, an itinerant vender of small wares, died at a farmstead. The neighbors attended his poor wake; and among them was this woman. In the course of the night some one said, "It is a pity to let him lie there like a cow or a horse; get up, Mary, and say some thing over him." "What can I say?" she answered; "I know nothing about him." She was prevailed upon; and thus began —

"Approach me, women:
If you grieve not for him who lies here,
You have yourselves lost many friends."

In this manner she continued to appeal to their private feelings and sorrows—reminding one ofthe loss of a husband, another of a lover, another of a father; and worked upon their feelings to such a degree, that every woman present was soon in tears, and all of them rose with one accord, and over the corpse of the unknown indulged each her own private grief.

Besides caoines, extempore compositions over the dead, thirrios, or written elegies deserve mention. They are composed almost exclusively by men, as the caoines are by women. Many of them are of no mean pretensions as efforts of genius. Specimens are to be found in manu script in the house of every peasant who cultivates the language of his country. They differ from the keens in little more than that they are written with more regard to metre. The measure, in English called heroic, is the most common, and suits them best.

We might greatly extend this portion of our inquiries; but, however interesting to some, we should do so at the risk of being tedious in the opinion of a large portion of our readers. The following, however, we must be permitted to transcribe; it is a translation from the original Irish by Mr. Callanan, the poet, whose lines on Gougane Barra we have already quoted. It is said to be the composition of "a fosterer" of Morty Oge O'Sullivan, the chieftain of Berehaven, who was shot in attempting to resist the service óf a warrant for his arrest on the charge of murdering a gentleman, his near neighbor. His body was conveyed to Cork, lashed to the stern of a king's cutter, and towed through the ocean. His head was subsequently exposed on the gaol of that city. He was, it is said, betrayed by one of his own followers.

"The sun on Ivera no longer shines brightly;
The voice of her music no longer is sprightly;
No more to her maidens the light dance is dear,
Since the death of our darling, O'Sullivan Bear.
"Scully, thou false one you basely betrayed him
In his strong hour of need, when thy right hand should aid him
He fed thee, he clad thee, you had all could delight thee,
You left him, you sold him: may Heaven requite thee!
"Scully, may all kinds of evil attend thee!
On thy dark road of life, may no kind one befriend thee!
May fevers long burn thee, and agues long freeze thee!
May the strong hand of God in his red anger seize thee!
"Had he died calmly, I would not deplore him,
Or if the wild strife of the sea-war closed o'er him;
But with ropes round his white limbs, through ocean to trail him,
Like a fish after slaughter, 'tis therefore I wail him. °

"Long may the curse of his people pursue them;
Scully, that sold him, and soldier that slew him!
One glimpse of Heaven's light, may they see never!
May the hearth-stone of hell be their best bed for ever!
"In the hole which the vile hands of soldiers had made thee,
Unhonored, unshrouded, and headless they laid thee;
No sigh to regret thee, no eye to rain o'er thee:
No dirge to lament thee, no friend to deplore thee.
"Dear head of my darling! how gory and pale
These aged eyes see thee, high spiked on their gaol
Thy cheek in the summer sun ne'er shall grow warm;
Nor that eye e'er catch light, but the flash of the storm.
"A curse, blessed ocean, is on thy green water,
From the haven of Cork to Ivera of slaughter'
Since thy billows were dyed with the red wounds of fear,
Of Muiertach Oge, our O'Sullivan Bear."

The wake usually lasts two days; sometimes it is extended to three, and occasionally to four.

Where the survivors are "poor and proud," however, the body is consigned to earth within twenty-four hours after death; for it is obvious that the expenditure is too great to allow of its continuance longer than is absolutely necessary. When the corpse is about to be taken out, the wail becomes most violent; but as then nature is most predominant, it is less musical. Before the coffin is nailed down, each of the relatives and friends kisses the corpse, then the coffin is brought out and placed on chairs before the door; and in some districts, the candles (which from the first were kept constantly lighted) are brought out also, and placed on other chairs in the same relative position they occupied within, and they are not taken away until the coffin is settled in the hearse, and the procession beginning to move.

The funerals are invariably attended by a numerous concourse; some from affection to the deceased: others, as a tribute of respect to a neighbor; and a large proportion, because time is of small value, and a day unemployed is not looked upon in the light of money lost. No invitations are ever issued. Among the upper classes, females seldom accompany the mourners to the grave; but among the peasantry the women always assemble largely.

The procession, unless the churchyard is very near, (which is seldom the case) consists mostly of equestrians—the women being mounted behind the men on pillions; but there are also a number of cars, of every variety. The wail rises and dies away, at intervals, like the fitful breeze.—

On coming to a cross road it is customary, in some places, for the followers to stop and offer up a prayer for the departed soul; and in passing through a town or village, they always make a circuit round the site of an ancient cross." In former times the scene at a wake was re-enacted with infinitely less decorum in the church-yard; and country funerals were often disgraced by riot and confusion. Itinerant venders of whiskey always mingled among the crowd, and found ready markets for their inflammatory merchandise. Party fights were consequently very common; persons were frequently set to guard the ground where it was expected an obnoxious individual was about to be interred; and it often happened that, after such conflicts, the vanquished party have returned to the grave, disinterred the body, and left it exposed on the highway. The horror against suicide is so great in Ireland, that it is by no means rare to find the body of a wretched man, who has been guilty of the crime, remaining for weeks without interment—parties having been set to watch every neighboring church yard to prevent its being deposited in that which they consider belongs peculiarly to them.

It is well known that if two funerals meet at the same churchyard, a contest immediately takes place to know which will enter first; and happily if, descrying each other at a distance, it is only a contest of speed; for it is often a contest of strength, terminating in bloodshed and some times in death. This arises from a belief that the last person buried in a churchyard is employed in bringing water to his fellew-tenants of the "narrow house," until he is relieved in turn by the arrival of a new sojourner in the dreary regions of mortality.

The lower classes of the Irish have always held in exceeding abhorrence the practice of dis interring the dead for the purpose of assisting science; and the men who, in former times, were employed by surgeons to procure "subjects," always held their lives by very slight tenures. {–

* Thus a corpse, passing through Fethard, in the county of Tipperary, is always carried round the pump, because the old cross stood there in former times; and there is a certain gate of the same town (for a considera ble part of the fortifications remain), through which a corpse is never carried, though in their direct course, be cause it was through that gate that Cromwell entered the town.

t In August, 1839, our informant saw lying amongst the nettles in the burial-ground at Mucross, a coffin, the lid of which had been removed, and in it there lay exposed to the unhallowed gaze of curiosity, a body in an awful state of decomposition, which had been left there by its relations, because they were not strong enough to
possess themselves of some particular nook in the abbey, which was defended by the friends of a body already
° which this party would have exhumed, but failing to do so, threw the coffin into the nettles, and ordered it to remain unburied.

: A distinguished lecturer on anatomy in Cork, Dr Woodroffe, whose name is familiar to men of science in every quarter of the world

* related to us some sterling anecdotes in illustration of the strength of this feeling
among the humbler Irish. He was once summoned hastily to visit a family of considerable respectability, the head of which had died of apoplexy. He was the only son of his mother—and she was a widow. Dr. Wood rofe described the scene with a degree of eloquence in which we should vainly attempt to follow him. The "neighbors," poor as well as rich, had gradually strolled into the room in which the corpse lay; and the nar row chamber was crowded. The departed had been loved and respected by all; and there was everywhere signs of earnest sympathy in his fate. The agony of the bereaved household was absolutely appalling. The doctor tried several experiments with a view to restore life—or rather to: satisfy the eager demands of the sur

Indeed, the surgeons themselves were generally objects of suspicion, and not unfrequently of dislike. In order to prevent the possibility of disinterment, we have known parties watch the grave night after night—always in large groups, and, in those days, never without an abundant supply of whiskey. To many of the country churchyards—(the church having vanished ages ago)—a rude hovel is attached, where the parties may sit at night; and where some man is paid to watch, by the friends of the deceased persons.

The most touching and sad, though interesting funeral, we ever attended, was at Mucross, during our recent visit. It was a damp and somewhat gloomy morning, and the waiter, who entered fully into our desire, told us, with evident pleasure, that "we were in great luck, for two widows' sons were to be buried that day,"—adding, "I'm sorry for their trouble, but sure it was before them; and as they could not get over it, and as you had the curiosity to see it, I'm glad they're to come to-day."

We walked about a quarter of a mile away, as it were, from the Cloghreen entrance to Mucross, to arrive at the gate appropriated for the passage of the dead to their last homes. Long before we could see any portion of the crowd, we heard the keen swelling on the ear, now loud and tremulous, anon low, and dying, dying away. Keening has fallen into disuse in this district; but the Kerry keen was more like what we imagine the wild wail of the Banshee to be, than the demonstration of human sorrow. The body had been placed in a plain coffin, what, in England, would be called a shell; and this was put upon a very common hearse, not unlike a four-post bed, drawn by an active but miserable-looking horse. The widowed mother, shrouded in her blue cloak, sat beside the coffin; and when the keeners cried the loudest, she rocked her body to and, fro, and clasped her hands, as if to mark the beatings of her stricken heart. Those who followed were evidently the poorer class of artisans from the town of Killarney, and peasants of the neighborhood; yet they were orderly and well-behaved—no drunken man disturbed the mournful ceremony. The humble grave was dug, not by any appointed sexton, but by a "neighbor," and before it was half-finished, the other funeral we had been told of had filled another corner of the churchyard. This one had no hired keeners, yet there was no lack of tears, and sighs, and bitta wailings. To us it was a wild and singular scene. While the narrow and shallow graves were preparing, the mothers were crouching at the head of each coffin. The deep blue hoods completely concealed each countenance; and so alike in attitude was one to the other, that they could no have been distinguished apart. Groups of men and boys were scattered throughout the church yard. In the distance, a young girl was kneeling beside a grave; sometimes she wept, and then threw herself upon the green sward with every demonstration of agony. Not heeding the crowd, who waited patiently for the lowering of the coffins, two aged women were seated, midway between the two funeral parties, on a broad flat stone, intent upon observing both : like the crones in the Bride of Laminermoor, they discoursed of the departed.

 "And which of the two widdy women do you pity most, Ally " " Och and troth, by dis and by dat, I can't tell. Sure I saw Mary O'Sullivan's boy alive and well yesterday mornin', an he said—it was mighty quare—'Mother,' says he to her, an he going out at the door—"

Survivors; for he well knew that all human efforts were vain. Every minute, the mother murmured, "Doctor, doc tor, give me back my good son!" At length, he prepared to depart, when the hall-frantic woman seized him by the arm, exclaiming, in a very angry voice, " I say, you shall give me back my brave son. " The doctor placed his hand on her shoulder, and said, in a deep and impressive tone, while the whole room was hushed,! woman, apply to God— can I raise the dead ". Instantly, the solemnity of the scene was broken by a voice screaming out from a far corner of the apartment. "Raise the dead! raise the dead! that ye can, ye thieving villain—didn't ye take my poor mother out of her quiet grave, in Douglas churchyard, bare three weeks ago. On another occasion, the doctor driving in one of the hired cars from Passage to Cork, observed that a pretty young country girl was his fellow-traveller; and on returning at night found she was again in his company.—
The circumstance led to a conversation; and the girl told him she had been to Kilcrea to see her grandmother buried, for the robber-doctor had sworn he would have the old woman's body; and she (the grand-daughter) had
sworn to baulk him. Our readers will easily imagine that a curious and amusing scene ensued; the unsuspecting girl fraukly explaining the mode she had adopted to keep her oath; which

consisted principally in her having interred the boy in a remote corner of the old abbey, and covered it with large stones. The dialogue was terminated only by the doctor's saying, "Well, Dr. Woodroffe said he would nave ner, you may be sure he will keep his word—for I am Dr. Woodroffe." The astonished and terrified girl screamed to the driver to stop the car; sprung off-ram back to Cork—instantly proceeded to Kilcrea, a distance of several miles: and having

...plained her case, had no difficulty in procuring assistance to remove her old grandinother rou, the plac° sue hai, in her simplicity, pointed out to the very person from whom she most desired to conceal it.

"Did he turn back to say it, alana?" interrupted the first speaker.

"He did."

"Inugh Inugh see that now. I wonder he hadn't better sinse than to turn back of a Sat urday mornin'."

"Mother,' says he, "what a handful you'll have of white silver to-night, and I in work all the week "

"' God bless you, my darlint, Amin ' she answered, and then he came about and kissed her. oh, wasn't she turned intirely from life when, in less than an hour after, he was brought in a corpse, and he her only comfort and help! I remember her a fine brave-looking woman, and see what she is now. Well, God look down upon us all!"

"Yarra! amen—there's Betsy Doolan out there, showing her bran new shawl at a funeral Well, the consate of some people! Do you know where the up funeral is from 7 other side of Mangerton, they say—an only son too!"

"Oh Peggy, you aint in airnest, are ye '''

"Fait, it's as thrue as gospel, Ally; or may I never light another pipe—two lone women's only sons: aint it a sorrowful sight? But her boy was going off in a consumption this many a day: and sure that was some comfort to her, to have him left in the sight of her eyes, and left to do what she could for him till the last; that was some comfort. Holy Mary did ye hear that cry from Widdy O'Sullivan What ails her I—"

"Yah! they've got down on her husband's coffin, and she can't abide his bones being disturbed, and small blame to her; he was a dacent man. Yah! yah hear to that screech, it bates the head-keener of them all—the strength of the trouble of the widdy's heart was in it; poor cray thur ! the Lord above look down and comfort ye." "I wonder will any of the quality in Killarney look to her ? It's a pity my Lady Kenmare's not in it; sure she looks to every poor craythur that wants. Oh, thin, sure the power of the blessings she resaves from the poor will carry her sowl to heaven. Its a comfortable blanket I had from her last frost. May she have all her heart's delight to the end of her days."

"Some people have grate luck," said the other woman, with a sneer; "but by dis and by dat, I never made a poor mouth to the quality." "And the dickons thank ye for your perliteness, and the man that owns ye in constant work ; not like a poor craythur such as me, who has no head, God help us, these ten years, to think her the childhre—only our own two hands to gather for them and ourselves the scrapings of the earth."

At last we saw the coffin lowered, but a little way beneath the turf, and the humble grave was quickly filled. There was no priest of any description present, nor do the Catholic priests in general attend the humble funerals. This we think exceedingly improper; it is distinctly and positively his duty—a duty he owes to the poor as well as the rich; and yet the victim of sudden death had prayers, many and sincere, offered up over his grave. When the coffin was completely covered, and the friendly grave-digger threw down his spade, every person in the churchyard knelt down; the men uncovered their heads, the females clasped their hands; the very children crowded to the spot, and knelt reverently and silently under the canopy of heaven; there was no word spoken — no sentence uttered; the desolate widow even suppressed the sobbings of her broken heart; and thus the people remained prostrate, perhaps for several minutes. When they arose, the funeral howl broke forth afresh, in all its powerful and painful modulations.

The other funeral was soon over; and the people from beyond the mountain exchanged greetings with those who dwelt in the town. After a little time, their immediate friends—for the poor are the friends of the poor—persuaded the widows to rise from the earth, and their tottering limbs were supported with the most tender care, while every epithet to soften and cheer was used to

* In Ireland, as we have said, they keen their relatives but a short time from the grave, after death. We expressed much pain at this hurrying mᵒrtality to decay. "Yah!" said an old Kerry man "sure they could not afford to keep it longer, even the richest of us." "How do mean "afford,' my good friend ? the dead require no entertainment." "Avick no ; but the living do. Sure no one would lave a corpse widout company, anᵒ company must have welcome ; and how could they afford the entertainment for more than three days at most 7 Sure they never turn the ueighbors out while the corpse is in ; that's the custom of the country, my lady, you see."

wards them. Much that was said was in the native Irish, and of that we understood little; but it was impossible to mistake the eager looks and sympathising tears of many who were present. It so happened that the two widows met when leaving the place where their last earthly blessings were consigned to the earth. "1'm sorry for your trouble, my poor woman,' said the mountain widow to the townswoman.

"Thank ye, and kindly too; the Lord's hand is heavy on us both;'
honestly, and yet with an almost meaningless gaze on the widow who addressed her, and who was a much younger woman. "Two only sons, ' she added—"they tell me, two only boys, yours and mine, and we to be left' but not for long. Tell me, avourneen"—and she laid her hand on her arm, and peered into her face—" did your boy die hard?"

"God be praised he did not; he wasted away without any pain or trouble. Long summer days and winter nights I watched and prayed for him—my gra boy! but the Lord took him for the best, if I could only think so." She paused to weep, while the people round her—some in Irish, some in English—exclaimed, "God comfort her "-" the Lord look down on her "– "Holy Mary pity her "–"Well, she has great strength intirely." "The breath left him," she added "as easy as the down of the wild rush leaves its stem."

"Then thank God always," said the old woman—" thank God that he did not die hard the neighbors will tell ye how I lost mine. He was alive yesterday, ay, he was as full of strength as the finest deer on Glena, and what is he now * Oh! but death was hard on him; I didn't know his face when I looked in it! think of that, my poor woman, think of that; the mother that bore him didn't know his face: Oh! it's a fine thing to have an easy death, and time to make our souls. Holy Mary" and she commenced repeating the litany to the Virgin with inconceivable rapidity, while her face wore the cadaverous hue of death, and her eyes gleamed like lamps in a sepulchre.

"She's turnin' light-headed," said a man in the crowd. "Get her home, Peggy, the throuble is too strong for her, intirely, and no wonder."

* This means—"Did he suffer severely at the last !"

N.A. Woods, *An Irish Wake* (1819)

Letters From The Irish Highlands Anon.,   1825

LETTER XXXIX. July.

It was when passing by the remains of the old church, on our return home the other evening, that the sounds of woe suddenly struck upon my ear: and, on listening attentively, I distinguished the national howl, not indeed in all its vehemence, but in low repressed tones, which were better in unison with the stillness of the evening air. The sound appeared to proceed from the burying-ground, and on looking towards it, we perceived some peasants kneeling over one of the graves. We sat down on the grass to observe them, but finding ourselves at too great a distance, we advanced, though with much caution, from the fear of disturbing them. They were all children except one, a young woman, whose grief appeared to be more violent than that of the others. She continued howling incessantly, rocking herself backwards and forwards, and from time to time throwing herself upon use of words in her lamentation: it certainly appeared to us that she did, but, being wholly unacquainted with the Irish language, we had no means of satisfying ourselves. She seemed to repeat the grave. The younger children only joined now and then, as if in chorus, and sometimes strayed from the melancholy spot, amusing themselves by gathering the wild flowers that were springing around. Though we had now approached pretty close, we could not determine whether the poor girl made the same sounds at stated intervals, and we fancied that the little ones added their voices, not accidentally, but as a chorus at a particular time. After a while, the poor mourners left the burying-ground, and set off on their return to the village. Their grief seemed forgotten as soon as they quitted the grave, and we became the objects of their attention; they talked much together, and often turned to look back upon us.

As we had not heard of any death among the tenants, we walked up to the chapel, anxious to ascertain whether there had been any recent interment. There was no appearance of a newly made grave: at the spot where the poor children had assembled, the turf appeared to have remained long undisturbed, and the head of the grave was marked by a wide wooden cross, which reminded us of Gray's beautiful lines. A number of white stones were laid upon the grave, probably placed there, in the first instance, to prevent the sods from being blown away, as the church stands in a very exposed situation, and perhaps further intended to preserve the sacred spot from being injured by the cattle, a necessary precaution, as the burying ground is uninclosed.

We were endeavouring to reconcile the appearance of the grave with the scene we had just witnessed, when we were met by one of the herdsmen. We asked him if anyone had been buried that day. "No, plaze your Honour." We then told him what we had just seen, and he readily explained the difficulty, by saying that it was very customary for the near relatives to assemble round the grave, on the anniversary of the funeral, and lament over their departed friend. "May be then, they are poor orphans, your Honour, grieving for a father or a mother: when they do be very sorry, they will keep the burying-day for three or four years after." This explanation accounts for the unconcern which the children shewed after they had left the grave. Our walk this afternoon brings to my mind a picturesque scene which I witnessed from the same spot some months ago.

Although the church is now a mere ruin, and no service has for years, perhaps for centuries, been performed within its walls, yet our poor neighbours still retain their attachment to their ancient place of burial.

I had just left the rising ground, on which these venerable ruins are situated, when I perceived a number of people descending the side of the opposite hill. I soon dis covered it to be a funeral procession, and, as it approached nearer to me, observed with surprise that the body was not in a coffin, but on a bier, with a linen cloth thrown over it, and confined at the four corners, to prevent its being blown away; which in deed was a very necessary precaution, as the wind was extremely high. I stopped to watch the mournful train wind down the steep declivity, and I can assure you the effect was truly picturesque. What would you, my dear friend, have thought of such a sight? So different from the funeral processions that you are accustomed to witness: no decent coffin or velvet pall—no clergyman to perform the burial service, for the edification of the survivors; for these poor people were not accompanied by their priest; the grave was dug, and the body committed to its parent earth, without a single prayer, without one word of exhortation to the bystanders I was surprised as well as shocked at this apparent neglect, the more so as the priests in general appear to be attentive to their sacred duties. I seized the first opportunity of asking Father John, whether it was not customary for him to attend the funerals of the poor. He told me that he had always done so, till he came into Cunnemarra; and that he had been much surprised by the custom which obtains here of burying the dead without the attendance of the priest. "I suppose they don't like to be troubling us," was the unsatisfactory but the only reason which he gave me. Do not, however, suppose that the body is always carried to the grave here without a coffin. It is the first instance of the kind that I have known in our immediate neighbourhood. Those who are too poor to buy a coffin will generally beg one of his Honour; and, indeed, we afterwards discovered that there was in this case a sufficient reason why the application should not be made. I believe it must be confessed to be no unusual occurrence on the other side of the bay. The people entertain a superstitious horror of selling wood for coffins, and our good Rector has told me that he found it impossible to buy timber for this purpose in Cliefden, and that the poor man, for whom he wanted it, must have been buried without, but for the humanity of Mr. - - - - - - who gave him the necessary materials. You have never acknowledged the receipt of one or two numbers of our county paper, which I sent you some time since, thinking you might feel interested in a scheme lately brought forward in the town of Galway, to lessen the expense of providing coffins for the destitute poor. Instead of furnishing, as usual, wooden coffins for each individual, it was proposed to introduce a patent one, made of metal, on a peculiar construction, in which the bodies might be successively carried to the grave, and dropped into the earth. The clamour excited by this proposal will, I doubt not, appear very natural to your English feelings. I am informed that it found but few partisans, even among those whose purses it was designed to spare, at the expense of the prejudices, if it must be so, of their poorer neighbours. Many were the appeals made on this occasion to the most sacred feelings of the human heart; but by some cooler reasoners, the point was argued on grounds that appeared well calculated to determine the question. They stated that when coffins were provided by the vestry grant, it was the custom for the relations of the deceased to bear the body to the grave; whereas, if the patent coffins were introduced, in opposition to the feelings of the people, they would most probably refuse to lend their assistance; and the expense of hired bearers would quite equal, I believe, indeed, it was estimated to exceed, the price of a wooden coffin. The proposal was dropped, and the coffins are now provided as before. Those who promoted this scheme represented it, I understand, as having been already adopted in many parts of England, but I could not learn where, nor can I ever remember to have before heard of such a plan. Before I leave the melancholy subject which I have chosen for this letter, I will mention a circumstance which has occasioned us not a little surprise; and having fallen under our notice in different parts of Ireland, is, I am inclined to think, a general custom. Children of an early age are buried in unconsecrated ground: a spot is set apart for this purpose, quite distinct from the burial place of adults, nor is it rendered sacred by any religious ceremony. Not far from our house, I could point out to you such an infant burying-ground, in a situation that would perhaps please your poetic fancy. It is on the verge of a sea-beaten cliff, the turf of the freshest green, overgrown by some straggling briers; and each little grave marked by a heap of the whitest, roundest pebbles that can be found on the shore below. You will be romantic, and imagine that Here scatter'd oft, the earliest of the year, By hands unseen, are showers of violets found, The red-breast loves to build and warble here, And tiny footsteps lightly print the ground. But the brake, alas ! cannot afford shelter sufficient for the robin, and though not in perfect unison with what might be expected from their natural warmth of feeling, yet the Irish are not accustomed, like the Welsh, to scatter flowers over the grave of their departed friends. I have just shewn this letter to my sister, who asks why I did not mention the "cairns", which form so picturesque a feature in Irish scenery. After wandering a mile or two along our mountain roads, where the scene is only varied by a rushy bottom, or a green hill side, you cannot fail to no tice a rude heap of stones, which you will sometimes find thrown up alongside your path. These are our "cairns"; they are raised, if I understand right, where a coffin rests on its way to the burying-ground, and, I believe, every good catholic who passes such a heap is expected to add a stone to the monument, while he offers a prayer for the soul of the departed. Of course, the more popular and distinguished the individual to whose memory the cairn is raised, the higher will be the heap, while the memorial of less illustrious characters will be little observed; and hence it is, that we meet with comparatively few of these rude monuments along our mountain paths. Making some inquiry about a cairm that I passed mot long since, I was told, "It belonged to one Coyne, plaze your Honour; a good man he was, and a man well known in the country." I walked on, pondering whether this was intended as an eulogy of his moral worth, or whether the epithet was used, in this case, according to a common Irish idiom, to signify a man of substance and well off in the world. Perhaps this was all my guide intended —perhaps in this wild and remote corner, as much as in your more civilized neighbourhood, the rich man will still be looked up to as the great man, and the most splendid monument will be purchased by the wealthiest purse. F.

LETTER XL JULY.
To your strictures upon Irish wakes I can make no reply; the custom is barbarous, I had almost said unnatural. To turn the house of mourning into a scene of festive rout, and drunken merriment, appears so repugnant to the common feelings of our nature, that we may be allowed to wonder how the corruptions of time could ever have given so misshapen a form to a custom which was undoubtedly at first both natural and praiseworthy. To wake the spirit of the departed, by calling to remembrance the actions of his past life, to recount his good deeds or noble exploits, must have been consolatory to the survivors, and must have had a powerful effect in stirring up their minds to an eager emulation of the virtues of the deceased; but many a poor hovering ghost has doubtless felt, with Sir Condy, that there was not such great talk about himself, after his death, as he had expected; and more thought of the pipes and tobacco." These wakes are attended with great, and to the poor, with serious expense, which is another strong objection to the custom. Often do the children of a

peasant spend more, on this occasion, in the purchase of tobacco, tea, and whiskey, with all the other requisites of a decent funeral, than is earned by them for many a long month after. It is not an uncommon thing for a fund to be reserved for this purpose by the parent himself; and many is the guinea which, in these times of extreme distress, has been reluctantly produced, in aid of a starving family, from the precious hoard. Their funeral cry or howl, as it is called, is not liable to the same objections, and must be allowed to be an innocent, although perhaps a barbarous, expression of grief. I grant you that it may appear disgusting when it is heard as the voice of a hireling; but that the aspect of real sorrow should be assumed and caricatured is not peculiar to Ireland; and the same regard to public decency, which bids a long train of mourning coaches, with all their gloomy trappings of woe, follow the hearse of one, who has lived unrespected, and died unlamented, may also lead our poor peasants, occasionally, to feign the sorrow which they do not feel; and to raise the funeral howl as a mark of public respect, where it cannot be given as a testimony of private affection. I was once called upon to attend the funeral of a lady, with whom I was distantly connected; the honourable post of bearer was assigned me. On reaching the house, I found an immense mob of people assembled without side, and within a number of gentlemen. Refreshments were liberally provided, of which they as liberally partook. The only sign of grief to be observed among them (for scarcely any one, beside myself, had thought it necessary to appear in mourning), was the putting on of scarfs and hatbands, which were offered to all whose rank was deemed sufficient to entitle them to the compliment. The coffin was at length brought down, amid the deafening clamour of the numerous female mourners assembled for the occasion, who, beating their breasts and tearing their hair, prepared to at tend the mortal remains of their mistress to the burial-ground, at the distance of two or three miles. When the coffin was placed upon the bier, a general howl was raised, and again when the hearse began to move, and afterwards, from time to time, as we proceeded slowly onwards to our destination. But although it would be absurd to contend that this pomp and parade of unreal woe is unknown in any rank, yet it would be inconsistent with the general character of the people to suppose, that it is often called in to supply the want of domestic and social affection; and to a resident in this country, the monotonous cry becomes naturally associated with the tears of the widow and the orphan. I was making some inquiries the other morning respecting a poor girl, who had lately lost her senses, and asked what had first brought on the disease. The answer was, "she was lying in the fever, just recovering, when she heard the cry raised in the house, and she knew it was for her father, who lay sick that same time, and who was just given up for dead, and that instant she went mad." I have often indeed thought that whatever ridicule may have been cast on these wild notes of sorrow, they are in truth very far from ludicrous, as they are heard bursting from a band of peasants, winding slowly among the hills, and bearing the body of the dead to the ruined chapel, which is here their favourite place of burial. I can well remember the thrilling effect of the howl, when it was raised upon occasion of the boat being overset, at the time the wreck came ashore last winter; and I once heard a young man describe the feelings with which he listened to it, as riding home, on a dark night, it was ° borne towards him on the breeze. He was returning to a cottage, situated by the sea-side, in a wild and solitary part of the county of Mayo. Evening drew in fast, and it became quite dark as he approached the village, when he was struck by the singular appearance of a number of fires kindled along the beach. He quickened his pace, and, as he drew nearer, heard the well-known funeral cry brought at intervals to his ear by the rising wind. Dark figures moving around, in attitudes of grief and lamentation, were soon distinguishable by the wavering light of the fires, and he hurried on to learn the melancholy tale. A boat, in the service of his family, had been overset that evening within view of the shore; the unfortunate crew, inhabitants of the village, had been all lost: lost within sight of their wives and children, who were thus doomed to watch their last struggles, and see them sink even before their eyes! The tide as it came slowly in washed the bodies ashore; night drew on ; and to assist their grievous search, they had kindled fires of the dried sea-weed, which lay in heaps on the beach—then, as the body of a son, a husband, or a father, was successively brought to land, it was welcomed again and again by the sad funeral cry. The neglected state of our burial-grounds may seem strangely at variance with these feelings. No care is taken by inclosures to keep off the foot of the intruder; nor is there any attempt made to preserve the mouldering skeleton from the unhallowed gaze of the stranger. The family vaults, in the old and ruined abbeys, are still used as places of interment; and many of these are without doors, and without covering; the coffins, with their silent tenants, as they moulder beneath the hand of Time, lie completely exposed to the curious eye of any one who may choose to inspect these frail remnants of mortality. In one of these abbeys, I noticed the niches in the walls quite filled with skulls, bleached by the wind, while bones of all kinds lay promiscuously scattered around. In one vault was pointed out to us the skeleton of a female, who had so recently been an actor in this busy scene, that not only her family, but her name was mentioned by the gentleman who acted as our guide. Yet, with all this apparent carelessness, the people are not wholly unmindful of what is due to the memory of their forefathers. The same gentleman, who was a catholic of some rank, checked me for leading my horse within the sacred precincts, by observing, that the poor people would feel hurt if they saw me: and it may be remarked, that the influence of these feelings gives to us a stronger protection than the iron coffin, or the triple guard can afford to you. We have the satisfaction of knowing that the tomb, however open, the coffin however slight, will not be violated by the sacrilegious hand of the nightly robber; and, if we have not the neatness, we have at least the security of a Welsh churchyard.

A Wake in Connemara, 1882

From: The Catholic World, Vol: XXXV,1882, p. 251

There is nothing more characteristic of the temperament of the Celtic race and the influence which the circumstances of life and the effects of national history have had upon the Irish branch of it, nor more misunderstood by its Saxon neighbors from the contrast of their custom and temperament, than the custom of the wake, once universal in Ireland, but now disappearing with other national peculiarities of the people. There is something peculiarly shocking to the Saxon habits of decorum in the idea of a boisterous merriment about the corpse of the dead, and it is attributed to an incurable shallowness of temperament and lack of deep feeling in those who practise it. It is considered both an indulgence and a desecration, and there is a total misunderstanding of its original purpose. Something of the difference between the Celtic and the Saxon custom of mourning, as exemplified by the solemn funeral of the one and the wake of the other, is unquestionably due to the radical differences in temperament, but much also to the hereditary difference of

circumstances that have made misery a constant companion
with the one and an infrequent guest with the other. When
sorrow comes seldom the impulse is to endure it, and even make
much of it. When it comes often the struggle is to escape from
it and throw it off by every means in the power. The Saxon
people, comfortable and prosperous, paraded their misery ; the
Irish, unfortunate and suffering, endeavored to conceal theirs.
The purpose of the merriment of the wake was to distract the
mind of the mourners, to give them some relief from the otherwise
unendurable sorrow, and its characteristics were as deeply
sad to the sensitive observation as all jests that " do conceal the
wound." It was not an evidence of the lightness but of the
depth of feeling, and if the contrast was to be made there was
likely to be more real grief and pangs of suffering under the distraction
and tumult of the Irish wake than under the sober decorum and
cold solemnity of the English funeral service. But
without any invidious comparison, and allowing the same
strength of natural feeling to all of humankind, the Celtic custom
was merely the expression of its temperament and by no
means an evidence of want of feeling.

There has been so much of degrading caricature concerning
the Irish wake, as in regard to other national customs, in that
English literature which was for a long time the accepted exponent
of Irish life, and which has been continued by such native writers
as Maxwell, Lever, and Lover—who wrote mainly
for English audiences, and of a purpose or from natural exaggeration
drew more for effect than for truth—that there is a generally false
idea concerning its nature. There is a general impression that
it is a scene of drunkenness, irreverence, and at best of
boisterous tumult; that its substance is a wild riot and its frequent
conclusion a general fight. How false this is, and how
much it is resented by the Irish people, has been shown to the
American people in one way by the fact that the wake scene in
Mr. Boucicault's " Shaughraun " cannot be given before an Irish
audience without vigorous hisses and sometimes with more emphatic
evidences of disapproval. The humors of the wakes as
described in the stock Irish novels like those of Maxwell and
Lover are no more natural or truthful than the vulgar comicality .
of the stage Irishman is like the real wit of the peasant, or the
coarse humor of the music-hall songs is like the deadly pathos of
such expressions of native feeling as " The Night before Larry
was Stretched." The real wake is by no means devoted to merriment
in any sense. Even where the sorrow does not break
through the attempts to hide it, it is only the alternation of the
set lamentation—the song and story follow the keen* He is a
very dull observer indeed who does not feel the real pathos of
the wake, or whose heart-strings are not touched by the depth

of its expression of grief as a whole as well as in the weird and
wild sorrow of the keen. Such as it is, however, the wake is disappearing,
fading with the native language and other peculiarities of the Irish
people. Wakes have long been disapproved of
by the Catholic clergy, and in the greater part of Ireland have
been reduced to little more than a simple vigil around the dead.
In the west they still retain many of their predominant features,
or did before the last famine, which is said to have made such
changes, although the custom which used to prevail of accompanying
the corpse to the grave with the keen along the road has
for some time been extinct, unless it be in some of the islands.
One late autumn I was a sojourner in a dwelling-place appropriately
nicknamed " Mount Misery," which overlooked a dark,
undulating landscape, brown heath and black bog, with the
patch of a green field here and there, gray walls and sod-roofed

* The correct Gaelic orthography is caoine.

cabins, that lay between it and the low, dark banks and gray
waters of the great Lough Corrib. The house was an appropriate
type of more than one to be found in the west of Ireland. It
had once borne the more hospitable title of the " Friar's
Head," and been inhabited for a generation or two by a family
of the inevitable Blakes, or Brownes, or Lynches of the pure
Galwegian stock. The house was not an old one, but probably had
never been finished, and in any event showed all the unredeemed
ugliness of premature decay. It was built of dark, gray stone in
the narrow and unrelieved style of architecture of the Georgian
era, and stood on a gentle eminence at a distance from the main
road. An empty and ruinous porter's lodge stood by the gate,
which hung heavily on one hinge, and an ill-trimmed and unthrifty
plantation flanked the muddy avenue, leading to a bare,
furze-grown pasture that was once the smooth, green lawn in
front of the mansion. A few ragged evergreens surrounded the
house, whose barren nakedness, however, was not relieved by
the curtain of ivy which in that country of ruins so tenderly unwraps
the wrecks of fortune and war and makes them an ornament instead
of a blot upon the landscape. The mansion was of
two stories in height and its walls were substantial; but its
rooftree had sunken from the horizontal; one chimney had blown
down and the other was ragged and visibly leaning; and the upper
windows were smashed in'or boarded up. The dog-kennels
were tenanted at will by a couple of pigs of the greyhound or
razor-back species. The extensive stables were now only occupied by
the poor old garran of the farmer and the doctor's bit of
a blood mare, with a piece cut out of her cheek where he had
driven her into a gate-post one dark night. Turf and manure
were piled against the walls of the house; the garden showed

tokens of potato ridges and the stumps of gathered cabbages;
and the stable-yard was a morass in which broken wheels and implements
showed like the grave-stones of departed prosperity.
Within the house the picture was not more cheerful or encouraging.
The hall-door, carefully pried open, admitted you
into the entry, on one side of which was the living-room of the
family, once the great dining-room. The plastering had fallen in
great patches and the mouldings were knocked off. The table,
on which the circles of the hot tumblers of twenty years ago
were marked, was propped in one corner on the uneven floor.
The chairs were broken-legged and broken-backed, and the
dresser showed a meagre display of cracked earthenware. In
the great chimney-place a prematurely sad and ragged young
woman watched the boiling- of a pot over a dull and feeble flame,
holding a child in her arms, while a couple more disputed possession
of the hearth with a dog and some guerrillas of fowls. The
tenant of the place was a " weak "—that is to say, poor—farmer,
who had lived there since the late Blakes, or Brownes, or Lynches
had succumbed to the combined evil effects of hunting, horseracing,
and hospitality, and the estate had fallen into the hands
of a receiving attorney, who exacted a rent that left a very slight
margin above a steady diet of potatoes.
There were, however, two other inmates of the house…

…I had expressed the wish to attend a genuine old-fashioned
wake, and upon the first occasion—the death of an elderly farmer
in a townland about ten miles from " Mount Misery "—we set
forth. At about four o'clock Fanny was brought out and put
into the shafts of the jaunting-car. We balanced each other on
the sides, Andy climbed into his seat in the centre, and we flashed
through the avenue and out into the post-road. Rain is the
normal condition of things at this season of the year in Connemara,
and we were not disappointed when the night fell in a
heavy mist, soon settling into the soaking deception of a fine
drizzle. With mackintoshes buttoned tightly, and the coal of the
pipe burning dimly under the nose with that special gratefulness
both of warmth and fragrance that comes from tobacco in the
wet, we rolled along in darkness mile after mile over one of those
solid limestone roads which are a special wonder to an American, and
for which he would be glad to exchange some of his
more pretentious paved streets. At long intervals we would pass
the light of a wayside cabin glimmering with a feeble halo
through the mist, and a dog would bark or a melancholy donkey
send his dismal hee-haw after us ; but there were long stretches
of the darkened land without sign of life. Finally the car turned
into the mouth of a narrow boreen which Andy must have discovered
by instinct, and went floundering along through the
mud, stray branches of the hedge now and then giving us a
sharp splash across the nose or a wet tickle in the ear, until we

came to a long, low house at the foot of a great, dusky mass of
hill. The windows were streaming with light, and as we drove
into the yard we could see that the doorway was filled with dark,
quiet forms.

Theft was no sound of merriment, not even of voice, from
the house. All was still, as if in expectation, when there came
from it a long, piercing, mournful wail—u-lu-lu ! * It rose to a
high, tremulous cry, filling the misty air with an indescribable
chill, and sinking into a low moan. It was thrice repeated, and
then followed by a rapid recitation in Gaelic in a sustained key.
The cry seemed the last excess of anguish and lamentation, and,
although I know that in one sense it was artificial, it overcame
me with an actual shudder. It was the keen.
After the recitative had ceased way was made for us into the
room where the corpse lay. It was large though low, and
around the bare rough walls candles were stuck up with lumps
of clay. Its only ornaments were a religious picture and a
faded lithograph of the " Liberator." In the centre a couple of
Stools supported a coffin of unpainted deal. No glass protected
the white, wan features of the corpse from the tobacco-cloud that
filled the air, eddying around the candles and under the cobwebs
of the thatch. The principal mourners sat at the side of the
coffin, and consisted of the son, a stout farmer of fifty, and his
wife, and a half-dozen of children in youth and girlhood. The
room was filled, except in the space immediately at the head of

* Fhuil le luadh—that is, blood and ruin.

the coffin, with all the neighbors for miles around, seated on
benches, stools, and turf kishes, or on the uneven floor. An impressive
quietude and solemnity reigned upon the countenances
of all. The faces of the assemblage were characteristic of the
locality. They were sharper in outline and wilder in expression
than their congeners of the south. Their features were more
regular, with darker complexions and hair, and less of the Milesian
outline. Some of them had the dark, flashing eye and the
regular oval of the Spanish face, and there was the carriage and
turn of the head of the dwellers of the mountain. They were
poorly clad, and few of the women had the comfortable long
blue cloaks of the southern farmers' wives, or the cap with its
frill of lace around the shining hair. Some of the men were
ragged beyond description, and the *suggaun*, or hay-rope, around
the waist was all that kept their garments in any degree of consistency.
Several of the men, and women also, were barefooted,
although the night earth and air were both damp and chill.
The keener sat on a low stool at the head of the coffin.
When she had finished her recitative, as we entered, she had
drawn the hood of her cloak over her face, and a slight rocking

of her body gave the only sign of life. It was as if she were
meditating under the excess of grief. After a silent interval of
some minutes she threw back the hood of her cloak, revealing
the pale face of a woman of about forty, with a fixity of look as
of one in a trance. Without lifting her eyes from the face of the
corpse she repeated her tremulous cry and continued with a
rapid recitative, apparently addressed to the dead rather than
the audience, and then subsided again into silence. The follow
ing is a literal translation of a portion of her invocation, and
characteristic of its entire language and substance:

U-lu-lu!

Ah ! he is gone ; ?
The sweet, clean old man is gone.
Happy was his face when he came to die ;
But his children lamented ;
His grandchildren lamented ;
There were tears and cries around him.
Ah ! he is gone.
He was honest ; he was true ; he was devout ;
His voice was low and kind ;
He wronged no man.
His cousins and all his relatives lament him,
All his neighbors lament him.
Ah! he is gone.

He is with the angels, above, above,
In brightness and happiness ;
We shed tears for him below
In darkness and sorrow.
May the winds blow soft on his grave;
May the turf grow green upon it,
As he sleeps with his fathers of many generations,
And pain and weakness feels no more.
Ah ! he is gone.
Uhla-uhla-gohla-goane !

As the keener continued silent the spirits of the company
were relieved from their tension. They began to talk and to
move. One or two got up and filled their pipes from a plate of
tobacco on the coffin, and there was a gradual relaxation of the
talk to gossip and joke. A little old man, wrapped in a gray
frieze overcoat much too large for him, with a face like a withered
apple and a look of. humor in his unfaded blue eyes, wiped
his *dhudeen* on his sleeve, and, handing it to his neighbor, commenced
the recital of a story in Gaelic. He gave out his narrative with
much comic emphasis, drawing the sympathetic attention and

laughter of his audience. The story was evidently well
known, but none the less pleasing on that account, the audience
anticipating with knowing smiles the jocose turns. The story
is a familiar one in the fireside legends of Ireland, and is a characteristic
specimen of them. It is called " The Well at the
World's End," and its substance is as follows:

There was a king, who had three sons. Being taken grievously sick,
he was told by a wise man that nothing could cure him but
a drink of water from a well at the world's end. His eldest son
volunteered to go and get the precious water over the seven seas
and seven lakes, and seven mountains and seven plains, that lay between
it and the palace. On his way he met a poor old woman,
who asked an alms, but the stingy prince refused to give her even
a bit of bread. When he came to the castle in whose courtyard
was the well he blew his bugle, and out rushed a giant lion that
bit him savagely, but, on consideration for the old father,' let him
go in. He went into a long hall, and there he found fifty knights
standing in armor and all sound asleep. On the throne was a
beautiful princess with a crown on her head, who told him
where the well was, and that if he did not get his bottle filled
and be out of the castle before the clock struck twelve it would
be the worse for him. He stayed so long gallivanting with her
that the clock struck and the knights woke up; the castle-door,
shut itself, and he was a prisoner. He was thrown into a dark
dungeon. As he did not return, the second son set off, but treat
ed the old woman no better and met with exactly the same fate.
Lastly the youngest son set out, and he gave the old woman an
alms as well as kind words, and she bestowed on him a magic
cake. This he gave to the lion, who was too busy in eating it
to do him any harm. When he spoke to the young lady, and she
told him about the well, he went off and filled the bottle the first
thing ,and returned to compliment her afterward. When the
clock struck twelve the knights did not wake, and the lady
showing him where the unfortunate princes were confined, he
released them and they all went home to the palace together,
where the king was cured, and the youngest prince and the lady
were married. " And if they didn't live happy together afterward,
that you may."

When the shanachy * had concluded his tale, which was embellished
with many flourishes and digressions here omitted,
whiskey was passed around, and a Connemara Hebe appeared
before us bearing in one hand a bottle and in the other a tum
bler with its bottom fixed in a stand of wood. Even in that
land of fair women I had not seen a more brilliant and striking face.
Hardly more than sixteen, there was a fulness to her
figure and a bloom on her cheeks, as the Irish song says,

" Like the apple's soft blossom,"

which the kindly air of Ireland alone gives in purest perfection
to womankind. Her eyes were as dark and limpid as those of
Andalusia, and the regularity of her features and the darker
tinge of her complexion gave token of that Spanish blood that
still survives in unabated strength after so many generations
since its original introduction in Galway. There was a dimple
in her chin and in her cheek that gave piquancy to the regular
features, and her crown of hair was silky and fine enough to be
the " brag of Ireland." She was better dressed than some of
the rest, a silk handkerchief being pinned across her bust with a
silver pin of an antique shape, a clean cotton gown fastened to a
roll behind displaying a bright scarlet petticoat. " Plase, if you
plase," she said, dropping a decided curtsey ; and we took the
least taste in life of the pure element to her good health, which
she repaid with a smile half timid and half gay, and altogether

* Correctly, seanchuidhe.

innocent and bright, and rapidly withdrew. The mirth continued
in various ways without becoming at all turbulent or even
boisterous. Occasionally some one would come in, cross himself
and pray by the side of the coffin, where the keener sat unmoved like a
statue of grief, and then rise up and join in the merriment ; but
at all times there were frequent ejaculations of sorrow
and sympathy, and a special endeavor to cheer and distract the
minds of the nearest mourners. The undercurrent of pathos was
visible under it all, and, strange as it may seem to some, the very
mirth and merriment did not seem incongruous with the presence of
death, while it was far from being in any feature the irreverent
festivity the wake is usually depicted. If such take place
in Ireland it has never been my fortune to see one.
An hour's stay in such a scene was enough to impress it
vividly on the mind, and we withdrew. Our departure seemed
to arouse the keener, who had remained silent and motionless
since our entrance, and as we passed out into the thick, damp air
once more the long, wailing cry thrilled in our ears and haunted
our minds as we moved heavily down the lane.
It commenced to rain soon after we started, but fortunately
a hamlet with a decent country inn was not many miles away.
In a short time we were steaming before a roaring turf fire in
the best room, and buxom Mrs. O'Farrell shook her fist at Katty
to hurry up the laying of the table, and turned to smile on us
with two steaming tumblers, saying, " Drink that, my poor boys,
for fear the cowld would get into your hearts."

The Observations of John Witakeer and Others, 1855

Dealings With the DEAD.

By: A SEXTON OF THE OLD SCHOO L. No. XCI
VOLUME II., 1855,
No. XCI

Wake—Vogo;--Waecan- import one and the same thing. So we are informed, by that learned antiquary, John Whitakeer, in his History of Manchester, published in 1771. Originally this was a festival, kept by watching, through the night, preceding the day on which a church was dedicated. We are told by Shakespeare--

He that outlives this day, and sees old age,
Will yearly, on the vigil, feast his neighbors,
And say tomorrow is Saint Crispian.

These vigils, like the agapa, or love-feasts, fell, erelong, into disrepute, and furnished occasion, for disgraceful revelry and riot.

The Irish Wake, as it is popularly called, however it may have sprung from the same original stock, is, at present, a very different affair. Howling, at a wake, is akin to the ululation of the mourning women of Greece, Rome, and Judea, to which I have alluded, in a former number. The object of the Irish Wake is to rouse the spirit, which, otherwise, it is apprehended, might remain inactive, unwilling, or unable, to quit its mortal frame—to wake the soul, not precisely, " by tender strokes of art," but by long-continued, nocturnal wailings and howlings. In practice, it has ever been accounted extremely difficult, to get the Irish soul fairly off, either upward or downward, without an abundance of intoxicating liquor.

The philosophy of this is too high for me—I cannot attain unto it. I know not, whether the soul goes off, in a fit of disgust, at the senseless and insufferable uproar, or is fairly frightened out of its tabernacle. This I know, that boon companions, and plenty of liquor are the very last means I should think of employing, to induce a true-born Irishman, to give up the ghost. I have read with pleasure, in the Pilot, a Roman Catholic paper of this city, an editorial discommendation of this preposterous custom However these barbarous proceedings may serve to outrage the dignity, and even the decency, of death, they have not always been absolutely useless. If the ravings, and rantings,

the drunkenness, and the bloody brawls, that have sometimes
occurred, during the celebration of an Irish wake, have proved
unavailing, in raising the dead, or in exciting the lethargic soul—
they have, certainly, sometimes sufficed, to restore consciousness
to the cataleptic, who were supposed to be dead, and about to be
committed to the grave.

In April, 1804, Barney O'Brien, to all appearance, died suddenly, in
the town of Ballyshannon. He had been a terrible
bruiser, and so much of a profligate, that it was thought all the
priests, in the county of Donegal, would have as much as they
could do, of a long summer's day, to confess him. It was concluded, on
all hands, that more than ordinary efforts would be
required, for the waking of Barney O'Brien's soul. A great
crowd was accordingly gathered to the shanty of death. The
mountain dew was supplied, without stint. The howling was
terrific. Confusion began. The altercation of tongues was
speedily followed, by the collision of fists, and the cracking of
shelalahs. The yet uncovered coffin was overturned. The
shock, in an instant, terminated the trance. Barney O'Brien
stood erect, before the terrified and flying group, six feet and
four inches in his winding sheet, screaming, at the very top of
his lungs, as he rose—" For the love o' the Bissed Jasus, jist a
dhrap o' the crathur, and a shelalah "

In a former number, I have alluded to the subject of premature interment.
A writer, in the London Quarterly, vol. lxiii. p.458, observes, that
" there exists, among the poor of the metropolitan districts,
an inordinate dread of premature burial." After
referring to a contrivance, in the receiving houses of Frankfort
and Munich,—a ring, attached to the finger of the corpse, and
connected with a lightly hung bell, in the watcher's room—he
significantly asks—" Has the corpse bell at Frankfort and Munich ever yet
been rung —For my own part, I have no correspondence with the
sextons there, and cannot tell. It may possibly have been rung, while the
watcher slept! After admitting the possibility of premature burial,
this writer says, he should be content with Shakspeare's test—
" This feather stirs; she lives."

This may be a very good affirmative test. But, as a negative
test, it would be good for little—this feather stirs not; she is
dead. In cases of catalepsy, it often happens, that a feather will
not stir; and even the more trustworthy test—the mirror—will
furnish no evidence of life.

To doubt the fact of premature interment is quite as absurd,
as to credit all the tales, in this connection, fabricated by French
and German wonder-mongers. During the existence of that terrible
epidemic, which has so recently passed away, the necessity, real or

imagined, of removing the corpses, as speedily as possible, has, very probably, occasioned some instances of premature interment.

On the 28th of June, 1849, a Mr. Schridieder was supposed to be dead of cholera, at St. Louis, and was carried to the grave ; where a noise in the coffin was heard, and, upon opening it, he was found to be alive.

In the month of July, 1849, a Chicago paper contained the following statement :—

" We know a gentleman now residing in this city, who was attacked by the cholera, in 1832, and after a short time, was supposed to have died. He was in the collapsed state, gave not the least sign of life, and when a glass was held over his mouth, there was no evidence that he still breathed. But, after his coffin was obtained, he revived, and is now living in Chicago, one of our most estimable citizens."

" Another case, of a like character, occurred near this city, yesterday. A man who was in the collapsed state, and to all appearances dead, became reanimated after his coffin was procured. He revived slightly—again apparently died—again revived slightly—and finally died and was buried."

I find the following, in the Boston Atlas of August 23, 1849:—

" A painful occurrence has come to light in Baltimore, which creates intense excitement. The remains of the venerable D. Evans Reese, who died suddenly on Friday evening, were conveyed to the Light Street burying-ground, and while they were placed in the vault, the hand of a human being was discovered protruding from one of the coffins deposited there. On a closer examination, those present were startled to find the hand was firmly clenched, the coffin burst open, and the body turned entirely over, leaving not a doubt that the unfortunate being had been buried alive. The corpse was that of a very respectable man, who died, apparently, very suddenly, and whose body was placed in the vault on Friday last."

The *Recherches Medico-legales sur L''incertitude des risques de la mort, les dangers des inhumations precipitees, les moyens de constater les dices et de rappeler a la vie ceux qui sont en etat de mort apparente*, by I. de Fontenelle, is a very curious production. In a review of this work, and of the Recherches Physiologiques, sur la vie et la mort, by Bichat, in the London Quarterly, vol. lxxxv. page 369, the writer remarks—" A gas is developed in the decaying body, which mimics, by its mechanical force, many of the movements of life. So powerful is this gas, in corpses, which have laid long in the water, that M. Devergie, the physician at the Morgue, at Paris, says that, unless secured to the table, they are often heaved up and thrown to the ground." Upon this theory, the writer proposes, to account for those posthumous changes of position, which are known, sometimes to have taken place. It may serve to explain some of these occurrences. But the formation of this gas, in a greater or less degree, must be universal, while a change in the position is com paratively rare. The curiosity of friends often leads to an in spection of the dead, in every stage of decomposition. However valuable the theory, in the writer's estimation, the generation of the most powerful gas would scarcely be able to throw the body entirely out of the coffin, with its arms outstretched towards the portal of the tomb ; of which, and of similar changes, there exist well authenticated records.

It is quite probable, that the Irish wake may have originated, in this very dread of premature interment, strangely blended with certain spiritual fancies, respecting the soul's reluctance to quit its tenement of clay.

After relating the remarkable story of Asclepiades of Prusa in Bithynia, who restored to life an individual, then on his way to the funeral pile—Bayle, vol. ii. p. 379, Lond. 1735, relates the following interesting tale. A peasant of Poictou was married to a woman, who, after a long fit of sickness, fell into a profound lethargy, which so closely resembled death, that the poor people gathered round, and laid out the peasant's helpmate, for burial. The peasant assumed a becoming expression of sorrow, which utterly belied that exceeding great joy, that is natural to every man, when he becomes perfectly assured, that the tongue of a scolding wife is hushed forever.

The people of that neighborhood were very poor ; and, either from economy or taste, coffins were not used among them. The corpses were borne to the grave, simply enveloped in their shrouds, as we are told, by Castellan, is the custom, among the Turks. Those who bore the body, moved, inadvertently, rather too near a hedge, at the roadside, and, a sharp thorn pricking the leg of the corpse, the trance was broken—the supposed defunct sprang up on end—and began to scold, as vigorously as ever.

The disappointed peasant had fourteen years more of it. At the expiration of that term, the good woman pined away, and appeared to die, once more. She was again borne toward the grave. When the bearers drew near to the spot, where the remarkable revival had occurred, upon a former occasion, the

widower became very much excited ; and, at length, unable to
restrain his emotions, audibly exclaimed—" don't go too near
that hedge "

In a number of the London Times, for 1821, there is an account of
the directions, given by an old Irish expert in such
matters, who was about to die, respecting his own wake—" Recollect
to put three candles at the head of the bed, after ye lay me
out, two at the foot, and one at each side. Mind now and put a
plate with the salt on it, just atop of my breast. And d'ye hear
—have plinty o' tobacky and pipes enough; and remimber to
have the punch strong. And—blundenoons, what the devil's the
use o' pratin t'ye—sure it's mysilf knows ye'd be after botching
it, as I'll not be there mysel."

The Wake Orgies

From: Ancient Legends, Mystic Charms, and Superstitions of Ireland
by Lady Francesca Speranza Wilde
[1887]

FROM ancient times the wakes, or funeral games, in Ireland were held with many strange
observances carried down by tradition from the pagan era. Some of the rites, however, were
so revolting and monstrous that the priesthood used all their influence to put them down.
The old funeral customs, in consequence, have now been discontinued almost entirely
amongst the people, and the ancient traditional usages are unknown to the new generation,
though the elders of the village can yet remember them. An old man still living thus
described to an inquiring antiquary and lover of folk-lore, his experience of the ceremonial
of a wake at which he had been present in the South of Ireland, when he was quite a youth,
some fifty years before.

"One dark winter's night, about seven o'clock, a large party of us," he said, "young men and
women, perhaps thirty or more, set out across the mountain to attend a wake at the house of
a rich farmer, about three miles off. All the young men carried lighted torches, for the way
was rugged and dangerous; and by their light we guided the women as best we could over
the deep clefts and across the rapid streams, swollen by the winter's rain. The girls took off
their shoes and stockings and walked barefoot, but where the water was heavy and deep the
men carried them across in their arms or on their backs. In this way we all arrived at last at
the farmhouse, and found a great assemblage in the large barn, which was hung throughout
with branches of evergreen and festoons of laurel and holly.

"At one end of the barn, on a bed decorated with branches of green leaves; lay the corpse.,
an old woman of eighty, the mother of the man of the house. He stood by the head of the
dead woman, while all the near relatives had seats round. Then the mourning women
entered and sat down on the ground in a circle, one in the centre cloaked and hooded, who
began the chant or funeral wail, all the rest, joining in chorus. After an interval there would
come a deep silence; then the chant began again, and when it was over the women rose up

and went out, leaving the place free for the next comers, who acted a play full of ancient symbolic meaning. But, first, whisky was served round, and the pipers played; for every village had sent their best player and singer to honour the wake.

"When a great space was cleared in the centre of the barn, the first set of players entered. They wore masks and fantastic garments, and each carried a long spear and a bit of plaited straw on the arm for a shield. At once they began to build a fort, as it were, marking out the size with their spears, and using some rough play with the spectators. While thus engaged a band of enemies appeared, also masked and armed. And now a great fight began and many prisoners were taken; but to save slaughter a horn was blown, and a fight demanded between the two best champions of the hostile forces. Two of the finest young men were then selected and placed at opposite ends of the barn, when they ran a tilt against one another with their spears, uttering fierce, loud cries, and making terrible demonstrations. At length one fell down as if mortally wounded; then all the hooded women came in again and keened over him, a male voice at intervals reciting his deeds, while the pipers played martial tunes. But on its being suggested that perhaps he was not dead at all, an herb doctor was sent for to look at him; and an aged man with a flowing white beard was led in, carrying a huge bundle of herbs. With these he performed sundry strange incantations, until finally the dead man sat up and was carried off the field by his comrades, with shouts of triumph. So ended the first play.

"Then supper was served and more whisky drunk, after which another play was acted of a different kind. A table was set in the middle of the barn, and two chairs, while all the people, about a hundred or more, gathered round in a circle. Then two men, dressed as judges, took their seats, with guards beside them, and called on another man to come forth and address the people. On this a young man sprang on the table and poured forth an oration in Irish, full of the most grotesque fun and sharp allusions, at which the crowd roared with laughter. Then he gave out a verse like a psalm, in gibberish Irish, and bade the people say it after him. It ran like this, being translated--

"'Yellow Macauly has come from Spain,
He brought sweet music out of a bag,
Sing *See-saw, Sulla Vick Dhau,
Sulla, Sulla Vick Dhau righ.*'

(That is, Solomon, son of David the King.)

"If any one failed to repeat this verse after him he was ordered to prison by the judges, and the guards seized him to cut off his head; or if any one laughed the judge sentenced him, saying in Irish, 'Seize that man, he is a pagan: he is mocking the Christian faith. Let him die!'

"After this the professional story-teller was in great force, and held the listeners enchained by the wonders of his narration and the passionate force of his declamation. So the strange revelry went on, and the feasting and the drinking, till sunrise, when many of the guests returned to their homes, but others stayed with the family till tile coffin was lifted for the grave."

*

Full details of these strange wake orgies can seldom be obtained, for the people are afraid of the priesthood, who have vehemently denounced them. Yet the peasants cling to them with a mysterious reverence, and do not see the immorality of many of the wake practices. They accept them as mysteries, ancient usages of their forefathers, to be sacredly observed, or the vengeance of the dead would fall on them.

According to all accounts an immense amount of dramatic talent was displayed by the actors of these fantastic and symbolic plays. An intelligent peasant, who was brought to see the acting at the Dublin theatre, declared on his return: "I have now seen the great English actors, and heard plays in the English tongue, but poor and dull they seemed to me after the acting of our own people at the wakes and fairs; for it is a truth, the English cannot make us weep and laugh as I have seen the crowds with us when the players played and the poets recited their stories."

The Celts certainly have a strong dramatic tendency, and there are many peasant families in Ireland who have been distinguished for generations as bards and actors, and have a natural and hereditary gift for music and song.

On the subject of wake orgies, a clever writer observes that they are evidently a remnant of paganism, and formed part of those Druidic rites meant to propitiate the evil spirits and the demons of darkness and doom; for the influence of Druidism lasted long after the establishment of Christianity. The Druid priests took shelter with the people, and exercised a powerful and mysterious sway over them by their magic spells. Druid practices were known to exist down to the time of the Norman invasion in the twelfth century, and even for centuries after; and to this Druidic influence may be traced the sarcasms on Christianity which are occasionally introduced into the mystery plays of the wake ceremonial. As in the one called "Hold the Light," where the passion of the Lord Christ is travestied with grotesque imitation. The same writer describes the play acted at wakes called "The Building of the Ship," a symbolic rite still older than Druidism, and probably a remnant of the primitive Arkite worship. This was followed by a scene called "Drawing the Ship out of the Mud." It was against these two plays that the anathemas of the Church were chiefly directed, in consequence of their gross immorality, and they have now entirely ceased to form any portion of the wake ceremonial of Ireland. Hindu priests would recognize some of the ceremonies as time same which are still practised in their own temples; and travellers have traced a similarity also in these ancient usages to the "big canoe games" of the Mandan Indians.

In the next play, the Hierophant, or teacher of the games, orders all the men out of the room; a young girl is then dressed with a hide thrown over her, and horns on her head, to simulate a cow, while her maidens form a circle and slowly dance round her to music, on which a loud knocking is heard at the door. "Who wants to enter?" asks the Hierophant. He is answered, "The guards demand admittance for the bull who is without." Admittance is refused, and the maidens and the cow affect great alarm. Still the knocking goes on, and finally the door is burst open and the bull enters. He also is robed with a hide and wears horns,and is surrounded by a band of young men as his guards. He endeavours to seize the cow, who is defended by her maidens, forming the dramatic incidents of the play. A general mock fight now takes place between the guards and the maidens, and the scene ends with uproarious hilarity and the capture of the cow.

There are other practices mentioned by writers on the subject, who trace in the Irish observances a tradition of the Cabyric rites, and also a striking similarity to the idolatrous practices of Hindustan as described in the "Asiatic Researches," and in Moore's "Hindu Pantheon."

It is remarkable also that in the Polynesian Islands the funeral rites were accompanied by somewhat similar ceremonies. These the early missionaries viewed with horror, and finally succeeded in extirpating them.

These ancient funeral rites have now disappeared in Ireland; still the subject remains one of intense interest to the ethnologist and antiquary, who will find in the details indications of the oldest idolatries of the world, especially of that primitive religion called Arkite, as in the dramatic performance called "The Building of the Ship," where one man prostrates himself on the ground as the ship, while two others sit head and foot to represent the prow and stern. This ship drama is, perhaps, a fragment of the earliest tradition of humanity represented by a visible symbol to illustrate the legend of the Deluge.

Preparing the Body

Washing the Corpse

Neighbours, who were specialists, usually women, washed and shrouded the body, and might help to prepare the house. Care was taken with the water used to wash the dead. Many accounts suggested it had to be discarded carefully, beneath a bush, in a corner, or where people didn't usually walk. It could cause the ground to grow *'fear gorta'*: hungry grass, that would make passers-by feel faint or shaky, or make a 'stray sod' that caused anyone walking on it to be lost. Artifacts used had to be treated with care. Dying people were put on woven straw mats which were burned or disposed of. Soap and towels would be burned, buried, or put in a fork of a tree.

There were customs for shaving of the dead and tools of shaving. In some area places all dead men were shaved, in others only those who were clean-shaven were shaved when dead.

For example, in Carne, Co. Wexford in the 1930s'If a man was wearing a moustache or side whiskers it was shaved off',[1]and in Sraheen, Co Mayo, it was said 'that if a man is not shaved before he is buried he will not go to heaven'.[2] In Kilcommon, Co. Tipperary,'A man who shaved during life is shaved, while those who wore beards are left there just as in life.'[3]The job of shaving the dead was generally done by a man, while women did the washing. The razor used should be given to the man who did the work, In places, like Shancurry, Co. Leitrim, it was buried '. No payment should be asked. Shaving a dead person was thought of as a tricky matter (cuts and nicks would not be acceptable). A person who was good at sharpening tools: 'He could put an edge on a scythe that would shave a corpse'.[5]
References to shaving the dead by men is found in stories concerning encounters between mortals and the 'Good People' – the fairies – who were widely feared . While women were held by the fairies to be midwives or nurses, men were roped in to play games, music or, to carry corpses or shave the dead –this was due to the Good People's aversion to iron.

The story of Pat Doherty From Shrule, Co. Galway:

There was once a man coming home from a wake. He had to cross a hill and on the top of the hill there was a little house. When he was near the house he heard a voice saying "Pat Doherty will shave the dead man". Out ran the fairies from the house and brought him in. Then he shaved the dead man and the fairies gave him tea. When he was going home the fairies struck a weed and it turned into a horse. He got up on the horse and went home. He was putting in the horse into the stable and he disappeared. Then he went in and went to bed.[6]

A Mayo Tale

 About a man inveigled into both shaving a corpse for some supernatural women and carrying his coffin. Tom Coffey 'was put astray' on his way home one night and, exhausted, sought shelter in a house. An old man there died just after Tom arrived, and the two women attending him told Tom 'he would have to shave him and he said that he never shaved a man in his life. They said that he would have to shave him.' The women then obliged Tom to make a coffin. 'They got a rope then and put it around the coffin. They told Tom that he would have to carry it and he [said he] would not be able. They said that he would. They put it on his back. He carried it all night until cock-crow. They told him to leave down the coffin and he did. The two women and the coffin disappeared.'[7}

A Haunted House, and an otherworldly barber [8]

Seamus de Brun of Croom, Co Limerick told

The Story of a Courageous Tramp

There was this great house, and nobody could stay there, because it was haunted. There was a notice on the gate stating that the person that would stay there three nights would get a thousand pounds.

There was a tramp walking the road and he saw the notice on the gate and read it. He went and told the owner that he would stay there. The first night the owner of the house gave him a bottle of whiskey. When he went in, he put down a big fire and sat down on a chair. At twelve o'clock a man dressed in black stood above on the stairs. The tramp said, what are you doing there, but he got no reply. He held on saying that until he fell asleep.

Next morning the owner unlocked the door and left out the tramp. Next night the owner gave him another bottle of whiskey. At about twelve o'clock, four men [came in] and a coffin on their shoulders. They set down the coffin and departed, and a corpse stood up from the coffin and asked him if he would shave him. He said he would, but he had no razor. The man in the coffin said that [it] was all right, as he himself had one. The tramp set to work and shaved him. Thanking him the corpse said that he had been coming here a long time, but had met no man with courage enough to shave him. The corpse told him where there were three crocks of gold and told him keep two for himself, and give one to the owner of the house. Next morning he done as he was told and got the thousand pounds. He was a rich man afterwards.[9]

Clearly prohibitions against payments for shaving the dead did not apply in the case of walking corpses.

-Traditional
Sources:

Dr Clodagh Tait, Mary Immaculate College, University of Limerick, - https://dralun.wordpress.com/

[1]https://www.duchas.ie/en/cbes/5009243/5001110/5122935
[2]https://www.duchas.ie/en/cbes/4428066/4374474/4462894?ChapterID=4428066
[3]https://www.duchas.ie/en/cbes/4922168/4857879/5018873
[4]https://www.duchas.ie/en/cbes/4605955/4605645/4644054
[5]*The Irish Press*, 2 June 1979, p.7.
[6]https://www.duchas.ie/en/cbes/5260385/5244869/5261376
[7]https://www.duchas.ie/en/cbes/4427950/4360421
[8]https://www.duchas.ie/en/cbes/5105151/4996451
[9]https://www.duchas.ie/en/cbes/4922034/4920807

On with the Wake!

Now you know why you should keen, and you have picked out a few good lines to keen and you know why keening is essential- When and where and how? It is not hard to tell!   Let the Wake proceed....

"...it was the signal for Finola to commence keening. She emitted a horrendous, piercing shriek that shivered the place and dropped to her knees and crawled toward the corpse.

"Kilty! Kilty! I knew you were leaving us, for I saw the banshee last night with my own eyes!" Well now, that sobered things up.
A frightened murmur arose."
-- Uris op.cit.p.15

"Liam, you will be telling the news. Be sure to go to the byres and the beehives and let the cattle and bees know that Kilty Larkin is gone.

Don't fail or the fairies will take his soul....
"are you carrying salt?"...
"Ma went to the large salt bowl in a niche on the side of the fire-place and doled out a pinch for my pocket, for Conor and for herself to ward off the evil spirits"

--Uris op.cit.p.5-6

To Begin

1. The women who prepared the body join the family.
2. The mourning family produces either muffled sobs or loud wailing related to the depth of sorrow.
3. In the event that the death was considered a "great loss" (a parent leaving a large family or tragic or early death) Keening is most intense and heartfelt.
4. After a period of Keening mourners are led away from the bedside by a few neighbors and are consoled.
5. Word is sent out to distant relatives and is spread with the help of a local shop or village.
6. Preparation and then keening does not wait for the arrival or others.
7. If the person dies late in the evening the main wake is not held until the following night so as to give neighbors and distant relatives time to attend.

Preparations and Requirements for the Wake

What do you need and how do you get it all done.

1. Two men - a relative and a neighbor take-part.
2. Coffin is ordered (traditionally made by a local carpenter at the wake house.). Croker (1824) notes that it was not unusual to find that the tombstone had been created well in advance of death. It would be found leaning on the cabin wall as a *"momento mori"* which would remind a person of death each time they left the house.
3. Supplies are brought in: bread, meat, food of all kinds, whisky, stout, wine, pipes, tobacco, snuff. (Tobacco and snuff are extremely important, as is alcohol)

Set Up of the Wake House

1. *A plate of snuff is taken to all for a pinch. A clay pipe filled with tobacco is given to all and all are provided with food and drink-traditionally a meal. Pipefulls of tobacco are offered.*
2. The place for the corpse is determined by the house itself. A table, settle or bed in the kitchen or one of the rooms is used. A loft may be used.
3. The clocks are stopped as a mark of respect.(Roslea)
4. All mirrors are turned toward the wall or covered.(Roslea)

Watching the body and Ritual of visiting the Corpse

This practice is closely related to that of the Hindus. It is very important as it is of the most ancient Indo-European aspect of Irish Culture derived from the ancient Celts.

1. A corpse must not be left unattended for the entire wake
2. A person, generally a woman, perhaps with others, sits nearby.
3. On entrance the mourner makes their way to
   the side of the corpse, kneels down and silently
   recites a few prayers for the departed soul.
4. Mourner is then welcomed by the relatives
   and expresses sympathy. "I'm sorry for
   your trouble" ...then the mourner speaks kindly
   of the deceased and then walks away.
5. The mourner is offered food and drink for
   the hours spent at the wake. If the weather
   is good the men congregate outside
6. The mourner stays for a few hours. The old men and old women come in the morning and with the end of the working day others in the community stop in.
7. The visitation lasts until midnight.
8. The Rosary is recited once or twice - at midnight and then towards morning. The Rosary is led by an important figure - teacher or leader who recites the first decade then the relatives take part. A truly traditional wake will have a special rosary for the dead and traditional prayers. The rosary is said around the corpse with those around the house reciting the responses.
9. Most visitors leave at midnight.
10. Close neighbors remain till morning. They drink tea or whisky or beer and talk about general affairs. Anecdotes are told with quiet laughter but within a solemn and decorous mood.

"It was only a matter of time for this fight to have occurred,
for there was bad blood between".....

.

"The two of them reeled about
the byre, more jarred by the poteen than
by each other's blows, with O'Kanes and
MacDevitts squaring off all over the place and the O'Neils
leaning toward the O'Kanes and
the O'Doherty's favoring the MacDevitts. It was shaping
up into
an epic when the peacemaker
arrived in the person of
Tomas Larkin"

-- Uris *op.cit.p.520*

Accounts of Wakes

Clearly *a quiet wake*
   ...is not traditional!

Account of Edward MacLysaght: Kildare 1683
"Their wakes also over dead corpses, where they have a table spread and served with the best that can be had at such a time, and after a while attending (in expectation the departed soul will partake) they fall to eating and drinking, after to reveling as if one of the feasts of Backus."

Account of Maria Edgeworth 1810:
Pipes and tobacco were first distributed along with cakes,
beer and whiskey. A verse was provided:
"Deal on, deal on, my merry men all,
Deal on your cakes and your wine;
For whatever is dealt at her funeral today
Shall be dealt to-morrow at mine;

Account of Rev. Horatio Townesend (Co. Cork) 19th century-
"The room, where the body is laid out dressed in white, is filled with people, regaling themselves with liquor and tobacco, and chatting on the various topics, one of which is praise of the deceased."

Account of T. Crofton Croker (1824)
"The wake of a corpse is a scene of merriment rather than of mourning. The body lies exposed in the coffin for two or three nights previous to interment, surrounded by many candles, and with the face uncovered. To avert misfortune arising from the death of the heads of families, when a man dies his head is placed at the foot of the bed; but this ceremony is not deemed necessary with women, and they are allowed to remain in the usual position. In the evening a general assembly of the neighbors takes place,
when they are entertained with whiskey, tobacco and snuff."

A Wake in the Old Times

When the corpses were washed and dressed, they looked uncommonly well, considerin'. Larry indeed looked as well as Sally; but you couldn't meet a purtier corpse than she in a day's traveling. I say, when they were washed and dressed, their friends and neighbours knelt down round them, and offered up a Pater and Ave a piece for the good of their sowls: when this was done, they all raised the keena, wooping over them a half bend, clapping their hands, and praising them, as far as they could say anything good of them: and indeed, the crethurs, they were never anyone's enemy but their own, so that nobody could say an ill word if after the first keening the friends and neighbours took their sates about the corpse.

Image above Left: From: Harper's Weekly, v 17 1873 March 15.

In a short time whiskey, pipes, snuff and tobacco came and everyone about the place got a glass and a fresh pipe. Tom, when he held his glass in his hand, looking at his dead brother, filled up to the eyes, and couldn't for some time get a word; at last when he was able to spake—"Poor Larry," says he, "you're lying there low before me, and many a happy day we spint with one another. When we were childher," he said turning to the rest, "we were never asunder; he was aulder nor me by two years, and can I ever forget the leathering he gave Dick Rafferty long ago, for hitting me with a rotten egg—although Dick was a great dale bigger than either of us. God knows, although you didn't thrive in the life, either of you, as you might and could have done, there wasn't a more neighbourly or friendly people in the parish they lived in; and now, God help them both, and their poor orphans over there. Larry *a cushla,* your health, and Sally, yours, and may God Almighty have mercy on both of your sowls."

After this, the neighbours began to flock in more generally. When any relation of the corpses would come, as soon, you see, as they'd get inside the door, whether man or woman, they'd raise the shout of the *keena*, and all the people about the dead would begin along with them, stooping over them and clapping their hands as before.

Well, as I said, it's that was the merry wake, and that was only the trugh, neighbours. As soon as night came, all the young boys and girls from the countryside about them flocked to it in scores. In a short time the house was crowded; and maybe there wasn't laughing, and storytelling and singing, and smoking and drinking and crying—all going on, helter-skelter, together. When they'd be all in full chorus this way, maybe some new friend or relation, that wasn't there before, would come in and raise the keena: of course the youngsters would keep quiet; and if the person coming in was from the neighbourhood with any of them that were so merry, as soon as he raised the shout, the merry folks would rise up, and begin to pelt their hands together, and cry along with him till their eyes would be as red as a ferret's. That once over, they'd be again down at the songs, and diversion, and divilment—just as if nothing of the kind had taken place: the other would then shake hands with the friends of the corpses, get a glass or two, and a pipe, and in a few minutes be as merry as the best of them.

Well as I was telling you, there was great sport going on. In one corner you might see a row of ould men sitting together, talking over ould times—ghost stories, fairy tales, and the great rebelling of '41, and the strange story of *Lamh Dearg*, or the Bloody Hand: they'd sit smoking—their faces quite pleased with the pleasure of the pipe--amusing themselves and a crowd of people that would be listening to them with open mouth. Or, it's odd, but there would be some droll young fellow among them, taking a rise out of them; and positively he'd find them able enough for him, particulary ould Ned Mangin, that wanted only four years of a hundred The Lord be good to him and rest his sowel in glory, it's he that was the pleasant ould man, and could tell a story with any that ever got up.

In another corner there was a different set, bent on pieces of divilment of their own. The boys would be sure to get beside their sweethearts, anyhow: and if there was a purty girl, as you may set it down there was, it was there the skroodging, and the pushing, and the shoving and sometimse the knocking down itself, would be, about seeing who'd get her. There ould Katty Duffy, that now is as crooked as the hind leg of a dog, and it'' herself was then as straight as a rush, and as blooming as a rose— Lord bless us, what an alteration time makes upon the strongest and fairest of us. It's she that was the purty girl that night, and it's myself that gave Frank MacShane, that's still alive to acknowledge it, the broad of his back upon the flure when he thought to pull her off my knee The very gorsoons and gishas were coorting away among themselves, and learning one another to smoke in dark corners…
After that time the house got too throng entirely, and couldn't hould half of them, so, by jing, off we set, maning all the youngsters of us, out to Tom's barn that was red up for us, there to commence the plays. When we were gone the ould people had more room, and they moved about on sates we had left them. In the mane time, lashings of tobacco and snuff, cut in plate fulls, and piles of fresh new pipes, were laid on the table for anyone that wanted to use them.

When it drew near morning, every one of us took his sweetheart and, after convoying her home, we went to our own houses to get a little sleep—so that was the end of poor Larry MacFarland and his wife Sally Lowry.

-"*Larry MacFarland's Wake,*" In: <u>Traits and Stories of the Irish Peasantry.</u>William Carleton, Vol. I. Pp.112-153. London 1896.

The Dead

Lady Wilde from: *Ancient Legends, Mystic Charms, and Superstitions of Ireland,* Ticknor and Co., Boston, 1887.

There are many strange superstitions concerning the dead. The people seem to believe in their actual presence, though unseen, and have a great fear and dread of their fatal and mysterious power.

If a person of doubtful character dies, too bad for heaven, too good for hell, they imagine that his soul is sent back to earth, and obliged to obey the order of some person who bids him remain in a particular place until the Day of Judgment, or until another soul is found willing to meet him there, and then they may both pass into heaven together, absolved.

An incident is related that happened in the County Galway, concerning this superstition.

A gentleman of rank and fortune, but of a free and dissipated life, became the lover of a pretty girl, one of the tenant's daughters. And the girl was so devoted to him that perhaps he might have married her at last; but he was killed suddenly, when out hunting, by a fall from his horse.

Some time after, the girl, coming home late one evening met the ghost of her lover, at a very lonesome part of the road. The form was the same as when living, but it had no eyes. The girl crossed herself, on which the ghost disappeared.
Again she met the same apparition at night, and a third time, when the ghost stood right before her in the path, so that she could not pass. Then she spoke, and asked in the name of god and the good angels, why he appeared to her; and he answered, that he could not rest in his grave till he had received some command from her, which he was bound to obey.

"Then," she said," go stand by the gate of heaven till the Judgment Day, and look in at the blessed dead on their thrones, but you may not enter. This is my judgment on your soul."

On this the ghost sighed deeply and vanished, and was seen no more. But the girl prayed earnestly that she soon might meet her lover at the gate of heaven, whither she had sent him, that so both might enter together into the blessed land. And thus it happened; for by that day year she was carried to her grave in the churchyard, but her soul went forth to meet her lover; where he waited for her by the gate of heaven; and through her love he was absolved, and permitted to enter within the gates before Judgment Day.

It was considered disrespectful to the dead to take a short cut when carrying the coffin to the grave.

In the Islands when a person is dying they place twelve lighted rushes round the bed. This, they say, is to prevent the devil coming for the soul; for nothing evil can pass a circle of fire. They also forbid crying for the dead until three hours have passed by, lest the wait of the mourners should waken the dogs who are waiting to devour the souls of men before they can reach the throne of God.

It is a very general custom during some nights after a death to leave food outside the house--a griddle cake, or a dish of potatoes. If it is one in the morning, the spirits must have taken it; for no human being would touch the food left for the dead. The great and old families of Ireland consider it right to be buried with their kindred, and are brought from any distance, however remote, to be laid in the ancient graveyard of the race.

A young man of family having died far away, from fever, it was thought advisable not to bring him home, but to bury him where he died. However, on the night of the funeral a phantom hearse with four black horses stopped at the churchyard. Some men then entered with spades and shovels and dug a grave, after which the hearse drove away. But next morning no sign of the grave was to be found except a long line marked out, the length of a man's coffin.

It is unlucky and a bad omen to carry fire out of a house where any one is ill. A gentleman one day stopped at a cabin to get a light for his cigar, and having wished good morning in the usual friendly fashion he took a stick from the fire, blew it into a blaze, and was walking away, when the woman of the house rose up fiercely, and told him it was an evil thing to take fire away when her husband was dying. On looking round he saw a wretched skeleton lying on a bed of straw; so he flung back the stick at once, and fled from the place, leaving his blessing in the form of a silver offering to neutralize the evil of the abducted fire.

After the priest has left a dying person, and confession has been made, all the family kneel round the bed reciting the Litany for the Dying, and holy water is sprinkled over the room until the soul departs.

Then they all rise and begin the mournful death -wail in a loud voice; and by this cry all the people in the village know the exact moment of the death, and each one that hears it utters a prayer for the departing soul.

At the wake the corpse is often dressed in the habit of a religious order. A cross is placed in the hands and the scapular on the breast. Candles are lighted all around in a circle and the friends and relatives arrange themselves in due order, the nearest of kin being at the head. At intervals they all stand up and intone the death-wail, rocking back and forward over the dead, and reciting his virtues; while the widow and orphans frequently salute the corpse with endearing epithets, and recall the happy days they spent together.

When the coffin is borne to the grave each person present helps to carry it a little way; for this is considered a mode of showing honour to the dead. The nearest relatives take the front handles first; then after a little while they move to the back and others take their place, until every person in turn has borne the head of the coffin to the grave-for it would be dishonorable to the dead to omit this mark of respect.

As the coffin is lowered into the grave the death-cry rises up with a loud and bitter wail, and the excitement often becomes so great that women have fallen into hysteria; and at one funeral a young girl in her agony of grief jumped into her father's grave and was taken up insensible.

Interference of the Clergy and Government in Cultural Practices

A Timeline of Confrontation

"Fortunately the wake was off bounds for Father Lynch and Father Cluny, but we all knew they were stationed in some shadowy place within earshot to amass evidence of bawdiness, nudity, dirty language together drinking, kissing, or worse...and all the other things in the endless catalogue of carnal sins...It was a good thing he (Father Lynch) was not in the house of Tomas Larkin this night because the loft was getting severely crowded. Our amusement turned to awe at the things they were starting to do to each other...."
-Uris *op.cit.p.19*

"Father Lynch had abolished some of the more grisly graveside customs such as thrusting the dead man's hand into a pail of milk to make the cream rise. However, he reinstated a loathed tradition of separating the men and women, burying each sex in its own section"-- Uris *op.cit.p.5-6*

"Slipping the fee into his pocket, he (Father Lynch) mounted the steps to the pulpit and faced a congregation that dropped to its knees in unison as though they had been felled by a single shot."
-- Uris *op.cit.p.5-46*

"...But God won't know who we are anyhow, because we've priests here who don't even know how to pray in the Irish language

Archdiocese of Armagh
The Synod of bishops on three occasions (1660,1668 and 1670) ordered that drinking at wakes should be abolished. On the third occasion, they forbade the distribution in wake-houses of whiskey or brandy; if this rule were disobeyed, they said, no priest would have any connection with either the wake or the funeral. Any priest who who was negligent in stopping this practice would be deprived of his parish. The abuse seems to have continued however; on October 8 1660 the Synod of bishops again forbade the drinking of alcohol at funerals.

Synod of Tuam (1660)
Statue 20 forbids excessive drinking and feasting at Catholic wakes. Money for wakes was to be diverted to the poor and to Masses for the souls of the dead.
Synod of Clones 23/8/1679 Orders an end to drinking and to wakes.

Diocese of Waterford and Lismore
1676- drinking at wakes should cease as it was an insult to God
1687- Drinking forbidden
1750- troubles with drinking at wakes reported.

Archdiocese of Cashel and Emly

.....it's that English they are"...
"The priest knew the faith of his people was bottomless. They obeyed meekly. Yet with all that faith there was one thing more powerful and that was their memory"
-- Uris *op.cit.p.45.*

1800-abuses at wakes detailed

"We likewise most strictly forbid all persons to distribute, or give out at wakes or funerals whiskey, or spirits or strong liquors of any sort, even so small a quantity, to any person, through any consideration or pretext whatever. And all heads of families, whoever they be, men or women, who order or suffer whiskey, or strong liquors of any sort, to be reprimanded in the chapel, and deprived of Sacraments, until they have made a public submission before the altar, for their criminal disobedience to the order of the church, with a solemn promise never attain to be guilty of the same transgression. And we most earnestly exhort all pious, devout persons, who may be at wakes or funerals where such odious, pernicious, and detestable practices take place, to give immediate notice thereof to the Parish Priest. Moreover, we strictly charge all our clergy, secular and regular, not to celebrate Mass at the wakehouse, nor bless the clay, nor accompany the funeral to the place of burial, where they discover that whiskey or spirits of any sort are given out..." These orders were to be read each Advent and translated into Irish as needed.

Archdiocese of Dublin 1831
"forbid congregations to provide tobacco at wakes or to spend money on things which would lead people to commit sin."

The Parish of Tydavnet, Co. Monaghan
1832- A responsible person would have to promise that tobacco would not be given out.

Diocese of Ardagh
1835- speaks out against alcohol at wakes.
Synod of Irish bishops, Maynooth 1875
Forbids Alcohol at wakes

Archdiocese of Dublin
1890- condemns drinking at wakes,

Diocese of Ferns- 1898- discourages using money for wake goods.

Diocese of Ardagh and Clonmacnoise 1903
Forbids alcohol at wakes under the pain of mortal sin.
Sources: Hartman, *Der Totenkult in Irland.* Handwoerterbuch des deutschen Abenglaubens, V, 1023-1167; Puckle, *Funeral Customs*, 61-

These are but a few of the decrees issued.

Whiskey was the usual drink of social occasions- fairs, markets, pattern days, weddings, wakes and funerals.

Over time the church has prevailed and therefore, the traditional customs have been limited in contemporary times. The earliest such interference dates from the year 306 AD. While the cost of wakes did impact the livelihood of a family the social ties which were really at the center of the wake would have brought rewards and advances worth many times over the cost.

One can not interpret the wake outside of this important social network. We must interpret the wake as a bridge linking two distinct, parallel, and, at times hostile, cultures. The Celtic people have often had to expend considerable energy to protect and defend their ancient traditions from the grasp of "mother church". It is this fierce struggle which makes our maintenance of the ancient wake traditions all the more important today.

Food and Drink

Food and drink work wonders upon the desire and tendency of people to give precedence to the schedules and timetables of their own small lives. With drink in hand and a plate of traditional home-cooked food, time stands still - the guests stay longer, they relax and talk. Hospitality binds the residents of the "wake" house to the community in the tradition of rounds and reciprocity of which the Irish social safety net was composed. The networking of the guests and of the community stretches the grid of social and cultural interrelationships over the wound and all is healed. A good spread is absolutely essential. Spare not calories, smoke, or alcohol.

Now....Back to the Wake!

1821, Charles Wiliams, "An Irish Wake…"

"...Brigid had filled dozens of small clay pipes with tobacco which had supernatural qualities at times
like this, and offered them about with a plate of snuff to hasten Kilty's Journey
and resurrection.Three lambs had been slaughtered and an immense stew boiled in the great pot and a
dozen loaves of fadge, a potato bread, browned on the baking boards,and likewise our own kitchen throbbed into action for the gathering would
be large. There were many foods we avoided because it reminded the elders of our poverty during the great famine and cheese was foremost among them, but cheese was always present at a wake, heaped unsparingly into wooden bowls".....""We will sup this meal with a spoon of sorrow"
- Uris *op.cit.p.514.*

1. Traditionally whisky and poteen (white/clear spirits distilled outside of the law using a small pot still) were the main drinks, beer and stout being rare in early days.
2. Drinking was generally not moderated. It was a part of mourning.
"a donkey belonging to the poteen-making widows was led into the room with creels filled with bottles of mountain dew"—*Uris, op.cit.p.515.*
3. Loud behavior and games were expected.
4. "The've paid the last respects in sad tobacco And silent is this wakehouse in its haze"
-Padraic O Conaire,Gaelic Storyteller-Higgins, Frederick Robert.
Tobacco- A sign of hospitality produced smoke that filled the air- another essential dimension.
5. The feasting at wakes was described in 17th and 18th century accounts as creating other problems.
6. People would take advantage of the household and overwhelm it as would local officials such as mayors who were at times banned by legislation.

A time to cast thoughts of grasping at life and of the counting of calories aside. To heal requires the living to live for the day. We must be joined through food!

A Few Recipes for the Wake

Irish Wake Cake

<u>Serves:</u> 10
3/4 cup unsalted butter
1 cup granulated sugar
2 tsp vanilla extract
2 large eggs
3 oz cream cheese
1 3/4 cups cake flour, sifted (roughly 6 oz by weight)
1 1/4 tsp baking powder
1/4 tsp salt

1 cup dried currants or raisins
2/3 cup buttermilk
1/2 cup powdered sugar
2 tsp lemon juice

Electric mixer with mixing bowl
9 inch loaf pan
Small bowl
Cooling rack

<u>Procedure</u>

1. Preheat your oven to 325 F degrees.

2. In the mixing bowl, use an electric mixer to cream the butter, sugar, and vanilla together.

3. Beat in the eggs one at a time, then add the cream cheese, mixing until thoroughly combined.

4. Add the flour, baking powder, and salt, mixing until thoroughly combined.

5. Gradually add buttermilk and mix until you have a smooth batter with no lumps, then fold in the currants.

6. Pour the batter into a greased 9-inch loaf pan.

7. Place the pan on the center rack in your oven and bake for about 1 hour 20-25 minutes, or until a knife comes out clean for a test.

8. Remove to a cooling rack and let the cake cool down for 15 minutes.

9. In a small bowl, combine the powdered sugar and lemon juice, then drizzle that icing over the cake while it is still warm. Let the cake cool down however before serving it.

10. Slice the cake and serve with a dollop of clotted cream or whipped cream.

Funeral Buns

Nov. 5, 1881.] The Oracle-a weekly journal of response, research, & reference,

Funeral Cake. Please give a recipe.—Severn Bank.

Funeral buns.—To make 48 cakes (called funeral
bread), at 3d. per cake, each weighing 1 lb. before they
are baked,

Take 2 stones of flour,
1 lb. of butter,
1 lb.of sugar,

Rub these well together, and then add

 3 lbs. of, currants, ginger , carraway seeds, cinnamon, , and a
little, rose , water,

Blend, the , whole , together , with
milk, and one pint of yeast,

 Make, them, round, and, , , ,

Bake a fine brown.

The Best Irish Soda Bread

Ingredients:

6 cups all purpose flour
2 teaspoons baking soda
2 teaspoons baking powder
3 tablespoons cornstarch
2 teaspoons sugar
1 teaspoon salt
2 ½ cups buttermilk
Highly traditional and recommended option: Two tablespoons caraway seeds.
Add them to the dry ingredients and sprinkle some on the top when ready for oven
Preheat oven to 375

Instructions:

Add all the dry ingredients in a large bowl and mix very well. Pour in all of the buttermilk into the bowl at once and stir. Stir only until the dough barely holds together. I mean barely! Do this quickly too!

Divide the dough into two portions. Shape each quickly into a round. Quickly!

Cut a cross 2/3 down into the top of each loaf so that you can see the cut. (spread dough slightly) The loaf should come apart about ½ inch. Paint the loaf over with buttermilk, being sure to get the bottom of the cross cut wet with it. Give the surface of the loaf a bit of texture by cutting into it with a knife or fork if it is too round and smooth. Let loaves rest for about ten minutes. Put into the oven-

The baking takes about 30-40 minutes.

The loaf is done when the buttermilk in the bottom of the cross is dry to the touch.

Do not handle, thump or cut hot soda bread! Let it cool down on a rack if possible.

Wrap in newspaper to keep lightly warm.

Guinness Cake

Ingredients:

1 cup butter or margarine,
1 cup brown sugar,
1 ¼ cups Guinness,
1 ½ cups raisins,
1 ½ cups currants,
1 ½ cups golden raisins,
¾ cup mixed candied citrus peel,
5 cups flour,
½ tsp.. baking soda,
1 tsp. mixed spice,
1 tsp. nutmeg,
3 eggs.

Instructions:

Butter a 9 inch cake pan. Put the butter, sugar and the Guinness in a pan and bring slowly to the boil, stirring all the time until the sugar and butter have melted. Mix in the dried fruit and peel and bring mixture back to the boil. Simmer for 5 minutes. Remove from heat and cool. Sift flour, spices and baking soda into a large bowl. Stir in cooled fruit mixture and beaten eggs. Put in a cake pan. Bake in center of preheated oven- 325 degrees for about 2 hours. Test with a skewer. When done cool in pan before turning out.

Black Cap Pudding

Ingredients:

3 oz. black currants
1 oz. sugar
drop of lemon juice
5 oz. Bread crumbs
2 eggs
2 oz. margarine
milk

Instructions:
1. Beat the eggs and mix with breadcrumbs.
2. Pour the currants into the greased pudding bowl
3. Put black currants into a saucepan and boil for 5 minutes with the sugar.
4. Mix bread crumbs with the melted margarine.
5. Put the mixture on top and cover with aluminum foil
6. Steam for 2 hours
7. Put on a plate and let cool.

Strawberry Scones

Ingredients:

1 cup strawberries,
2 ¼ cups all-purpose flour,
3 tablespoons sugar,
2 teaspoons baking powder,
¼ teaspoon salt,
6 tablespoons butter or margarine,
2/3 cup milk.

Instructions:

Make sure you have cream to go with these fantastic scones. You can substitute sour pie cherries for the strawberries. While we feel it necessary to indicate that margarine might be substituted for butter we do so only as a point of interest and curiosity as no one in their right minds would ever make this recipe without real butter of the highest quality. This is one of our St. Patrick's day delights. In America you can make it for George Washington's Birthday celebrations with sour pie cherries. Use a bit more sugar if using sour cherries.

Preheat oven to 425 degrees. A well pre-heated oven is absolutely essential. Hull strawberries, cut into ½ inch pieces. Complete the following instructions as quickly as possible. Mix together flour, sugar, baking powder and salt. Add butter. With pastry blender cut butter in until mixture resembles coarse crumbs. Lightly but quickly stir in strawberries. Toss well to coat. Add milk all at once. Toss together but only until mixture holds together. Flour hands and form dough into ball. On floured board with floured rolling pin roll out dough ½ inch thick. Cut dough into 2

½ inch circles with floured biscuit cutter. Place on greased cookie sheet. Bake until golden, about 12 minutes. Serve warm. Makes 12 scones.

Fadge

Ingredients:
2 lb. baking potatoes
1 egg beaten
1/2 stick butter
2-3 tablespoons flour
herbal flavoring of choice
milk
salt
pepper
bacon fat/butter

Instructions:
1.boil potatoes- peel when cooked. Drain and dry lightly in dry pan then mash coarsely.
2. Add egg, butter, flour, herbs, salt and pepper.
3. Add milk if mixture is stiff- careful! It should be fairly solid.
4. Fry in bacon fat or butter on the griddle. Should be crusty and brown on both sides (about 4-5 minutes)

Limerick Ham

A great flavor and easy to make-great for a festive meal.
Ingredients:
One ham-cured and cooked- not a salted country ham.
1/4 cup juniper berries (if dried soak until soft)
1 1/2 cups French style mustard (country style coarse if possible)
1 cup Gin
1 cup brown sugar

Instructions
Score the ham to a depth of 1/2 inch on all sides.
Rub juniper berries into the cuts all over.
Mix the gin, brown sugar and mustard.
Cover the ham with the mixture. Bake in a hot oven covered
with foil until heated through. Remove foil and bake until
skin is crisp. From time to time baste with liquid from bottom of pan.

A Savory Pie! Bacon and Egg Pie:

Eaten cold or warm at home or on country outings savory pies turn up everywhere as popular dishes.

Ingredients:
2 cups all-purpose flour,
1 level tsp. salt
1/3 cup lard
3-4 tbsps. cold water
5-6 rashers bacon (thick sliced bacon-if you can't get Irish sliced bacon use 12-15 slices of American style bacon.)
6 eggs.
Instructions:
Sift flour and salt into a bowl. Cut up fats and rub them into the flour. Gradually add the water, mixing it in with a knife until the mixture forms a ball and leaves the bowl clean. Lightly shape on a floured board and cut in two pieces. Grease a 10-inch pie plate, roll out half the pastry and line the plate with this. Place the rashers like the spokes of a wheel and break an egg into each space. Roll out the other half of the pastry and carefully cover the filling with this. Crimp the edges all around lightly. Mark segments with a knife so that each person gets a rasher and an egg-- brush the top with milk. Place in a preheated oven at 400 degrees for 40-45 minutes

The Whiskey and Drink

While today drink is becoming politically incorrect the host of an Irish Wake simply must have Whiskey and in quantity. Here are some recipes which might appeal to 21st. century guests.

Whiskey is traditionally consumed without dilution! One should also have sherry (both sweet and dry) and cordials on hand. Wine is also acceptable. I also include some traditional Irish favorites. Quantity is very important. Well known Irish brands should be obtained if possible but the highest quality is not essential. At the present time safe commercial varieties of Poteen are available. One should be very careful of any Poteen from an untrusted source. It could be deadly. A good pot of tea should always be available. An Irish blend of Ceylon and Assam is recommended. A good guide is to know your guests and be sure that there is something for everyone, however, the wake is not the time to cater to each and every sensitivity to the point where the preferences of others are restricted. To each guest their own.

Some traditional favorites.....

Whisky Punch
Serves 1 Ingredients:1 measure of Whiskey (*uisce beatha*-the water of life), 2 teaspoons white sugar, 4-6 cloves,2 slices fresh lemon, 200 ml (7 oz.) boiling water.1. Put the Whiskey sugar, cloves and lemon slices into a strong preheated glass.2.Pour on the boiling water and stir until the sugar has dissolved.

Version 2: 1 1/2 teaspoons brown sugar, 3 cloves, 1 slice lemon,1 jigger Irish Whiskey, boiling water.

Irish Coffee-

*Version 1-*1 1/2 teaspoons sugar, Hot strong black coffee,1 jigger Irish whiskey, 1 tablespoon whipped cream. Heat a stemmed whiskey goblet. Add the sugar and enough of the hot coffee to dissolve the sugar. Stir well. Add the Irish whiskey and fill the glass to within an inch of the brim with more very hot black coffee. Float the cream on top. Do not mix the cream and the coffee. The hot whiskey-laced coffee is sipped through the velvety cream.
*Version 2:*1 teaspoon sugar, hot strong black coffee,1 jigger Irish whiskey,1 tablespoon double cream. Pour cream over a teaspoon held over coffee so that it floats on the coffee.

Scalteen

1-2 teaspoons honey, 2 tablespoons Irish Whiskey, 1/2 cup hot milk. Blend honey and whiskey together and stir the mixture into hot milk.

Egg Flip

Version 1- 3/4 cup milk, 1 egg yolk,1 teaspoon sugar,1 jigger Irish whiskey, grated nutmeg. Scald the milk. Beat the egg yolk and sugar together. Add the whiskey and pour the scalding milk on top. Add the grated nutmeg and serve in a heated glass.
*Version2-*Make as above but fold in the stiffly beaten white of an egg before serving.

Is deacair amhra`n a ra`dh gan gloine! It's hard to sing with an empty glass!

Ginger Beer

Ingredients: 1 1/2 ounces gingerroot, cut into 3 pieces,1 1/4 pounds sugar,1 tablespoon cream of tartar, 2 lemons peeled and thinly sliced, 1 gallon spring water, boiling,1/2 ounce yeast, creamed with 1 teaspoon sugar. Instructions-Bruise the pieces of ginger to release the essence and combine in a large bowl with the sugar, cream of tartar and the peel and pulp of the lemons. Add the boiling water and stir well to dissolve the sugar, set aside to cool. When lukewarm, add the yeast. Cover the bowl with a clean cloth and set aside in a warm place for 24 hours. Skim, strain and bottle the liquid making sure that the bottles are securely corked, consume after 3 days.

Mulled Rum

Ingredients -(per Person) 1 1/2 ounces Jamaica rum,1 teaspoon brown sugar, 3 whole cloves, stick of cinnamon, slice of lemon very thin .Instructions: combine all ingredients in an old-fashioned glass or any thick 6-oz tumbler or pewter mug, warmed first by rinsing in scalding water. Add about 3 1/2 oz. boiling water, stir with the cinnamon stick. It is traditional to heat the drink just before serving by thrusting a hot poker out of the fire into the drink.

Elderflower Wine

Ingredients-1 quart elderflowers, 1 gallon spring water, 3 pounds white sugar, 1 lemon juiced with the peel sliced thin,1 tablespoon active dry yeast,1 pound golden raisins. *Instructions*-On a hot summer day, gather the flowers from elder bushes - they should be in full bloom. Strip the flowers gently from their stalks and loosely pack a 1-quart container to measure the flowers. Transfer the flowers into a stoneware crock large enough to contain all of the ingredients. In a large saucepan combine the water sugar and lemon peel. Boil for one hour, skimming from time to time. Pour the mixture over the flowers to scald them and stir well. When cooled to a little more than lukewarm add the lemon juice and yeast. Cover the crock with a clean tea towel, stir with a long wooden spoon daily for 7 or 8 days until fermentation ceases. Put the raisins into a wooden wine cask and strain the wine into the cask. Discard the flowers and the peel. Let stand in a cool place. Seal the cask after 24 hours and keep for 6 months before bottling.

Ginger Wine

Ingredients-3 oranges, juiced, 3 lemons, juiced,8 pounds brown sugar, 3 egg whites beaten, 1/4 pound fresh gingeroot, coarsely chopped, 1/2 teaspoon yeast, 2 bottles good gin or poteen. *Instructions:* Bruise the ginger and strain the orange and lemon juices. In a large non-corrodible pot combine 3 gallons of water with the sugar and egg whites and bring to the boil. Skim and add the ginger and boil for 45 minutes - set aside to cool. When lukewarm, add the strained juice and stir in the yeast. Set aside to ferment for 3 days. Stir in the gin and pour all into a wooden cask, bung it up loosely. Bottle after 8 weeks and cork securely.

Always remember that liberal dispensing of spirits and tobacco is a requirement! And let no person rise to speak against it at the wake.

Storytelling, Song, Dance, and Verse

"With the heavy lamenting over for a time, the older folks tucked in their niches, smoking away on clay pipes, playing cards and telling stories some of the young wanes scampered about stuffing pepper into the teapots and tobacco jars, setting off sneezing seizures, while outside the bachelor boys and spinster girls snuck into the shadows to play kissing games and perform mock marriages..."- Uris. Op. Cit. P. 18.

It is said that wakes were far merrier than weddings

One would look forward to the death of an old man or woman and to the festivities of the wake, which would follow. Celebrations and activities associated with the wake were held as very important traditional customs. People were reluctant to give them up. These events were much more than burials. They linked the community together and provided stages for many other cultural activities.

Today the old time wake in Ireland is almost a thing of the past, however, with a bit of time and study it can be easily re-created. The important traditions can be given new life and the wake can become a way to repair and maintain the inner structures of society and culture.

Storytelling

No wake should be without stories and sayings. Put them on cards and hand them out. Short stories are easily learned. Do not underestimate the ability of guests to tell stories. Simply provide them with time and get the ball rolling with a few of your own. Storytelling began late at night after midnight following the Rosary. Listening to storytellers was a main amusement in early times. One would always have the entertainment of storytelling even if one could afford nothing else. While one could hire a storyteller or invite the local *seanachie* (storyteller) in to tell, in the old days, most everyone had a story or several to try out on the assembled group. You do not have to have anything fancy. Storytelling is done to small groups without the need for microphones, amplification or stages. And for payment well, hospitality took care of that. The local storyteller would often be an elderly man. As he would tell a story to one group in the house it would be repeated to another at a great distance from the speaker. Stories functioned to keep the listeners from falling asleep as they watched the corpse. A bishop one time found fault with stories at wakes:

Dr. John Breanan Bishop of Waterford and Lismore noted in 1676 that: "Tales were "*ineptae fabulae*" (silly stories). Prayers should be recited at wakes instead!"

A few good stories...

Remember that adaptation is the rule. There is no need to be an actor or to memorize. Put the stories on cards and pass them out. Ask your guests to read them over and then find someone to tell them to in their own words. This will get them talking and participating in an ancient tradition.

Shortening the Road

Himself and his son were walking the road together one day, and the Goban said to the son, "Shorten the road for me." So the son began to walk fast, thinking that would do it, but the Goban sent him back home when he didn't understand what to do. The next day they were walking, and the Goban said again to shorten the road for him, and this time he began to run, and the Goban sent him home again. When he went in and told the wife he was sent home the second time, she began to think, and she said, "When he bids you shorten the road, it is that he wants you to be telling him stories." For that is what the Goban meant, but it took the daughter-in-law to understand it. And it is what I was saying to the other woman, that if one of ourselves w as making a journey, if we had another along with us, it would not seem to be one half as long as if we wouldn't be alone.

And if this is so with us, it is much more with a stranger, and so I went up the hill with you to shorten the road, telling you that story.

Two Women or twelve Men

There was a fox that had three young ones, and when the time came to teach them how to fend for themselves, the old fox took them to a house. There was great talk going on inside the house. He asked the first two young ones if they could tell him who was in the house. They couldn't. Then he tried the third.

"Who is inside?" asked the old fox.

"Either two women or twelve men," said the young one.

"You'll do well in the world," said the old fox.

No man goes Beyond His Day

A fisherman must follow the sea, and how can a man escape the day of his death? There is such and such a time marked out for a man on this earth, and, when his day is come, if he went into an ant's hole, death would find him there. We have only our time, and, young or old, a man must go when he is called.

There was a boat going out to Inis Tuaisceart once to fish from the rocks, and when they were halfway out they found that they had left the mast behind them. So they went back for the mast. And there was a man on the slip who was the best man on the island at fishing from the rocks, for at every craft there is one man is better than all others, if it were only at driving nails with a hammer. They set out again, taking this man with them, and, when they came to Inis Tuaisceart, they went about the island putting one man out on a rock here and another there, till at last they were all in their places fishing. After they had been thus for a time, the day began to rise on them, and the boat went again to pick up the men. But when they came to the rock where they had put this man out, he was not to be found. A wave had come up out of the sea, they said, and taken him, for death wanted him and his day was come, and when they went back at the beginning of the day it was not for the mast they went, as they thought, but for the man. No man goes beyond his day.

The Best Road to Heaven

There was a woman I knew was very charitable to the poor; and she'd give them the full of her apron of bread, or of potatoes or anything she had. And she was only lately married. And one day, a poor woman came to the door with her children and she brought them to the fire, and warned them and gave them a drink of milk; and she sent out to the barn for a bag of potatoes for them. And the husband came in, and he said:"Kitty, if you go on this way, you won't leave much for ourselves." And she said: "He that gave us what we have, can give us more." And the next day when they went out to the barn, it was full of potatoes--more than were ever in it before. And when she was dying, and her children about her, the priest said to her:"Mrs. Gallagher, its in Heaven you'll be at twelve o'clock tomorrow.

St. Mael Anfaidh and the Bird's Lament for St. Mo Lua

This was the Mael Anfaidh who saw a certain little bird wailing and sorrowing. "O God," said he, "what has happened there? I will not eat food until it is explained to me." While he was there he saw an angel coming towards him. "Well now, priest," said the angel," let it not trouble you any more. Mo Lua son of Ocha has died, and that is why the living things bewail him, for he never killed a living thing, great nor small; not more do men bewail him than the other living things do, and among them the little bird that you
see" -Irish 9th-10th century

Mo Chua's Riches

...Mo Chua and Colum Cille were contemporaries. And when Mo Chua (that is Mac Duach) was in a hermitage of the wilderness, he had no worldly wealth but a cock and a mouse and a fly.. The work the cock used to do for him was to keep matins at midnight. Now the mouse, it would not allow him to sleep more than five hours in a day and a night; and when he wished to sleep longer, being tired from much cross vigil and prostration, the mouse would begin nibbling his ear and so awoke him. Then the fly, the work it did was to walk along every line he read in his Psalter, and when he rested from singing his psalms the fly would stay on the line he had left until he returned again to read his psalms. It happened soon after this that these three treasures died; and Mo Chua wrote a letter afterwards to Colum Cille when he was in Iona in Scotland, and complained of the death of this flock. Colum Cile wrote to him, and this is what he said; "Brother, said he, "you must not wonder at the death of the flock that has gone from you for misfortune never comes but where there are riches".... -Irish, Geoffrey Keating 1634

A Light tokens the Death of Mr. Corrigan

Well, I was coming along the road convenient to Drumbargy Lane and I seen this light And it seemed for to start- I couldn't say whether it started from Francy's or whether it come past it. But it was a little below Francy's when I seen it first.

And it was a powerful light and what struck me was that wasn't it a wonder that it wasn't blacked out, do you see, for the way it was at that time it was only the underpart of a bicycle light that you'd see the upper part of the glass had to be either blackened or there had to be a black cloth over it. It was during the war do you see.

But this was a full light.
And it came on very, very, very, very quick.
And it was just coming forward to where the turn is on the road when it disappeared.
So I was on this side of Drumbargy Lane at that time. And the thought that struck me was that they either got a burst or a puncture or something had happened to the bicycle.
So I came on anyway expecting for to come across some man in difficulty or some person, man or woman.
But there was nobody on the road.
So I took from that that it was some kind of token
John O'Prey was working here with Francy's father at the time.
And he was coming home one night.
And this light came along as he thought meeting him
But it went out before they met
And there was nobody on the road.
I just don't know how long it was before I seen it that John O'Prey seen it. But Francy's father died about a week or a fortnight a short time after....

A Clock Token

One night the clock in my room struck six and it had not struck for years and two nights after on Christmas night it struck six again and afterwards I heard that my sister in America had died just at that hour. So now I have taken the weights off the clock that I wouldn't hear it again.

The Banshee Cries for the Boyles

I saw the Banshee when old Boyle's mother died. I was coming home in the dusk with a load of sods, and the old gray horse and me mother with me. And says she to me "Some poor woman has lost her man or maybe a son."
And the thing wore a shroud as if it had come from a coffin, and its hair was streaming in the wind, we both saw it. And me mother she said a prayer or maybe two. "That's the Banshee", says she
Aye it cried for many an old family here and some say it's one that has gone before.
Be that as it may no human heart could utter such grief so mind ye I doubt it.

The Best and Worst Nail in the Ark

The shipwright who made the Ark left empty a place for a nail in it, because he was sure that he himself would not be taken into it. When Noah went into the Ark with his children, as the angel had told him, Noah shut the windows of the Ark and raised his hand to bless it. Now the Devil had come into the Ark along with him as he went into it and when Noah Blessed the Ark the Devil found no other way but the empty hole which the shipwright had left unclosed, and he went into it in the form of a snake; and because of the tightness of the hole he could not go out nor come back and he was like this until the Flood ebbed and that is the best and the worst nail that was in the Ark.

--Irish 16th century

How Cobhthach Contrived his Brother's Death

Cobhtach the Lean of Bregia, son of Ughaine M/or, was king of Br/egia; but Loeghaire Lorc, son of Ughaine, was king of Ireland. He too was the son of Ughaine M/or. Cobhtach was jealous of Loeghaire for the kingship of Ireland, so that a wasting sickness seized him, and his blood and his flesh withered from him, whence he was called "the Lean of Bregia"; but he had not succeeded in killing Loeghaire. Loeghaire was summoned to him after that, to give him his blessing before he died..."Come tomorrow," said Cobhthach, "to build my tomb and set up my gravestone and conduct the wake for me, and perform my funeral lament, for I shall shortly die." "Good", said Loeghaire, "it shall be done" "Well now, " said Cobhtach to his queen and his steward, "say that I am dead, without anyone else knowing, and let me be put in my chariot with a razor-knife in my hand. My brother will come hastily to bewail me, and will throw himself on to me; perhaps he will get something from me. " That came true. The chariot was brought out; his brother came to bewail him, and threw himself down on him. He planted the knife in him at his midriff so that the point came out of him at the tip of his heart, and he killed Loeghaire so... –Irish, Ninth Century

The Ivyed Tree-Top

My little hut in Tuaim Inbhir, a mansion would not be more delightful, with its stars as ordained, with its sun, with its moon.

It was Gob/an that made it (that its tale may be told you) my darling, God of Heaven, was the thacher who has thatched it.

A house in which rain does not fall, a place in which spears are not feared, as open as if in a garden without a fence around it. -Irish 9th century

The Terry Alts

The Terry Alts were a bad class; everything you had they'd take from you. It was against herding they began to get the land, the same as at the present time. And women
they would take; a man maybe that hadn't a perch of land would go to a rich farmer's house and bring away his daughter. And I, supposing, to have some spite against you, I'd gather a mob and do every bad thing to destroy you. That is the way they were, a bad class and doing bad deeds. One of them went to confession to the priest that asked him how many crimes did he do, and he said, "I was at thirteen killings between Clare and Connacht." He met with a dreadful death. His tongue came four inches out, that neither priest nor doctor could put it in.

One Queer Experience

A good many believe that the fairies will spirit away children. They will carry off a healthy child and leave instead a weazened little dwarf. One day they played that trick on a tailor, and he kept the dwarf several years and it didn't grow any, and was just the same shriveled little thing it was in the beginning. Finally, the tailor made up his mind what the matter was. So he heated his goose red hot and held it over the dwarf, and said, "Now, get out of here-- I know you!" But the dwarf never let on it noticed him; and the tailor lowered the goose little by little till it almost touched the dwarf's face. The n the dwarf spoke and said, "Well I'll leave, but first you go to the door and look round the corner."

The man knew if he did that the dwarf would get the best of him and he said he would not. Then the dwarf saw 'twas no use, and it sprang out of the cradle and went roaring and cackling up the chimney, and a good child lay there in its place. I had one queer experience myself. It was the time of the Fenian troubles. I was sitting up late--I suppose it must have been after midnight --but I hadn't taken anything,and was as sober as I am this minute. Well, it got to be very late, as I said, and by and by, I heard strange noises, hundreds of them, and they were dragging dead bodies and all that. I could hear their breathing, and I could hear their clothing rub along against the wall. Then the ceiling and the sides of the room I was in began to wave. I took a candle and went out in the hall, and there was nothing there, doors all fastened, everything all right. Now, what do you make out of that? I never have been able to account for it myself.

The Cow that Ate the Piper

There were three spalpeens coming home to Kerry from Limerick one time after working there. On their way, they met a piper on the road. "I'll go along with ye," said the piper.
"All right," they said. The night was very cold, freezing hard, and they were going to perish. They saw a dead man on the road with a new pair of shoes on his feet.
"By heavens! "said the piper. "I haven't a stitch of shoes on me. Give me that spade to see can I cut off his legs."
"Twas the only way he could take off the shoes. They were held on by the frost. So he took hold of the spade and cut off the two feet at the ankles. He took them

along with him. They got lodgings at a house where three cows were tied in the kitchen. "Keep away from that gray cow," said the servant girl, "or she'll eat your coats. Keep out from her." They all went to sleep. The three spalpeens and the piper stretched down near the fire. The piper heated the shoes and the dead man's feet at the fire and got the shoes off. He put on the shoes and threw the feet near the gray cow's head. Early next morning he left the house wearing his new pair of shoes. When the servant girl got up, she looked at the door. It was bolted, and the three spalpeens were asleep near the fire. "My God!" she cried. "There were four of ye last night, and now there are only three. Where did the other man go?" "We don't know," they said. "How would we know where he went?" She went to the gray cow's head and fond the two feet. "Oh my! She cried. "He was eaten by her." She called the man of the house."The gray cow has eaten one of the men," said she. "What's that you're saying?" asked the farmer. "I'm telling the truth " she said "There's only his feet left. The rest of him is eaten." The farmer got up. "There were four of ye there last night, men," said he. "There were," said one of the spalpeens, "and our comrade has been eaten by the cow."

"Don't cause any trouble about it," said the farmer. "Here's five pounds for ye. Eat your breakfast and be off. Don't say a word." They left when they had the breakfast eaten. And they met the piper some distance from the house, and he dancing on the road. Such a thing could happen!

The Coffin

A long time ago when I was a young lad I was in a farmer's house below near Monagea one evening and I saw a very strange thing there. It was what looked like a coffin without any cover on it standing up against the wall and it had shelves across it like a small cupboard and there were tins and things in it the same as you would find on the shelves of a dresser. Well the old man of the house noticed how curious I was and he told me about it.

It seems that one night when he was a young married man they were sitting around the fire in the kitchen, himself and the wife and the old people and a few of the neighboring boys, when the door opened and four men came in with a coffin between them, and they laid it down in the middle of the floor without saying a single word and then they turned and walked out again. They were strangers to the people in the house.

Well what was in the house of them had not a word to say with the fright- they were staring at the coffin and they petrified.
Well after a while the young man of the house plucked up his courage. "Here in the name of God," says he, "it would be better to see what is inside in it and to be ready to send for the priests or the peelers according to what is there".
The cover was loose on top of it and he lifted it up and the rest of them came around and looked at what was inside it. It was a young girl and she lying back the same as if she was asleep. "She is not dead with that color on her" says the old woman, the young man's mother, "and let ye lift her out of it, and put her down in the bed in he room below". They did it and she was breathing away, just the same as if she was asleep. They all stood around the bed watching her, and in about a half an hour she

woke up the same as anyone would wake up out of their sleep. And she was greatly puzzled and very much in dread of them, for she did not know where she was or who all the strangers might be.

Well the old woman and the young woman hunted the men up into the kitchen and they started to comfort the poor girl and to tell her that they were respectable people and that she need not be in dread, that nothing would happen to her. And they gave her a drink of hot milk and the like of that to bring back her courage until finally she told them that she was from near Newton in County Kerry and that she was after going to bed the same as always at home and that the next thing she knew was to wake up in this house.

The next day she was a lot better and they tackled the sidecar and started off for Newton. It was a journey of about fifteen miles to her own place.

And when they arrived at her people's place, they found that the whole place was very upset for when the people of the house were after getting up in he morning three or four days before they found their daughter or what they thought was their daughter dead in her sleep and they were after waking and burying her.
And when she had them persuaded that she was their real daughter didn't they send a few hundred men to the churchyard to open the grave, and God between us and all harm wasn't the coffin in the grave empty.

The Four leafed Shamrock and the Cock

There was a great fair being held in Dingle one day long ago. Tis a good many years ago, I think. All of the people were gathered there as usual. Whoever else was there, there was a showman there, and the trick that he had was a cock walking down the street ahead of him drawing a big, heavy beam tied to his leg. At least, all the people thought that it was a beam, and everyone was running after him, and as he went from street to street, the crowd was getting bigger all the time . Each new person who saw the cock and the beam joined in the procession. Then there came up the street a small old man carrying a load of rushes on his back. He wondered what all the people were looking at. All that he could see was a wisp of straw being dragged along by a cock. The thought that everybody had gone mad, and he asked them why they were following the cock like that. Some of them answered him, "Don't you see the great wonder?" they said. "That great beam of wood being dragged after him by that cock, and he's able to pull it through every street he travels and it tied to his leg?"

"All that he's pulling is a wisp of straw," replied the old man. The showman overheard him saying this. Over to him he went, and he asked him how much he wanted for the load of rushes he had on his back. The old man named some figure-- to tell the truth, I can't say how much he wanted for the load of rushes he had on his back--but whatever it was, the showman gave it to him. He would have given him twice as much. As soon as the showman took the load of rushes off the old man's back, the old man followed after the crowd, but all that he could see was the cock pulling a heavy beam tied to his leg. He followed him all over Dingle.
What happened was that the old man had a four -leafed shamrock, unknown to himself, tied up in the load of rushes. That's what made what he saw different from

what the people saw, and that's why the showman paid him three times the value for the rushes. He told the people, and they gave up the chase. I heard that story among the people, and it could be true, because the four-leafed shamrock has that power.

The Hour of Death

The old people used to say that in the olden times everybody knew the exact time when he would die. There was a man who knew that he would die in autumn. He planted his crops the previous spring, but instead of building a fine firm fence around them, all he did was to plant a makeshift hedge of a few rushes and ferns to guard the crops. It so happened that God (praise and glory to Him!) sent an angel down on earth to find out how the people were getting on. The angel came to this man and asked him what he was doing. The man told him. "And why haven't you a better fence than that makeshift to protect your crops?" asked the angel. "It will do me," said the man, "until I have the crop stored. Let those who succeed me look after their own fences. I'll die this autumn."

The angel returned and told the Almighty what had happened. And from that day on, people lost foreknowledge of the hour of death.

The Burial of the Priest's Concubine

This is a tale about a priest's concubine when she died, Many people came to her to carry her away to bury her, and they could not lift her because she was heavy.

And they all wondered greatly at this, and everyone said, "O One God Almighty Father, how shall she be taken to be buried?" And they consulted a cunning professor and the Professor said to them as follows: "Bring two priest's concubines to us to carry her away to the church." And they were brought, and they carried her away very lightly to the church; and the people wondered greatly at this, and the professor said to them, " There is no cause for you to wonder at their actions, O people; that is, that two devils should carry off one devil with them." Finit. -Irish 14th-15th Century

Nera and the Dead Man

"Ailill and Medb, King and Queen of Connacht, are in their palace at Ráth Cruchan. It is the eve of Samhain, the modern Hallow-e'en, and great was the darkness of that night and its horror. Ailill promises to reward anyone who will put a withe round the foot of either of two captives who had been hanged the day before. A number of men make the attempt, but return in terror with their errand unfulfilled. At length Nera sets off for the gallows. He put a withe round the foot of one of the two captives. Thrice it sprang off again. Then the captive said to him unless he put an extra spike on it the spike of the wood itself would not close on it. Then Nera put an extra spike on it. The hanged man then asks Nera to take him on his back to the house which is nearest to us, saying that he was thirsty when hanged and now wants a drink. When they arrive at the nearest house there is a lake of fire round it. There is no drink for us in that house, says the captive. The fire is always raked there. Nera carries him to the second house but they cannot enter as a lake of water surrounds the house. There is never a washing nor a bathing tub nor a slop pail in it at night after sleeping. They go to the third house and here the dead man enters.

There were tubs for washing and bathing in it and a drink in each of them. also a slop pail on the floor of the house. He (the hanged man) then drinks a draught from each of them (he tosses a handful of ashes at the barking dog and it falls down dead and before the people have a chance to wake) He scatters the last sip from his lips at the faces of the people that were in the house so that they all died. Henceforth it is not good to have either a tub for washing or bathing or a fire without raking or a slop pail in a house after sleeping." Nera at this point is really scared- so much so that he runs off into the night and still to this day that dead man is still occupying the small house in the hills of Ireland somewhere……

Well… that is a start! There are many more! See what you can find!

Sayings of Death and of Wakes

Sayings are the bridges, which link bits of conversations together. They also make great turning points. Sometimes they serve as condensed knowledge and take a few moments or a few sips of a drink to completely comprehend. These too can be put on cards and handed out when silence strikes. Have fun!

Many a day we shall rest in the clay.
Death is the poor man's best physician.
Death doesn't come without a cause.
There's neither herb nor care for death.
To die and to lose one's life are much the same thing.
There'll be many a dry eye at his death.
There is hope from the mouth of the sea but none from the mouth of the grave.
A man at sea may return but not the man in the churchyard.
Sleep is the brother of death.
One can't tell which skin will hang from the rafter first, the old sheep's or the lamb's.
The trace of the hand will live but not the hand that made it.
Death stares the old in the face and lurks behind the backs of the young.
There is many a person with a high head today who will be lying lowly tomorrow.
May God spare anyone who has a hand in his own death.
It is not the tree that is a long time shaking that is the first to fall.
Death does not take a bribe.
The graveyard growth is in him.
Death never comes too late.
You'll be going yet and your two feet before you
There are two things that cannot be cured- death, and want of sense.
God never closes one door but he opens another.
May you be in heaven a half hour before the Devil knows you are dead

Superstitions Concerning the Dead

From: Ancient Legends, Mystic Charms, and Superstitions of Ireland
by Lady Francesca Speranza Wilde
[1887]

MANY strange spells are effected by the means of a dead man's hand--chiefly to produce butter in the churn. The milk is stirred round nine times with the dead hand, the operator crying aloud all the time, "Gather! gather! gather." While a secret form of words is used which none but the initiated know.

Another use is to facilitate robberies. If a candle is placed in a dead hand, neither wind nor water can extinguish it. And if carried into a house the inmates will sleep the sleep of the dead as long as it remains under the roof, and no power on earth can wake them while the dead hand holds the candle.

For a mystic charm, one of the strongest known is the hand of an unbaptized infant fresh taken from the grave in the name of the Evil One.

A dead hand is esteemed also a certain cure for most diseases, and many a time sick people have been brought to a house where a corpse lay that the hand of the dead might be laid on them. *

The souls of the dead who may happen to die abroad, greatly desire to rest in Ireland. And the relations deem it their duty to bring back the body to be laid in Irish earth. But even then the dead will not rest peaceably unless laid with their forefathers and their own people, and not amongst strangers.

A young girl happened to die of a fever while away on a visit to some friends, and her father thought it safer not to bring her home, but to have her buried in the nearest churchyard. However, a few nights after his return home, he was awakened by a mournful wail at the window, and a voice cried, "I am alone; I am alone; I am alone!" Then the poor father knew well what it meant, and he prayed in the name of God that the spirit of his dead child might rest in peace until the morning. And when the day broke he arose and set off to the strange burial ground, and there he drew the coffin from, the earth, and had it carried all the way back from Cork to Mayo; and after he had laid a time dead in the old graveyard beside his people and his kindred, the spirit of his child had rest, and the mournful cry was no more heard in the night.*

The corner of a sheet that has wrapped a corpse is 'a cure for headache if tied round the head.

The ends of candles used at wakes are of great efficacy in curing burns.

A piece of linen wrap taken from a corpse will cure the swelling of a limb if tied round the part affected.

It is believed that the spirit of the dead last buried has to watch in the churchyard until another corpse is laid there; or has to perform menial offices in the spirit world, such as carrying wood and water until the next spirit comes from earth. They are also sent on messages to earth, chiefly to announce the coming death of some relative, and at this they are glad, for then their time of peace and rest will come at last.

If any one stumbles at a grave it is a bad omen; but if he falls and touches the clay, he will assuredly die before the year is out.

Any one meeting a funeral must turn back and walk at least four steps with the mourners.

If the nearest relative touches the hand of a corpse it will utter a wild cry if not quite dead.

On Twelfth Night the dead walk, and on every tile of the house a soul is sitting, waiting for your prayers to take it out of purgatory.

There are many strange superstitions in the western islands of Connemara. At night the dead can be heard laughing with the fairies and spinning the flax. One girl declared that she distinctly heard her dead mother's voice singing a mournful Irish air away down in the heart of the hill. But after a year and a day the voices cease, and the dead are gone for ever.

*

It is a custom in the West, when a corpse is carried to the grave, for the bearers to stop half way, while the nearest relatives build up a small monument of loose stones, and no hand would ever dare to touch or disturb this monument while the world lasts.

When the grave is dug, a cross is made of two spades, and the coffin is carried round it three times before being placed in the clay. Then the prayers for the dead are said, all the people kneeling with uncovered head.

The Death Sign

From: Ancient Legends, Mystic Charms, and Superstitions of Ireland
by Lady Francesca Speranza Wilde
[1887]

A woman was out one day looking after her sheep in the valley, and coming by a little stream she sat down to rest, when suddenly she seemed to hear the sound of low music, and turning round, beheld at some distance a crowd of people dancing and making merry. And she grew afraid and turned her head away not to see them. Then close by her stood a young man, pale and strange looking, and she beheld him with fear.

"Who are you?" she said at last; "and why do you stand beside me?"

"You ought to know me," he replied, "for I belong to this place; but make haste now and come away, or evil will befall you."

Then she stood up and was going away with him, when the crowd left off their dancing and ran towards them crying--

"Come back; come back; come back!"

"Don't stop; don't listen," said the young man, "but follow me." Then they both began to run, and ran on until they reached a hillock.

"Now we are safe," said he "they can't harm us here." And when they stopped he said to her again, "Look me in the face and say if you know me now?"

"No," she answered, "you are a stranger to me."

"Look again," he said, "look me straight in the face and you will know me."

Then she looked, and knew instantly that he was a man who had been drowned the year before in the dark winter time, and the waves had never cast up his body on the shore. And she threw up her arms and cried aloud--

"Have you news of my child? have you seen her, my fair-haired girl, that was stolen from me this day seven years. Will she come back to me never no more?"

"I have seen her," said the man, "but she will never come back, never more, for she has eaten of the fairy food and must now stay with the spirits under the sea, for she belongs to them body and soul. But go home now, for it is late, and evil is near you; and perhaps you will meet her sooner than you think."

Then as the women turned her face homeward, the man disappeared, and she saw him no more.

When at last she reached the threshold of her house a fear and trembling came on her, and she called to her husband that some one stood in the doorway and she could not pass. And with that she fell down on the threshold on her face, but spake no word more. And when they lifted her up she was dead.

Legends of the Dead in the Western Islands

From: Ancient Legends, Mystic Charms, and Superstitions of Ireland
by Lady Francesca Speranza Wilde
[1887]

WHEN young people die, either men or women, who were remarkable for beauty, it is supposed that they are carried off by the fairies to the fairy mansions tinder the earth, where they live in splendid palaces and are wedded to fairy queens or princes. But sometimes, if their kindred greatly desire to see them, they are allowed to visit the earth, though no enchantment has yet been discovered powerful enough to compel them to remain or resume again the mortal life.

Sometimes when the fishermen are out they meet a strange boat filled with people; and when they look on them they know that they are the dead who have been carried off by the fairies with their wiles and enchantments to dwell in the fairy palaces.

One day a man was out fishing, but caught nothing; and was just turning home in despair at his ill-luck when he suddenly saw a boat with three persons in it; and it seemed to him that they were his comrades, the very men who just a year before had been drowned in that spot, but whose bodies were never recovered, and he knew that he looked upon the dead. But the men were friendly, and called out to him--

"Cast your line as we direct, and you will have luck."

So he cast his line as they bade him, and presently drew up a fine fish.

"Now, cast again," they said, "and keep beside us, and row to shore, but do not look on us."

So he did as directed and hauled tip fish after fish till his boat was full, and then he drew it up to the landing-place.

"Now," they said, "wait and see that no one is about before you land."

So the man looked up and down the shore, but saw no one; then he turned to land his fish, when, behold, the men and the second boat had vanished, and he saw them no more. however, he landed his fish with much joy and brought them all safely home, though the wise people said that if he had not turned away his head that time, but kept his eyes steadily on the men till he landed, the enchantment would have been broken that held them in fairy-land, and the dead would have been restored to the earthly life, and to their kindred in the island who mourned for them.

A few jokes

Jokes help us reach beyond the worries of our own mortality to allow us to project our faith and let us crow out a bit from that foundation. Jokes also work because they are built upon universals. They demonstrate that we are part of a larger continuity and that we have not been singled out for special torment. Let them liven the silences and tensions for you.

Paddy was found dead in his back yard, and as the weather was a bit on the warm side, the wake was held down to only two days, so his mortal remains wouldn't take a bad turn. At last his friends laid him in the box, nailed it shut & started down the hill into the churchyard. As it was a long, sloping path and the mourners were appropriately tipsy, one fellow lurched into the gatepost as they entered the graveyard. Suddenly a loud knocking came from in the box. Paddy was alive! They opened the box up and he sat up, wide eyed, and they all said, Sure, it's a miracle of God! All rejoiced & they went back and had a few more drinks but later that day, the poor lad died. Really died. Stone cold dead. They bundled him back into his box, and as they huffed and puffed down the hill the next morning, the priest said, "Careful now, boys; mind ye don't bump the gatepost again."

His wife had been killed in an accident and the police were questioning Finnegan.
"Did she say anything before she died?" asked the sergeant.
"She spoke without interruption for about forty years," said the Irishman.

Mrs. Pete Monaghan came into the newsroom to pay for her husband's obituary. She was told by the kindly newsman that it was a dollar a word and he remembered Pete and wasn't it too bad about him passing away. She thanked him for his kind words and bemoaned the fact that she only had two dollars. But she wrote out the obituary, "Pete died." The newsman said he thought old Pete deserved more and he'd give her three more words at no charge. Mrs. Pete Monaghan thanked him and rewrote the obituary: "Pete died. Boat for sale."

Padraic Flaherty came home drunk every evening toward ten. Now, the Missus was never too happy about it, either. So one night she hides in the cemetery and figures to scare the bejeezus out of him. As poor Pat wanders by, up from behind a tombstone she jumps in a red devil costume screaming, "Padraic Sean Flaherty, sure and ya' don't give up you're drinkin' and it's to Hell I'll take ye." Pat, undaunted, staggered back and demanded, "Who the hell ARE you?". Too that the Missus replied, "I'm the divil ya' damned old fool." To which Flaherty remarked, "Damned glad to meet you sir, I'm married to yer sister."

O'Connell was staggering home with a pint of booze in his back pocket when he slipped and fell heavily. Struggling to his feet, he felt something wet running down his leg.
"Please, God," he implored, "let it be blood!"

At Paddy's wake a crowd had begun to form and the chairs had become scarce. Paddy was propped up on the middle parlor upon three chairs when in walked three men in excess of the number of chairs available. For a while they stood around eating, drinking and talking with the lads in the kitchen but eventually Seamus noticed and ran out into the middle parlor, set Paddy in his coffin up against the side wall and took the chairs to the men in the kitchen. After a while the parish priest arrived. He walked into the front parlor and chatted with the ladies for a while over tea. Eventually he asked of the corpse and was directed into the middle parlor. When the priest went into the middle parlor he saw Paddy leaning up there against the wall in his coffin and was not pleased with the sight. The priest immediately yelled in to the men in the kitchen saying: "Three chairs for the corpse." Well you see it had been a long day at the wake- one of the men replied in a loud voice: "hip, hip, Hooray", "hip, hip, Hooray", "hip, hip, Hooray". All joined in- including the priest!

What's the difference between an Irish wedding and an Irish Wake?
To be sure….There is one less drunk at the wake!

Singing

"Sing a song at a wake and shed a tear when a child is born."

-Irish Saying

A good singer was highly valued and singing at wakes was very popular. Songs are described as being "merry." As with other traditions singing was attacked by the clergy and has largely died out. Recording machines also have taken their toll. Singing was not present where the wake involved a great loss but neither were there other diversions at such events. Sir Henry Piers writing in 1682 of Wakes in Westmeath referred to lewd songs being sung at wakes there. At such wakes singing also would become a penalty for the loss of a wake game.

At times songs were sung at the request of the deceased while still living. The singer received a drink to continue singing and the refusal of a good singer to sing would be an insult. Singing contests were also known between groups in different parts of the wake house.

Songs were lively and extended to love songs, patriotic ones, religious songs or songs of sad occurences. Songs of Connemara: *Baile Ui Li* (Ballylee), *An Muilleoir Bán* (The White Miller), *Bhi Triúr Mac Agam* (I had Three Sons), *Oileán Éide* (Edie Island), *Buchaill na Gruaige Doinne* The Brownhaired Boy), *An Caillin Rua*, (The Redhaired Girl) *Sile Ni Ghadhra* (The Cottage Maid), The Streams of Bunclody and Don't Marry were very popular. Other songs from the tradition suitable for wakes are*: Bheir Mí Ó, Fill A Rún Ó, Gleanntáin Ghlas Ghaoth Dobhair*, and *An Mhaighdean Mhara.* The song The Old Bog Road is often sung at wakes.

I have included a variety of songs and notation. Some songs are included because they are currently popular. Not all of the songs are strictly of the Irish Tradition. However, all are of the "popular" Celtic tradition.

Although singing faded out at the turn of the century there is still nothing more moving than the sound of the human voice singing a classic traditional song. You don't need to get fancy. In traditional music one doesn't need always to have a professional musician.

Amplification should be used when only absolutely necessary.

Joining in with a good song can bring people together as in no other way.

Songs of and For Wakes

At wake or at fair I would twirl my shillelagh
**And trip through the jigs with my brogues bound
with straw
And all the pretty maidens from the village, the
valley
Loved the bold Phelim Brady, the bard of Armagh**-

--The Bard of Armagh

Young Roger looked so handsome I could weep

With his hair of brown and eyes of blue so deep,
At the wake I got excited
But my love went unrequited
On the way back from the wake he fell asleep.

-The Unlaid Maid (Sugden & Nudds--The Kipper Family)

Then I came upon a friggin' wake for a friggin' rotten swine,
By the name of Jock O'Leary and I touched his head with mine,
And old Jock sat up in his box and raised his friggin' head.
His wife took out a forty-four, and shot the bastard dead.

-Song From Lucifer's Hammer

And at the wake
They were lashin' down
'The drops of brandy'
'The old fashioned habit'
In the church they were lashin' down pounds and fivers
So Mattie would be fine in the old by and by.

-Mattie (Johnny Mulhern)

And when I'm on my back and my soul is at peace
The women will crowd for to cry at my wake,
And their sons and their daughters will utter their prayers
To the Lord for the sake of their father.

- Limerick Rake

At the learning I wasn't such a genius I'm thinking,
But I soon bet the master entirely at drinking,
Not a wake or a wedding for five miles around,
But meself in the corner was sure to be found.
- The Juice Of The Barley

Said the guard, testing him, "Say these words if you can:
'Around the rugged rock the ragged rascal ran."
"Tell them I'm not crazy, tell them I'm not mad
'Twas only the sup of the bottle I had.
A man died in the Union by the name of McNabb
They washed him, they laid him outside on a slab
And after O'Connor his measurements did take
His wife took him home for a bloody fine wake
Well, about twelve o'clock and the beer it was high
The corpse he sits up and says he with a sigh
"I can't get to heaven, they won't let me up
'Till I bring them a quart of Johnny Jump-Up

- Johnny Jump-Up

He rambled to an Irish wake on one St. Patrick's night,
They asked him what he'd like to drink, they meant to treat him right.
But like the old Kilkenny cats, their backs began to arch,
When he called for orange phosphate, on the seventeenth of March.\

- Didn't He Ramble (Will Handy)

Neither wedding nor wake was worth an old shake,
If Denny was not first invited,
For at emptying legs or squeezing the bags,
He astonished as well as delighted.
In such times poor Denny could not ear a penny,
Martial law had a sting like a viper -
It kept Denny within till his bones and his skin
Were a-grin through the rags of the piper.

-The Cow that Ate the Piper

Young boys they were lying where crops were ripening,
From the strength of youth they were borne away,
In their wedding clothes for their wake they robed them,
Oh King of Glory man's hope is vain.

-Anac Cuain

Yes, they beat the drum slowly, they played the pipes lowly,
And the rifles fired o'er me as they lowered me down,
The band played "The Last Post" in chorus,
And the pipes played "The Flowers of the Forest."

- Willie Mcbride's Reply Stephen L. Suffe

Well, how do you do, Private William McBride,
Do you mind if I sit down here gy your graveside?
And rest for awhile in the warm summer sun,
I've been walking all day, and I'm nearly done.
And I see by your gravestone you were only 19
When you joined the glorious fallen in 1916,
Well, I hope you died quick and I hope you died clean
Or, Willie McBride, was it slow and obscene?
-NO MAN'S LAND (Eric Bogle)

Heart's Ease

Sing care away with sport and play for past time is a pleasure
If well we fare for naught we care, in mirth consists our treasure
Let stupids lurk and drudges work, we do defy their slav'ry
He is a fool that goes to school, all we delight in brav'ry

What doth avail, far hence to sail, and leave our life in toiling
Or to what end should we here spend our days in irksome moiling
It is the best to live at rest and tak't as God doth sent it
To haunt each wake and mirth to make, and with good fellows spend it

Finnegan's Wake

If you have no other song at the wake this should be it! The wake should resemble

this song!

Finnegan's Wake   Traditional

Tim Finnegan lived in Walkin' Street
A gentleman, Irish, mighty odd;
He had a brogue both rich and sweet

And to rise in the world he carried a hod.
Now Tim had a sort of the tipplin' way
With a love of the whiskey he was born
And to help him on with his work each day
He'd a "drop of the cray-thur" every morn.

cho Whack fol the darn O, dance to your partner
Whirl the floor, your trotters shake;
Wasn't it the truth I told you
Lots of fun at Finnegan's wake!

One mornin' Tim was feelin' full
His head was heavy which made him shake;
He fell from the ladder and broke his skull
And they carried him home his corpse to wake.
They rolled him up in a nice clean sheet
And laid him out upon the bed,
A gallon of whiskey at his feet
And a barrel of porter at his head.
cho:

His friends assembled at the wake
And Mrs. Finnegan called for lunch,
First they brought in tay and cake
Then pipes, tobacco and whiskey punch.
Biddy O'Brien began to bawl
"Such a nice clean corpse, did you ever see?
"O Tim, mavourneen, why did you die?"
Arragh, hold your gob said Paddy McGhee!

cho:

Then Maggie O'Connor took up the job
"O Biddy," says she, "You're wrong, I'm sure"
Biddy she gave her a belt in the gob
And left her sprawlin' on the floor.
And then the war did soon engage
'Twas woman to woman and man to man,
Shillelagh law was all the rage
And a row and a ruction soon began.

cho:

Then Mickey Maloney ducked his head
When a noggin of whiskey flew at him,
It missed, and falling on the bed
The liquor scattered over Tim!
The corpse revives! See how he raises!
Timothy rising from the bed,

Says,"Whirl your whiskey around like blazes
Thanum an Dhul! Do you think I'm dead?"

Finnegan's Other Wake
(Charlie Miller 1983)

Tim Finnegan was a moral man
A member of the Majority,
A fine, upstanding Republican
With but one vice --- to water ski.
Now one fine day to Pleasant Point
The dozers came --- ka-chug, ka-chug
They pumped the Delaware River dry
And Tim was skiing in the mud.

cho: Whack-fol-a-dol, now where's our river?
Give it back for goodness sake,
There's dead fish and rocks and mud
But no more water in Finnegan's wake.

Now Tim he left the office early
Strapped his skis on at the pier,
He shouted to the motor boat driver,
"Come on! Get this thing in gear!"
The driver gunned the Chrysler engine
Tim grabbed the tow rope without fear,
The prop churned gravel, the motor exploded
Found Tim in mud up to his rear.

Tim, he looked around with horror
Said, "I voted for Ron, they can't do this to me!"
I guess I'll have to use my noodle
To figure out how I can ski."
He got himself a big Ford Bronco
Four-wheel drive and power brakes;
Tied his tow rope to the bumper
A spray of mud was Finnegan's wake.

Now twenty miles south of there
Philadelphians looked out to see
A muddy gap between Penn's Landing
And the State of New Jersey.
But tho' container ships are stuck
The Olympia turned on her side
They'd sooner drive the Delaware
Than to take I-95.

Now Tim awoke, to his relief,
To find that it was all a dream.
They hadn't pumped out all the water
We still had a running stream.
But PECO's nukes are very thirsty
They'll drink all the water they can take
Hear the people, dump the pump
So we can swim in Finnegan's wake.

Pat Malone Forgot That He Was Dead

Times were hard in Irish town; everything was going down,
Pat Malone was pushed for ready cash.
He'd the life insurance spent; all his money, too, had went
And all of his affairs had gone to smash.
His wife spoke up and said, "Now, dear Pat, if you were dead
This twenty thousand dollars we could take."
And so Pat laid down and tried to make out that he had died
Until he smelled the whiskey at the wake.
Then Pat Malone forgot that he was dead.
He raised himself in the bed and what he said,
"If this wake goes on a minute, to be sure the corpse is in it
You'll have to keep me drunk to keep me dead, "

So they gave the corpse a cup, and afterward they filled it up
And laid him down again upon the bed.
And before the morning grey, everybody felt so gay
They forgot that Pat was only playing dead.
So they loaded him from the bunk, still alive but awful drunk
And put him in the coffin with a prayer.
And the driver of the cart said, "Be God, I'll never start
Until I see that someone pays the fare."
Then Pat Malone forgot that he was dead.
He raised himself in the coffin, while he said,
"If you fairly doubt my credit, you'll be sorry that you said it
You drive on or else the corpse will break your head.

So the funeral started out on the cemetery route,
And the neighbors tried the widow to console.
'Til they got beside the base of Malone's last resting place
And gently lowered Patrick in the hole.
Then Pat began to see, just as plain as one could see
That he'd forgot to reckon on the end.
And as clods began to drop he broke loose the coffin top
And quickly to the earth he did ascend.
Then Pat Malone forgot that he was dead,
And from the cemetery quickly fled.

He came nearly going under, it's a lucky thing, by thunder,
That Pat Malone forgot that he was dead.*

Molly Brannigan

This song is an old-time classic from the days of John McCormick and the song hall.
It is a great parlor song, which will provide a wonderful old-time atmosphere to any
gathering.

Molly Branigan   Traditional

Ma'am dear, did ye never hear of pretty Molly Brannigan?
In troth, then, she's left me and I'll never be a man again.
Not a spot on my hide will a summer's sun e'er tan again
Since Molly's gone and left me here alone for to die.

The place where my heart was you'd aisy rowl a turnip in,
'Tis large as all Dublin, and from Dublin to the Divil's glen:
If she'd wish'd to take another, sure she might have left mine back again
And not have gone and left me here alone for to die.

Ma'am dear, I remember when the milking time was past and gone
We strolled thro' the meadow, and she swore I was the only one
That ever she could love, but oh! the base and cruel one,
For all I that she's left me here alone for to die.

Ma'am dear, I remember when coming home the rain began,
I wrapt my frieze-coat round her and ne'er a waistcoat had I on
And my shirt was rather fine-drawn, but oh! the false and cruel one,
For all that she's left me here alone for to die.

The left side of my carcase is as weak as water gruel, ma'am,
There's not a pick upon my bones, since Molly's proved so cruel ma'am
Oh! if I had a blunder gun, I'd go and fight a duel, ma'am,
For sure I'd better shoot myself than live here to die.

I'm cool an' determined as any salamander, ma'am,
Won't you come to my wake when I go the long meander, ma'am?
I'll think myself as valiant as the famous Alexander, ma'am

When I hear ye cryin' o'er me, "Arrah! why did ye die?"

Steve O'donnell's Wake

Steve O'Donnell was a Gentleman so everybody said, He was Loved by all His Friends both Rich and Poor, And everyone felt sorry when They heard that Steve was Dead, And They saw the piece of Crepe upon the Door.

The Barber came to shave the Galway Slagga from His Throat, And cut His Hair in A La Pompadore, A Red Necktie and Buttonhole Boquet was in His Coat, And a Bunch of Shamrocks in His Hand He wore.

Undertaker Feeney had the Job to lay O'Donnell out, In a Casket of the very finest make, He dressed the Corpse in Broadcloth and said "Boys there'll be no doubt", That They'll all get Drunk at Steve O'Donnell's Wake

There were Fighters, Biters,and Irish Dynamiters, There was Beer,Gin,Whisky,Wine and Cake, There were Men in high positions there were Irish Politicians, And They all got Drunk at Steve O'Donnell's Wake.

There were 50 Candles at His Head & 20 at His Feet, Plenty Flowers sent for Friendship sake, O' Steve Me By'e why did You Die? the Grieving Widow said, And We all felt sad at Steve O'Donnell's Wake.

Mike McGovern said that Steve O'Donnell was an awful Bum, Of course He only meant It for a Joke, But Paddy Mack got up His Back and He made McGovern run, Cause He hit Him in the Eye an awful Poke.

They all joined in the Fightin' then cause everyone was mad, And Blood enought was spilled to form a Lake, They knocked the Corpse down on the Floor and blew off all the Lights, There was Murder down at Steve O'Donnell's Wake.

Then the Cops came in to stop the Brawl to make them understand, And the Corpse was picked up by His Brother Dan, But someone stole the Necktie from around O'Donnell's Throat, Mike McGovern Said O'Reilly was the Man.

O'Reilly's Friends got crazy mad and swore They'd have His Life, McGovern saw He made a great Mistake, They fought and fought and Danced around until the Cops came in, And arrested all at Steve O'Donnell's Wake

Macushla is another old-time favorite from the days of John McCormick. It is a song that adds a certain gravity to the gathering.

Macushla

Macushla, Macushla your sweet voice is calling
calling me softly again and again
Macushla Macushla I hear it's dear pleading
my blue eyed Macushla I hear it in vain

Macushla, Macushla your white arms are reaching
 I feel them enfolding, caressing me still
fling them out from the darkness my lost love Macushla
let them find me, and bind me again if they will

Macushla, Macushla your red lips are saying
that death is a dream and love is for aye
then awaken Macushla, awake from your dreaming
my blue eyed Macushla awaken to stay.
Rowe/MacMurrough

The Irish Wake, 1826

(Dibdin.)

Life's as like as can be to an Irish wake,
Where their tapers they light,
And they sit up all night,
Wid their, why would you leave your poor Paddy
to mourn
Arrah! how could you will be such a cake?
Musha ! what will I do?
Oh. Lilly, lilly, lilly a loo,
Oh, hone !
Faith' we're left altogether alone.
But when the grief the liquor puts out,
The fun is all changed in a crack;
Away; like smoke, goes the whiskey about,
And they foot it, cross over, and back to back,
Wid their tiptelary whack.
Poor miss, bolted safe with a good lock and key,
Like Thisbe may call,
Through the hole in the wall,
How hard's my misfortune, I'm left here to
 mourn,
Will no one take pity on me?
Musha "what will I do?
Lilly, lilly, lilly la loo,
Oh, hone!

    I shall be after lying alone.
But when the rope-ladder affords her relief,
And she turns on her mother her back,
'Mong friends and relations she leaves all her
grief,
And away to Scotland they trip in a crack.
With their tiptelary whack.
The toper, next morning, low, sick, and in pain,
The glasses all breaks,
Beats his head, 'cause it aches,
And wishes that wine may to poison be grown,
If ever he gets tipsey again. -
With his, what shall I do?
Lilly, lilly, lily la loo,
From this moment I'll drinking disown.
But when in a posse come Bacchus's troop,
He changes his tone in a crack,
They drink and they sing, they halloo and whoop,
Till they don't know the colour of blue from
black.
And its tiptelary whack.
And so 'tis through life, widows left in the nick,
Dying swains in disgrace,
Patriots turned out of place,
Don't they, cursing their stars, make a horrible moan
Just like when the devil was sick.
Wid their, what will I do?
Lilly, lilly, lilly la loo,
Oh, hone!
Faith: we're left all to grunt and to groan.
But when the widow gets married again,
When the lover is taken back,
When the patriot ousted a place shall obtain,
Away to the devil goes care in a crack,
And 'tis tiptelary whack.

-Fairburn, The Universal Songster and Museum of Mirth, Vol. 2, 1826.

The Old Bog Road

My feet are here on Broadway
This blessed harvest morn,
But oh! the ache that's in my heart
For the spot where I was born.
My weary hands are blistered
Through work in cold and heat!
And oh! to swing a scythe once more
Through a field of Irish wheat.
Had I the chance to wander back,
  Or own a king's abode.
I'd sooner see the hawthorn tree
  By the Old Bog Road.

When I was young and restless
  My mind was ill at ease,
Through dreaming of America,
And the gold beyond the seas.
Oh, sorrow rake their money,
  'Tis hard to find the same,
And what's the world to any man
If no one speaks his name.
I've had my day and here I am
  A-building bricks per load.
A long three thousand miles away

From the Old Bog Road.

My mother died last springtime,
When Erin's fields were green.
The neighbours said her waking
  Was the finest ever seen.
There were snowdrops and primroses
  Piled high above her bed,
And Ferns Church was crowded
When her funeral Mass was read.
And here was I on Broadway
  A-building bricks per load.
When they carried out her coffin
  Down the old Bog Road.

There was a decent girl at home
  Who used to walk with me.
Her eyes were soft and sorrowful

Like moonlight o'er the sea.
Her name was Mary Dwyer,
But that was long ago.
The ways of God are wiser
Than the things that man might know.
She died the day I left her,
A-building bricks per load,
I'd best forget the days I've spent
On the old Bog Road.

Ah! Life's a weary puzzle,
Past finding out by man,
I'll take the day for what it's worth
And do the best I can.
Since no one cares a rush for me
What need is there to moan,
I'll go my way and draw my pay
And smoke my pipe alone.
Each human heart must bear its grief
Though bitter be the 'bode
So God be with you, Ireland,
And the Old Bog Road.
-Teresa Brayton

The Parting Glass

The parting glass is a great transitional song, which can help move mourners from grief to celebration of life. It is also great with a toast.

Oh, all the money that e'er I had, I spent it in good company, And all the harm that e'er I've done, Alas it was to none but me And all I've done for want of wit, to mem'ry now I can't recall, So fill to me the parting glass, Good night and joy be with you all.

Of all the money that e'er I spent
I've spent it in good company
And all the harm that ever I did
Alas it was to none but me
And all I've done for want of wit
To memory now I can't recall
So fill to me the parting glass
Good night and joy be with you all

If I had money enough to spend
And leisure to sit awhile
There is a fair maid in the town
That sorely has my heart beguiled
Her rosy cheeks and ruby lips
I own she has my heart enthralled
So fill to me the parting glass
Good night and joy be with you all

Oh, all the comrades that e'er I had
They're sorry for my going away
And all the sweethearts that e'er I had
They'd wish me one more day to stay
But since it falls unto my lot

That I should rise and you should not
I'll gently rise and softly call
Good night and joy be with you all

The Night That Paddy Murphy Died
The Night Paddy Murphy Died

traditional

Version I

The night that Paddy Murphy died I never shall forget
The whole damn crew got stinking drunk and some ain't sober yet;
The only thing we did that night that filled my heart with fear
We took the ice from off the corpse and put it in the beer

cho: And that's how we showed our respect for Paddy Murphy
That's how we showed our honor and our pride;
That's how we showed our respect for Paddy Murphy
Our respect for Paddy Murphy on the night that Paddy died.

The night that Paddy Murphy died I never shall forget
The whole damn crew got stinking drunk and some ain't sober yet;
The other thing we did that night that filled our hearts with fear
We took the coins from off his eyes, and spent it all on beer.

The Night Pat Murphy Died
Version II

The night Pat Murphy died is a night I'll never forget
Everyone got roarin' drunk and some not sober yet;
As long as the bottle was passed around and everyone feeling gay
And a lady came with bagpipes and music for to play

Mrs. Murphy sat in the corner, pourin' out her grief
While Kelly and his friends, those dirty, robbin' thieves
They crept into the anteroom and a bottle of whiskey stole
They placed the bottle on the corpse to keep the liquor cold CHORUS

cho: And that's how they showed their respect for Paddy Murphy
That's how they showed their honor and their pride;

They said it was a sin and a shame and they winked at one another
Now everything in the wakehouse went, the night Pat Murphy died

At three o'clock in the morning, some dirty blue-eyed scamp
He wrote upon the coffin lid, ""Herein lies a tramp,""
They stopped the clock so Mrs. Murphy couldn't tell the time
And at a quarter after three, Sure they told her it was nine.

And everyone got merry, they didn't care for prayer
Mrs. Murphy said she'd wait 'til all the gang were there
Of all the sights I've ever seen that made me shiver with fear
They took the ice right off the corpse, and they placed it on the beer

Now everything was doin' fine, there was no ill at all
'Til Finnegan told Flannagan, "You've got an awful gall."
I thought that that might start a row, And sure enough it did
For Callahan had carved his name upon the coffin lid

Then the fight got fierce & strong and everybody in
Someone knocked the whiskers off poor old Darby Flynn
And Dirty Andy Burke was there, Now whadda ya think he done?
He placed the corpse right on its head, In the corner just for fun

Someone hollered for the cops; they busted down the door
They jumped upon ol' Paddy's back and they laid him on the floor
They knocked him twice behind the ears and they knocked him on the head
When they jumped up from his back, Sure they found out he was dead

Mrs. Murphy started in, battled with them cops
She chased 'em, every one of them; She chased 'em several blocks
A lovely time was had by all, eighteen in court were tried
For having caused a riot on the night Pat Murphy died

At eight o'clock in the morning, The funeral left the house
And everyone but poor ol' Mrs. Murphy was out soused
They stopped on the way to the churchyard at the old Red Door Saloon
They went in there at nine o'clock And they didn't come out 'til noon

Someone asked ol' Finnegan if anyone had died
"Lou," says he, "I'm not quite sure, I just came for the ride."
They started out for the graveyard all in a very straight line
But when they reached the grave, they found they'd left the corpse behind
CHORUS

Lyke Wake Dirge

A ancient Yorkshirre/ Scottish song which I included for fun and for a Celtic touch.

This ae night, this ae night
Every night and a'
Fire and sleet and candle lighte,
And Christ receive thy saule

When from hence away art past
Every ...
To whinny moor thou com'st at last
And ...

If ever thou gavest hosen and shoon
Sit thee down and put them on.

If hosen and shoon thou ne'er gav'st nane
The whinnies shall prick thee to the bare bane.

From whinny moor when thou may'st pass
To Brig o' Dread thou com'st at last.

If ever thou gavest meat or drink
The fire shall never make thee shrink.

If meat or drink thou ne'er gav'st nane
The fire will burn thee to the bare bane.

This ae night, this ae nighte
Fire and sleet and candle lighte.

The Funeral

Well the other night I got an invitation to a funeral
But to me disappointment the fellow didn't die
He said that he was sorry for having disappointed us
And seeing he apologized we let the thing go by
To ease our disappointment he took us out and treated us
He bought a quart of porter for a company of ten
When somebody asked him whose money he was squandering
The fellow took his wallet out, we didn't ask again.

Well we bought a concertina for to keep up the rascallity
 But none of us could play it though we tried our best and worst
And we made an awful noise on it and if its any benefit
We played the thing so carefully that all the bellows burst
We bought a boiled potato to fix the concertina with
When someone hit Maloney with the carcase of a cat
 He bundled up his whiskers and he read us out the riot act
And swore that he'd put two heads on the *bottle rack.

 Well the owner of the beer shop when he saw us a rioting
 He ordered us to get out, ah, but that we all refused
So he whistled up some locals that were standing round the corner
And for ten or fifteen minutes we were bodily abused
Well when we left the beer shop and down the road we started
A bunch of hungry urchins they pelted us with mud
We ordered them to chuck it, they said that they were doing that
And then they all ran off and they left us where we stood.

Well the next thing we saw was a bunch of Salvationists
They rifled all our pockets and they asked us were we saved Poor Little John
McGinty got escorted to the station house For
 asking a policeman if his appetite was shaved
 Well all to free McGinty we all took off our under shirts
And down to the pawn shop we marched the blooming lot
 We told them that we only wanted ten and six on them
 Enough already on them was the answer that we got.

Well we got the ten and sixpence all for to free McGinty with
Bad luck to the beer shop we met along the way
Of course we couldn't pass it without having some refreshment
And we squandered every penny of the fine we had to pay
The beer it being in us the sense it soon was out of us
And for a bit of rioting we quickly did repair
We battled one another till we weren't worth three ha'pens
Ye'd a carpet on the floor with all the skin and hair.

 Now McGinty hit McGantsy and McGansty hit some other man
 And any man hit any man against who he had a spite
 And poor little MacNamara who was sitting doing nothing
Got a kick that broke his jawbone for not indulging in the fight
We fought away like Turks till the police separated us
And took us to the station with broken noses and black eyes I got
sixty days in jail, to me it was a lesson
I will go no more to funerals until the fellow dies.

- traditional

Isn't It Grand Boys

This song has become very popular and has been recorded by the Clancys. It is a grand song of celebration, and a good one to end the wake celebration with.

Isn't it Grand Boys   trad.

Look at the coffin, with golden handles
Isn't it grand, boys, to be bloody-well dead?

Let's not have a sniffle, let's have a bloody-good cry
And always remember: The longer you live
The sooner you'll bloody-well die

Look at the flowers, all bloody withered
Isn't it grand, boys, to be bloody-well dead?

Let's not have a sniffle, let's have a bloody-good cry
And always remember: The longer you live
The sooner you'll bloody-well die

Look at the mourners, bloody-great hypocrites
Isn't it grand, boys, to be bloody-well dead?

Let's not have a sniffle, let's have a bloody-good cry
And always remember: The longer you live
The sooner you'll bloody-well die

Look at the preacher, a bloody-nice fellow
Isn't it grand, boys, to be bloody-well dead?

Let's not have a sniffle, let's have a bloody-good cry
And always remember: The longer you live

The sooner you'll bloody-well die

Look at the widow, bloody-great female
Isn't it grand, boys, to be bloody-well dead?

Let's not have a sniffle, let's have a bloody-good cry
And always remember: The longer you live

The Flowers Of The Forest

This is another Scottish song, which is included because of its beauty as a slow air. A wonderful song for meditation and contemplation especially when played slowly.

I've heard them liltin', at the ewe milkin,'
Lasses a-liltin' before dawn of day.
Now there's a moanin', on ilka green loanin'.
The flowers of the forest are a' wede away.

As boughts in the mornin', nae blithe lads are scornin',
Lasses are lonely and dowie and wae.
Nae daffin', nae gabbin', but sighin' and sobbin',
Ilk ane lifts her leglin, and hies her away.

At e'en in the gloamin', nae swankies are roamin',
'Mang stacks wi' the lasses at bogle to play.
But ilk maid sits drearie, lamentin' her dearie,

The flowers of the forest are a' wede away.

In har'st at the shearin' nae youths now are jeerin'
Bandsters are runkled, and lyart, or grey.
At fair or at preachin', nae wooin', nae fleecin',
The flowers of the forest are a' wede away.

Dool for the order sent our lads to the Border,
the English for ance by guile wan the day.
The flowers of the forest, that fought aye the foremost,
The prime of our land lie cauld in the clay.

We'll hae nae mair liltin', at the ewe milkin',
Women and bairns are dowie and wae.
Sighin' and moanin' on ilka green loanin',
The flowers of the forest are all wede away.

An Mhaighdean Mhara

This old song from the Sean Nós tradition of Connemara is a wonderful haunting
melody which is well suited for meditation and contemplation.

An Mhaighdean Mhara   Traditional Irish Gaelic

Is cosu/il gur mheath tu/ no/ gur thre/ig tu/ an greann,
Ta/ sneachta ga freasach fa/ bhe/al na mbeann',
Do chu/l bui/ daite 's do bhe/ili/n sa/mh,
Siud chugaibh Mary Chinidh 's i/ ndiaidh an E/irne 'shna/mh

A mha/ithri/n dhi/lis, du/irt Ma/ire Bha/n,
Fa/ Bhruach an chladaigh 's fa/ bhe/al na tra/
Maighdea/n Mhara, mo mha/ithri/n ard,
Siud chugaibh Mary Chinidh 's i/ ndiaidh an E/irne 'shna/mh

Ta/ mise tuirseach agus beidh ga la/
Mo Mha/ire bhroinngheal 's mo Pha/draig ba/n
Ar bharr na dtonna 's fa/ bhe/al na tra/
Siud chugaibh Mary Chinidh 's i/ ndiaidh an E/irne 'shna/mh

'Cailín Rua' ('Red-haired Girl')

Nach doiligh domhsa mo chailín a mholadh,
Ní hé amháin mar bhí sí rua,
Bhí sí mar gha gréine ag dul in éadan na ngloiní,
Is bhí scéimh mhná na Finne le mo chailín rua.

Curfa:
Thug mé lion í ó bhaile go baile,
Ó Gheaftaí Dhoire go Baile Átha Luain,
Chun fhuil aon mhíle dár shiúil mé ar an fad sin,
Nach dtug mé deoch leanna do mo chailín rua.

B'fhearr liom í ná bó is ná bearrach,
Nó a bhfuil de loingis ag tarraingt chun cuain,
B'fhearr liom arís na cíos Chluain Meala,
Go mbeinn is mo chailín i mBaile Átha Luain.

Curfa

Chuir mé mo chailín go margadh Shligigh,
Ba é sin féin an margadh bhí daor,
Bhí scilling agus punt ar an mheánpheicín ime,
Is go dtug mé sin le fuinneamh do mo chailín rua.

Curfa

Chuaigh sí siar agus bróga breac' uirthi,
Ribíní glasuaithne teannta ar a gruaig,
D'éalaigh sí uaimse le buachaill an tsiopa,
Is a Rí nár dheas í, mo chailín rua.

Curfa

The Red-haired Girl

Isn't it hard for me to praise my red-haired girl,
Not only because of her red hair,
She was like a ray of sun reflected through glass,
And she had the beauty of the Finne women.

Chorus:
I took her from town to town,
From the gates of Derry to Athlone,
There's not a mile of the way I traveled,
That I didn't give my red-haired girl a drink of ale.
I prefer her to any cow or heifer,
Or all the long ships drawing into the harbor,
I would rather than have all the rent of Clonmel,
To be in Athlone with my red-haired girl.

Chorus

I sent my girl to the Sligo market,
That was the market that was expensive,
A weight of butter cost one guinea,
And I gave it willingly to my red-haired girl.

Chorus

She went west wearing striped shoes,
Her hair tied up with the greenest ribbons,
She left me for a shop-boy,
God, wasn't she lovely, my red-haired girl.

Chorus

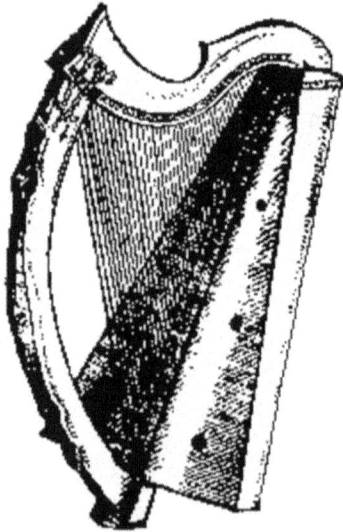

Music And Dancing

Instrumental music was restricted to accompaniment for dancing. John Dunton observed "a rough dance" accompanied by pipe music in the mid 17th century. Thomas Dineley in 1681:

> "At these meetings the young frye, viz Darby, Teige, Morough, Leeam, Rinett, Allsoon, Norah, Shevaune, More, Kathleen, Ishabel, Noualla, Mayrgett, Timesheen, Shinnyed, etc...appeare as gay as may be, with their holyday apparell, and with piper, harper or fiddler, revel and dance the night throughout, make love and matches,"

Thomas Campbell mentions dancing as part of a game in 1778 as does Rev. James Hall (1813) when he mentioned the game as Mending the Old Coat. Dancing at wakes is mentioned in Maria Edgeworth's Castle Rackrent (1810). T. Crofton Croker noted a dance performed by young men with blackened faces and sticks, which seemed like a Morris Dance. Brewer wrote in 1825 of a merry dance and pipe music and Woods-Martin describes an obscene dance called Droghedy performed at Munster wakes. J.G. Prim calls it an old-time Morris dance. These reports highlight the division between the "Celtic" wake and the "Roman" burial. The tension this created with the Irish Bishops highlights the antagonism between the Catholic Church and the Irish people. (it is often said that the Irish have two minds, one Celtic the other Catholic, and that they are alway at war with each other!)

The death of a dancing master in Liscarroll in Co. Limerick was followed by a wake in his hometown for a few days then one in a neighboring parish for another few. It has been told that sometimes the corpse itself was taken out to dance.

Dances mentioned in association with wakes were single or double reels, jigs, hornpipes and sets- essentially all of the traditional Irish Dance forms. If there was no piper a mouth organ, mouth music or lilting took its place.

Croker notes that a dance where one person stood in the center of a ring of dancers who danced around them was popular as was a dance resembling Morris dancing involving "gestures with sticks" and the blackening of faces.

Recorded Music To Consider-

Lamentation and Keening:

Lament, Various Artists, Nigel Rolfe, Womad Real World, Caroline Records, CAROL- 2525-2.- Many fine lamentations. Highly recommended.

For the Emigration or American Wake-

In Ireland the custom was to provide a wake for those individuals emigrating, as in truth- they would be seen no more in the village.

Farewell to Eirinn. Dolores Keane and John Faulkener, Eamon Curran.,Green Linnet, DanburyCt., 1981., GLCD 3003.-Many fine traditional songs of parting.

Long Journey Home., The Chieftains and others.,Unisphere Records.,09026-68963, 1998. Captures the spirit of emigration.

A Few Laments

Irish Lamentation Traditional

Kerrywoman's Lament Traditional

Air

Lament for the death of Owen Roe o'Neill O'Carrolan

The Valley of Knockanure

After the Keening- Lively music to uplift the spirit:

The Congress Reel Traditional
Reel

The Widow's Daughter Reel Traditional
Reel

Swans Among the Rushes Traditional
Jig

The Boys of Bluehill Traditional
Hornpipe

Sheebeg Sheemore   Turlough O'Carolan

See the tune to "The Flowers of the Forest." Above

Some Good Recordings for Lively Music

The Best of the Chierftains., The Chieftains,
Columbia/Legacy,CK 48693.1992- good
    for the games and dancing round the house

Carolan's Receipt.,Derek Bell.,Shanachie Records.,
79013.-Great quiet parlor background muisic.

Grand Airs of Connemara.,Various., Ossian Publications., Cork,Ireland, OSS CD 28-

Not all sad but provides a good Gaelic   atmosphere.

The Wake Games of Ireland

These games have been collected by Sean O'Suilleabhain in his central reference work on the topic: <u>Irish Wake Amusements</u>.(Mercier, Dublin, 1976) These games were also played at other functions and celebrations.

I include a representative sample and will be adding more of my favorites soon!

I hope you will feel free to modify to play them in this politically correct and hypoallergenic world of ours!

Lifting the Corpse

A very large man would lie down on his back on the floor. The legs must be kept straight and rigid. Four men then tried to lift him off the floor with their thumbs placed under the shoulders right and left and on the calf of the legs right and left. Each lifter used only one of his thumbs. If the man was lifted places were exchanged. If they failed they would have their heads bashed against the floor (especially if they dropped the man!)

Pulling the Stick- Sweet Draughts

Two man sat facing each other on the floor. Legs were extended so that the soles of their shoes touched. A strong stick: a handle of a spade or pitchfork, was laid across the tops of their shoes. Both gripped the stick, one hand inside and one outside and each tried while holding his legs rigid to lift his opponent off the floor even as much as an inch. After three pulls places were exchanged and the test continued similarly. Sometimes a man who was to be lifted off the floor would make his foot slip from the opponent's shoe. Friends would stand on the coat tails of the person they did not wish lifted.

Lifting a Chair

A chair was gripped at the base of one of the legs by each contestant in turn in an attempt to raise it above his head. It was by no means an easy thing to do, as the old chairs were quite heavy.

Breaking an Egg

An egg was held between the contestant's two hands with the pointed ends against the palms. He then tried to crush the egg, and generally failed.

The Stronger Hand

Two men stood facing each other, with their right hands raised against each other. Pressure was then exerted by each in an attempt to force down his opponent's hand.

Wrestling-

A man would enter the house dressed in a suit of straw and challenge all present to wrestle the Connachtman.

A. A man gripped a stick with his hands at either end and tried to jump over it. Without breaking his hold. An open razor edge upwards was used instead of a stick.

B. 12 men faced each other in two lines, six in each row. The men in each line stood about two feet apart from their neighbours. Each player extended his two arms and gripped the hands of the man facing him. Other active men at the wake then tried in turn to jump over each pair of hands in turn, down between the lines without stopping. This was a very difficult feat to perform.

C. Two men stood with a spade handle or other stick resting on their shoulders. Two others then tried to excel each other in performing acrobatic tricks on the stick, like circus performers.

D. Two men competed to do somersault on the floor returning to a standing position.

Driving the Pigs across the Bridge

Those who arrived late at the wake house were the pigs . They are scolded for not having arrived earlier and then someone would shout "We must drive the pigs across the bridge" The bridge consisted of a number of men, who stood in line behind one another, with their shoulders bent forward. The "pigs" were then forced with blows to mount like riders, on the backs of the others; when all had mounted, they were suddenly thrown on the floor in a heap on the floor.

Riding the Wild Ass

A rope with a noose at one end was thrown over one of the rafters of the house. The man who wished to show his agility then grasped the other end of the rope and put one of his feet into the noose. He then pulled on the free end of the rope and tried to raise himself high enough to enable him to kick against another rafter or couple with his free foot. The difficulty and danger of the trick came from the fact that one part of his body (the hands) was pulling against another (the foot) and he might easily fall on to the floor and injure his head or back.

Stealing the Goats

The player grabbed two sods of turf, one in either hand, and faced the floor with his hands and legs extended; only the turf sods and the toes of his shoes were allowed to touch the floor. The player's objective was a potato, which lay on the floor below his face. He had to pick this up with his mouth without allowing his stomach to touch the floor or bending his arms or legs. This was difficult enough to do while uninterrupted, but it became more so when he had to reply to questions during the attempt:

> Questioner: Where are you going now?
> Reply: Stealing the goats from Hell.
> Questioner: Swear that you are.
> Reply: I swear that I am.

Lifting a horseshoe

The shoe was placed three or four inches out from the foot of the kitchen wall. The person who tried to pick it up took his stand about three feet from the wall, and had to pick up the shoe without bending his knees. Whenever he bent forward in making the attempt, his head would touch the wall, and he was not allowed to use his hands to help straighten himself again.

Going around Under a Table

The player would lie face downwards on a table, catching the edges with both hands. He then was required to bring his body around under the table, between its legs, and return to his starting point without touching the floor. His main difficulty was to keep the table from overturning in the process.

Walking on the legs of a Stool

A fairly long stool would be laid on the floor, legs upwards. The contestant had to mount the stool, placing his two hands on the front legs and his two feet on the back ones. To do the trick he had to walk around on the stool legs with his hands and feet until he returned to his original position.

The Donkeys and Baskets

A man lay face down on the wake house floor. Two others sat facing each other at either side of him and extended their legs across his back toward each other. Each took hold of the other's legs. The prone man was now the donkey and the other two the baskets. His task was to rise up as a real donkey would raising the baskets on his back. Two groups of three often took part in this test each striving to be the first in completing it.

Spinning the Tin Box

Each of the male players was given an even number while each female got an odd number. The players sat here and there in the kitchen while a tin box was spun in the center of the floor by the man in charge of the game. As the box spun around he would call out the number of some player whose duty it then was to rush forward and catch the box before it ceased to spin. A player who failed to do so was given some penalty.

The Mock Court or The Police Game

Eight or so of the players remained in the kitchen, while everybody else went outside the door. Those who were inside then divided themselves up according to their duties in the game; one would act as judge, two as lawyers; one as court-clerk, and three or four as policemen. The police would then go outside and drag in somebody as prisoner, while the others pressed in also to hear the case being tried. The judge too k his seat, and the clerk read out the name and address of the prisoner, as well as the offense with which he was being charged. The trial then proceeded as it would in a legal court, one lawyer prosecuting, the other defending. The main source of the fun, apart from the charge itself, was to be found in the sly references made by both counsel to the private affairs of some of those present, who were dragged into the case. These mischievous, though irrelevant, hints caused great laughter, as they were understood by all. Having heard the evidence, the judge announced his verdict, which was witty and light or severe, according to how he regarded the defendant. The police had then the task of seeing that the verdict was carried out; if guilty, the defendant might be handled roughly as punishment or even doused nine or ten times in a tub of water. If the first trial produced a good deal of amusement, as second or third would follow, until all were tired of the game.

A somewhat similar game, which involved a court-case, was the following. A man lay down on the floor, feigning illness, and a doctor would be sent for. The doctor arrived into the kitchen on horseback, the horse being two fellows clad in straw to resemble an animal. The horse would be a very wild one and, in the course of prancing around the kitchen, the doctor would be thrown down on top of the sick man on the floor. When examined, it would be found that both the patient and the doctor were dead, and the two who played the part of the horse would be tried for causing their deaths.

Building the Ship

John L. Prim has provided a garbled account of the way in which this game was played at wakes in Kilkenny over a hundred years ago. He mentions how the keel was first laid, followed by the prow and stern of the ship; then a woman, who was taking part in the game, would raise the mast with some gesture and speech that convinced Prim that the game had its origin in pagan times. His account is so unclear that it would be difficult, for want of additional details, to imagine how the game was really played. Henry Morris has noted that his uncle had seen a similar game played about one hundred years ago in Co. Monaghan. It was a lively game, with lots of activities going on, he said; the only part he could remember was the tarring of the ship (soot being smeared on somebody). Morris said that the game died out in Farney, Co. Monaghan, before the year 1880.

A Co. Galway man has described the game, as he saw it played there. Three men sat down astride a stool, one behind the other, all facing in the same direction. The man in front was the prow of the ship; the man in the middle, the body of the ship; and the third man the stern. A fourth player stood on the floor beside them; he was the builder of the ship. He would ask the company for a hammer or sledge, which he needed for the work, and he got it-a hard sod of turf, a piece of turnip, or something like that. Having got the implement, he would walk around the stool, talking loudly to himself about his accomplishments as a ship-builder. He would then insert the right hand of the center man under the right arm-pit of the man in front, and continue to walk around the ship, striking hard blows with his hammer on the three, as he went. He would next put the left hand of the center man under the left arm-pit of the first man, striking blows all the time to make things firm. He then placed the legs of the hind pair around the body of the person in front of each, hammering away to keep the timbers from splitting. The trio would then have to lie back, as far as they could, and the builder would start to raise the mast. This part of the game was often obscene. Another game is mentioned by Prim called Drawing the Ship Out of the Mud, but it is not described.

Building the Bridge

Twelve men or so stood out on the floor and formed into two lines of six each, facing one another. Each man took hold of the two hands of the man opposite, thus forming the bridge from which the game took its name. The bridge had now to be tested for strength. Another player mounted on the crossed hands and walked to and fro along them. Finding no apparent fault with its construction, he dismounted. Somebody would then suggest that the bridge be tested to see if it would take a flood of water through its eye. This would be done by some rogue who sluiced the legs and feet of the players with a bucketful of dirty water.

Making the Poteen

This game is both imitative and a booby-trap. Somebody who had not seen it played previously would be asked to sit on a chair or stool in the center of the floor. He would be, as it were the still. The man who was working the still would walk fussily around him, getting ready for the work, while some others remained outside the house to keep an eye out for the police or "Revenue men". As the busy preparations were at their height within, the watchers would rush in to say that the police were coming. Speedy action was now necessary; the first thing to be done was to hide the still outside in the dark. The stiller gave this order to his helpers, and they set to work with a will. Pity the poor still! The innocent fellow who simulated that was dragged out into the darkness and flung headlong into the cess-pool of the dung -hill or some equally unpleasant hiding-place from which he had to extricate himself without light or help.

Coining the Money

Another booby-trap! Counterfeit money was to be coined, as it were, and some innocent fellow was got to sit in the middle of the floor to represent the mint. The players circled around him chanting "Coin the money! Coin the money!" until somebody rushed in from outside to say that the police were approaching. The mint had now to be hidden as quickly and as disagreeably as the still in the preceding game.

Sledging

Booby-trap again! The master smith and his helpers announced that they had to make some plough-"socks", or horseshoes or something like that. A man who had no experience of the game was asked to sit in the centre of the floor to represent the anvil. As soon ass the victim was seated, the master, and his apprentices began to thump him with their fists, as hammers, chanting in time with the blows:
"Strike him strike, strike together!"
"Strike, strike, all together! "
Having pummeled the anvil well for a time, one of the apprentices would suddenly shout that the anvil was on fire! It had to be taken out quickly
lest the forge be burned. The poor anvil was taken hold of by three or four strong fellows and dumped into the cess-pool outside, or else was douched with buckets of water.

The Kiln on Fire

In this game, players simulated a miller and his men drying corn. The floor represented the kiln. The miller would order his men to bring in sacks of corn to put into the kiln. Each man went outside and came back with a man on his back; this process went on until some twenty men, as sacks, were lying in a heap on the floor. The were left there for a while to dry, as it were, and were then turned, those under neath being placed on top. When this had been done, and the process of drying the corn was progressing well, one of the workmen would suddenly should that the kiln was on fire. The miller and his helpers would rush to pour buckets of water on the sacks, drenching all who were heaped on the floor, especially those on top. In some areas, only two players took part, the miller and his daughter.

The Deaf Miller

A player (the miller) sat on the floor, mixing soot and water in a dish with a stick. As he worked, he carried on a conversation with himself, his remarks causing great laughter among the audience. One of his mill-hands would enter carrying another player, as a sack of corn, on his back, and would tell the miller that the sack was to be ground. The miller would pretend not to be able to hear him, owing to the noise of the mill, and would finally order the helper to lay the sack down behind him. When five or six sacks had thus been deposited behind the miller, who all the while continued to mix the soot and water (to simulate grinding) and keep up his remarks in a loud voice, the helper would shout that the mill was on fire.

The miller would have no trouble in hearing this and would throw the sooty water over his shoulder on top of the sacks behind his back to quench the blaze.

Lifting the Old Nag

A heavily-built man would hobble into the kitchen, pretending to be an old foundered horse, and throw himself down on the floor, grunting and complaining. Some players would gather about him, and he would ask them to raise him to his feet. Two or three would attempt this and would fail; others would come to their assistance, but even nine or ten would not be able to lift the nag. The leader of the game would then order them to remove their coats. They did so, throwing aside the coats here and there, and started to lift again, straining every muscle, but to no avail. The nag was too heavy. The leader would then order them to remove other garments, and when they had finally got rid of their socks, they would succeed in their task. At this point, some mischievous fellow would quench all the lights in the wake-house; the others would let the nag collapse on the floor and, in the darkness, set about finding their clothes, which would have been hidden away by members of the audience. Rough-and-tumble searching went on until the lights were restored, and the game was over.

Cutting the Timber

A man lay down across the threshold of the kitchen feet outside, head within. He was to represent the saw. Two players now took hold of his feet outside, while two others caught his head and shoulders in the kitchen. They pulled against one another, forward and backwards, as if they were sawing wood, until one pair proved too strong for the other.

The Dry Barber; The Shaving Game

In The Shaving Game, the leader and his assistants went through the crowded kitchen of the wake-house to find out who needed a shave. They would pick on somebody whom they might dislike for some reason,and drag him out to sit on a chair in the middle of the floor. The barbers then gathered about him and started to rub water, in which many kinds of dirt had been mixed, onto his face and head. He was powerless to resist or escape. Two would then begin to shave him with bits of stick or something, as razors. The shaving was, needless to say, an ordeal in itself, and it was finished by drenching the victim with water to get rid of the soap!

Other Diverse Diversons

Board Games

Croker (1824) describes favorite board games called The Walls of Troy and Short Castle. He describes Short Castle as follows:
It is "played on lines (usually marked with chalk) in this form.

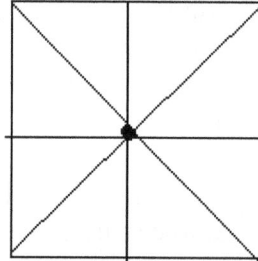

Each player is provided with three counters, (small black and white pebbles, or shells) which are singly deposited on the board in turn: the game is won by getting these three counters in a straight line. The center point is considered the most advantageous, and is always taken by the first player; when all the counters are deposited, moves are made from one point to the next, should it be unoccupied and so on, until a careless move on either side decides the game, by allowing the adversary to form his three counters in a row.

Card Playing

James Farewell describes a wake in 1689-
"Some play the trump, some trot the hay;
Some at macham, some noddy play
(Macham was a type of card-game)

There are many references to card games in association with wakes. Such games are often mentioned when the deceased was old and when attendance was small. If the deceased was a card player his friends always remembered him with a game of cards played in the kitchen with the corpse given a hand. Card tricks were also performed.

Riddles

Younger people found that the time at wakes was best spent with riddling. If you did not find the correct answer you were awarded a penalty. Tongue twister questions were also popular. Riddles however took second place to the major games.

Tongue Twisters

These could be in either Irish or English. Tongue twisters often were part of games such as *Scaoil Thart an Chearc Shearr* (Pass the Short Hen About). One end of a small stick was reddened in the fire. One player held it while reciting a long tongue-twister and kept waving the stick to prevent the red end from becoming black. If he succeeded in doing this he quickly passed the stick to his neighbor, who had to repeat the same rigmarole, while keeping the burnt end from dying out. Each player was allowed to blow on the red part during the rhyming. The player in whose hand the Short Hen died had to suffer some penalty. Other names for the game are: Deal/an D/e, An Birin Beo and Tom's Alive.

Versifying

Versifying is the composition of extempore verses with music while working. This was done as in the fields and during household tasks at wakes in between games.

Repetition of Jingles

Often popular set lines of poetry were repeated in association with games. Players would stand in a circle with one in the center. The one in the center would be a leader would give something to the first player who would ask him. "What is this" "a fat hen" said the leader would reply. The first player then gave the object to his neighbor who would ask the same question. The reply would be "A fat hen and two ducks". It went on until it reached the last player who was told that he or she had just received eight pairs of bullocks, seven pairs of boars, six pairs of red calves, five whales, four fat pigs, three grey geese, two ducks and a fat hen! The penalty was given to any player who could not repeat correctly in turn his own jingle. This penalty might be having to kiss some person have soot smeared on the face.

Here is one of the jingles:
"This is the ship that came from Spain
That carried the iron over the main
That made the spade of both stout and strong
That dug the grave both deep and long
That held the huntsmen, hounds and horns,
That chased the fox from under the thorns...."

Into the Clay

Life below the ground was often just as interesting as life above it....

Croker (1824) notes that often there was disagreement concerning the place of burial. Because being buried with family was so important these disagreements were quite intense. Often one party would win and would triumphantly carry the corpse to a cemetery many miles away from the site of the family residence.

Croker (1824) also noted that due to the belief that the last buried in a cemetery had to wait on and serve all the others buried there until the next was buried, those reaching the cemetery from different funerals would often come to blows over the issue of who should be buried first.

Hospitality was also a problem even for the souls buried in the churchyard. It is said that unlike in life, the souls of the dead would not welcome the newcomer . This was especially true of a *cuggeriegh* or intruder buried in a family or clan plot.

11. There are two funerals for the corpse,
one in the evening and   the second to the graveyard
on the next day.
12. The corpse is delivered to the church.
(if horses are used their hoofs were
blackened and straw was laid in the
street outside the wake house to deaden
the sound-Roslea.) Catholic
coffins would be covered in a brown
cloth, while the coffins of the Protestant
dead were covered in black. (Roslea)

"His coffin was lifted from its four supporting chairs which were then kicked over in accordance with custom that also dictated the coffin leave the cottage feet first...
Finola had to remain at home, for a pregnant woman might surely have a stillborn if she attended a funeral and obtained the curse of the dead"...
..."The friends and neighbors rotated as pallbearers, carrying the coffin on their shoulders and switching around every several yards. Tomas walked directly behind them, his hands and forehead resting on Kilty's box. His children marched at his side. Behind Tomas a dozen men carried spades and behind them the entire village formed an entourage. Father Lynch approached the procession wearing   a black vestment for death which had been embroidered along with his other vestments by the women of the village. Chanting and sprinkling holy water, he turned and led the way to the church."-- Uris op.cit.p.44.

The Procession

"An Irish funeral procession will present to the English traveler a very novel and singular aspect. The coffin is carried on an open hearse, with a canopy supported by four pillars, not unlike the car used at Lord Nelson's funeral: it is adorned with several devices in gold, and drawn by four horses, and is, perhaps, more impressive to the beholder, than the close caravan-like-conveyanyance used in England: but what is gained in solemnity by the principal feature, is suddenly destroyed by the incongruity of the rest of the train, generally composed of a few postchaises, the drivers in their daily costume of a long great coat and slouched hat. In addition to these, I have seen a gig in which the clergyman (I imagine, by his being equipped in a white scarf and hat-band) drove a friend; afterwards came a crowd of persons of all descriptions on foot. No noise, no lamentations were to be heard; but the figure in the flowing white scarf brandishing his whip, gave, at a little distance, very much the effect of an electioneering procession"

."…The open hearse is common throughout Ireland, and that used by the poorer classes becomes perfectly grotesque, from the barbarous paintings of saints and angels with which it is bedizened. The concourse of persons who attend the funeral of an opulent farmer, or a resident landlord, is prodigious. Not only those to whom the deceased was known, but every one who meets the procession turns to accompany it, lest his haste be ever so great, for a mile or two, as nothing is accounted more unlucky, or unfriendly, than to neglect doing so.

The funeral of a gentleman acknowledged as the head of a clan (now an event of rare occurrence, and almost solely confined to the county Kerry) is one of those sights it is impossible to behold without feeling sublime sensations. The vast multitude, winding through some romantic defile, or trailing along the base of a wild mountain, while the chorus of the death-song, coming fitfully upon the breeze, is raised by a thousand voices. On a closer view, the aged nurse is seen sitting on the hearse beside the coffin, with her body bent over it; her actions dictated by the most violent grief, and her head completely enveloped in the deep hood of her large cloak, which falls in broad and heavy folds producing a most mysterious and awful figure.

Then at every crossroad, such roads being considered symbolic of their faith, there is a general halt; the men uncover their heads and a prayer is offered up for the soul of their departed chief."-Croker (1824, pp.171-172).

13. Relatives and maybe a few neighbors return to the house .
14. The Corpse is buried and a few relatives or neighbors stay to help clean the house putting things back in order.

"After Tomas arrived, the coffin was set down into the ground and covered. Each mourner passed by in turn and placed a rock on it until the pile became a small cairn. In twos and threes the men drifted to McCluskey's public house and the women back to the village."

-- Uris op.cit.p.47

One Woman, a resident of Cork was too poor to rent a hearse or even a cart to carry her body to the cemetery. Her daughter learned of this, found a rope and tied her mother's coffin onto her back and carried it ten miles to the cemetery.
–Croker (1824)

Croker (1824) notes that due to the perceived sanctity of priests clay from their graves was taken, mixed with water and consumed for health and the cure of diseases. When Sir Richard Musgrave, leader of the White Boys died the soil covering his body was taken away for its curative properties in such quantity that the officials of the church had to make several trips bringing more earth to cover the grave.

-Croker (1824)

Literature

Dialogue VI. The Wake

Rose, Nancy.

Rose. POOR Ned Kinselagh is dead, and has left a distressed family indeed !

Nancy. Is he? poor soul!—I am very sorry.—Will you come to the Wake to night?

Rose. I intend, when I have cleaned up the house, to go and sit awhile with the poor old neighbour. Shall I call on you to come with me?

Nancy. No. I'll not go so soon. I'll sit up all night.

Rose. Ah, now Nancy, don't do that. Why should you lose your natural rest?

Nancy. And why should you lose yours? you sate up two nights with him while he was sick.

Rose. Oh, that was quite different, you know; but now, when the poor man is gone, sitting up will be of no use to him.

Nancy. It's not to be of use to him I'll sit up, but to have a little diversion.

Rose. Well to be sure, I wonder, of all things, how people can be playing and diverting themselves, and a poor fellow-creature dead before their eyes, and don't know how soon themselves may be lying in the same way!

Nancy. O yes, I remember how you behaved at Nelly Murphy's wake; how you looked at her under the table, and burst out crying; you spoiled all our comfort and satisfac.tion. I am sure not one of us ever desired to meet you at a wake again.

Rose. How could I help crying *to* see the clever, clean, likely young woman, cut down like a flower, in a few days, and her poor old mother rocking with grief in the chimney corner! I wondered how any one could laugh and be merry in such a place.

Nancy. Why it would help to keep up the poor woman's heart to see a little fun going on.

Rose. Oh, not at all, but make her a great deal worse; and I'll engage she thought it very cruel to have such a noise in the place, and no one minding her, except some old people that bid her not fret, and she fretted the more for that.

Nancy. Really they say that Nelly got her death at Pat Doghery's wake, for he died of a fever, and she remarked the heavy smell that was in the room, and she took sick and died very soon after.

Rose. I don't doubt it, and I

would not wonder if many a one got sickness at a wake; so many crowd in, and often into a close room, and when it is a heavy sickness, sure it must be dangerous.

Nancy. Then indeed, people should consider that, and know what disorder the person died of; for one's own wake is not a pleasant thing to think of.

Rose. Ah, my dear Nancy, if we thought more about that time, it would be better for us; and how can we help thinking of it, when a neighbour lies before us, stiff and cold, that was as well and as hearty as ourselves a little while before. Oh sure it's no time for play*!

Nancy. Would you leave the poor corpse by itself, as I hear they do in some places?

Rose. No, I would not: to be sure there are different customs in different places, and we show our love and respect to our neighbours by sitting quietly by them when they are dead, and talking over all their goodness, and crying for them; and we feel our hearts soft and tender, and we love our neighbours that are alive better, when we think in how short a time all our lives will be over, and that we don't know how soon it will be our turn to go. If I had my will I would never let more than half a dozen sober neighbours sit up at a wake.

P. 29. 8' *When a neighbour lies stiff and cold, ' that was well and hearty as ourselves, a little ' while before, O, sureit's no time for flay!'*

It has been sufficiently explained to the English reader, that a wake in Ireland does not, as in England, mean a dance, a merry making, but a sitting up with a corpse, a waking of the dead. Formerly in the Irish lamentations over the dead, the relations called upon the deceased to awake, as if they did but sleep. These meetings soon became parties of pleasure for the living, instead of mournings for the dead. Some years ago, every servant girl in the lower and middle 'ranks of life thought she had a right to be allowed to go to the wake of a relation, or neighbour; and with a certain air of confidence that she should not be refused, and a certain mixed tone of sorrow, and real face of festivity, would come up to her mistress, and ask to be allowed to go to the wake.— * Ma'am, my *shister's* husband's dead, and ' I'd be glad if you'd be pleased to let me go ' to the wake to night:' or, 'Ma'am, it's ' Cecily Gallagher's wake to night, that was ' a great neighbour of my mother's, and if ' you'd be pleased to give me leave, I'd be ' sorry not to be *in it.'*

Nancy says, that she would not give a pin to go to a wake, except at night: but we are happy to state, that of late years it has become disreputable, in some counties in Ireland, for young women to attend wakes by night. And female servants now ask permission only to go to the wake in the day time, ' because they could not do such a thing as to go to a wake by night; the priest would not allow of it.' This is a great improvement.

-P. 3. 1 The life was out of it.

Here is an example of the Irish poetical mode of expression. Instead of saying that a person is killed, or dead, they say *you'll never hear him speak again;* or, *he'll never taste a bit, or swallow a drop more;* or, *he'll never trouble any body more—the life is out of him. the breath is gone out of him.*

Like the ancient expressions—he has ceased to be—he is no more—the vital spark is fled.—

' And from the lips the vital spirit fled
' Returns no more to wake the silent dead.

- Edgeworth, Maria, <u>Cottage Dialogues Among the Irish Peasantry</u>, with Notes and a Preface, 1811, p.26.

According to William Carleton

Bucxramback, The Country Dancing-Master, p.15, Moll Roe's Marriage, p. 221, Mary Murray, the Irish Match-maker, p.30, and Tom Greissey, The Irish Sanachie, p.189.   from: <u>Tales and Stories of the Irish Peasantry</u>. William Carleton, 1834.

...There are, however, others which are serious,
and may be looked upon as the exponents of the pathetic spirit
of our country. Of the latter, I fear, several are altogether
lost; and I question whether there be many persons now alive
in Ireland who know much about the Hero Lheig, which, from
the word it begins with, must necessarily have been danced
only on mournful occasions. It is only at wakes and funereal
customs in those remote parts of the country where old usages
are most pertinaciously clung to, that any elucidation of the
Hora Lheig, and others of our forgotten dances, could be
obtained.

Immediately after the relaxation of this legend, he passed at
once into a different spirit. He and Frank Magavren marshalled

their forces, and in a few minutes two or three dozen
young fellows were hotly engaged in the humorous game of
"Boxing. the Connaughtman." Boxing the Connaughtman
was followed by the "Standing Brogue" and the "Sitting
Brogue," two other sports practised only at wakes. And
here we may remark generally, that the amusements resorted
to on such occasions are never to be found elsewhere, but are
exclusively peculiar to the house of mourning, where they
are benevolently introduced for the purpose of alleviating
sorrow. Having gone through a few more such sports, Tom
took a seat, and addressed a neighbouring farmer, named
Gordon, as follows :—"Jack Gordon, do you know the history
of your own name, and its original fluency ?"
" Indeed no, Tom, I cannot say I do."
"Well, boys, if yee derogate your noise a little, I'll tell
yez the origin of the name of Gordon ;'" it's only about ould
Oliver Crummle, whose tongue

- Tom Greissey, The Irish Sanachie, p.189.

Moll Roe's Marriage.

IT is utterly impossible for any one but an Irishman fully to
comprehend the extravagance to which the spirit of Irish
humour is often carried, and that even in circumstances which
one would suppose it ought least to be expected. In other
countries the house of death is in reality the house of mourning,
and so indeed it is also in Ireland, where domestic grief is felt
with a power that reaches to the uttermost depths of the heart.
But then in Ireland this very fulness of sorrow, unlike that
which is manifested elsewhere, is accompanied by so many
incongruous associations, apparently incompatible with, or
rather altogether opposed to, the idea of afliiction, that strangers,
when assured of such an anomalous admixture of feelings,
can scarcely bring themselves to believe in their existence. I
have said that in Ireland the house of death is without doubt
the house of mourning ; but I must not conceal the additional
fact, that it is also, in consequence of the calamity which has
occurred, the house of fun, and of fun, too, so broad, grotesque,
and! xtravagant, that in no other condition of society,
even in Ireland, is there anything to be found like it. This,
no doubt, may appear a rather startling assertion, but it is
quite true.

And now many of my sagacious readers will at once set
about accounting for such a singular combination of mad mirth
and profound sorrow. Let them, however, spare their meta
physics, for I will save them a long process of reasoning on the

subject, by stating, that all this clatter of laughter and comic uproar proceeds from a principle that does honour to Paddy's heart—I mean sympathy with those whom the death of some dear relative has thrown into affliction. Indeed no people sympathize more deeply with each other than the Irish, or enter more fully into the spirit that prevails, whether it be one of joy or sorrow. The reason, then, why the neighbours and acquaintances of the deceased flock at night to hold Wakes— the merriest of all merry meetings—frequently in the very house where he or she lies dead, is simply that. the sense of the bereavement may be mitigated by the light-hearted amusements which are enacted before their eyes. The temperament of the Irish, however, is strongly susceptible of the extremes of mirth and sorrow, and our national heart is capable of being moved by the two impulses almost at the same moment. Many a time I have seen a widow sitting over the dead body of an affectionate 'husband, midst her desolate orphans, so completely borne away by the irresistible fun of some antic wag, who acted as Master of the Revels, that she has been forced into a fit of laughter that brought other tears than those of sorrow to her eyes. Often has the father—the features of the pious and chaste mother of his children composed into the mournful still ness of death before him—been, in the same manner, carried into a fit of immoderate mirth on witnessing the inimitable drolleries exhibited in "Boxing the Connaughtman," or the convulsive fun of the " Screw-pin Dance." The legends and tales and stories that are told at Irish wakes all bear the impress of this mad extravagance ; and it is because I am now about to'relate one of them, that I have deemed it expedient to introduce it to my readers by this short but necessary pre— face. Those who peruse it are not to imagine that I am gravely writing it in my study; but that, on the contray, they are sitting in the chimney-comer, at an Irish wake, and that some droll Senacbie, his face lit up into an expression of broad farcical humour, is proceeding somewhat as follows: "Moll Roe Raffertywas the son—daughter I mane—of ould Jack Rafferty, who was remarkable for a habit he had of always wearing his head undher his hat; but indeed the same family was a quare one, as everybody knew that was acquainted wid them. It was said of them—but whether it was thrue or not I won't undhertake to say, for 'fraid I'd tell a lie—that whenever they didn't wear shoes' or boots, they always went bamfooted; but Ihard afther...
-Moll Roe's Marriage, p.221.

Tom, was at a wake in the neighbourhood; for it somehow happened that there was seldom either wake or dance within two or three miles of us that we did not attend ; and, God forgive us! when old

Poll Doolin was on her death-bed, the only care that troubled us was an apprehension that she might recover, and thus defraud us of a right merry wake! Upon the occasion we allude to, it being known that Tom Gressiey would be present, of course the house was crowded. And when he did come, and his loud good-humoured voice was heard at the door, heavens ! how every young heart bounded with glee and delight ! The first thing he did on entering was to go where the corpse was laid out, and in a loud rapid voice repeat the *Deprofundis* for the repose of her soul, after which he sat down and smoked a pipe. Oh, well do we remember how the whole house was hushed, for all 'was expectation and interest as to what he would do or say. At length he spoke—" Is Frank Magavrcn there ?"

" All that's left o' me's here, Tom."

" An' if the sweep-chimly-general had his due, Frank, that woul'dn't be much; and so the longer you can keep him out of that same, the betther for yourself." '

" Folly on, Tom! you know there's none of us all able to spake up to you, say what you will."

'It's not so when you're beside a purty girl, Frank. But sure that's not surprisin' ; you were born with butther in your mouth, an' that's what makes your orations to the fair sect be so soft an' meltin, ha, ha, ha! Well, Frank, never mind; there's worse where you'll go to : keep your own counsel last :

let's salt your gums, an' you'll do yet. Whisht, boys; I'm goin' to sing a rann, an' afther that Frank an' I will pick a couple o' dozen out o' yez ' to box the Connaughtman.'" Boxing the Connaughtman is a play or diversion peculiar to wakes; it is grotesquely athletic 'in its character, but full, besides, of comic sentiment and farcical humour. He then commenced an Irish rann or song, the substance of which was as follows, according to his own translation : "' St. Patrick, it seems, was one Sunday morning crossing a mountain on his way to chapel to say mass, and as he was an humble man (coaches weren't then invented at any rate} an' a great *pedestrium* [pedestrian], he took the shortest cut across the mountains. In one of the lonely glens he met a herd-candy, who spent his time in eulogizin' his masther's cattle, accordin' to the precepts of them times which was not by any means so larned an' primogenitive as now. The countenance of the day was clear …

- Tom Greissey, The Irish Sanachie, p. 184.

Sources

Sources for specific materials are provided within the text.
This is a list of general references.

Carlson, Lisa Caring ForYour Own Dead, Upper Access Publishers, PO Box 457,
Hinesburg, Vermont 05461.

Colum,Padraic. A Treasury of Irish Folklore., Crown, 1967.

Croker, T. Crofton, Researches in the South of Ireland.,Irish Academic
Press,1981(1824).

Danaher, Kevin.,The Year In Ireland., Mercier/Irish Books and Media,1972.

Ó Súilleabhìn, Seán., Caitheamh aimsire ar thórraimh./ Irish wake amusements.

Cork, Mercier Press,1969, c1967.

Appendix I:

Doing it Yourself

The Irish Wake has traditionally been a hands-on family centered and home-based ritual; however, enlisting the assistance of local professionals to mourn, prepare the body, perform music and tell stories and provide keens has also been an important part of the tradition. While entrusting preparations to professionals is an option, it is also important to realize that it is often possible to take care of many of the arrangements yourself or at least in the setting of your own home. I have provided some information below. I hope that it will be of assistance for those who wish to return to a more cultural home and family-based ritual of death and burial. Please be advised that the following information is provided only as a guide. Be sure to contact your local authorities to obtain the most accurate and current information.

In the United States:

From the Web Page of the Funeral Consumers Alliance:
Caring for your own dead is permitted in ALL states with these conditions or exceptions:

Colorado—The statutes specifically refer to the rights of religious groups and their members to care for their own dead. In practice, the "religious conviction" of any family is likely to be honored. Funeral directors are not licensed in Colorado, so anyone can be a "funeral director."

Connecticut—The laws in Connecticut are in conflict with each other, begging for a lawsuit. The laws specifically provide that the "custody and control of remains . . . shall belong to the surviving spouse . . . or . . . next of kin . . . "[Sec. 45-253]. On the other hand, a funeral director's signature is required on the death certificate. Only a funeral director or embalmer may remove the body of a deceased person from one town to another" when a person dies in Connecticut, but towns and ecclesiastical societies may provide a hearse and pall for burial of the dead. Go figure. A licensed embalmer must be in charge when death is from a communicable disease. Because the laws are conflicting in this state, a family wishing to care for its own dead may wish to seek the help of legal counsel. The FAMSA office may be able to help by filing a friend of the court brief.

Illinois—/As of 1990, next-of-kin or a designated agent may be in charge, although the coroner in Dupage County has flatly stated that he would refuse to release a body to a family. Families in that county who run into difficulty may need to seek an emergency court order. If so, contact FAMSA for a friend of the court testimony.

Indiana —The statutes in Indiana are in conflict and begging for a lawsuit here, too. The business statutes, dictate that a disposition permit may be given only to a funeral director, the passage of which was surely influenced by the industry. None of the health statutes, however, have such restrictions and refer to the "person in charge," defined as next-of-kin. Families that wish to care for their own dead may be able to find a local mortician who will cooperate in getting permits. Otherwise, be prepared for a court challenge to get your rights.

Louisiana—Again, in this state, laws are in conflict with a family's rights and should be challenged in court. A family in Louisiana may transport a body once all permits are acquired. A mortician, however, is needed for all other aspects such as obtaining those permits and at final disposition, so information in the above books is primarily helpful only to those taking the body to another state.

Massachusetts—In 1996, the Memorial Society here convinced the State Board of Health that Commonwealth laws permitted families to care for their own dead. It was left to the discretion of the individual boards of health whether or not to comply with the state's opinion. Although many towns have agreed to do so, a court case will be pursued if difficulty arises. Personnel in the Department of Health have been very helpful with recalcitrant local officers. Call the FAMSA office for assistance: 800-765-0107

Michigan—A 1995 court decision affirmed a family's right to possess a body "for the purpose of preparation, mourning and burial." This state also has one of the best home burial statutes. Families wishing to care for their own dead in this state may run into officials who are not aware of the court case. If you have difficulty, call the FAMSA office, 800-765-0107.

Nebraska—Statutes regarding family rights (and obligations to pay the bill) are in conflict with statutes requiring a funeral director to be in charge of all deaths.

New Hampshire—A new statute passed in 1999 goes into effect January 2000 permitting next-of-kin or designated agents to care for their own dead.

New Jersey—Statutes give next-of-kin the right to control disposition. Regulations, not statutes, promulgated by the Mortuary Science Board require the involvement of a funeral director. However, the Mortuary Board has NO authority over private citizens, only licensees.

New York-- As in Louisiana, a family may transport a body once all permits are acquired. A mortician, however, is needed for all other aspects such as obtaining those permits and at final disposition, so this information is primarily helpful only to those taking the body to another state.

Appendix II:
Burial On the Isle of Ireland

Health and a long life to you.
Land without rent to you.
A child every year to you.
And if you can't go to heaven,
May you die in Ireland-Old Irish Toast

You can't always get what you want!

But you can do the next best thing!

Those interested in arranging for burial on the Isle of Ireland should note that two governments are currently involved: the United Kingdom and the Republic of Ireland. Before leaving the United States bodies must be carefully prepared and forms must be completed. Here is the information provided by the National Funeral Directors Association publication: <u>Recommended Foreign Shipping Guidelines</u>, Revised May 1999: (Please note that you should check to make sure that this information is still current. Call: National Funeral Directors Association, Brookfield, Wisconsin 800-228-6332   or   262-789-1880 or at 202-547-0441.)

 In addition to the procedures outlined below, the Association notes that it is also essential to contact the embassy of the country involved for further details on their end: the embassy of the Republic of Ireland: 202-462-3939 the embassy of the United Kingdom, 202-588-6500.

According to British Airways one would need the certificates mentioned below with the addition of a certificate from relevant authorities noting that the body is being removed with permission for transport and interment elsewhere. Because only certain aircraft can carry bodies you may need to contact the airline shipping office as soon as possible. You can also present your paperwork including weight and dimensions (a limit of 100 kilos and length of 72 inches was given) to the shipping office before you are entirely ready for shipment. The office can then have the shipping office at the destination review the documents to make sure no additional paperwork is required.

RECOMMENDED GUIDELINES:

I.   The human remains shall be subject to the following health measures:

A.   When the body is embalmed

1.   Thorough washing with an effective disinfectant; disinfection of all orifices; packing all orifices with cotton saturated with an effective disinfectant.
2.   Proper embalming (arterial and cavity) in accordance with standard U.S. procedures.
3.   Placed within an impervious metal sealer casket (coffin) or any casket (coffin) made of wood and other materials that can accommodate a metal utility case capable of being sealed to prevent the possibility of the escape of fluids and offensive odors.
4.   Encasement of casketed remains in a wood shipping box or a new certified airtray.

B.   When embalming is not possible

1.   When possible, thorough washing with an effective disinfectant, disinfection of all orifices with cotton saturated with an effective disinfectant, and wrapping in a sheet saturated with effective disinfectant.
2.   Placement of the human remains within an impervious metal sealer casket (coffin) or any casket (coffin) made of wood or other materials that can accommodate a metal utility case capable of being sealed to prevent the possibility of the escape of fluids and offensive odors.
3.   Encasement of the casketed remains in a metal lined/wood shipping box; the metal liner (zinc or steel) to be soldered or welded so as to be completely sealed by fusion.

C.   Cremated remains

1.   Not subject to health or other measures and may be shipped by any method; need no quarantine clearance.
2.   Must be accompanied by the following:

a.   Certificate of cremation from the crematory
b.   Cremation affidavit
c.   Certified copy of death certificate

3.   Statement of funeral director that urn contains only ashes of the deceased.
(Note: The embassy may require all or certain documents be authenticated.)

II. *Preliminary packaging specifications*

A.   Human remains must be secured in a casket or alternative container and placed in a wood shipping box ¾" thick with six handles (4 on sides, 2 on ends), closed with screws (not nails) no more than 18" apart or in a new certified airtray.

B.   Outer shipping containers must provide an identification window or insert into which documentation and certificates are placed.

C.   The head end of the outer shipping container must be identified to assist cargo handlers in aircraft loading and unloading operations.

D.   The casket may be covered with a protective plastic cover prior to placement in the outer shipping container to protect against scratches and mars.

III. *Documentation required*

A.   Two certified copies of the death certificate

B.   Burial/transit permit

C.   Communicable disease affidavit (form enclosed)

D.   Two copies of notarized embalmers or cremation affidavit (form enclosed)

E.   A letter from the funeral home stating the flight itinerary and the consignee

Doc: 99foreign shipping

COMMUNICABLE DISEASE AFFIDAVIT

To whom it may concern:

This is to certify that_____
                                                         (deceased)

died on_____at_____
            (date)   (address)

in the United States of America; the undersigned has no knowledge that the

deceased died of a communicable disease; the body of the deceased has been

thoroughly and properly embalmed by the U.S. standard arterial and cavity methods

in accordance with the public health rules and the laws applicable to the place of

death; said body has been placed in a strong metal impervious casket with lid locked

on a gasket; said casketed body has been placed in a wood outer shipping box; and

said casket and outer wood shipping box contain nothing but the body of the

deceased.

_____   _____
        (date)   (firm)

                                  _____
                                       (signature)

Subscribed and sworn to before me at_____
                                                  (city)

_____in the United States of America, this
        (state)

_____
        (date)

_____   _____
        (date)   (notary pubic, (city))

EMBALMER AFFIDAVIT

To whom it may concern:

This is to certify that_____
                                   (deceased)

died on_____at_____
         (date)   (city)

_____,_____has been thoroughly embalmed
      (state)   (county)

by the U.S. standard arterial and cavity methods in accordance with the public

health rules and laws applicable to the place of death and the undersigned has no

personal knowledge that the deceased died of a communicable disease.

_____   _____
        (date)   (signature of embalmer)

_____
(firm)

_____in the United States of America
(state)

this_____.
(date)

_____   _____
(date)   (notary public, (city))

CREMATION AFFIDAVIT

To whom it may concern:

This is to certify that this container contains only the cremated remains

of_____who died on_____

at_____

in the United States of America
_____   _____
(date)   (signature)

                                  _____
                                  (firm)

Subscribed and sworn to before me at_____
                                                (city)

_____in the United States of America,
(state)

this_____.
(date)

Appendix III

"Keens and Death Ceremonies", From: Researches in the south of Ireland, Thomas Crofton Croker, 1824

"Keens and Death Ceremonies", From: Researches in the south of Ireland, illustrative of the scenery, architectural remains, and the manners and superstitions of the peasantry. With an appendix, containing a private narrative of the rebellion of 1798 , Thomas Crofton Croker, 1824.

CHAPTER IX.
keens and death ceremonies.

" The women mix their cries, and clamour fills the fields. The warlike wakes continued all the night, And funeral games were played at new returning light." Dryden.
" AN easy death and a fine funeral" is a proverbial benediction amongst the lower orders in Ireland. Throughout life the peasant is accustomed to regard the manner and place of his interment as matters of the greatest importance ;" "to be decently put in the earth, along with his own people," is the wish most frequently and fervently expressed by him. When advanced in life, it is usual, particularly with those who are destitute and friendless, to deny themselves the common necessaries of life and to hoard up every trifle they can collect for the expenses of their wake and funeral. Looking forward to their death as to a gala given by them to their acquaintances, every possible preparation is made for rendering it, as they consider," creditable;" their shroud and burial dress are often provided many years before they are wanted ; nor will the owners use these garments whilst living, though existing in the most abject. state of wretchedness and rags. It is not unusual to see even the tombstone in readiness, and leaning against the cabin wall, a perpetual " memento mori" that must meet the eye of its possessor every time he crosses his threshold.

There is evidently a constitutional difference in the composition of the English and Irish peasant; but this peculiarity may be more satisfactorily accounted for by the prevailing belief with the latter of a future state being a material one, and subject to wants even more urgent than those of this life ; under this impression, shoes, considered a luxury quite unworthy a thought, are believed almost indispensable after death, when it is supposed much walking has to be performed, probably through rough roads and inclement weather. The superstition evidently proceeds from the tenet of purgatory or qualification for heaven, held by the Romish church ; and on this particular, the general belief of the Irish peasantry is somewhat at variance with the representations of their pastors : the priest describes it as a place of fire, but the people imagine it to be a vast and dreary extent, strewed with sharp stones and abounding in thorns and brambles. The influence of this doctrine affects rich and poor, according to their circumstances, and is a most valuable one, for I have been assured

the emolument it yields to the Catholic church of Ireland, by a late limited calculation, exceeds 650,000/. per annum. The attachment manifested towards particular burial-places arises from the same cause; and the anxiety amongst the vulgar to be interred with their deceased relatives, bestows even on death a feeling of social interest. A remarkable instance occurred not long since. An old beggar woman, who died near the city of Cork, requested that her body might be deposited in White Church burial ground. Her daughter, who was without the means to obtain a hearse or any other mode of conveyance, determined herself to undertake the task, and, having procured a rope, she fastened the coffin on her back, and, after a tedious journey of more than ten miles, fulfilled her mother's request. This national trait may be recognized in an advertisement copied from the Sydney Gazette of the 1st October 1814, the existing regulations of which colony oblige every person to give public notice of their departure. " Dennis Hurley, intending to quit the colony in the Seringapatam, to visit the land of his forefathers, where he hopes, after this life of toil and trouble, to rest under his native turf, requests that all claims against him may be presented for payment." Mr. Hurley, I presume, was one of those " real patriots"
-" who, be it understood, Have left their country for their country's good."

Separate interests (as in the case of marriage) often cause disputes at funerals; and as no acknowledged rule exists in such cases, a battle usually ends the dissension, and the corpse is borne away in triumph by the victorious party to a cemetery perhaps twenty miles distant from that originally intended. At a Roman Catholic clergyman's funeral, which took place recently in the South of Ireland, the fathers of his order were opposed by the relations of the deceased, who wished the coffin to be conveyed to their family vault, but the attempt proved fruitless, as the fathers, anticipating opposition timely, procured so strong a force that the Assailing faction was beat off, and a guard was stationed on the grave for some weeks after to prevent the dead man's resurrection, should it be attempted. I remember once overhearing a contest between a poor man and his wife, respecting the burial of their infant. The woman wished to have the child laid near some of her own relations, which the husband strongly opposed, concluding her attachment to her friends. was superior to her love for him ; but he was soon convinced by his wife's argument, that as her sister had died in child-birth only a few days previous, she would afford their poor infant suck, which nourishment it might not have if buried elsewhere.

Another instance of similar superstition occurred in the case of a woman, who presented several beggars with a loaf and porringer, that her deceased child might not want a porringer or bread in the next world. She accounted for her knowledge of the wants of an after-state by saying that a very good man, who used to have occasional trances, in which it was known his soul left his body and became familiar with disembodied spirits, returning to its former habitation after a short absence, told her, on his recovery from one of these fits, that children, dying at an early age, whose parents' neglect deprived them of the use of a porringer, were obliged to lap milk out of their hands; whilst others, who were provided in life with one, had a similar article prepared for their comfort in a future state ; and " now," continued the woman, as she bestowed her last loaf and porringer on a mendicant, " my mind is eased of its burthen, and my poor child is as happy as the best of them." Many other anecdotes of the same nature might be related, but these are sufficient for the purpose of illustration. The belief also of a similarity between spiritual and mortal existence extends, not merely to necessities, but to points of etiquette. It is a general opinion amongst the lower orders, that the last buried corpse has to perform an office like that of " fag" in our public schools by the junior boy, or at a regimental mess by the youngest officer ; and that the attendance on his churchyard companions is only relieved by the interment of some other person. The notion may seem too absurd, yet serious consequences have sometimes resulted from it ; and an instance comes within my recollection where two funerals, proceeding to the same burial-ground, arrived within view of each other a short distance from their place of destination. Both immediately halted, and a messenger was mutually despatched to demand precedence; their conference terminated in blows, and the throng on both sides forsaking the coffins, rushed impetuously forward, when a furious contest ensued, in which some lives were lost.

It is a prevalent notion that the ghost of a stranger is seldom well received by the ancient possessors of a churchyard, particularly if it has long been reserved to a clan or sept, when the *"cuggeriegh,"* or intruder, is sadly annoyed by his associates. There is in this a strange variation between life and death in the Irish character, as the trait of hospitality towards strangers is proverbially predominant while living. When priests, or others noted for their sanctity, die, their graves are resorted to for some of the clay, which is mingled with water and drank for the cure of various diseases.

Sir Richard Musgravc mentions that earth from the grave of Father Sheehy, who was executed about the middle of the last century as the leader of some White Boy outrages, was held in great repute, and taken away so rapidly, on account of its supernatural powers, that the sexton had more than once to renew the covering. Recent cases may be named, where this custom has been carried to such lengths that it was interdicted under the threat of exemplary punishment. The wake of a corpse is a scene of merriment rather than of mourning. The body lies exposed in the coffin for two or three nights previous to interment, surrounded by many candles, and with the face uncovered. To avert misfortune arising from the death of the heads of families, when a man dies his head is placed at the foot of the bed ; but this ceremony is not deemed necessary with women, and they are allowed to remain in the usual position. In the evening a general assembly of the neighbours takes place, when they are entertained with whiskey, tobacco and snuff. On these occasions songs are sung and stories related, while the younger part of the company beguile the time with various games, and sports, such as blind man's buff, or hunt the slipper. Dancing, or rather running in a ring, round an individual, who performs various evolutions, is also a common amusement; and four or five young men will sometimes, for the diversion of the party, blacken their faces, and go through a regular series of gestures with sticks, not unlike those of the English morris dancers.

Amongst the games played at wakes, are two which I have never observed out of Ireland, and from their being so universal with the peasantry, they are probably of considerable antiquity. One of these is called " the walls of Troy," and the other " short castle." Of the former, although I took some pains to acquire it, I now find myself unable to give a satisfactory description; the latter is played on lines (usually marked with chalk) in this form. Each player is provided with three counters, (small black and white pebbles, or shells,) which are singly deposited on the board in turn: the game is won by getting these three counters in a straight line. The centre point is considered the most advantageous, and is always taken by the first player; when all the counters are deposited, moves arc made from one point to the next, should it be unoccupied, and so on, until a careless move on either side decides the game, by allowing the adversary to form his three counters in a row. An Irish funeral procession will present to the English traveller a very novel and singular aspect. The coffin is carried on an open hearse, with a canopy supported by four pillars, not unlike the car used at Lord Nelson's funeral ; it is adorned with several devices in gold, and drawn by four horses, and is, perhaps, more impressive to the beholder, than the close caravan-like conveyance used in England ; but what is gained in solemnity by the principal feature, is suddenly destroyed by the incongruity of the rest of the train, generally composed of a few postchaises, the drivers in their daily costume of a long great coat and slouched hat. In addition to these, I have seen a gig in which the clergyman (I imagine, by his being equipped in a white scarf and hat-band) drove a friend; afterwards came a crowd of persons of all descriptions on foot. No noise, no lamentations were to be heard; but the figure in the flowing white scarf brandishing his whip, gave it, at a little distance, very much the effect of an electioneering procession. The open hearse is common throughout Ireland, and that used by the poorer classes becomes perfectly grotesque, from the barbarous paintings of saints and angels with which it is bedizened. The concourse of persons who attend the funeral of an opulent farmer, or a resident landlord, is prodigious. Not only those to whom the deceased was known, but every one who meets the procession, turns to accompany it, let his haste be ever so great, for a mile or two, as nothing is accounted more unlucky, or unfriendly, than to neglect doing so. The funeral of a gentleman acknowledged as the head of a clan (now an event of rare occurrence, and almost solely confined to the county Kerry) is one of those sights it is impossible to behold without feeling sublime sensations. The vast multitude, winding through some romantic defile, or trailing along the base of a wild mountain, while the chorus of the death-song, coming fitfully upon the breeze, is raised by a thousand voices. On a closer view, the aged nurse is seen sitting on the hearse beside the coffin, with her body bent over it ; her actions dictated by the most violent grief, and her head completely enveloped in the deep hood of her large cloak, which falls in broad and heavy folds, producing altogether a most mysterious and awful figure. Then at every cross-road, such roads being considered symbolic of their faith, there is a general halt ; the men uncover their heads, and a prayer is offered up for the soul of their departed chief. The Irish funeral howl is notorious, and although this vociferous expression of grief is on the decline, there is still, in the less civilized parts of the country, a strong attachment to the custom, and many may yet be found who are keeners or mourners for the dead by profession. In the fourth volume of the <u>Transactions of the Royal Irish Academy</u>, the musical notation of one of these lamentations may be seen ; and Dr. O'Brien, in his Irish dictionary, describes the keen* as " a cry for the dead, according to certain loud and mournful notes, and verses, wherein the pedigree, land, property, generosity and good actions of the deceased person, and his ancestors, are diligently and harmoniously recounted, in order to excite pity and compassion in the hearers, and to make them sensible of their great loss in the death of the person whom they lament." Having a curiosity to hear the Keen more distinctly sung than over a corpse, when it is accompanied by a wild and inarticulate uproar as a chorus, I procured an elderly woman, who was renowned for her skill in keening, to recite for me some of these dirges. This woman, whose name was Harrington, led a wandering kind of life, travelling from cottage to cottage about the country, and though in fact subsisting on charity, found every where not merely a welcome, but had numerous invitations, on account of the vast store of Irish verses she had collected, and could repeat. Her memory was indeed extraordinary; and the clearness, quickness, and elegance with which she translated from the Irish into English, though unable to read or write, is almost incredible. Before she commenced repeating, she mumbled for a short time, probably the beginning of each stanza, to assure herself of the arrangement, with her eyes closed, rocking her body backwards and forwards, as if keeping time to the measure of

* " This Irish word, written by our late grammarians *Caoine,* but anciently, and properly *Cine,* is almost equal in letters and pronunciation to the Hebrew *Cina,* which signifies lamentation, or crying, with clapping of hands, *lamentatio, planctus, ploratus* vide 2 Sam. i. 17; and in its plural *Cinim,* lamentations vide Ez. ii. 10. Welch *Kuyn* is a complaint."

the verse. She then began in a kind of whining recitative, but as she proceeded and as the composition required it, her voice assumed a variety of deep and fine tones, and the energy with which many passages were delivered, proved her perfect comprehension and strong feeling of the subject, but her eyes always continued shut, perhaps to prevent interruption to her thoughts, or her attention being engaged by any surrounding object. From several keens which I took down from this woman's dictation, I have selected four, and to each I have attached a short explanatory introduction. They will doubtless appear to the English reader odd combinations of the sublime and vulgar.

NUMBER I.
A keen composed on Sir Richard Cox the historian, who died in 1733; the first verse presents a curious picture of Irish hospitality. " My love and darling, though I never was in your kitchen, yet I have heard an exact account of it. The brown roast meat continually coming from the fire ; the black boilers continually boiling ; the cock of the beer-barrel for ever running; and if even a score of men came in, no person would inquire their business ; but they would give them a place at your table, and let them eat what they pleased, nor would they bring a bill in the morning to them." " My love and friend, I dreamed through my morning slumbers, that your castle fell into decay, and that no person remained in it. The birds sung sweetly no longer, nor were there leaves upon the bushes; all was silence and decay! the dream told me that our beloved man was lost to us that the noble horseman was gone! the renowned Squire Cox! " My love and darling, you were nearly related to the Lord of Clare, and to O'Donovan of Bawnlehan ; to Cox with the blue eyes and to Townsend of White Court. This is the appointed day for your funeral, and yet I see none of them coming to place even a green sod over you."

NUMBER II.
Is the lamentation of a man named O'Donoghue, of Affadown, or Roaring Water, in the west of the county Cork, for his three sons and son-in-law, who were drowned. " The wild geese," an idiom used in the last verse, was a popular name given to such young men as volunteered into the Irish brigade. " It was on a rainy Monday; a fair gale blew, and my sons left the shore an half an hour before sun-rise to fish in the sea; my children were driven far away to be drowned. This year has been the year of my ruin for ever " " Cormick (Charles), my eldest child, he could kill with his gun every bird that flew in air, the wild duck, and the partridge, and the grouse, and black plover of the lonesome mountains !" " Cormick, my dear! flower of young men, who was mild and well educated, who was just and pure and good ! Oh! glorious King of Heaven, if thou hadst but spared him to me ! It was the loss of him that broke my heart entirely; I might I could have parted with the rest." " Daniel, my dear Daniel, the youngest of my sons, it was this day fortnight he was Avashed on shore, without strength or life in his body. I saw him as he lay lifeless upon the shore, and my heart was cold and dumb and motionless at the sight!" " Children, dear children, do you pity me? do you see me ? look on me, your poor father crying and lamenting for the sunshine of his eyes; for the life of his life, for the soul of his soul; what is he now? a poor broken hearted old man, weeping alone in the cold corner of a stranger's house " " Great is my grief and sorrow ! sadness and tears weigh heavy on my Christmas. To have my four young and stout men thrown on the will of the waves! If the great ocean, or the dark caves of the ocean

would restore the three bodies that now lie in its depths, how beautifully they would be keened and lamented over in Affadown!" " Great is my grief and sorrow that you did not all go from your father on board ship ! or if my sons had left me for a season, like the wild geese, to go to a foreign land, then might I have expected from my Maker the help of my four mild and clever young men at some future time."

NUMBER III.

About the middle of the last century, Mr. O'Sullivan the younger, of Beerhaven, or, as he was called, Morty Oge O'Sullivan, possessed considerable influence in the west of the county Cork. The chief of a rude and mountainous district and supported by a numerous and hardy body of dependants, he had long set both the laws and magisterial authority at defiance. Grown confident in his own strength, and fearless of legal punishment, he became an agent for the French and Spanish governments, enlisting men for their service in Ireland, and transporting them in a vessel of his own to the continent. Mr. Puxley, a neighbouring gentleman of respectability, laid informations before the secretary of state, of such notoriously disloyal conduct, and O'Sullivan, actuated by revenge, having by some means gained intelligence, waylaid and shot Mr. Puxley on his return from church. This daring assassination called for a particular visitation, and on the 2d May,1754, a party of military, commanded by Lieutenant Appleton, was despatched from Cork to Beerhaven, where they arrived on the Saturday following about midnight. O'Sullivan, expecting an attack, had fortified his residence, and posted sentinels, who were surprised ; but the barking of a dog alarmed the inmates, and they obstinately defended themselves for some time, until the house was set on fire, when O'Sullivan, appearing at the door, was shot through the heart. Many of his men were killed or severely wounded in this engagement, and two were made prisoners, one of whom was Council, the reputed author of the following lamentation. The vessel employed by O'Sullivan in carrying on his illegal traffic with France was immediately sunk by a king's cutter sent round for the purpose, to the stern of which his body being lashed, was towed through the water to Cork ; his head was afterwards spiked on the south gaol of that city, and his remains interred in a bastion of the New Fort. Connell was the confidential servant of this disaffected character. and is reported to have composed and sung the present threnody, tin; night previous to his execution. " Murty, my dear and loved master, you carried the sway for strength and generosity. It is my endless grief and sorrow sorrow which admits of no comfort, that your white head should be gazed at as a shew upon a spike, and that your noble frame is without life."

"I have travelled with you, my dear and muc- loved master, in foreign lands, and through various provinces and counties, and in the royal prince's army, when we moved with kings. But it is through the means of Puxley that I am left in grief and confinement in Cork, locked in heavy irons, and without the hope of being released." " The great God is good and merciful! I ask his grace and pardon, and his support, for I am to be hanged at the gallows to-morrow without doubt; the rope will squeeze my neck, and thousands will lament my fate, but may the Lord have mercy upon my master ! it was for his sake that I am now in their power." " Kerryonians (Kerrymen), pray for us ! sweet and melodious is your voice, my blessing I give to you, but you will never see me again amongst you alive ; our heads will be upon a spike as a shew, A A
under the cold snow of the night, and the burning sun of the summer, and every other change of weather." " Oh! that I was ever born! oh! that I ever returned to Beerhaven! Mine was the best of masters that Ireland could produce; may our souls be floating to-morrow in the rays of endless glory!" " The lady his wife, heavy is her grief, and who may wonder at

that, were her eyes even made of green stone; when he, her dear husband, was shot by that ball? If he had retreated, our grief might have been lighter, but the brave man would not, for the pride of his country, retreat." " He has been in kings' palaces, and in Spain he got a pension; the lady of Clare gave him robes bound with gold lace as a token of remembrance. He became a captain on the coast of France, and yet should he return to Ireland for us to lose him." " There is a lady in London who expects him every day with his vessel." *

The rest wanting.*

* Since this volume has gone to press, I have observed in Blackwood's Magazine, a paraphrase on O'Sullivan's elegy, or rather verses founded on the circumstances of his death. The relation by which they are prefaced in that publication strangely coincides with what 1 have written, except in ascribing the death of O'Sullivan to the treachery of a menial, named Scully, and attributing to his nurse the framing of this composition. The reader may thank me for transcribing these spirited verses. The sun on Ivera no longer shines brightly ; The voice of her music no longer is sprightly; No more to her maidens the light dance is dear, Since the death of our darling, O'Sullivan Bear. Scully ! thou false one, you basely betrayed him, In his strong hour of need when thy right hand should aid him ; He fed thee, he clad thee, you had all could delight thee, You left him, you sold him, may Heav'n requite thee !
Scully! may all kinds of evil attend thee ! On thy dark road of life may no kind one befriend thee!

The account given of this lamentation, called the" Smith's Keenan," is at once simple and romantic. A young man (a smith) left his widowed mother and sisters, who resided at Killavullian on the Blackwater, and married in a distant part of the country. Sometime after, one of his sisters, hearing that he was ill, set out to see him, but before she reached her destination, the night came on, which compelled her, being ignorant of the way, to seek shelter at a cottage on the road side; here she found the inmates preparing to proceed to a wake in the village where her brother resided, and going forward with them, on arrival discovered it to be her brother's wake, at the sight of whose

May fevers long burn thee, and agues long freeze thee!
May the strong hand of God m his red anger seize thee!
Had he died calmly I would not deplore him;
Or if the wild strife of the sea-war closed o'er him;
But with ropes round his white limbs through oceans to trail him,
Like a fish after slaughter, 'tis therefore I wail him.

Long may the curse of his people pursue them;
Scully, that sold him, and soldier that slew him!
One glimpse of Heav'n's light, may they see never;
May the hearth-stone of hell be their best bed for ever.
In the hole, which the vile hands of soldiers had made thee;
Unhonoured, unshrouded, and headless they laid thee;
No sigh to regret thee, no eye to ram o'er ee,
No dirge to lament thee, no friend to deplore thee.

Dear head of my darling ! how gory and pale
These aged eyes see thee, high spik'd on their gaol!
Thy cheek in the summer sun ne'er shall grow warm ;
Nor that eye e'er catch light, but the flash of the storm.
A curse, blessed ocean, is on thy green water,
From the haven of Cork, to Ivera of slaughter ;
Since thy billows were dyed with the red wounds of fear,
 Of Muiertach Oge, our O'Sullivan Bear.

lifeless body she burst into the following exclamations. The conclusion is singular; nor is it possible for a translation to do justice to the strain of powerful sarcasm in the original, directed against the wife of the deceased. " Brother, dear brother! your long absence from home did not raise you in this world, you left us, and you found a wife who knew not how to love you. No one here knows your family, you are in the midst of strangers; they only know that you were a smith, and son of a smith, from the Blackwater's side!" " Oh ! if I had your cold limbs by the Blackwater's side, or on the banks of the small river (the Awbeg), or by the Bride ; Mary and Kate and Julia would cry over you, and our mother would cry most sweetly for you ; and I, oh ! I would cry more than them all for you!" " Oh ! brother, dear brother I might have known that you were laid low, when I did not hear the sound of your forge, or of your sledges, striking strong and noisy I" " Dear brother, and my darling brother, you have the marks of a wife that did not love you; she left my brother hungry in the winter, and dry in the summer ; without a Sunday dress, and the sufferer from long fasting :" " You woman, his wife! my brother's wife, you woman with the dry eyes ; you woman who are both dumb and deaf; go home! go any where, leave your husband to me, and I will mourn for my brother." " You woman above with the dry eyes! my brother's wife, come down, and I will keen you; you will get another husband if you are young enough: but I can never get a brother!" (The priest comes forward and speaks.) " Hold your tongue, stubborn stranger, why will you provoke your brother's wife?"

(She answers.) " Hold your tongue, stubborn priest! read your Litany and Confiteor: earn your half-crown and begone : I will keen my brother." These examples of the keen, notwithstanding their inequality of sentiment, and the injury sustained by a literal translation, will not, I am confident, appear wholly destitute of merit, although it is evident there are many passages and allusions, which those unacquainted with local manners and history, can neither feel nor understand correctly. But under any circumstances, the natural expression of sorrow awakens our sympathy, for the simple language of grief is always poetical. The national exclamations used on the death of a friend or an acquaintance are often very figurative:

May the heavens be his perch to-night!" is no uncommon ejaculation, on first hearing of the loss of such. What an original metaphor is this, and what a fine allegorical picture does it present! the soul springing upwards like a bird, and resting its weary wings after the flight, in some " bower of bliss." Nor are keens merely orally preserved amongst the peasantry. 1 have three original Irish death-songs in M.S. now lying before me, the most recent of which, on a namesake of my own, is dated 21st January, 1822, and consists of thirteen verses, not worth translating, but the English preface prefixed to it is curious, as a specimen of the modern bardic spirit, and is transcribed verbatim. " I can most undoubtedly testify that since the death of Captain O'Sullivan Beer Haven, I did not see nor hear any man died so much regretted for, nor even so free from the least stain or blemish attached to his character, as the most worthy and much lamented Edward Croker, Esq. near Curriglass. Declared and certified by me the poet, William Cremon."

Keens are also a medium through which the disaffected circulate their mischievous principles, and this they do without much attempt at concealment, the Irish language being a sufficient cloak for the expression of seditious sentiments ; few, if any, of the gentry being acquainted with it, as they consider it too vulgar and inelegant to form a part of their studies. Those criminals whose lives have been forfeited in the cause of rebellion, derive no small consolation from the idea of martyrdom, which they imagine they have attained, and in this they are encouraged by the popular voice, apostrophising their shade as that of an hero and a patriot. Their countrymen are called upon to revenge their death, and to recover the estates of their Milesian ancestors, whose spirit has alone descended to them; on that spirit and what it will achieve, many verses are frequently bestowed. It is compared to the mountain-eagle, that, even in bondage, the hand of strangers could not tame ; to the mountain-torrent, that would suddenly burst forth with overwhelming inundation, and destroy the lands where the cold hearted Saxons revelled. When the awful sentence of death has been pronounced by the judge on an Irish culprit, it is not unusual for him to petition that his body may be given to his friends after execution, and, if this is granted, he meets his fate with fortitude and resignation. Those, who from their official capacity have been obliged to witness such distressing scenes, have often expressed their surprize at the dying declaration of men who were convicted on the clearest and most unquestionable evidence, that they were innocent of the crime for which they were about to suffer, and this assertion has been supported by the most solemn appeals to the Deity. It is only charitable to consider so palpable a falsehood uttered by those on the very brink of eternity, as the result of absolution on the ignorant mind ; the doctrine by which the murderer can conscientiously declare his innocence has something in it irreconcilably opposed to truth and reason.

If a complete account of the crimes and conduct at the place of execution of those who had been convicted by the law in Ireland since the Articles of Limerick, could now be drawn up, I am persuaded it would afford a moral and political view of the country, the result of which would surprize even the best acquainted with these subjects. Dean Swift appears to have entertained the same idea, and he accordingly made a collection of the printed dying speeches of Irish culprits, which he enriched with his own invaluable comments : one of the volumes of this series was in my possession for a short time, whence I take some extracts, to give an idea of the general tenour of the dying speeches of the last century. The first of these explains the point of copyright in such matters, the others are distinguished by their soundness of reasoning. " The last speech and dying words of Valentine Kealy and Cornealus Sulivan, who is both to be executed near St. Stephen's green, this present Saturday, being the 13th instant, March, 1724-5, for robberys committed by them. The Speech of Valentine Kealy. Good people, I am advised by several of my acquaintances to give my speech from my own mouth to some printer, in order to prevent others of that trade from printing sham speeches of me; therefore (by their perswatiom) I sent for the printer in MONTRATII STREET, to whom I made the following true speech, and if any other prints it,

I assure you it is false," &c.

The Speech of Cornealus Sulivan.

Dear Christians, I at first had no thoughts to make any speech, by reason I am far from my friends or relations, but seeing my fellow sufferer doing it 1 thought fit to do the same, which is in manner following/' &c
.

Captain M'Dermot, who was hanged at Cavan on the 30th March, 1725, for murder, explains his situation thus " And I, who was taught to read the Latin, English, and Irish tongues, and was naturally complaisant to all mankind, am here made an example for the sins of my forefathers." As a companion to this, is " an elegy on the death of Mr. Jo. Foe, who unfortunately departed this life at Kilmainham gallows, October 20th, 1725." The first edition of the Cork Remembrancer, a book which should rather be entitled the Cork Criminal Recorder, published in 1783, and compiled by a Mr. Fitzgerald, contains the particulars of almost every execution in that city, during the preceding half century. I have been told that the author of this singular chronicle made a point of being present at the death of every criminal whose exit he has recorded, and he generally marched in the procession from the gaol to the gallows : on one occasion it is reported of Mr. Fitzgerald, that, being confined to his bed by a severe illness, he actually petitioned the judge to postpone an execution, until he was sufficiently recovered to become a spectator.

Parting Lines

Wasn't it a shame I didn't bear you along with me to Kate Cassidy's wake, a fine stout lad, the like of you, for you'd never see the match of it for flows of drink the way when we sunk her bones at noonday in her narrow grave, there were five men, aye, and six men stretched out retching speechless on the holy stones-Synge, John Millington, <u>The Playboy of the Western World</u>

"In Ireland, they say, the sleep that knows no waking is often followed by the wake that knows no sleeping!"
-Ancient Irish Truth

FUNERAL AT SHEPPERTON LAKES

"After leaving Clonakilty, each step that we took westward brought fresh evidence of the truth of the reports of the misery, as we either met a funeral or a coffin at every hundred yards, until we approached the country of the Shepperton Lakes. Here, the distress became more striking, from the decrease of numbers at the funerals, none having more than eight or ten attendants, and many only two or three."

-Illustrated London News, February 13, 1847.

Many thanks to Mary the Proofreader

This is a Production of Hutman Productions

Harper's Weekly, v 17 1873 March 15,

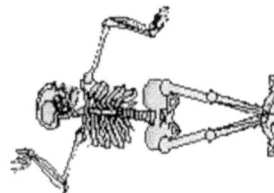

www.ingramcontent.com/pod-product-compliance
Lightning Source LLC
Chambersburg PA
CBHW082350270326
41935CB00013B/1569